Classroom Teaching

D1247420

This book is part of the Peter Lang Education list.
Every volume is peer reviewed and meets
the highest quality standards for content and production.

PETER LANG
New York • Bern • Berlin
Brussels • Vienna • Oxford • Warsaw

Classroom Teaching

An Introduction

SECOND EDITION

Joe L. Kincheloe and Shirley R. Steinberg, EDITORS

PETER LANG
New York • Bern • Berlin
Brussels • Vienna • Oxford • Warsaw

Library of Congress Cataloging-in-Publication Data

Names: Kincheloe, Joe L., editor. | Steinberg, Shirley R., editor.
Title: Classroom teaching: an introduction / edited by Joe L. Kincheloe and Shirley R. Steinberg.
Description: Second edition. | New York: Peter Lang, 2018. | Previous edition: 2005.
Includes bibliographical references and index.
Identifiers: LCCN 2018013867 | ISBN 978-1-4331-5727-1 (paperback: alk. paper)
ISBN 978-1-4331-5688-5 (ebook pdf) | ISBN 978-1-4331-5689-2 (epub)
ISBN 978-1-4331-5690-8 (mobi)
Subjects: LCSH: Teaching. | Classroom management.
Classification: LCC LB1025.3.C55 2018 | DDC 371.102—dc23
LC record available at https://lccn.loc.gov/2018013867
DOI 10.3726/b13692

Bibliographic information published by **Die Deutsche Nationalbibliothek**.
Die Deutsche Nationalbibliothek lists this publication in the "Deutsche
Nationalbibliografie"; detailed bibliographic data are available
on the Internet at http://dnb.d-nb.de/.

Front cover artwork: *Hello Friend.* © 2018 Roymieco A. Carter.
Used with permission of the artist.

The paper in this book meets the guidelines for permanence and durability
of the Committee on Production Guidelines for Book Longevity
of the Council of Library Resources.

© 2018 Peter Lang Publishing, Inc., New York
29 Broadway, 18th floor, New York, NY 10006
www.peterlang.com

All rights reserved.
Reprint or reproduction, even partially, in all forms such as microfilm,
xerography, microfiche, microcard, and offset strictly prohibited.

Printed in the United States of America

Dedication

And we continue to advocate to make a difference

For the victims and families of gun violence: students, teachers, support staff, and administration
who have been unable to be nurtured and protected in their schools
As we remember and mourn those lost, we understand that safe schools are an unalienable right,
and we continue to advocate to make a difference

In memory of Joe L. Kincheloe, whose legacy and radical love continues inspire and inform

Table of Contents

INTRODUCTION

And So, We Teach

Shirley R. Steinberg

I f you are reading these words, you have determined you are destined to teach or, possibly, that you *must* teach. Was it those Saturday mornings, after cartoons, when you hauled out the little blackboard, coloring books, crayons, blocks, and forced younger siblings and neighborhood kids to be your students? Was it that favorite teacher, the one who changed your life? Was it because school was a bad place, and you knew you could do better? Are you the offspring of a teacher? Or, was teaching your second choice, your *fall back-on* profession? All legitimate reasons, and you're here: a pre-service teacher ready to enter a most essential, exhausting, complicated, and challenging profession … and, oh yeah, btw, you will *never* collect a salary commensurate with your profession. In the next few school terms, you are expected to become cognitive theorists, curriculum designers, assessment aficionados, and behavior managers. Good luck on that. My advice to you is to absorb *the stuff*, but pay attention to *the passion*. Know that the rubrics, taxonomies, and outcomes are only tools to get you into the schools, then your authentic teacher education begins.

Simulation, stimulation, and recitation serve to legitimate the degree you will receive, and make no mistake, you need that knowledge. However, being educated to become a teacher *must happen in the schools*, that's when we begin to understand just exactly what it means to teach. Just as this short *Introduction* is part of your preparation for this class, teacher education is the preliminary setup for legitimating you in order to enter into the real thing. There are volumes written about teaching, meticulously created to launch you into your chosen vocation, read them with an eye of commitment *and* suspicion. Absorb the advice, throw away any antiquated, pedantic notions, and create your own self-teacher … remember your own school story and use it as a model to understand who you wish to become as a teacher (or, who you do *wish* to become). Be reflective, become a student of yourself as a teacher, create a life-long self-study of your chosen profession. Know your kids … *know them*. Become a researcher of your students, observe what curricula they bring into your class: their experiences, beliefs, backgrounds, differences, and subcultures … continually inquire into the ways in which each one learns and performs. Remind yourself that your goal is not to parent, nor to become their friend … it is to be their teacher, their mentor, their support, their advocate, and their safety.

Along with observing and learning your students, be continually aware of the power agencies which govern teaching and education. The authors in this book are united in the understanding that *teaching is a political act.* Two centuries ago, North American public schools were created for one purpose: to teach a previously illiterate societal class to become docile and obedient workers. The Industrial Revolution recreated work to be done by the masses, factories became centers of production, and workers needed to be trained. For a population previously not disciplined to work en masse, North American workers needed to be educated and controlled. Indeed, this explains why our schools are modeled on factory organizations. The bells, the timetables, keeping attendance, grouping, these all stem from schools being modeled after factories. And, factories served to sustain an ideological citizenry involved in the creation of capital, of goods for revenue. The idea of the arts, or learning for learning's sake was not part of the original mandate for public schooling. Aesthetics, physical activity, and enjoyment were the curricula of the privileged, the rich … and public schools were ways in which to serve the economy and the nation.

Theorists and school reformers began to advocate to admit the arts, physical education, discovery, and imagination into education, and by the early part of the twentieth century, new ways in which to imagine schooling were slowly infused into schools. There has, however, never been an agreement as to what public education should look like, what it should mean. And curriculum wars have raged, instituted and legislated by national, state, and provincial law makers … progressive schools, experimental schools, back-to-basics schools, core curriculum schools: all attempts to find the *best way to educate.* The best way, the best curriculum, the best methods … and all of it, political. As you will read in the chapters of this book, political power, ideological power influences, creates, and recreates schools and curriculum. The education of each generation is heavily influenced by those in power, those who lead, and we see how curriculum and assessment are guided by this leadership. Sometimes, when education is not a political (and economic) priority in a government, the previous decade continues to lead the current decade … eventually leading to a static, nonprogressive education. I remember my oldest son, Ian, coming home from his grade 1 class, blankly handing me a *Dick & Jane Reader.* First published in the 1920s, these readers were identified with North American children learning to read. The series was revamped in the 1960s, and my son was taught to read with them in the 1980s. An early and avid reader, he was mystified about his first textbook. It was silly, decontextualized in his world, and over 60 years old. The readers weren't inherently bad, just without context, without cultural connection to Ian, and depicted out-of-date notions of children and family. When I approached the principal of Ian's school, pointing out the antifeminist text, the stereotypical roles of boys and girls, I was told that I was "too radical," and that children in the 1980s were the same as any other decade's children. This issue is an example of how the political and ideological enters into even the most seemingly innocent text. Depictions of race, class, gender, play, and work in these readers reflected an era which may or may not have existed, but certainly did not for my son. Publishers are also complicit in deciding upon which books are selected, which politicians respond to their ideological stance, and in the case of school texts in the past few decades, even laid the groundwork for curricular legislation. Schooling is Political.

We hope this book creates a space for alternate views of teacher education predicated upon notions of equity, social justice, negotiated curriculum, and self-reflection. No "lesson plans" are included, no recipes, no charts, and no fail-safe methods. While the curriculum is prescribed, there is nothing preventing us to intuit and contextualize the way we teach what our states and provinces lay out as content for teachers. Being a good teacher is understanding the way in which knowledge can be taught and learned, and *how* we present this knowledge, within context, for our particular students. The job is tough, often lacking material rewards … but it is worth every drop of sweat, every late night, and every student.

PART I

Teaching:
Becoming and Doing

CHAPTER 1

What Are We Doing Here?
How Do We Build a Framework for Teaching?

Joe L. Kincheloe and Shirley R. Steinberg

This book is grounded on the premise that we can do better—we can build a far better society and far better schools. One of the most important prerequisites of such an effort involves our ability to imagine what such a society and such an education might look like. That's what this book attempts to do—to provide a compelling vision of what classroom teaching could become. The authors offer a hopeful, democratic, challenging, and pragmatic portrait of classroom teaching that engages the mind, heart, and creative impulse. Since Joe published his first work almost thirty years ago, some readers have said that "all that sounds good, but it'll never work in the real world." There is nothing impractical about developing visions of what could be. Indeed, constructing such visions is a very practical enterprise, for all innovation begins with vision. Without vision we are existentially dead or at least dying. As creatures without vision, we walk a meaningless landscape attending only to immediate urges. We want more, as do the authors in this book. Moreover, we believe that human beings have only begun a journey of meaning-making and achievement that will take them to presently unimaginable domains. Education is intimately tied to—and even makes possible—this amazing journey.

Gaining a Sense of Where We're Going

Classroom teaching that takes place outside of a rigorous examination of the larger goals of education is always trivialized and degraded. All of the chapters in this book are premised on the notion that great classroom teaching is always grounded on larger understandings of purpose, a vision of the social role of education, and a sense of what type of people we want to be. What's sad is that so much of what takes place in higher education, teacher education, the public conversation about schooling, and elementary and secondary schools themselves is disconnected from these dynamics. When analyses of purpose and vision are relegated to the domain of "the impractical," we have issues. In such a situation the culture has lost a central dimension of its humanness, its *élan vital*, its life force.

The authors and editors believe that human beings are enriched by:

- an understanding of the physical and social universes;

- the historical context that has shaped them;

- the literary and other aesthetic creations that express their hopes and fears;

- the philosophical insights that can help clarify and construct meaning;

- an awareness of the hidden cultural and ideological forces that tacitly influence their identities and values;

- new cognitive insights that help students move to more powerful modes of thinking;

- the political ideas that help them in the struggle to control their own lives;

- different ways of knowing: Indigenous, feminist, non-Western, alternate knowledges.

We want classrooms that help produce a society—and a world—worthy of our status as citizens.

The way such classrooms are created involves gaining a sense of social and educational purpose. The title question of this chapter, *what are we doing here?* must be answered by teachers in order for them to construct compelling, challenging, motivating, socially responsible, and just classrooms. Without an answer to this question and a pedagogy constructed around that answer, there is little chance of creating a classroom that makes a difference in students' lives—especially students marginalized by the forces of race, class, gender, and sexuality—and a difference in the larger society. We are asserting here that merely getting students to prepare for the standards tests administered by the school district or the state is not enough. In fact, there is evidence that moves us to argue that such a test-based teaching and learning process may do more harm than good.

In these test-based contexts the very question of what we are doing here too often gets profoundly distorted. On numerous occasions over the last few years of standards hysteria we have heard a variety of political and educational leaders assert these sentiments: "Why are we here? What is our main goal? That's right, to raise the test scores." Obviously, raising standardized test scores is not the *raison d'être* of classroom teaching. There is something profoundly disturbing about such pronouncements regarding our goals. Indeed, there is a "rational irrationality," when in the name of reason we lapse into irrational beliefs and behavior.

For example, standardized tests measure so little of what education involves. The previous list of some of the ways a rigorous education can enrich our lives can't be measured by such tests. At most, such exams pick up on some of the fragmented, unconnected data one has obtained from schools. In this book we argue that such data are relatively unimportant in the larger vision of education and classroom teaching that we are laying out here. This is *not* to say that knowledge is not important. But the way we confront knowledge and make sense of it is every bit as important as committing particular "facts" to memory. Being prepared to ask *why* we are studying "this knowledge" and not "this other knowledge" is a skill that is far more useful than scoring high on a standardized test.*

What makes the question, "What are we doing here?" so complex for teachers is that North Americans are so divided over the answer. All educational questions are primarily political questions. Even what many might think are simple questions—such as "What do we teach?"—are riddled with political inscriptions. Do we teach the knowledge that she or he thinks is most important? Do we teach in the way Dr. Smith says is the best for student learning or in the way Dr. Brown maintains creates the best learning environment? The answers to such questions are complex, and we answer them depending on our larger social, cultural, political, and philosophical assumptions whether or not we are conscious of them. It is impossible to be neutral about these questions. Along with the authors, we hold particular social, cultural, political, and philosophical perspectives. These perspectives influence our vision of what constitutes a good classroom. We will tell you about the biases we bring to each of the following chapters. None of us claim that what we are providing you is *objective* information about classroom teaching. No information is objective. It is our perspective.

We will try to convince you that it's not such openly admitted biases that should worry you. What concerns us is the information that is provided to you as a form of objective truth, free from interpretation and human perspective. Whenever a teacher or educational expert claims that she/he is giving us "the truth," we need to feel uncomfortable. A central assertion of this book is that all claims of good classroom teaching are based on particular political/social visions—there is no one, objective political/social vision. In this context as human beings who want to be teachers, we are faced with an existential dilemma: no one else can tell us the right way to teach; we have a human responsibility to decide for ourselves what constitutes good teaching and appropriate educational goals in a democratic society. We believe that every teacher must make this decision and struggle against systems that unreasonably attempt to deny teachers of this professional prerogative. This doesn't mean that teachers are free to indoctrinate students with fascist dogma, racial hatred, or inaccurate information. It does mean that teachers can make curricular and pedagogical decisions within particular democratic and scholarly boundaries.

The Importance of Healthy Debate about the Goals of Classroom Teaching

If we are to have a genuine and productive public debate about educational goals, we must insist that such debate focuses on the clarification of guiding principles on which our teaching is based. Is the goal the improvement of test scores, or does it involve the well-being of the children entrusted to our care? Is well-being defined as the particular needs that specific students bring with them to school, or is it a vague notion that means little? We believe that a variety of social, cultural, political, and economic factors have operated to diminish public life. In an age of mediocrity the public conversation about these matters is truncated. Often what we consider "normal" is socially constructed by modes of repression, oppression, fear-mongering, and forces of economic, political, racial, and gender power.

When we talk about having an honest conversation about the goals of education and the nature of good classroom teaching, these forces often represent such activities as some form of anti-governmental action. For example, when we argue that we should have access to an education that provides diverse viewpoints from people around the world about history, science, literature, politics, religion, and other topics, this is often defined as subversive. We believe that such perspectives are dishonest, disastrous in their social impact, anti-intellectual, and destructive to a free society. We are confident that a rigorous debate about the principles on which such educational perspectives rest will expose their antidemocratic and repressive nature. We hope that after reading this and many other sources about these issues that you will insist on and participate in such debate in your teacher education programs, the schools in which you teach, and the communities in which you live. We believe that the curriculum *should* be challenged, that diversity is essential, and that the voices of students matter (Paraskeva & Steinberg, 2016).

The debate that we're trying to foster—about the goals of education in general and classroom teaching in particular—therefore deals with the foundations of diverse perspectives. In this context we ask, what is the basis for the curriculum? When we speak of curriculum we are not only referring to the knowledge or subject matter that is taught in schools. In addition, we are referencing the goals and purposes of teaching and learning, methods of classroom teaching and organization, and the ways we assess the quality of the teaching and learning taking place. We also move outside the classroom in our definition of curriculum, asserting that classroom teaching has to do with a myriad of things that happen in the world surrounding the school. In our expanded and critical understanding of education, we are also interested in the ways knowledge is produced and human consciousness is constructed and the role that power plays in these processes (Steinberg, 2010).

We maintain that a public debate about the goals of education and classroom teaching must ask hard questions about the role of corporations in shaping the social and pedagogical agenda. Corporations have become increasingly powerful over the last few decades, paying less taxes as they grab more power and influence via their control of media and public information. As part of this increasing corporate domination of society, they have become less willing to provide taxes to public institutions that they cannot control. Sensing that an empowered and self-directed teaching profession in public schools might be inclined to criticize their socially harmful behavior, corporate leaders have aligned themselves with right-wing politicians to use their control of information to subvert the idea of public education.

We hear talk about the privatization of schooling and the value of corporate-operated, for-profit education, home schooling is on the rise, lotteries are created to bring money to education. We are deeply concerned with the social and political impact of such a corporatized school system. As unelected, unaccountable power wielders, corporations would not tolerate criticism in their schools. Teaching would be deprofessionalized and teachers would be subjected to rigid forms of control. No elected school boards or political bodies would operate under this corporatized arrangement to address these problems. The public's educational right to knowledge and democratic empowerment, already compromised, would no longer exist in this brave new world of for-profit schooling. This scenario is not a fantasy. Plans exist both to win public support for such changes and to implement these schools once approval is granted. For-profit organizations are increasing in popularity, offering to teach a curriculum to students (often in STEM); instead of creating more provocative opportunities for teachers in a district, hiring "out" to shiny and glamorous corporate curriculum providers becomes a norm. Parents are warned that their children will not *be competitive* in a global market, creating an unfounded fear which leads to the need to "purchase" their child's education.

The classroom teaching that we advocate holds an optimistic view of what humans can become (Griffin, 1997). Our pedagogy is grounded on the belief that humans are destined for greatness and can be motivated to learn on these premises. The classroom teaching promoted in this book is premised on an honest discussion of these competing belief systems and the ways they affect the nature of society and education themselves. One of the most powerful dimensions of becoming an educated person involves understanding the great issues of the day. We also believe that it is a government's obligation to support and provide equal and excellent education to all children.

In this spirit we argue that the curriculum should present a variety of perspectives on what should be taught in schools. A central feature of such a curriculum would involve understanding a variety of different viewpoints in a variety of academic domains and the ideologies, values, and worldviews on which they are based. A classroom grounded on this curriculum would expose students to diverse interpretations of history, science, linguistics, literature, and philosophy while encouraging them to support and defend their own interpretations in these areas. An understanding of diverse perspectives and the justifications for the differences between them promotes intellectual and ethical maturity (Harrington & Quinn-Leering, 1995). Many of the forces that want to do away with public education are frightened by the possibility of students engaging multiple perspectives. Those who support indoctrination and regulation of human beings are always opposed to a democratic engagement with intellectual diversity.

These are the types of insights that will emerge in a healthy democratic debate about what we should be doing in education. Such debate will move us away from imposed, standardized, decontextualized, scripted modes of classroom teaching. It will help us empower teachers and students to become scholars who understand the contexts of meaning-making in which schooling is structured. In this context they will gain the mature understanding that knowledge is not simply given humans but is actively constructed by individuals coming from particular locales in the sociohistorical web of reality. Individuals like us, operating in the observational confines of their historical time and social location, produce the knowledge taught in school. This means that school knowledge like all knowledge is fallible; it is prone to error.

When educational institutions restrict what can be questioned and what interpretations of the world are allowed, they undermine a society's capacity to deal with change and novelty. And, in the contemporary globalized, electronic, information-saturated world of the twenty-first century, change is the status quo. Thus, a key dimension of a critical and rigorous education for such a hyper-reality involves the ability to interpret and make meaning of a barrage of information thrown at us by corporate-owned media and education. This interpretive ability becomes extremely important in this context because the motive for such information bombardment may be to induce us to buy into or give our consent to ways of thinking that are not in our own best interests. Such ways of thinking may serve the needs of corporate power wielders more than they serve our own. We want classrooms to help students survive in this contemporary power-driven climate of deceit by developing a literacy of power—an ability to discern the fingerprints and effects of power on the knowledge thrown at them.

Traditional Debates about the Goals of Classroom Teaching

Instead of being relegated to the dumpster of official history, the chronicle of our past and present disagreements should rest at the center of a democratic curriculum. Teachers need to understand the philosophical, historical, political, social, and cultural assumptions that support their classroom decisions. It is important to note in this context that it is just these types of assumptions that right-wing advocates of the privatization of public education don't want pre-service teachers to study and understand. An important aspect of the agenda of those who would seek to deprofessionalize teaching is to abolish teacher education as it now exists. The first step in this abolition process involves getting rid of the social, political, philosophical, historical, and cultural analysis that engages teachers in asking about the purpose of education in a democratic society.

This type of analysis is very frightening to those who seek to privatize education because such study induces teachers to ask deeper questions about the real motivations for such educational change. Once we begin to study the privatization movement we begin to see that, in addition to the huge profits to be made in the process, new forms of political and ideological control over teachers' work can be achieved. In privatized and corporate schools teachers will be unable to appeal to principles such as academic freedom or freedom of speech to protect their critiques of such power wielders. Teachers who point to the oppressive power of corporations and various forms of oppression will simply be dismissed. They will have no legal recourse to protect themselves from or overturn such firings.

In this repressive context questions of how certain educational purposes affect particular groups of people or specific individuals are not asked. What happens to poor people when we define intelligence in a particular way? Indigenous people? Newcomers? Non-English speakers? If we define politics as the domain where power operates and questions about the best ways to share power are asked, then we can begin to see the intimate connections between politics and education. Depending on our definitions of dynamics such as intelligence, success, and higher-order thinking, different people will win (gain power) and lose (lose power) in educational situations. When we accept the validity and universal predictive power of IQ tests, for example, we set up students from poor backgrounds for failure. The types of skills evaluated and the language used in the tests are more commonly found among English speaking middle/upper-middle-class students. If educators decide that these test scores are "real" indications of students' abilities, then schools will treat such students as uneducable and thus guarantee their academic failure. As a classroom teacher, how you view such issues will make all the difference to your students, especially your most vulnerable students.

We can begin to see contemporary manifestations of larger historical debates over the goals of education. Is it the function of schooling to help people reach their highest potential, providing them in the process with the understanding of the forces that impede them on such a quest? In such a context, students armed with this insight can work to bring about a more inclusive and just social order. Or is it the function of schooling to support and perpetuate the dominant social order by efficiently producing individuals who will serve functional roles within businesses, industries, and various organizations? With this notion, the social role of such students is not to strive for their fullest potential or to critique the justice of present sociopolitical arrangements, but to accept the status quo and keep it operating. Or is it possible for schools to help accomplish both goals? Are there points at which they come into direct conflict? Can, for example, marginalized students work for intellectual self-improvement and socioeconomic mobility and a more just social order while working to preserve the dominant social order? Such activities may collide head on.

Should the goal of schools should involve teaching about and promoting the mores and values of the so-called dominant culture or provide validation and respect for the subcultures that make up the society as a whole? This question lays the foundation for discussions of multiculturalism and the role of diverse cultural knowledges and values within the curriculum (Bruner, 1996; Kincheloe, 2001; Kincheloe & Steinberg, 1997; Steinberg, 2001). In this context some fundamentalist religions, for example, argue that the role of the schools is to perpetuate the belief structures of dominant patriarchal culture. Teaching such belief structures would include inculcating the superiority of Western civilization and a particular religious viewpoint in the minds of all students. Obviously, different groups of people are very emotional about these issues, and teachers will have to confront the debate and its effects at some level in their professional life.

Another debate involves what exactly it might mean to pursue the goal of cultivating the intellect of students. It is unfortunate that the effort to cultivate the intellect has been reduced to inculcating subskills in math and reading. Too often students are subjected to standards test-driven curricula characterized by skill-and-drill lessons on circling the verb and drawing an X through the noun. As a first-year language arts teacher in a middle school in Tennessee, Joe was faced on the night of his first open house with a parental rebellion. Several parents had organized to hijack the language arts teachers' presentation on the curriculum we had developed. As we attempted to explain the communication skills that we planned to teach and how parents could help in this process, angry parents shouted that they saw no provision for teaching how to diagram sentences. As Joe tried to explain that sentence diagramming was only one technique for teaching about the structure of language, angry parents drowned out his voice. They wanted no "intellectual" explanation. They saw the teaching of sentence diagramming as important to the academic success of their children. It was important because teachers in high school might require it.

The larger notion of cultivating the intellect by helping students gain important writing, reading, and other communication skills was not relevant to the parents. One can understand on one level the social and cultural forces that move many parents to think only of the "success" of their children. We are very sensitive to such concerns, especially among parents who have never enjoyed socioeconomic success. Nevertheless, the question of our larger purpose in the educational context—a purpose, of course, that cannot be removed from these contexts—is overlooked in such circumstances. In the process education is reduced to a means toward an end of socioeconomic success, and the intrinsic value of education and the critical consciousness it might develop are dismissed. The debate about the goals of education must bring up these issues for public examination. Teachers must be keenly aware of these issues as they prepare their everyday work in their classrooms.

The Goals of Classroom Teaching and Questions of Power

No matter how much many people might wish it were not the case, schools and classrooms are battle-grounds where competing interests attempt to define who we are as a society (Anderson & Summer-field, 2004). In many domains we see forces that want to retain a monolithic vision of our homelands as White, Christian, patriarchal, English-speaking, heteronormative nations and demand that class-rooms reflect such uniformity. Diversity around issues of race, Indigeneity, religion, gender, language, and sexuality does not play well with these forces. Different races are "inferior"; different religions are "ungodly"; men are the heads of the household; nondominant languages are considered inappropriate; and nonmainstream sexual orientations are ignored. Indeed, so many of the issues surrounding educational policy, teaching, and learning relate to these issues. All of these concerns are issues of power that raise the question of who gets to teach their viewpoints as the truth that all others must learn.

In this context, we believe that rigorous, life-changing teachers must have a complex understanding of power and how it shapes the world in general and individual lives in particular. Many of the ideas we employ in this chapter come from critical pedagogy (for an introduction to the field see Kincheloe, 2004). In our case and those of the authors of the following chapters, we take some ideas from this school of thought and mix them with ideas from other schools. We share several basic precepts about the need for a rigorous education that explores a wide variety of knowledges and is grounded on a belief in democracy and socioeconomic justice, but we do not hold uniform perspectives. All of us do believe, however, that understanding issues of power and their relation to the purposes of education is central to becoming a great classroom teacher.

Indeed, the people we are and the nature of our consciousness of ourselves in general and as teach-ers are directly tied to power. Our critical orientation to classroom teaching is always mindful of the interrelationship between teachers', students', and administrators' consciousness and the sociohistorical contexts in which they work. These historical power forces have shaped all of us.

The teachers we want to see operating in schools, regardless of their own backgrounds, understand such sociocultural dynamics and their relationships to themselves and their students. In relation to themselves, critical teachers value self-exploration. In relation to these power dynamics and their own lives, they work to expose buried fragments of themselves constructed by their connections to such forces of power.

Critical classroom teachers seek to expose what constitutes reality for themselves and for partici-pants in educational situations. How do educational leaders, administrators, other teachers, parents, and students come to construct their views of educational reality? Critical teachers see a socially con-structed world and ask what forces construct the consciousness and the ways of seeing of the actors who live in it. Why are some constructions of educational reality embraced and officially legitimized by the dominant culture while others are repressed? Why do I feel so uncomfortable with teaching about particular issues or raising certain questions, yet I have no trouble bringing other knowledges into my classroom. What contexts, what experiences, what belief systems have moved me to operate in these ways? Why do I react so emotionally (positively or negatively) to what I have written in this introduc-tion? What are the origins of such feelings?

Teaching and knowledge production are never neutral but constructed in specific ways that privi-lege particular logics and voices while silencing others. Why do science and math courses in the North America, for example, receive more attention and prestige in public schools than liberal arts (Roth, Tobin, & Ritchie, 2001)? Critical teachers who are searching for the way power helps shape individual and social consciousness uncover links between the need of large corporations to enhance worker productivity and the goals of contemporary educational reform and standards movements to reestablish "'excellent' schools" (Horn & Kincheloe, 2001). We discover relationships between the interests of business and the exclusion of the study of labor history in Western schools. We expose the connections between the patriarchal Eurocentrism of educational leadership and definitions of classics that exclude the contributions of women, minorities, and non-Westerners to the literature, art, and music curricula.

Power regulates discourses, and discursive practices are defined as a set of tacit rules that regulate what can and cannot be said, who can speak with the blessing of authority and who must listen, whose socioeducational constructions are scientific and valid and whose are unlearned and unimportant. In the everyday world of teachers, legitimized discourses insidiously tell teachers what books may be read by students, what instructional methods may be utilized, and what belief systems, definitions of citizenship, and views of success may be taught. Schools may identify, often unconsciously, conceptions of what it means to be educated with upper-middle-class White culture; expressions of working-class or non-White culture may be viewed as uneducated and inferior.

In this context teachers are expected to sever student identification with their Indigenous, minority-group or working-class backgrounds, as a result alienating such students through the degradation of their culture. Thus, the culture of schooling privileges particular practices and certain methods of discerning truth. Michel Foucault argues that truth is not relative (i.e., not all worldviews embraced by different teachers, researchers, cultures, and individuals are of equal worth) but relational (constructions considered true are contingent upon the power relations and historical context in which they are formulated and acted upon). The question that grounds critical teachers' efforts to formulate a system of meaning for their classroom teaching is whether what we designate as truth is relational and not certain. If it is, then what set of assumptions can we use to guide our activities as professionals, to inform our questions as teachers and producers of knowledge? This question is one that such teachers attempt to answer for the rest of their lives. This is a question that runs throughout my work as a scholar and a teacher.

Power is an extremely complex topic. In the context of this discussion of the goals of classroom teaching we want to focus on the political notion of hegemony. Antonio Gramsci was an Italian political philosopher in the first decades of the twentieth century who was arrested by Benito Mussolini's Fascist government in the 1920s and imprisoned until his death in 1937. During his imprisonment Gramsci kept notebooks in which he developed some of the most sophisticated understandings of power ever conceptualized. One of these concepts was hegemony. In contemporary democratic states, Gramsci argued, dominant power is no longer exercised simply by physical force but through sociopsychological attempts to win people's consent to domination through cultural institutions such as the schools, the media, the family, and the church.

Gramsci's hegemony posits that winning the popular consent is a very complex process. Power groups win popular consent by way of a pedagogical process, a form of learning that engages people's conceptions of the world in such a way that transforms, not displaces, them with perspectives more compatible with various elites—White supremacy, economic power wielders, patriarchy, heterosexuals, and so on. The existence and nature of hegemony are among the most important and least understood features of contemporary life in industrialized, democratic countries. We are all hegemonized, as our knowledges and understandings are structured by limited exposure to competing definitions of the sociopolitical world. The hegemonic field, with its bounded sociopsychological horizon, garners consent to an inequitable power matrix—a set of social relations that are legitimized by their depiction as natural and inevitable. We come to believe that the world could have existed in no other way: there will always be poor people, and there will be a bell curve distribution of student abilities in every classroom, so many students simply don't have the ability to learn.

The methods of hegemony move social domination from a yellow alert to a red alert. Critical teachers find themselves in a state of full alert in regard to the capacity of power wielders to dominate in the late twentieth century and the first decade of the twenty-first century. This contemporary social condition—this hyperreality—is marked by cultural dislocation because of the bombardment of information that is thrown at us by electronic media. This social vertigo is marked by a loss of touch with traditional notions of time, community, self, and history. This proliferation of signs and images characteristic of information-soaked hyperreality functions as a mechanism of control in contemporary Western societies. The key to a pedagogy that fights dominant power and is counterhegemonic involves the ability to point out the way power operates to produce various representations, images, and signs, and the capacity to illustrate the complex ways that the reception of these images and signs affect individuals located at various race, class, and gender coordinates in the web of social reality.

What this means in everyday life, of course, is the ability of power to produce meaning in ways that move people to adopt particular behaviors that are in the interests of the power wielders. One example is the way Nike has inscribed their athletic shoes with a signifier of status that moves kids of all socioeconomic strata to want them. How did shoes gain such an importance? Nike pours millions of dollars into social research and into advertising to obtain its desired effect. McDonald's (Kincheloe, 2002) and its successful use of advertising cultivates young children as consumers. When corporations such as Nike and McDonald's have produced positive views of their products and the act of consuming them, they generate tremendous goodwill toward the present corporate-dominated sociopolitical environment. Add hundreds of other corporations spending billions of dollars to create positive corporate images, and we have a powerful political force in support of the status quo with its low corporate taxes and good business climates.

The power of these corporate information producers to shape our political viewpoints, our view of success, our view of ourselves, and our view of the world makes them the most important teachers in human history. Classroom teachers need to understand that much of the most powerful pedagogy in the world takes place *outside* of the classroom in contexts carefully produced by corporations promoting TV, radio, movies, video gaming, smart phones, and so on. Corporate-owned media can set agendas, mold loyalties, depict conflicts, and undermine challenges to the political status quo without a modicum of public notice. Critical teachers must work to expose the insidious ways that power shapes our consciousness and the knowledge we are exposed to both in and out of the classroom. This is a central concern of the rigorous classrooms we promote in this book. Such a concern, we argue, moves us to be aware of the fragility of democracy in the our current political climates.

Understanding the Alienation of Contemporary Experience: The Authoritarianism of Positivism

A primary goal of a critical education in the contemporary globalized world involves not a quest for universal truths but an effort to heal the alienation everyday life (Reason & Bradbury, 2000). In this alienation we are removed from the world and other people, the advent of the Internet and social networking has sealed our existence into individual pods, and personal relationships are constantly redefined. Indeed, we are often quite alienated from our own selves, our erotic, passionate, loving, interactive selfhood. In the prevailing knowledge climate of academia we often observe a quest for certainty that alienates us by denying the complexity and ambiguity of everyday life. From the birth of the Scientific Revolution in Western societies in the seventeenth and eighteenth centuries, René Descartes, Sir Isaac Newton, and Francis Bacon—the founders of modern science—sought a perfect form of knowledge. Such "truth" would provide individuals guidance in what to do in professional and personal life. This certainty could only be derived by using the correct method in knowledge production. This correct method we would come to understand as the scientific method. It is the foundation for the knowledge theory (epistemology) of positivism.

Positivism is a key contributor to the alienation we experience in contemporary times. Positivism believes that:

- All true knowledge is scientific knowledge—it is knowledge about which we are positive. *Only Western societies produce such knowledge; other cultures must give up their ways of producing knowledge and follow us.*

- All scientific knowledge is empirically verifiable—through the senses we can count, see, and hear things and thus represent the world in numbers. *Knowledges not grounded empirically and quantitatively about complexities such as feelings, emotion, hurt, humiliation, for example, are often dismissed in the positivist context.*

- One must use the same methods to study the physical world as one uses to study the social and educational worlds—a key dimension of knowledge work in this context involves predicting and controlling natural phenomena. *Human beings are treated like any other "variable" in this framework.*

- If knowledge exists, it exists in some definite, measurable quantity—mathematical language is best suited to express our knowledge of the world. *Many claim that the most important dimensions of education cannot be expressed in this language.*

- Nature is uniform and whatever in it that is studied remains consistent in its existence and behavior—there is an underlying natural order in the way the physical, social, psychological, and educational domains work. *Humans, many argue, are not as predictable and regular as positivists claim.*

- The factors that cause things to happen are limited and knowable, and in empirical studies these factors can be controlled—the best way to study the world is to isolate its parts and analyze them independently of the contexts of which they are a part. *It is profoundly difficult, many assert, to control all of the factors that shape human actions, and when we remove individuals from their social context, we may have destroyed their natural setting that makes them who they are.*

- Certainty is possible, and when we produce enough research we will understand reality well enough to forgo further research—research is like a jigsaw puzzle, a search for all the pieces that give us a final picture of the phenomenon in question. *Such a quest focuses our attention on the trivial, those things that lend themselves to easy measurement.*

- Facts and values can be kept separate, and objectivity is always possible—good research is always politically and morally neutral. *Nonpositivists argue that values, a variety of assumptions, and power dynamics always shape knowledge production.*

- There is one true reality, and the purpose of education is to convey that reality to students—positivist research tells us the best way to teach this reality. *Those who argue that different research methods and different values will produce different views of reality are simply misguided, positivists maintain.*

- Teachers in the positivist framework become "information deliverers," not knowledge-producing and knowledge-questioning professionals—there is no need for teacher education in this context, for teachers should simply pass along the truths that experts have given them. *Scholarly teachers with analytical and interpretive abilities do not fit in the positivist world of schooling.*

- Traditional, Eurocentric ways of knowing are superior to "other" ways of knowing.

Positivism extends alienation, as it induces individuals to focus on knowledge that has little to do with the well-being of human beings as a species. Questions about environmental protection, sustainability, the relationship between humans and the cosmos, tendencies toward militarism, the lost of community, ethical responsibilities, and the disparity of wealth are dismissed in this context. Indeed, the very insights that would lead to a reduction of alienation are devalued in a positivistic epistemology. Our efforts to engage teachers in helping students develop criteria for making ethical choices, to imagine alternatives to present alienating social arrangements, are consistently opposed by positivists. Standardized testing, running records, ready-made curricula all contribute to a positivistic way to educate, as does politically conservative notions of schooling.

We must be able to ask questions of educational goals in a democratic society (Goodson, 1999). These questions cannot be considered out of place and irrelevant, Questions about social alienation have been quashed within curriculum, and attempts to devise new ways of understanding the pedagogical cosmos have been undermined. Right-wing notions of schooling are overtaking school boards and state/provincial education offices. Religious fundamentalists are attempting to control curriculum development.

There is an urgency within these conservative efforts to develop a set of content standards that have to be learned by everyone in order to standardize the nation's curriculum. Right-wing political/educational reformers feel they need a way to control teachers who might be prone to question the traditional positivist verities. If something is not done quickly, many conservatives believe, schools could become places where genuine democratic dialogue took place, where indoctrination about the inferiority of diverse ways of seeing was not tolerated, where classrooms valued the insights and contributions of students from a wide range of cultures and belief systems.

Addressing Alienation: Moving to Multiple Perspectives

Our social and educational imagination cannot be destroyed. As we asserted at the beginning of this chapter, more is possible than conservative educators and their positivist allies ever conceptualized. These regressive forces have attempted to place a lid on human possibility and have induced good minds to focus on the trivial. We can do better. We urge you to advocate a constructive and affirmative critical pedagogy that values human dignity and the sacred relationship between human beings and their physical (environmental), social, cultural, political, economic, and philosophical contexts. The new terrain of insight we envision works to end and transcend positivistic forms of:

- *abstract individualism*—viewing humans apart from the natural contexts that have shaped them

- *technicalization*—valuing the technical over questions of human purpose and wellness

- *mechanization*—understanding humans as machine-like and computer-like, missing in the process the complex dynamics that make humans human

- *economism*—looking at human beings as primarily cogs within the economic domain rather than as sacred and unique entities with infinite capacities for doing good

- *nationalism*—conceptualizing human purpose in light of the competitive needs of the state and a narrow "patriotism" that undermines our capacity to ask ethical and moral questions about our collective behavior (Griffin, 1997)

- *rationalism*—viewing humans those who operate in ways that dismiss the importance of intuition, feeling, affect, emotion, and compassion in the effort to understand self and world

- *objectivism*—understanding that the goal of education and scholarship is to produce and consume a body of neutral data that fails to engage a variety of knowledges produced in diverse ways in differing cultures and historical eras.

Liberated from the positivist discourse of certainty, critically grounded students and teachers come to the realization that there are always multiple perspectives with which they are unfamiliar. Searching for new ways of seeing and multiple perspectives, they find for instance, that art and aesthetics provide a rich domain for such perspectives, new modes of reasoning that have been dismissed by a positivist culture high on the tradition's hyperrationality. Art challenges what the great critical theorist Herbert Marcuse (1955) labeled: "the prevailing principle of reason" (p. 185). Art, imaginative literature, and music grant teachers and students an alternative epistemology, a way of knowing that transcends objective forms of knowledge (Rose & Kincheloe, 2003). Literary texts, drama, painting, sculpture, and dance help individuals see, hear, and feel beyond the surface level of sight and sound. They can alert the awakened to the alienated, one-dimensional profiles of the world promoted by positivistic culture.

Art illuminates the problematic, as it creates new concepts and new angles from which to view the world. In this way art, through its interpreters, gives birth to meaning, as it breaks through the alienated surface to explore the submerged social and political relationships that shape events. In contemporary popular culture, one can see these aesthetic dynamics at work. Observing *The Simpsons* for example, one can see brilliant writers parody the assumptions that lead to alienation in contemporary society. The prejudice, pomposity, self-righteousness, and gravitas of the rich, famous, and powerful are open targets for the critical arrows of the screenwriters. As the socially, politically, and culturally problematic are exposed, the pedagogy of *The Simpsons* becomes an act of defamiliarization. The classroom pedagogy we promote here takes a similar path, as teachers learn not only to defamiliarize the "common-sense" worlds of their peers and students but also to create situations where student experience can be used to defamiliarize the world of schooling.

As aesthetic concerns with the "now" defamiliarize contemporary education's tendency to standardize and formalize the role of instruction, teachers and students seek pleasurable ways of reconceptualizing and reconstructing the institution (Steinberg, 2016). Overcoming the tyranny of reliance on delayed gratification for future success and the demonization of learning that is fun, critical teachers set up a mode of scholarship that is unbowed by the alienating power of positivist truth. Emerging from this playful haughtiness is the realization that the arts promote a form of teaching that requires interpretation and understanding of context. In this context critical teachers fight forces that suppress intellectual and other types of freedom. Addressing alienation necessitates the exposure of these forces, these dominant cultural fictions that attempt to regulate us.

We bring hidden social, political, artistic, and cultural infrastructures to consciousness to facilitate larger efforts to empower teachers and students to make conscious choices concerning their lives. Many educators move through their years of teaching without ever thinking about their own thinking and the infrastructures and discourses that have shaped it. The discourse of positivist science, for example, with its obsession with measurement has shaped the nature of dominant learning experiences in schools. Educational and psychological science has devoted much attention to the development of more precise systems of measurement and the application of such measurement to the minds of students. As a result, many educators and laypeople cannot think of intelligence in any terms other than the number on an IQ test.

Measurement has fragmented the world to the point that individuals are blinded to particular forms of human experience. Attempting to study the world in isolation, bit by bit, educational scientists have separated the study of schools from society. For the purpose of simplifying the process of analysis, disciplines of study are divided arbitrarily without regard for larger context (Kincheloe & Berry, 2004). Educational reforms of recent years, including top-down mandated standards and standardized curriculum, have been formulated outside of the wider cultural and political concerns for where students come from or where they find themselves in relation to education. As politicians of all major parties promote a test-driven, one-size-fits-all curriculum, they create new strains of cognitive and ontological alienation. Finding its roots in positivist fragmentation, recent educational reforms have produced a "factoid syndrome," where students learn isolated bits and pieces of information for texts without concern for relationships among the data or their applications to personal struggles or the problems of the world.

The classrooms we promote are not grounded on an objective curriculum, which refuses to discuss its intellectual roots, its cultural, economic, philosophical, and social assumptions, and its location in history. They are built upon socio-cultural, contextual life world experiences and multiple knowledges. They are built by teachers who understand the diverse nature and needs of different classrooms and students. In the alienated standardized curriculum of the middle of the first decade of the twenty-first century, the claim that "we treat all students the same" is a cruel hoax. A critical curriculum and classroom are grounded on the understanding that this ostensibly benign proclamation shields some harmful practices. Our critical pedagogy commences with an appreciation of the divergent sociocultural locations of schools and students in the web of reality and the power asymmetries that complicate any classroom experience (Apple, 1993). Any attempt to provide an egalitarian and socially-just experience for students in these classrooms begins not with suppression of differences and context, but with a recognition of them that moves us to informed action.

References

Anderson, P., & Summerfield, J. (2004). Why is urban education different from suburban and rural education? In S. Steinberg & J. Kincheloe (Eds.), *19 urban questions: Teaching in the city*. New York, NY: Peter Lang.

Apple, M. (1993). The politics of official knowledge: Does a national curriculum make sense? *Teachers College Record, 95*(2), 222–241.

Bronner, S. (1988). Between art and utopia: Reconsidering the aesthetic theory of Herbert Marcuse. In R. Pippin, A. Feenberg, & C. Webel (Eds.), *Marcuse: Critical theory and the promise of utopia*. Westport, CT: Bergin and Garvey.

Bruner, J. (1996). *The culture of education*. Cambridge, MA: Harvard University Press.

Carr, W. (1998). The curriculum in and for a democratic society. *Curriculum Studies, 6*(3) [Online]. Retrieved from http://www.triangle.co.uk/pdf/validate.asp

Covaleskie, J. (2004). Philosophical instruction. In J. Kincheloe & D. Weil (Eds.), *Critical thinking and learning: An Encyclopedia*. Westport, CT: Greenwood.

Gee, J., Hull, G., & Lankshear, C. (1996). *The new work order: Behind the language of the new capitalism*. Boulder, CO: Westview.

Goodson, I. (1999). The educational researcher as public intellectual. *British Educational Research Journal, 25*(3), 277–297.

Griffin, D. (1997). *Parapsychology, philosophy, and spirituality: A postmodern exploration*. Albany, NY: State University of New York Press.

Harrington, H., & Quinn-Leering, K. (1995, April 25). *Reflection, dialogue, and computer conferencing*. Paper presented to the American Educational Research Association, San Francisco.

Herrnstein, R., & Murray, C. (1994). *The bell curve: Intelligence and class structure in American life*. New York, NY: The Free Press.

Horn, R., & Kincheloe, J. (2001). *American standards: Quality education in a complex world—The Texas case*. New York, NY: Peter Lang.

Kincheloe, J. (1999). *How do we tell the workers? The socioeconomic foundations of work and vocational education*. Boulder, CO: Westview.

Kincheloe, J. (2001). *Getting beyond the facts: Teaching social studies/social sciences in the twenty-first century*. New York, NY: Peter Lang.

Kincheloe, J. (2002). *The sign of the burger: McDonald's and the culture of power*. Philadelphia, PA: Temple University Press.

Kincheloe, J. (2003). Critical ontology: Visions of selfhood and curriculum. *JCT: Journal of Curriculum Theorizing, 19*(1), 47–64.

Kincheloe, J. (2004). *Critical pedagogy*. New York, NY: Peter Lang.

Kincheloe, J., & Berry, K. (2004). *Rigour and complexity in educational research: Conceptualizing the bricolage*. London: Open University Press.

Kincheloe, J., & Steinberg, S. (1997). *Changing multiculturalism*. London: Open University Press.

Marcuse, H. (1955). *Eros and civilization*. Boston: Beacon Press.

Paraskeva, J., & Steinberg, S. R. (Eds.). (2016). *Curriculum: Decanonizing the Field*. New York, NY: Peter Lang.

Reason, P., & Bradbury, H. (2000). Introduction: Inquiry and participation in search of a world worthy of human aspiration. In P. Reason & H. Bradbury (Eds.), *Handbook of action research: Participative inquiry and practice*. Thousand Oaks, CA: Sage.

Rose, K., & Kincheloe, J. (2003). *Art, culture, and education: Artful teaching in a fractured landscape*. New York, NY: Peter Lang.

Roth, W., Tobin, K., & Ritchie, S. (2001). *Re/constructing elementary science.* New York, NY: Peter Lang.

Steinberg, S. R. (2001). *Multi/intercultural conversations.* New York, NY: Peter Lang.

Steinberg, S. R. (2010). Power, emancipation, and complexity: Employing critical theory. *Power and Education, 2*(2), 140–151.

Steinberg, S. R. (2016). Curriculum? Tentative, at best. Canon? Ain't no such thing. In J. Paraskeva & S. R. Steinberg (Eds.), *Curriculum: Decanonizing the field.* New York, NY: Peter Lang.

Willinsky, J. (2001). Raising the standards for democratic education: Research and evaluation as public knowledge. In J. Kincheloe & D. Weil (Eds.), *Standards and schooling in the U.S.: An Encyclopedia.* Santa Barbara, CA: ABC-Clio.

CHAPTER 2

The Meaning of Pedagogy

Philip M. Anderson

Pedagogy determines how teachers think and act. Pedagogy affects students' lives and expectations. Pedagogy is the framework for discussions about teaching and the process by which we do our jobs as teachers. Pedagogy is a body of knowledge that defines us as professionals. Pedagogy is a belief that all children can learn and that it is the duty of the adult to participate in that growth and development. Pedagogy is a definition of culture and a means to transmit that culture to the next generation.

As one can see, pedagogy is one of the difficult words, one of the words that has many meanings. Every important word represents complex concepts and ideas and is, of necessity, not easily defined. The lack of precise definition in this case also results from at least one other circumstance. This circumstance is the continuing battle over the very idea of pedagogy, the modern version of which dates back to the founding of the first teacher education institution by Horace Mann in Massachusetts in 1839. That debate is about whether anyone can learn to teach or whether anyone can really teach anyone anything at all. The most recent version of this debate goes to such extremes as witnessing Texas state legislators passing laws limiting the amount of pre-service pedagogical study in which teachers can participate (to prevent new teachers from studying too much pedagogy because it is bad for them).

The main reason for the complexity of the definition of pedagogy evolves from the complications of definitions in scholarly discourse around the "big" terms, the terms that matter. For example, everyone appears to have a favorable opinion of "democracy" until we get around to agreeing on the definition of democratic activity. Is democratic activity learning to be patriotic supporters or the loyal opposition of the status quo? Educational terms designed as compromises between competing ideas, such as "balanced literacy" (designed as an inclusive term in the phonics and whole language debate), become bitterly contentious when advocates of balanced literacy—liberal or conservative—define the tasks of the teacher and learner. What is balanced to one group is limited or biased to the other. In either circumstance above, much of the debate is over definition. But, then again, the definition of terms is about real practice, philosophy, and policy. In a rational world, words have consequences.

If one looks at the definition of pedagogy in the *Merriam-Webster OnLine* Dictionary, one begins to see why the definition is complicated. It reads: "The art, science, or profession of teaching." The dictionary says that pedagogy can be an "art" or a "science" or a "profession." So, which is it? Merriam-Webster reports that pedagogy may be defined from one worldview or the other. The artistic view of the world and the scientific view of the world are very different, and some would say in opposition to one another. Since modern dictionaries are reports of usage, the way words are actually used in talk and text, pedagogy must be defined in these multiple ways in everyday discourse. In a discussion of pedagogy that is not carefully articulated, we could be talking at cross-purposes or talking from different sets of assumptions.

The dictionary also defines pedagogy as a professional concern. Professional language tends to be technical and limited to the special meanings used by the members of the particular profession. One of the definitions of a professional is someone who understands the technical language of the field of knowledge as well as its practice. The same dictionary says that a profession is "a calling requiring specialized knowledge and often long and intensive academic preparation." I suppose we will need to deal with the word "calling" at some point in this chapter, but let's save it for later. The dictionary appears to be saying that pedagogy is a sophisticated concept and requires some significant study and understanding.

Merriam-Webster additionally refers the reader to a secondary meaning of the word "education" for a further definition of pedagogy: "The field of study that deals mainly with methods of teaching and learning in the schools." This definition is the more limited definition of pedagogy but is more site-specific. Functionally, pedagogy is about teaching in schools. The meaning of pedagogy, whatever it is, has to do with teaching and learning in schools. Though pedagogy is about teaching, it is clearly more than teaching, since it is about learning and learning takes place inside and outside of schools and other institutions. The answer to the definition of pedagogy may be in all three worldviews: the art and the science and the profession of teaching. A look at the development of these approaches to the pedagogy question is necessary to understand where we are now in the task of defining and employing pedagogical study and action.

Talking about Teaching: A Very Short History

Treatises on teaching existed in the ancient world, and books on education were important cultural landmarks in the Renaissance. Most of these discussions of teaching were concerned with teaching for purposes we are not so interested in any more. Most were interested in the humanistic problem of educating the ruling elite or the spiritual problem of preparing the clergy. The modern debate over pedagogy really begins with the development of the common school, the school for everyone, the democratic school for the improvement and maintenance of democracy. The earliest influential thinking in this area came from Horace Mann, mentioned above, and resulted in the (then) radical notion of preparing teachers to teach in a special institution, the "normal school." Throughout the nineteenth century, one finds increasing interest in the art of teaching to promote democratic or republican ideas to replace the educational systems, or lack thereof, in the old monarchies of Europe. Germany was particularly influential during this period, and we see the development of the kindergarten and other innovations in childhood education. By the end of nineteenth century, the progressive thinking of the modern age begins to transform all social thinking, and we have the beginnings of serious re-thinking of social and cultural assumptions. In education, we see the first publication of John Dewey and the beginnings of pragmatist philosophy and experiential learning theories that transform the education of teachers, particularly the development of new methods of teaching in addition to the transformation of the content of the curriculum.

But there have been teachers since ancient times, so there must have been some thinking about how teaching could be accomplished in better or more interesting ways. Over the years the primary discussions of teaching have been about teaching the content of the curriculum, the "stuff" of teaching. In fact, most educational writings of the past—and the conservative writings of the present—focus on the *what* of teaching, the content, rather than the *how*. The modern debate about whether pedagogy is even something that can be studied is a debate between those who see teaching as a complex professional undertaking and those who believe, like conservative icon William Bennett (US Secretary of Education in 1986), that teachers need only show evidence of their knowledge of subject matter, their good character, and their ability to communicate with students in order to teach. If you think pedagogy is difficult to define, try coming up with precise definitions or even functional definitions of "good character" or "knowledge of subject matter."

The important issue here is that Bennett represents a conservative reaction against the modern development of the profession of teaching. The neo-conservatives, writing immediately after the *Nation at Risk* report of 1983, produced a veritable onslaught of anti-pedagogical books. Neo-conservatives such Diane Ravitch, Chester Finn, and E. D. Hirsch railed against the very notion of pedagogy and attacked the knowledge base of teacher education and the knowledge base of schooling. In their various books, the concept of "teaching method" is held up to ridicule, and Bennett's definition of teacher knowledge defines their notions of how teachers might be prepared to teach children. The movement is conservative, indeed reactionary, in its explicit and articulated desire to return to a pre-Dewey emphasis on content learning.

The most recent progressive movement in pedagogy arrives out of that cauldron of controversy and tries to reconcile the argument between the liberal progressive methodologies and the neo-conservative reaction. In the 1980s, the federal government set out to find what made teachers *good* teachers, and various contracts were awarded to study the issue and develop model state guidelines for teacher preparation. State governments were expected to re-think the content of the curriculum in their schools, in particular, to develop common tests of knowledge for students to progress in school and to graduate from high school. Federal contracts for "state frameworks" were also issued during that time to lead the state's efforts. Out of the work of these researchers came the concept of pedagogical content knowledge, a new way to think about our word "pedagogy." Most current state teacher certification guidelines operate under the assumptions within the pedagogical content knowledge model.

Pedagogical content knowledge (PCK) is a hybrid concept that attempts to reconcile the various definitions of pedagogy as an art or a science or a profession. Not understanding the nature, or the roots, of the hybridization in the concept of pedagogical content knowledge can lead to great confusion. PCK is a concept related to professionalization and therefore cannot be commonsensical. In the pages that follow, each of the definitions of pedagogy that have evolved over time will be explained as part of our modern notion of pedagogy, and we will explore the ways in which these very different views of teaching have been brought together as a program of study for teachers.

The Art of Teaching/Craft of Teaching

Pedagogy was originally defined as an art. The teacher learns from the accumulated wisdom and knowledge of teachers of the past, much like an apprentice to any other sort of craftsman. When talking to most people outside of the profession of teaching, one needs to assume that this is the definition of teaching to which they are referring. Pedagogy is about observing and refining one's skill as a teacher, however the culture defines teaching and learning. The Puritan teacher of seventeenth-century Massachusetts had different expectations about the role of the teacher and how children learn than does a twenty-first century teacher in southern California, but both of them still engage the art of teaching passed down through the centuries. Some methods of teaching employed by both remain the same despite the mind-numbing changes between the two teachers and their times.

Within the art of pedagogy position there lies another small but significant debate. Some folks want to insist that teaching is a craft, not an art (or a science or a profession for that matter). The craft definition of teaching is really a form of the art of teaching model, but it wants to limit teacher knowledge and status to a "lower" form of knowledge gained by something less than even apprenticeship standards require. An apprenticeship model assumes that one learns one's craft from a practitioner. The limiting notion of the craft model is not just its lowering of the teacher's status but its assumption that teaching is not that difficult to learn (or, that "anyone" can do it). Craft models are inherently conservative. Craft knowledge changes very slowly and assumes that something is already being done the way it should be, and one learns all one would ever need to know about teaching from working with an experienced master teacher. In contemporary talk about teaching one does hear talk of master teachers. Master teacher-apprentice teacher discourse assumes many features of and animates much of the art and craft model.

The craft model—the art of teaching—has a long history, and one finds the educational thinking within the art of teaching model always returning to the past for answers. The educational reform of medieval learning (500 years of Latin and canonical works of the Bible) in the Renaissance consisted of returning to the even more distant past of ancient Greece and the Roman Empire. Latin, the traditional language of learning, was still retained (and Greek added) in the reform model. The main difference was a shift from the Roman Catholic educational model to the new Reformation-minded religions and then some movement toward secular study. There were efforts to provide a vernacular education of a sort (e.g., most of the new translations of the Bible out of Latin and into modern languages occur at this time), but the traditional methods held sway and one needed access to the traditional language of learning, Latin, to gain access to the texts. The texts were the content of the curriculum; to be educated was to have that knowledge.

The arts and craft model of pedagogy provides us with many features of the curriculum we still retain: the formal study of grammar is one, a holdover from the formal study of Latin, a language no longer spoken by the population at large. Formal study of grammar was not only necessary for scholars to learn Latin, but the study was considered a means for developing "rigor" or discipline of the mind. This sort of formal knowledge was also a good way to strengthen the memory, it was believed. There is a bit of a circular argument here: those who could remember all the rules did indeed have good memories. Did the rule learning strengthen the memory, or did a strong memory help in learning all the rules?

Formal written Latin was also a very regular language, with a very logical sort of grammar as part of its make-up (unlike a living and changing language such as English). Medieval scholars and teachers saw regularity in God's creation, the earth, the people, the language and believed in a very logical way of constructing a curriculum and regular ways of engaging in pedagogy. By logical, I do not mean modern scientific logic but the logic of the medieval world. Pedagogical practice reflected an orderly word, a spiritual world, and a world unchanging. One's education was a spiritual education. Much of the moral tradition of pedagogy, that teachers teach appropriate or "good" behavior, goes back to the beginnings of teaching.

Discipline, or teaching children how to behave, is a traditional craft concern. One of the first things a new teacher hears from veteran teachers are "tricks" for "controlling" a classroom. "Don't smile until Christmas" is an all-time favorite and is also a suggestion about the demeanor a teacher should bring to the classroom.

This sort of craft knowledge, or teacher lore, is usually based on a somewhat old-fashioned view of the role of children in society; many times this view reflects a continuing Puritan ethic about being seen and not heard. But craft knowledge does change when society changes. Corporal punishment has a long history in schools but has now generally disappeared with the new children's rights movement. Parents have challenged the *in loco parentis* tradition of the art of pedagogy in recent years, arguing that teachers do not have the right or the responsibility of a parent in teaching children. On the other hand, the notion that the teacher is acting in the place of the parent is still a strong assumption of any school system, and the teacher's present legal responsibilities are predicated on *in loco parentis*.

In the craft model, much is made of the "way we used to do things." Tradition is revered, while change is suspect. Another fact of the craft model is that many adults, including teachers without other pedagogical training, rely on their perceptions of teaching which they experienced as a student (see Cuban, 1993). The logic appears unassailable: generations of kids before have done well under these craft pedagogies, so why should we change? The traditional model does not support change for the sake of change; those who support the craft model question why someone would want to change the pedagogy in the first place. Traditionalists fear that the teacher with different pedagogical assumptions has a social or political agenda he or she wishes to promote. Are we "experimenting" on the children? Are the children "missing out" on the "basics" in this new curriculum? Isn't the important stuff from the past just as important now as then? Are we forgetting our history? In any case, why change when there is nothing wrong?

One contemporary version of the art of teaching approach to pedagogy is very different from the traditional craft model. The "art of teaching" sometimes means an "aesthetic view of teaching." An aesthetic view of teaching, such as that presented by Elliot Eisner (1979), assumes that teachers engage in behavior that promotes the perspective and performance of the artist. This particular model of the art of teaching, which is not a craft model, requires extensive pedagogical training, theoretical grounding, and new modes of thinking and discourse. The aesthetic view of teaching fits under the pedagogical content knowledge discussion in the pages to come. The point here is not to confuse the art and craft traditional model of pedagogy with the essentially postmodern aesthetic model of teaching and learning. The aesthetic view of teaching and learning is grounded in theory.

I make special mention of theory here because the traditional art of teaching definition of pedagogy is "atheoretical"—that is, it is not contingent upon or advanced by theories of learning or teaching. Instead, the art of teaching, as suggested above, is an experiential model of learning. Does this mean that the art of teaching definition of pedagogy relies on experiential learning, similar to that articulated by John Dewey and the progressives? No, it does not. And here resides one of the paradoxes of the art/craft of teaching definition that demonstrates its limitations for defining all of pedagogical study.

Though one does experiential learning in art/craft classrooms, that phenomenon is a result of "contamination" by 100 years of progressive education. Underlying most traditional craft pedagogies is an assumption that learning is a set of information. The neo-conservative version of the argument (cultural literacy) is an information-processing model of thinking (analogous with computer database storage) and measures student success on recall of specific information. Much of the art/craft of teaching model is based on this assumption of academic formalism in student learning. The teacher's job in the art/craft model is to provide formal academic knowledge, and pedagogical study is defined as learning that formal knowledge and learning ways to present the knowledge to kids. The biggest change in the art/craft model in recent years, though it has been there since the beginning, is the increased emphasis on student testing (thereby further confusing means with ends).

The Science of Teaching and the Science of Learning

The scientific definition of pedagogy is the major contribution of the modern age of pedagogical study. The origin of the scientific definition comes from the study of psychology, particularly the study of how children and adolescents learn. In fact, it was a psychologist who defined adolescence as a developmental stage back at the turn of the twentieth century (Hall, 1904). John Dewey's first book was a book on educational psychology, written in the 1890s. During the great age of reform, 1890–1945 (see Hofstadter, 1955; Cremin, 1961), science was the new knowledge and the standard by which the significance of knowledge was measured. Dewey's pragmatic philosophy was predicated on a scientific ontology. In education, psychologists such as E. L. Thorndike created a new pedagogy out of the study of human behavior. Most of our modern notions of how humans grow and develop were shaped in this era and continue as a major part of what is defined as educational research.

From the science of pedagogy we developed our notions of age-appropriate curriculum. Whatever rationale one uses, most modern pedagogy is based on the assumption that little children learn in different ways and need different content than do adolescents and adults. The work of Jean Piaget demonstrated that children tend to be concrete learners who become more capable of abstraction as they grow older (Piaget, 1973). Teachers who spent time focusing on abstraction at the expense of concrete learning taught something younger students could not yet learn. Piaget and other scholars' work also appeared to suggest that there was an orderly fashion in which people developed and that there were common potentials at various stages of development. Learning began to be talked of in terms of the scope (range) and the sequence (order).

The idea that foundational knowledge assisted students in their later development also comes from the science of pedagogy model. In language development, one sees good examples of the scientific model in the phonics programs in schools. Much of the pedagogical wisdom on sound/letter correspondence (i.e., phonics), vocabulary learning, reading comprehension measured as recall of text, and silent reading are a result of the scientific study of how children learn language. The focus on reading at the expense of writing, however, was not a scientific choice but a political one (see below).

Unlike the "logical" organization of the curriculum in the art of pedagogy model, this new way of pedagogical thinking used "psychological" organization (Dewey, 1910). In a logical model, one looks at a body of knowledge, breaks it down into its parts, and teaches from what appears to be the simplest, usually smallest, component of the task or information. In this logical frame, the teacher moves from that small or simple bit of information to what appears to be the more difficult, usually the largest chunk of information. For example, the art and craft model of teaching has always taught writing to children by beginning with writing single sentences. It was assumed that not only was a single sentence the simplest element of writing (it is called the simple sentence in formal grammar, after all), but that writing a good sentence was prerequisite to writing a paragraph. When researchers actually studied how adults write, and subsequently how children write, it became clear that all writers saw the task of writing as "holistic." No writer asks, "What is my first sentence, and then what is my second sentence?" He begins by conceiving the larger rhetorical task for the audience and purpose established. It was also clear that writing was a multiple-draft effort and that correctness of spelling and other grammatical and rhetorical issues could be dealt with in various revisions instead of focusing on writing one "correct" sentence after another as we went along. The long-held tradition of reading first and writing second was also found to be unhelpful in the larger development of literacy, since the tasks of learning each were reciprocal in their cognitive and behavior imperatives.

What I am describing above, of course, is the whole language approach to reading and writing. Oddly, supporters of the phonics approach attack the whole language approach to reading pedagogy. Since both approaches draw their legitimacy from the scientific approaches to pedagogy, how can they be at odds with one another? Phonics advocates argue that the fundamentals of sound/letter correspondence (matching letters with possible sounds) come before all literacy behavior and must be mastered first. The phonics approach also privileges reading over writing based on the same assumption (though cognitively it makes little sense). But if one looks closely, the phonics pedagogy is not just about sound/letter correspondence but "correctness" and a logically organized curriculum. The one correct sentence at a time method is clearly a syntactic or grammatical exercise, not a rhetorical or writing task. The phonics approach tends to emphasis correctness and formal grammar and a range of other traditional art/craft methods. It is about a logical organization of the curriculum, more a craft model of pedagogy than a scientific one. The scientific study of phonics was turned into a traditional pedagogy, primarily to provide a pseudo-scientific rationale for the traditional curriculum. The "balanced literacy" model attempts to reconcile both approaches, which is why balanced literacy advocates can agree on the term but not on the implementation.

The other key element of the science of teaching definition of pedagogy comes from a belief in Western science that equates efficiency with efficacy. In other words, science not only creates new knowledge but also helps us make better use of our resources and time. Part and parcel with the scientific movement in the reform age is the notion of scientific management and social efficiency. It was the scientific study of the social efficiency of teaching and learning Latin in 1912 that finally removed Latin from the required curriculum. Scientific evidence of Latin's efficacy in teaching thought, grammar, or important cultural content was found to be lacking. The traditional curriculum passed down through the centuries and dating back to medieval teaching was summarily eliminated by the new scientific view of the world and its methods of dealing with the world.

The science of teaching also gives us the "content versus process" debate in teaching, so forcefully re-articulated by the neoconservatives in the 1980s. The content versus process debate is the central argument between the art/craft and science approaches to pedagogy. Much of the educational psychology research was concerned with the process of teaching. Traditionally, the art/craft of teaching model tended to focus on a single defined content: the traditional curriculum. The scientific study of the process of learning uncovered many traditional practices that inhibited learning or at least made learning less efficient. Latin, as cited above, was one victim. Latin was argued to be inefficient for schooling that was not conducted in the language. Experimental and observational study of the way children actually learned English led to all sorts of new pedagogical methods in classrooms. One of those new methods was silent reading. Oral recitation, a standard practice of the art/craft model, was determined to be inefficient and not helpful in developing reading skills and was replaced by silent reading techniques and testing. The process of learning, embodying sound psychological developmental research, became the standard for pedagogical thinking.

Here is where experiential learning became a priority in pedagogical thinking. The famous Dewey attribution, "learning by doing," comes from the scientific model of pedagogy. Concern with educating the "whole child" comes from scientific study of the human organism; a healthy mind and a healthy body are seen as complementary. Physical education (and even recess) is invented to improve the health and well-being of children (in scientific terms). Nutrition programs (including school lunch) become part of the school's functions and part of a comprehensive approach to the education and growth of children and adolescents. The building and administration of schools, based on sound scientific research and scientific management imperatives, is introduced into training of administrators. Scientific pedagogy and its social efficiency concepts made the case for the movement toward comprehensive schooling (educating the whole child and educating all children regardless of social class) as opposed to simple academic schooling of the art/craft model.

Scientific study also demonstrated the value of student "interests" in developing age-appropriate curriculum. New curriculum content was introduced to match up with the new methods of teaching designed from the process of learning research. If students did learn better when the content reflects their interests, then new reading materials focusing on their everyday experience were needed. New texts that reflected appropriate vocabulary learning levels were introduced into the schools. Eventually, studies found that only 220 words are fundamental to most human communication, and that word list became the basis for controlled vocabulary in the new developmental reading texts. Whereas reading aloud was the traditional pedagogical model, new studies demonstrated that silent reading was more efficient, and techniques improving fluency and comprehension through silent reading were introduced into teacher's pedagogical approaches.

The scientific movement approach to pedagogy changes the content of the curriculum in schools and colleges. The social sciences came into being and challenged history as the main curricular emphasis in schools. The science curriculum, virtually absent from the liberal arts curriculum until the twentieth century, takes precedence over other subjects. The scientific method also transforms whole disciplines other than psychology, applying scientific method to study of English, for instance, with the emergence of the New Criticism. A long-term project to replace normal schools as craft institutions and absorb teacher preparation in the new colleges begins in the 1930s and is completed in the mid-1960s. The study of teaching should be scientific; it should be modern, and it should shed itself of the old ways just as the new scientific age was shedding the past. Only the universities contained the academic rigor and the range of intellectual opportunities necessary to the study of pedagogy, and universities became the site of pedagogical study under the watchful eye of the state education authorities.

Pedagogy and the Professionalizing of Teaching

The latest movement in pedagogical study focuses on the efforts to make teaching a profession. Teacher licensing has been with us for decades, but it was the academic resurgence of the 1980s that promoted new standards for teacher certification, raising the academic standards for entry into the teaching profession. Most of the impetus for this change was the federal report called *A Nation at Risk* (National Commission on Excellence in Education, 1983), which was severely critical of a perceived lack of academic rigor in US K–12 schooling. Predictably, the effort to raise academic standards became an implicit (and sometimes explicit, see William Bennett and the neo-conservatives) attack on the value of—and even the need for—pedagogical study. Despite the continuing debates in the culture about pedagogy at large (see, for instance, the spate of Teach for America-type "alternate route" programs now operating on the assumption that the "good" people need little pedagogical training), the states have developed new certification rules and regulations for teachers that assume that teachers need a body of knowledge that is not the basic liberal arts curriculum of their college years and that there is sufficient scientific research about teaching and learning to demonstrate teachers need advanced study as well as experience.

There have been various attempts to bring teacher preparation into colleges in an intellectually sound manner—that is, to provide a full liberal arts education and still keep the best of the old teacher colleges, especially the child psychology—but the marriage was clearly an arranged one for convenience without much love lost between the partners. Very little effort has been made in the academic disciplines to modify the curriculum to reflect the content that teachers required for teaching children and adolescents. The elementary education elements of teacher preparation have remained largely separate from the rest of the college until recently and not because the elementary faculty and students were not interested in the liberal arts. The recent movement toward professionalization has resulted in elementary education majors now being required to major in a second area, a traditional academic major, to be certified to teach. The logic here is that the study of a college discipline is an important part of developing intellectual capacity. This sounds like the craft model by any rationale.

And so, the modern preparatory work for teacher preparation has been an attempt to bring together the craft tradition and the scientific tradition. The assumption was that teachers, both general education and discipline-based majors, still needed a traditional liberal arts education. The knowledge future teachers received while pursuing the liberal arts and sciences (note the split in the name between arts and sciences) was supposed to be whatever other "non-education" students were gaining, the somewhat circular notion of being "liberally educated." But we do know what this means: the belief that education builds tolerance, that knowledge brings wisdom, that intellectual activity brings success and happiness, and that the technical, managerial, and leadership classes should have a humanistic education (much as the Renaissance treatises on educating the ruling elite argued).

The teacher preparation area of the higher education of K–12 teachers was tri-partite. The first part was educational foundations, which taught, as implied by the name, the intellectual foundations of education in Western society, mostly focused on philosophical and historical writings. The foundations part was a liberal arts model focused on educational questions and traditions. What teachers learned about teaching from the liberal arts and the educational foundations was merely craft knowledge if that. Very little attention was paid to the job of teaching kids, and foundations professors, who did not spend much time thinking about schools or working in them, frequently saw themselves as liberal arts faculty trapped in the school of education. The actual liberal arts faculty in the academic disciplines spent no time on pedagogical questions except to frequently attack the poor preparation of high school students and question the intellectual capacity of students wishing to become teachers rather than professors.

The second part of teacher preparation in higher education, which accommodated the scientific model of pedagogical study, produced courses in human growth and development and educational psychology. These courses, as well, tended to emphasize content and knowledge extraneous to the specific task of teaching kids and instead provided future teachers with knowledge gleaned from a hundred years of scientific research on human development. The educational psychology part of the equation tended to focus on studies of learning, both human and animal, and required the teacher to apply these principles of learning to the craft knowledge the teachers took to the classroom. Studies of learning frequently find the teacher an obstacle to efficient learning, and educational psychologists are wont to suggest that the best learning situations are the ones that eliminate the "teacher variable" (the euphemism is "individualized learning"). Tension between classroom teachers and educational researchers has always been based on this problematic assumption.

The third part of teacher preparation and certification is the so-called "methods courses," so named because they have traditionally focused on the methods of teaching. The original structure and content of the professional education courses appeared to be fundamentally craft knowledge. These courses were frequently connected to experiential learning in classrooms and normally preceded practice teaching apprenticeships. Though some of the professional education course work aimed to teach "general methods" (i.e., how to discipline children, how to write a lesson plan, how to keep a grade book, and other elements of the day-to-day life of teachers), most professional education courses in this new era are "discipline specific." The discipline specificity reflects some of the most important work on pedagogy done in the past century, the research on teacher knowledge and skills, primarily through the pioneering work of Lee Shulman (1986) and his associates, that has been termed pedagogical content knowledge. The transformation of "methods" from craft knowledge to professional knowledge came about through the development of articulated pedagogical content knowledge in the academic disciplines.

Shulman's research on good teaching led to several interesting new ways of conceiving of teacher knowledge and teacher development and preparation. Shulman found that there were identifiable characteristics in the knowledge and skills of successful teachers, teachers he termed experts. Teachers who did not possess the knowledge and skills were either ineffective or newer, less experienced teachers, whom Shulman termed novices. The pedagogical content knowledge of successful teachers fell into several important categories. I quote from a science teachers website (Herr, 2001)] a discipline notorious for resisting pedagogical study, simply to show how deeply the concept of PCK has affected thinking about pedagogy:

According to Shulman (1986), PCK includes "the most useful forms of representation of [topics], the most powerful analogies, illustrations, examples, explanations, and demonstrations—in a word, the ways of representing and formulating the subject that make it comprehensible to others. ... Pedagogical content knowledge also includes an understanding of what makes the learning of specific topics easy or difficult: the conceptions and preconceptions that students of different ages and backgrounds bring with them to the learning of those most frequently taught topics and lessons."

The author of the website goes on to define the basic categories of pedagogical content knowledge, stating that pedagogical content knowledge is an accumulation of the following common elements:

- Knowledge of subject matter

- Knowledge of students and possible misconceptions

- Knowledge of curricula

- Knowledge of general pedagogy

The author goes on to state that PCK is knowing what, when, why, and how to teach using a reservoir of knowledge of good teaching practice and experience (Herr, 2001).

This is an accurate representation of the basic categories of pedagogical content knowledge, but it seems a bit formalistic in its outline form. One of the central features of Shulman's research was that pedagogical content was discipline based. Teachers of English taught somewhat differently than teachers of mathematics based on the expectations of their academic disciplines and the professed aims of those knowledge and skill sets in the larger culture. There were characteristics that were common to all effective teachers, but teachers of different disciplines exhibited different mindsets, or stances, depending on the discipline.

The pedagogical content knowledge approach, which currently governs most teacher testing and certification, poses some intradisciplinary problems, the most interesting being the articulation of DBAE, or discipline-based art education (see Eisner, 1979). In art teaching one finds a traditional split between artistry, the production of art, and the appreciation or history of art, the spectator function. Many art teachers who emphasize the production of art in their classes objected to the idea that certification knowledge should focused on knowledge of art history. The split between the artistry approach and the art history/cultural appreciation approach is institutionalized in higher education as the art department and the art history department, two separate majors in the art department. The emphasis on cultural history in the pedagogical content knowledge of art teacher certification is then also a statement about the direction and content of art teaching. In the end, most state teacher certification promotes a combination of the two domains though the testing is overwhelmingly from the DBAE approach.

The PCK approach to pedagogy does try to reconcile the craft tradition with the scientific, but in the end, the pedagogical content model is empirical and scientific in its orientation and assumptions. PCK is in opposition to the craft model; it is a challenge to the craft model. There are conservative elements, in particular the assumption of disciplinary knowledge as the basis for teaching content, but in general the PCK even challenges the hegemony of the disciplines. PCK challenges the disciplines simply by its emphasis on teaching children and adolescents in a developmentally appropriate way. As Dewey pointed out a long time ago, the logical organization of any discipline is an adult understanding—the psychological organization of the curriculum is necessary to bring children to the eventual adult understanding.

Among the various researchers engaged in Shulman's PCK studies was one in particular, Pamela Grossman, whose research on new English teachers reported in *The Making of a Teacher* (1990) played out the distinction between the art/craft model and the pedagogical content model. Grossman actually examined the two paradigms of craft knowledge and pedagogical content knowledge through studying two groups of novice teachers, alternate route teachers with little pedagogical content preparation and teachers who completed a teacher preparation program.

Grossman's assumptions about pedagogical content knowledge, drawn from Shulman's work, are more sophisticated than our laundry list above. Here are the four central tenets of pedagogical content knowledge that directed her investigation of new teachers from the art/craft (only) model and pedagogical content knowledge paradigms:

- knowledge and beliefs about the purpose of teaching a subject at various grade levels;

- knowledge of students' understanding, conceptions, and misunderstandings of particular topics in a discipline;

- knowledge of curriculum materials available for teaching particular subject matter as well as knowledge about both the horizontal and vertical curricula for a subject; and

- knowledge of instructional strategies and representations for teaching particular topics. (pp. 8–9)

Grossman's research demonstrated rather forcefully that those who did not engage in professional preparation—that is, did not have pedagogical content knowledge—taught in fundamentally different ways than those who were prepared to be teachers. Many of the art/craft model teachers were unsuccessful in teaching students and, worse, had very little basis for making instructional decisions or growing as teachers. They could not be reflective about their practice because they had no basis for reflection. Their knowledge tended to focus on adult understandings of the logically organized knowledge from their college studies. Asked to explain their failures, they frequently blamed the kids.

The social function of PCK is part of the professionalization of teaching, and its value lies in defining professional knowledge. As one can see, both the craft knowledge model and the scientific model can be employed without treating the issue of professionalization of teaching. It is PCK that brings the two competing models together by reconciling the value of both, however uncomfortably. For teachers to be accountable "professionals" there must be a special language and practice arrived at through study. Professionals are decision-makers who draw upon the best resources in their fields of practice. The range and complexity of the pedagogical field require an intellectual framework worthy of its complexity. Pedagogical content knowledge serves such a purpose, and some important research shows its functional value in the day-to-day work of the teaching professional.

Post-Modern Critiques of Modernist Pedagogy

Post-modernism is a critique of modernism, particularly the use of science as the primary focus of knowledge legitimization. Post-modernist thinking rejects the "objectivism" of science and promotes multi-logical and culturally sensitive approaches to knowledge (Kincheloe, 2004). There is strong case for the argument that the pedagogical content knowledge approach is a modernist construct, but the attempt to bring together the craft and scientific approaches to teaching itself is based on the postmodern impulse to account for the seemingly irreconcilable. What pedagogical content knowledge signifies is a return to complexity in thinking about pedagogy while maintaining several elements of scientific approaches and traditional craft knowledge. There is a strong element of reflective pedagogy in the pedagogical content knowledge paradigm, assuming that the teacher's function is that of a professional practitioner who is a creator of new knowledge in the field of practice.

Post-modernism has influenced each of the areas of pedagogical content knowledge, beginning with foundational work and disciplinary work, both deeply affected by the movement called cultural studies. The educational psychology movement has been transformed by attention to what is called constructivism. The professional knowledge has been transformed and critiqued by something called critical pedagogy. Each of these postmodern movements is interrelated in the critique of the art/craft and scientific pedagogies.

The scientific model has run into various criticisms in recent years from differing fronts, in particular the emerging field of cultural studies. Cultural studies, despite what some seem to claim, is not the singular domain of the social sciences. The scientific movement legitimated the social sciences and transformed foundational work in education from the craft model, adding social foundations to the philosophical and the historical. Cultural studies is as prevalent in the arts and humanities as in the social sciences, perhaps more so—the aesthetics of teaching mentioned at the beginning of the chapter is an example of a post-modern challenge to science-based pedagogy. Feminist pedagogy, an interdisciplinary approach to knowledge that crosses all the arts and sciences, presents itself as another critique of science and its cultural biases associated with the tradition of male-dominated science.

Constructivism is a response to the implied stimulus-response, behaviorist structure of educational psychology research and its attendant pedagogical principles. The extreme version of the behaviorist paradigm, growing out of a long tradition of "teacher-proof" materials is "scripted teaching," the most extreme version of which provides both the questions and the answers for the teacher, who is not expected to deviate from the written script. Reflective teaching is also part of the constructivist model of pedagogy in that it assumes that not only is knowledge self- and socially constructed, but that, by definition, what the teacher does in teaching follows a constructivist set of assumptions.

Critical pedagogy is a special case, in that it does not always focus on classroom teaching but is a critique of knowledge itself. Critical pedagogy involves reflective practice but reflective practice that is a critique of the status quo. Critical pedagogy is a post-modernist critique of the nature and purpose of schooling that makes several assumptions missing from the craft and science models, one very important one being that all educational practice is political in nature and is concerned with access and equality in society.

The Future of Pedagogy

The future of pedagogy really breaks down to a battle between professionalism and dilettantism. Can anyone who is "committed" to teaching do it, or does it require serious study and professional preparation? Teacher researcher pedagogy suggests that teachers teach and, properly situated, construct new teacher knowledge in their classrooms. Originating with Dewey's notion of experimental education, the newest version of teacher professionalism asks the teacher to engage in a pedagogy that is simultaneously both researcher and teacher driven. The future of the teacher as professional lies in the hands of teachers in their own classrooms and the creation of a new pedagogy based on the PCK model but reflecting the new movements in cultural thinking. Teachers must also resist some of the current efforts to reduce teaching to a technical craft in the employ of the government officials who appear to wish to limit the curriculum and the purposes of schooling to simple information and basic skills.

The "calling" of teaching, in the sense of *Merriam-Webster's* assertion that a profession is a calling, returns to the heart of the matter, the original ethical and religious models for teaching the young. The notion of a calling can be part of a neo-conservative trend in society to return to the spiritual, meaning the moral, as played out in the United States as a form of Puritanism. But there is nothing wrong with feeling a calling to teaching. Whatever the impulse, the desire to be a teacher should be paired with a desire to learn as much about your calling as possible, to keep an open mind, and to be prepared to not only know everything you can but also to envision and produce the future of your profession.

References

Cremin, L. (1961). *The transformation of the schools.* New York: Vintage Books.

Cuban, L. (1993). *How teachers taught: Constancy and change in American classrooms, 1890–1990.* New York: Teachers College Press.

Dewey, J. (1910/1997). *How we think.* Mineola, NY: Dover.

Eisner, E. (1979). *The educational imagination: On the design and evaluation of school programs.* New York: Macmillan.

Grossman, P. (1990). *The making of a teacher: Teacher knowledge and teacher education.* New York: Teachers College Press.

Hall, G. S. (1904). *Adolescence: Its psychology, and its relation to physiology, anthropology, sociology, sex, crime, religion and education.* New York: Appleton.

Herr, N. (2001). Pedagogical content knowledge in science teaching. *Sourcebook for teaching science.* http://www.csun.edu/~vceed002/ref/pedagogy/pck

Hofstadter, R. (1955). *The age of reform: From Bryan to F.D.R.* New York: Random House/Vintage.

Kincheloe, J. (2004). *Critical pedagogy primer.* New York: Peter Lang.

National Commission on Excellence in Education (April, 1983). *A nation at risk: The imperative for educational reform* (A report to the nation and the Secretary of Education, United States Department of Education by the National Commission on Excellence in Education). Washington, DC: USDE.

Piaget, J. (1973). *To understand is to invent: The future of education.* New York: Grossman.

Shulman, L. (1986). Those who understand: Knowledge growth in teaching. *Educational Researcher 15*(2), 4–14.

CHAPTER 3

About Power and Critical Pedagogy

Shirley R. Steinberg and Joe L. Kincheloe

The question of power and its effects on what we do in education is the focus of this chapter. The dramatic changes in our political perspectives over the last forty years have taken place because of the efforts of dominant power to develop better business climates. These changes in political perspectives—this reeducation—have profoundly reshaped many people's viewpoint on the goals of education. The idea that one of the central purposes of schools is to strengthen our democracy has been overshadowed by a view of schooling as an aid to personal advancement. Of course, personal advancement is a very important purpose of school but not to the exclusion of education's civic functions (Bracy, 1997). While enabling the transition from school to work is an important dimension of schooling, the nature of this process is all-important. Again, this is an issue of power (Steinberg, 2010). Whose interest does this worker education serve? Do students being trained for work after high school develop the skills to be informed, empowered workers in a democratic and egalitarian society? Do they have the opportunity to critically analyze the occluded social norms, cultural practices, political economic assumptions, and the frameworks of the worker education programs themselves that operate in the shadows?

Power and the Production of the Regulated Self

In the political climate of the last forty years, vulnerable, non-university preparatory students are unfortunately not told the whole story. They are not informed that business and corporate leaders often tell schools what types of workers they want. And the type of workers they want are not usually the empowered, democratic, power-literate, justice-seeking, analytical students whom we want to see graduating from high school. Indeed, union-hating, docile, authority-respecting, anti-intellectual students are much more attractive to many business and corporate leaders than the ones we treasure. Such leaders often speak about adjusting students to the demands of the free market, not about changing the market to their needs as human beings. They speak often about adjusting students to the status quo, not about adjusting the status quo to students. Questions of social justice and the cultivation of the intellect often run ideologically counter to the needs of the market. The concept of graduating students who offer social critiques is unacceptable to the corporatized political landscape of the twenty-first century.

Our vision of curriculum and classroom pedagogy is suspect in this corporatized terrain. The mission of corporate advertisers and knowledge producers is not simply to sell products but to shape consciousness so consumption becomes a central preoccupation of human life. The production of this corporatized, hegemonized state of consciousness is the primary pedagogical act of the contemporary era. Whenever we forget that this is the case, we lose our ability to make sense of twenty-first century educational politics. We can find the influence of this pedagogical impulse in all aspects of social, cultural, political, psychological, and educational life in the globalized world we inhabit. We can begin to understand why classroom pedagogies designed to render students passive, docile, and receptive still thrive in the contemporary era (Covaleskie, 2004). What doesn't make sense viewed in isolation becomes more understandable when viewed in context. Many teachers enter elementary and secondary classrooms without any prior study of these sociopolitical dynamics.

The failure of teacher education to help teachers situate teaching and learning in larger historical contexts is tragic. When the influence of what Joe has elsewhere called a mechanistic (Kincheloe, 2005) educational psychology is added to the mix, we obtain a clearer picture of how education often operates to regulate individuals in the interests of dominant power. It is mechanistic in that it uses machine metaphors to understand the complex workings of the mind. Over the last half century it has conceptualized the mind as a computer, thus reducing the interactive complexity of cognition to a self-contained software program. As a discourse of positivism, mechanistic educational psychology, from its inception in the early twentieth century to the present, has served as a discourse of ordering, categorizing, and regulating.

The poor, the non-White, refugees, Indigenous peoples and immigrants have been the individuals deemed to be in the most need of regulation because of the perceived danger they present to the larger society. Thus, educational psychology was there to "prove" that these people did not possess the intellectual ability to succeed in school and therefore needed to be socially regulated so they would not stain the social fabric. As a form of regulatory power, educational psychology has operated to discover universal "truths" about individuals that were used to determine their worth to the social order. Those who score low on standardized tests, for example, cannot enter the domain of sociopolitical decision-makers.

One of the most important dimensions of the power to regulate comes from educational psychology's authority to objectively describe an individual's intellectual ability. Such pronouncements are ideological as they work to maintain dominant power relations. It is no surprise that it is the well-to-do who are deemed intelligent and the poor and racially marginalized who are deemed incapable by the psychological establishment. As the positivistic hyperrationality of the mainstream of the discipline refuses to consider the sociopolitical dimension of psychological activities, the field produces a bureaucracy of rule-following technocrats. Such functionaries study the mechanical parts of the watch but have never thought about the nature of time. Many educational psychologists' pernicious use—see Richard Herrnstein and Charles Murray's *The Bell Curve* (1994)—of African American IQ scores to illustrate Black inferiority to White represents an obvious deployment of psychology as a regulatory force. Of course, when such assertions are made, analysts find that tough questions about the nature of intelligence, factors that affect one's relation to the test, the motives of the psychologists involved, or the perspectives of dissenting psychologists are often repressed.

Critical educators are profoundly interested in these dynamics and what they tell us about the politics of teaching and learning. We argue that such understandings should be central dimensions of what teachers need to know. The more we know about classroom teaching, the more we understand that all dimensions of education hold political implications. How we think (cognition) is a profoundly political act. It is not, as mechanistic educational psychology has contended, an individual mental activity. As with learning itself, cognition is both an individual and a social action. Where its individual dimension ends and the social begins is not discernable; indeed, the individual and the social cannot be separated. This is what positivistic observers have missed in the process, causing great harm to children and adults. The classroom teachers we want to occupy our schools will not miss this lesson; they understand that student ability is not simply an individual matter and will develop teaching strategies that takes this insight into account.

One of the simplest teaching strategies that take this lesson into account involves operating under the assumption that all children can learn, no matter what their background. In the positivistic and mechanistic universe, such an assumption has become a radical position. Critical classroom teachers refuse to buy into the deficit model of positivism and mechanism. In this deficit context academic failure is viewed as a personal failure of individual students. When student problems are psychologized in this way, educators are induced to blame the victims of oppressive social, cultural, and economic conditions. Classroom teachers must be able to read the imprints of such oppression on the minds and bodies of their students. We understand that such a task is difficult when the power of mechanistic psychology and positivist forms of education to label and categorize is so pervasive. Critical educators are not afraid to fight these insidious forms of regulation.

We can do better. We can work for an educational psychology that understands the ways it reflects the prejudices and power hierarchies of dominant culture, the ways it transubstantiates cultural traits into universal norms. The educational psychology that imposes its view of students on schools and classrooms is an ethnocentric psychology that reflected the norms of a particular segment (the socially, culturally, and economically privileged) of Western societies. The frameworks of understanding employed by these groups were institutionalized in cognitive studies as "intelligence." The view of the individual as existing apart from society as a self-formed and self-directed entity was institutionalized in personality psychology as "normal development." Once we have the humility to examine other cultures' ways of understanding the world and the nature of human development, we begin to understand that these descriptions of intelligence and normal development are more porous than we thought.

There may be diverse ways of demonstrating intelligence and development if we are smart enough to recognize them. We may come to realize that the use of rigid, monological definitions of these dynamics can result in the regulation of "different" individuals in ways that demand they be more like Western, White, male, upper-middle-class Christians. In this ideological context education becomes a type of colonization. Students from "inferior" backgrounds are regulated to fit the needs of the "superior" culture. Is it surprising in this context that many Black students equate being educated with becoming White (Emdin & Adjapong, 2018)? They are resisting the colonizing elements of positivist education and mechanistic psychology. Teachers who have never been exposed to this critique of educational regulation will see their mission as saving the souls of their poor and non-White students (Henke, 2000). Salvation in this context involves bequeathing them the gospel of dominant cultural morals, aspirations, and behavior.

Creating Counterhegemonic Classrooms: Critical Pedagogy and Curriculum

Positivist and mechanistic perspectives and colonizing pedagogies must be countered by scholarly, empowered, and well-organized teachers. Critical teachers refuse to accept standardized, externally developed, scripted curricula that appeal to the lowest common denominator of teacher and student ability. Critical teachers maintain that students should study the world around them, learning who they are and what has shaped them in the process. In this context students are challenged to analyze and interpret data, conduct research, and develop a love for scholarship that studies things that matter. Critical middle school math teachers in this counterhegemonic context see their goals as cultivating a love for math, developing student interest in finding more and more uses for math in their lives, and producing a passion in students to know more about the subject.

No discussion of counterhegemonic classroom teaching would be complete without the insights of Paulo Freire, the Brazilian educator. Both Freire (1970) and Ira Shor (1992) have studied curriculum development in this context, employing the concept of a "generative theme." A generative theme is a topic taken from students' lived experience that is compelling and controversial enough to elicit their excitement and commitment. Such themes are saturated with affect, emotion, and meaning because they engage the fears, anxieties, hopes, and dreams of both students and their teachers. Generative themes arise at the point where the personal lives of students intersect with the larger society and the globalized world. Freire's work in *The Pedagogy of the Oppressed* (1970) revolutionized education by advocating for empowerment through understanding of one's own world and context. The notion of using lived experience creates a natural interest and thirst for knowledge based on our students' own worlds. An example of contemporary critical pedagogy and teaching can be seen in the use of hip-hop to enhance students' understanding of curriculum through rhyme and beats (Emdin and Adjapong, 2018).

One can observe similarity between Freire's generative themes and John Dewey's progressive education. In the early decades of the twentieth century, Dewey advised teachers to build their classroom lessons around the life experiences of students. Only by starting with these experiences, Dewey maintained, can we ever reach higher forms of knowledge and cognition. Starting with student life experiences and devising generative themes that connect to them, critical teachers can help students to question their experiences and to ponder the important points at which those experiences intersect with larger social, political, scientific, aesthetic, and literary concerns.

For example, beginning with a generative theme taken from students' fears of unemployment after graduation, a teacher and her students could construct a curriculum for a semester around the reasons for jobs becoming sparse. Research on corporations' gains, and workers' losses, on opportunities, education, vocational access, becomes a class project while students are researching not only for course requirements, but contextually about their own lives. This also ties into federal and local governments' participation (or nonparticipation) to create employment, encourage education, and find future-oriented ways in which to ensure the next generation will be gainfully employed.

In light of this generative theme and these questions, students and teachers could develop historical curricula that explore the relationships between corporations and governments, between factories and schooling/education. They could develop lessons that explore the human, physical, political, and economic geography of particular areas. In this context they could explore literature—novels and short stories that depict particular elements of life in these settings. They could develop political science lessons that study the different positions of government officials in relation to responding historical rises and drops in employment. Activities within these lessons are limited only by the teachers' and students' imagination. Not only would such lessons engage student interest but students would also gain valuable research and analytical skills. In addition, they would learn not only about the topic at hand but the value and uses of disciplines such as history, geography, literature, political science, anthropology, and cultural studies. In the test-driven, standardized, and scripted classrooms of the present era, students learn that school is not connected to the world around them. As students endure such classrooms, they relegate their enthusiasm and passion to nonacademic dimensions of their lives. In using applicable generative themes, students are engaged in learning and in understanding not only the future, but in taking agency in their own future.

Such generative themes and the lessons they support help students not only acquire knowledge but learn about who they are and where they stand on the issues of the day. A counterhegemonic classroom frees students from the indignity of being told who they are and what they should know. It gives them the right to direct the flow of such inquiries on their own terms. This doesn't mean that students make all the decisions about what they should learn and simply teach themselves. It means that students make *some* of these decisions in negotiation with an expert teacher who constantly works to help them develop their analytical and interpretive abilities, their research skills, and their sense of identity as empowered democratic citizens. In this context students gain the capacity to distinguish between oppressive and liberating modes of seeing the world and themselves. In this way students are able to identify forms of faux neutrality that permeate mainstream schooling. They are empowered to pick out the distortions, unexamined assumptions, and hidden philosophical beliefs that shape the official standardized curriculum of the contemporary epoch.

These are the core skills of the counterhegemonic classroom. Students with such skills are able to identify the fingerprints of dominant power on the pages of particular textbooks and in the requirements of mandated curricula. They deploy their literacy of power. With such skills they unmask the ways that ostensibly common-sense ways of seeing undermine their own and other people's best interests. Teachers and students operating with these counterhegemonic skills are undoubtedly dangerous and threats to the status quo. Indeed, we are the types of scholars who question the problematic ways that students are categorized, differences between students are represented, educational purposes are defined, schools are organized, and relationships between communities and schools are developed.

In counterhegemonic classrooms, teachers reframe the ways that school looks at students, in the process discovering student talents invisible to everyone at school. Here teachers use such talents as bases of opportunity to which they can connect academic skills and affective dynamics. Making use of students' interests and talents in everything from skateboarding to music, we can have the student develop a reading/resource list and devise a curriculum that could be used to teach other students and teachers about the topics in question. Such students learned so much, developed better reading and writing skills, and often gained a new relationship with both learning and schooling. For once they were the experts, teaching those around them about something they understood better than anyone else. Such pedagogical methods consistently helped students see their lives in school in new and more positive ways.

Nihilistic Classrooms in a Purposeless World

Contemporary hegemonic educational leaders, in their efforts to privatize schooling, work to remove education from the public sphere, the province of democracy (Giroux, 2015). Conversations about pedagogical purpose fade from the radar screen of public concerns. In this context, isolated individuals seek credentials from schools that have no positive civic value or social purpose. As traditional supporters of the value of education fail to clarify the purposes of education in a democratic society, regressive goals are asserted for educational institutions. In this context, school becomes a place where students are indoctrinated with a belief in the

- superiority of North Americans over other peoples around the world

- infallibility of the unregulated market economy

- supremacy of the conservative religious traditions

- virtue of an authoritarian morality that represses the joy of the erotic and sexual dimensions of human existence

- value of a decontextualized, cause–effect hyperrationality that reduces the act of learning to rote while devaluing the importance of interpretation

- harm of studying power relations and raising questions of justice.

The classrooms we want to produce extend democracy by implementing pedagogies that develop analysis, interpretation, policy discussion, the ability to advocate a position, and the quality of debate.

The classrooms promoted here are democratic spaces that are informed by the principles of democracy. Such classrooms are not compatible with classrooms that are grounded on a market vision of the world, a vision where everything is reduced to consumption and profit making. The notion of the public good is replaced with the values of self-interest and competition (Apple, 1993). In market-driven classrooms the teaching of history becomes a Disneyland-like process of passing along trivial—and untrue—verities about the nation's goodness. The idea of taking a hard look at who we are as a nation in the process of attempting to learn from our successes and our failures is repugnant in this context. In such classrooms the idea of learning to be historians who recognize the complex interpretive dimensions of producing knowledge about the past is repugnant, even un-patriotic.

In these nihilistic classrooms the idea of building a conceptual framework is irrelevant. Without conceptual frameworks, individuals are not able to understand the ways their various environments construct their perception of the world and shape their consciousness. Conceptual frameworks help students step back from the way we normally see the world and discover the ways our linguistic codes, cultural signs, race, class, gender, sexualities, and embedded modes of power shape what we know. In the nihilistic classrooms of the contemporary era these are the exact understandings many political and educational leaders don't want students to develop. The nihilistic classroom rests on naïve realism that asserts that the world of physical objects exists separately from human beings' perception of it. No matter what we believe about the world or ourselves or where we are located historically and culturally, people see the world in the same way.

In a sense, the properties of an object are physically contained in the object and, as a result, everybody understands it the same way: the physical properties never change (Cary, 2004). In this naïve realist frame, knowledge is nothing more than a warehouse of representations of particular objects. No conceptual framework need be created to understand that these representations are influenced by particular and often hidden assumptions. Of course, these mental representations may be seriously misleading and lead to oppressive modes of behavior. Classrooms grounded on this naïve realism make their main task the transfer of these unproblematized representations into the heads of students. In such classrooms when students' representations of the world match their teachers' perspectives and that of the curriculum guides, then education has taken place (Bredo, 1994). Thus, we are very ambitious in this book. We are calling not simply for much-needed changes in classroom teaching strategies but for changes in the worldview that shapes education in general.

Beyond Nihilism: Demanding New Configurations

Corporations, sports teams, TV networks, religious groups, social media, and educational systems reorganize all the time, without really changing the conceptual configurations, cognitive frameworks, or political structures of the old organization. Such nihilistic conceptual configurations involve educational goals that attempt to adjust students to certain norms and transfer a body of official information into their minds. Such cognitive frameworks involve using IQ and other standardized tests to separate the intellectual sheep from the goats by judging the efficiency of their lowest cognitive functions. And such political structures involve working to maintain the status quo and existing power relationships between national, racial, class, gender, and sexual groups. If we study many of the educational reforms that have been implemented in North America over the last 170 years of schooling, we find that most of them do not challenge these structures. The classroom teaching promoted in this book is characterized by a deep restructuring that is based on:

- a new vision of human potential

- a reassessment of how organizations operate

- a new and elevated view of the professional role of teachers

- a new understanding of the relationship between schools and communities

- a reframed understanding of human interrelationships

- a new appreciation of the way schools can be used for oppressive purposes

- a new awareness of the abilities of students no matter how young they may be

- an appreciation of multiple ways of knowing and understanding

The implementation of these principles in the classroom cannot occur by simple mandate or without struggle and deep analysis. Such changes will draw upon the great strengths teachers bring to classrooms as well as the idea that all teachers should be scholars who produce knowledge and conduct research as a key dimension of their pedagogical role. This exalted view of the teacher is in everyone's best interests. Instead of expecting little from teachers and developing scripted lessons and standardized, "teacher-proof" materials, our new configuration respects teachers as professionals who diagnose and make decisions about what is needed in classrooms. Again, this ostensibly simple and respectful maneuver will necessitate great struggle because it demands a critique of prevailing worldviews and the promotion of other ones.

We must have the intellectual ability to construct a better system of meaning that can be examined by other teachers and students. Without the vision of professional teacher-scholars who produce their own knowledges and operate as curriculum developers, political and educational leaders will continue to bounce from one ungrounded educational fad to another. Such fadism understandably causes teachers to become cynical and even hostile to educational reform. After many years in the profession, they know that today's fad will be replaced by a new and often diametrically opposite fad in just a few years (Horn, 2000). Teachers victimized by these dynamics refuse to even engage in the what-are-we-doing-here conversation. We can often revisit our own schooling and recall times in which information regurgitation was more important than creativity and alternative answers.

The new educational configurations that we promote involve understanding that all educational activities and all curricula promote particular ways of viewing the world. The knowledge contained in a textbook, curriculum standards, and the information that a standardized test demands are all particular, selected traditions. All of these knowledges are constructed out of social, economic, political, philosophical conflicts. Some knowledges are included in a society's certified knowledges, while many knowledges are erased. Knowledges that mean the most to us in a quest for just, ethical, egalitarian, and democratic ways of being in the world have often been these erased ones (Apple, 1993, 1999; McLaren, 2000). Which knowledges are legitimated and which knowledges are erased always reflect who possesses power and who does not.

In critical classrooms scholar-teacher researchers uncover erased (subjugated) knowledges, produce and help their students produce new knowledges, and develop the ability to study and question mandated knowledges. Ivor Goodson (1999) describes such scholarly acts of classroom teaching and learning as a form of moral witnessing. Moral witnessing insists that the world is still under construction and that no knowledge is finalized, complete unto itself. School in this context does not exist to pass along final truths about the world; instead, it operates to construct the world in a just and ethical way. Here the differences in worldviews and political orientation return with extreme vengeance. Questions of educational purpose and the ethical goals of education are not questions that can be settled by the deployment of scientific evidence. No data exist that establish the correct goals for schooling. Educational reformers make an epistemological error when they attempt to muster scientific evidence for what is an interpretive question (Cary, 2004). This mistake is made daily on the contemporary educational landscape.

No scientific study, for example, can tell us that classrooms should be concerned with the way students are affected by sociocultural and economic inequality. Empirical studies may point out the ways that inequality shapes education and classroom teaching, but they cannot make us care about such a reality. The classrooms we shape are based on society's values. And if a society does not value efforts to address great disparities of privilege, access, opportunity, and wealth, then classrooms will reflect such a value position. When we think about classrooms within these conceptual configurations, we begin to understand the ways that classrooms are often designed for the privileged. If Paulo Freire was concerned with a pedagogy for the oppressed, then many contemporary US classrooms are grounded on a pedagogy for the privileged (Reason & Bradbury, 2000). A central question we ask in our critical classrooms thus involves how we address privilege so that privileged students become aware of their privilege and marginalized students become aware of their marginalization. How do we pursue such awareness in a way that empowers both groups to work to maximize the possibility of social mobility for the oppressed and critical consciousness of the way power works for everyone? These are central goals for our critical classrooms.

Critical Classrooms and the Power of Relationships

One of the key aspects of the critical classrooms we envision involves engaging teachers in a conversation about the power of relationships in teaching and learning. The types of relationships that we are promoting are multidimensional. For example, the importance of relationships in education involves interactions with other human beings and social groups, the ecosystem and the human role in it, power relations, conceptual relations, and ontological relationships (as previously discussed, our relationship to the world and the way it shapes who we are). Speaking from so many domains—physics and theology to popular culture—many individuals have expressed a desire for a more connected vision of self, vocation, and education.

Viewed from the vantage point of our no-nonsense politics of agency, justice, democracy, and rigorous scholarship, the quest for relationship can get past the tendency to trivialization. Critical teachers can begin to understand the ecological base of our concept of relationality and the ways it can help us rethink classroom teaching and knowledge production. Monological forms of information produced in reductionistic disciplines are typically unconnected modes of knowledge alienated from other ways of knowing and being. Thus, classrooms get one-perspective forms of curriculum that don't allow multiple points of view. An epistemology is at work here that operates best when all parties work in isolation, within the closed boundaries of monolithic and self-sufficient disciplines. When things are proceeding as dominant power thinks they should, abstract individuals produce data about the fragment of the world the discipline is authorized to examine. The proper ontological state in this context is solitary: human beings in contextual isolation. Even the political state in which these *solitary beings* live is described as a contractual arrangement of "social atoms." Even the *concept*—not to mention the lived *enaction*—of community in this context is truncated.

Thus, the many categories of relationship mentioned above are subverted.

- In electronic hyperreality individuals are isolated from one another—we don't know our neighbors, teachers don't know the students in their schools; smart phones have increased this isolation like no other activity or device;

- Different socioeconomic classes. races, sexualities, ages, religious groups are segregated from one another;

- Human beings lose touch with the ways we are part of the natural world, the ecosystem, and thus forget the need to keep it healthy and in balance;

- People fail to discern their connections with power and how dominant power plays an exaggerated role in shaping our identities and our consciousness;

- Students and teachers are not taught how to understand the relationships among facts provide their meaning—schools induce students to memorize unrelated bits and pieces of meaningless data for tests;

- Individuals lose sight of the ontology of relationships and the ways their connections with people, places, things, culture, and power make us who we are.

In this isolation—this absence of relationship—Westerners have ignored difference. Critical teachers, aware of these Western failings, seek relationship and dialogue with those who see the world differently. The point is not to romanticize such individuals and appropriate their knowledges but to generate new edified perspectives and more sophisticated ways of knowing and inquiring. We believe that this generative process takes place when present perspectives are connected to larger structures and supersystems. As individuals and groups come to see their assumptions in light of diverse knowledges (epistemologies), ways of being (ontologies), and understandings of the universe (cosmologies), they begin to imagine other ways of thinking about everyday life and the quest to make sense of it. Thus, the concept of relationship is at the core of our critical worldview.

What Does It Mean to Be an Educated Person? Cultivating Historical Consciousness

Isn't it amazing that public discourse about educational reform rarely mentions graduating "educated people," and what constitutes an "educated person" is not a common question in educational circles? Discussion of these topics inevitably brings us back to issues of ethics, power, compassion, justice, democracy, and social responsibility, and in the twenty-first century these topics are "too dangerous" for public analysis. We believe that most teachers want to educate questioning, discerning and confident students.

To understand the dimensions of their work, teachers must be able to see themselves, their profession, the schools, their society, and the world itself in a larger historical context. We are arguing here that a central dimension of becoming a teacher—and, for that matter, an educated person—should be the development of a historical consciousness. Developing a historical consciousness is viewed by many as a dangerous and subversive act. Indeed, the effort to help teachers and students develop a historical consciousness can be denigrated as impractical, unrelated to the everyday functions of being a teacher. A historical consciousness helps us develop a perspective toward the goals of education whether we are teachers or students; it helps us change and sophisticate our view of the educational enterprise. Once we begin to historically contextualize the competing goals of education, we begin to get a sense of what schools are really trying to do and where we stand in relation to these efforts. We begin to understand what we are doing here.

Teachers should walk into class with a meta-historical consciousness, meaning that she grasps the human struggle as a whole (meta). Teachers see everyday life as the present installment of a set of much larger stories that go far back into the past and reach far into the future. Our meta-histories—there are many of these stories—help us discover where we are, the forces that contributed to this situation, and where we might want to go from this stage of the journey. If we don't know where we and other people came from and what motivated them to get to this point, we don't possess a very good grounding for figuring out if we want to keep going in the same direction or change the course. Every class a teacher teaches should contribute to the development of her own and her students' meta-historical consciousness. Of course, critical teachers will take into account the age level and sociocognitive needs of their students when developing such pedagogy. But there is no reason such a goal cannot be pursued in kindergarten, middle school, high school, and college settings. It can be brought into every disciplinary orientation from biology and math to literature and government, without exception. All subjects can be taught to some degree as history.

Developing a historical consciousness is not a simple act of collecting unquestioned data about the past. Individuals with a meta-historical consciousness avoid a worshipful relationship with the past but, instead, attempt to make sense of it, interpret it, and apply the background it provides to contemporary questions (Wilschut, 2001). The worshipful approaches to the past we find in contemporary schools render teachers and students vulnerable to the contemporary corporatized politics of knowledge with its ability to shape consciousness. After the content standards movement of the last few years, many political and educational leaders have tried to make history education little more than an awareness of the past that is part of a larger indoctrination of particular views of our own infallibility. In this regressive context, efforts to develop larger conceptual frameworks that lead to savvy historical interpretation are suppressed. Such frameworks are exactly what many of the present right-wing/conservative educational reforms are designed to preclude.

There is nothing simple about the meta-historical frames of reference that critical teachers endorse. The pedagogical act of constructing them is delicate, subtle, and rigorous. We are living in a period of history that is marked by dramatic historical changes in numerous domains. In many ways we are in the middle of reconsidering how we relate to the world around us, who we actually are, and how we produce knowledge about all of these things. Particular questions emerge at this juncture of human history:

- Are we separate individuals who develop personalities in a universal set of stages, or are we socially constructed in ways connected to where we are standing in the web of reality?

- Are we in conflict with nature and must we work to tame "her" for human benefit, or do we live in a delicate interaction with the natural world that must be understood and nurtured by all the nations and peoples of the world?

- Are we born with certain mental capacities that must be measured so we can sort everyone into their best-fitting social role, or are we always becoming and depending on our circumstances, capable of developing new abilities and improving old ones?

- Have we reached the end of political history where the adoption of free-market economies represents the highest achievement of which humans are capable, or are there other forms of social and personal evolution that would bring about redirected and more cooperative societies?

- Can we objectively understand the world based on a body of scientific research that piece by piece, like a jigsaw puzzle, reveals the whole, or is such a final understanding impossible given the new ways of seeing the world that constantly reveal themselves in diverse circumstances?

Historical Consciousness, Power, Colonialism/Neocolonialism, and Student Failure

Our historical awareness helps us see the social and political dimensions to the educational/psychological process by which individuals from particular groups are labeled as failures. An analysis of the meaning of "academic ability" leads us inevitably to a student's access to the cognitive resources of society. Educational psychologist Jerome Bruner (1996) labels these cognitive resources "cultural amplifiers." Instead of focusing on a hereditary notion of intelligence, Bruner argues, psychologists and educators should identify the situations, experiences, contexts, and the intellectual tools that help us think better and more clearly. Upon identification, we should bring such tools, situations, experiences, and contexts into the educational process.

How can we measure intellectual ability without taking into account an individual's or a group's access to such cultural tools? In light of the Eurocentrism embedded in the ways we designate failure, certain political and educational leaders may step back from policies set up to represent social and cultural outsiders as slow and incapable. Their difference from the White, male, upper-middle-/upper-class conformist mainstream is viewed as an unfixable deficiency. Without a critical education that finds insights in diverse traditions, epistemologies, worldviews, and macro-histories, these attributions of the failure of those not at the colonial center will continue to rule the day. Colonial and other power relations shape the ways that students are viewed in classrooms.

Who owns knowledge? What are the motives of those who own knowledge? Why are there so few alternatives to official interpretations of the world on TV and in the school curriculum? Why are perspectives that differ viewed not simply as diverse knowledges but as dangerous ideas? In a neocolonial world, the answers to these questions are quite disturbing. The study of such questions should be central to any system of schooling in a democratic society. However, such studies are viewed by many as expressions of radicality, of being too liberal. Critical teachers must work to change the perceptions of the public about the politics of knowledge. As we survey questions of educational goals at this period of history, addressing the question of the politics of knowledge becomes a central concern for the future of both democratic schooling and democracy itself.

Neocolonialism continues to shape and distort what teachers must contend with in the world of contemporary schools. In light of the preceding insights, George Dei and Stanley Doyle-Wood (2005) maintain that teachers must understand clearly the ways unequal colonial relations are constructed and extended in schooling practices. Critical classroom teachers seek multiple knowledges and diverse perspectives to reshape their classrooms. Such teachers understand that many educators from the mainstream hold a cultural and socioeconomic class affinity with many of their more successful students (Cherednichenko, 2005). Because of this connection, these students become the chosen ones who are provided special privileges and the benefit of a more complex and textured curriculum. This is another way that marginalized students operating in a neocolonial school system are denied access to the intellectual tools of dominant culture—Jerome Bruner's cultural amplifiers—and, thus, are punished for the problems they bring with them to school.

In the present era of neocolonial standardized curricula and top-down standards these understandings fall on deaf ears. In this situation when educational leaders and classroom teachers fail to consider difference in its human and knowledge-related forms, schools too often operate to stupidify, to construct a power-compliant form of consciousness. Here boys and girls from minority and economically marginalized contexts realize that academic success often demands that they give up their ethnic and cultural identities. Indeed, they must work to become as much like individuals from the dominant culture as possible. What is especially poignant is that even such an effort doesn't assure them of acceptance and success in the scholarly domain.

After jumping through all the scholarly and advanced degree-mandated hoops, they often find that such certification is not enough. They must prove themselves again and again to those from the elite halls of racial, class, gender, and ethnic privilege. Critical teachers can play a key role in pointing out the ways these hurtful dynamics play themselves out in the everyday life of school. Such critical teachers use their understanding of power and the structures of inequality to help alleviate the suffering of students caused by the school's equation of difference with deficiency. These racially, ethnically, and economically different students must be protected from the label of "failure" and the neocolonial justification of their "inability." Again, critical teachers understand these dynamics.

New Forms of Consciousness, New Ways of Being Human: A New Sense of Purpose

Taking the power literacy mentioned earlier in this chapter, connectedness, and the meta-historical insights described above and combining them with an appreciation of the power of difference, we begin the process of creating a new form of human consciousness. Such a consciousness focuses on the integrated nature of individual human beings, the social world, and the physical universe. When teachers develop such a consciousness they are able to understand everyday issues of classroom practice within this larger integrated whole. Nothing stands alone; no decision is devoid of larger consequences; everything fits together in some way. This is the opposite of the fragmented worldview, the positivism, the disconnected alienation, and the standardization that powers the contemporary world of education. The consciousness critical teachers seek involves what Philip Wexler (1997) calls a "drive for being," an effort to act upon the connectedness of the diverse dimensions of the universe. A key dimension of such an effort involves combining one's understanding of colonialism and power with insight into heart and emotion at the individual level. In this spirit, we connect the conceptual with the world of sensation and feeling. Thus, a rigorous education is always combined with sensitivity and concern for individual needs, for the alleviation of human suffering.

This connected form of critical consciousness makes education an enterprise for developing new, more ethical ways of being human. Developing this consciousness and these ways of being are central goals of critical classrooms. Teachers with a critical consciousness possess the ability to step back from the world as we are accustomed to perceiving it. They understand the ways our perception is constructed via media, linguistic codes, cultural signs, race, class, gender, colonial blinders, sexualities, and other hidden modes of power. Such a consciousness leads us into critical analysis, emancipatory teaching, and the production of dangerous, world-changing knowledge. Teachers with a critical consciousness become world makers. In this role we ask penetrating questions. How did that which is come to be? Whose interests do particular institutional arrangements serve?

Teachers with such a consciousness are empowered to ask often-neglected questions about the sociopolitical purposes of schooling. In a critical pedagogical context they can more clearly discern how education operates to reproduce or challenge dominant sociopolitical and economic structures. Such understandings are profoundly important in learning to think, teach, and live democratically. Educational purpose cannot be separated from social justice, human liberation, self-direction, resistance to regulation, community building, deeper forms of human interconnection, and the fight for freedom. When educators fail to gain these theoretical frames, schools inexorably become sorting machines for the neocolonial corporate order. Without such informed modes of making meaning, schools tend to reinforce patriarchal structures, Eurocentric educational practices, homophobia, and racism. Teachers with a critical consciousness help us understand the ways that dominant power wielders have worked to create an educational system that benefits the most privileged among us at the expense of those marginalized by race, class, gender, and sexuality.

Classrooms that teach a critical consciousness turn out students who understand the world, themselves and their relationship to the world and the connections that shape them. They understand the nature of higher orders of thinking and how such thinking can be applied to the duties of global and local citizenship. Such a consciousness becomes second nature to students involved in critical, active, creative, and challenging classrooms. Students with a critical consciousness see the world in a new way; the test of such learning does not revolve around their ability to recall irrelevant and unconnected data on demand for standardized exams. Evaluation in this context has to be conducted in a much more complex, contextualized, and nuanced manner as we search together for new and unexplored connections and relationships. In this way a critical consciousness seeks new ways of seeing, new ways of being human.

New ways of seeing and being are grounded on deeper levels of understanding. Moving beyond the traditional model of educational and cognitive psychology, a critical consciousness addresses modes of criticism, creativity, theorizing, imagination, and meaning making. We (1993) have worked to develop a new view of cognition in our version of postformalism (Kincheloe, 2004; Kincheloe, Steinberg, & Hinchey, 1999; Kincheloe, Steinberg, & Villaverde, 1999). This postformal psychology attempts to blur boundaries separating cognition, culture, epistemology, history, psychoanalysis, economics, and politics.

Without this boundary crossing, search for connection, and contextualization, the consciousness that supports contemporary classrooms promotes an alienated cognition. Such a truncated form of learning manifests itself in an inability to keep up with changes in the world of commerce, ideas, scholarship, information, social, and technological needs. These types of thinking are not sufficient for the present. They are not adequate for the need to understand and resist dominant ideological efforts to construct our consciousnesses to better fit with the corporatized, globalized, and imperial world of the twenty-first century.

Challenged by these new ways of seeing and being, the conversation about educational reform can never be the same. Understanding the impact of sociocultural, political, environmental, and economic contexts, teachers with a critical consciousness expose the ways a more traditional view of cognition has tended to construct ability or aptitude as a quality found only among the privileged few. Viewing intelligence as an unchangeable biological thing-in-itself, positivist educational psychology creates a pedagogy of hopelessness that assigns students to lifelong categories. When critical teachers begin to examine the ways cultural, economic, political, and social forces inscribe both this psychology and the teaching it promotes, the category of persons who we consider capable of learning begins to change. The cognitive sophistication of those denigrated students who fall outside the domain of the cultural mainstream—non-White, lower socioeconomic class, non-English-speaking, and without formally educated parents—begins to materialize before newly focused eyes.

This new view of learning and human capability modifies classroom practice with its understanding that not only is cognitive ability expressed in diverse ways but that it is learnable. Individuals of various ages and backgrounds can learn conceptual systems that help them make meaning, that facilitate their understanding of and ability to negotiate the deceptive world around them (Emdin, 2016). Given this realization, there is no reason for teachers to assume the failure of a large group of students. Indeed, in critical classrooms a key goal involves making sure that a far greater number of students perform better in school. One of the barometers of evaluation in this context involves a greater percentage of high student achievement—especially by students from low socioeconomic and non-White backgrounds.

A critical consciousness and the classrooms it supports generate great hope, as they reject the cognitive hopelessness of rigid hereditarian psychologies that assert that we inherit our intelligence (Seidel & Jardine, 2013). Not only is intelligence learnable, but it can be taught in numerous places: the schools, workplaces, political action organizations, civic organizations, and in any other place where people interact. Such understandings induce educators to make use of these places and to enter into collaborative educational relationships with people involved with them. Such insights can revolutionize the concept and practice of education in this society. Such an education will be villainized by regressive forces who want to maintain disparate power relations. Of course, these forces will challenge teachers with a critical consciousness who understand the complexity of the interrelationships that make the world what it is. But what is the alternative? Do we want to live a life of conformity to power wielders who want to regulate people to operate against their own interests and the well-being of the weakest among us? Education is too potentially beneficial a force to be reduced to a boring, conformist servant of the powerful.

Classroom teaching can become a magic process. Teaching becomes a process of connecting students to the universe, the earth, the human race, social groups, and other individuals. Students begin to discern their place in these relationships and their intellectual and social responsibilities to them. Both students and teachers come to understand the intricate web of reality from many perspectives and enter into it. We see the world from many vistas, from diverse cultural perspectives, as part of numerous processes, and in light of differing contexts (see our work on bricolage, Kincheloe, 2001; Kincheloe & Berry, 2004; Steinberg, 2018, 2015, 2011; Kincheloe, McLaren, & Steinberg, 2012). Using these multiple perspectives, we begin to see things about the world and ourselves that we never saw before. Once we recognize the power of confluence of these different viewpoints, we begin to seek them out like miners seek for gold. Indeed, we come to realize that an awareness and appreciation of these diverse perspectives are in many ways worth more than gold.

As critical teachers and their students gain new experiences and insights and make new connections, the purpose of their classrooms evolves. In turn, as purpose evolves the nature of teacher–student interaction develops in new and exciting ways. We begin to connect our classrooms to institutions outside of school, in the process involving ourselves and our students more and more in the lived world. Students begin to realize that there is no way to separate classroom learning from political, religious, cultural, business, and other institutions. Indeed, the critical teaching and learning promoted here cannot take place if such lived world connections are not made. The authors of the following chapters pick up on these themes and present visionary and practical insights into diverse ways of creating these types of classrooms. They know that there is not one way of teaching or one vision of what constitutes an engaging classroom. Echoing one of our themes here, there are diverse ways to be a critical teacher and to engage students. We hope you gain in this book not only helpful but also life-changing insights into classroom teaching. We hope it gives you a compelling answer to the question of what we are doing here.

References

Apple, M. (1993). The politics of official knowledge: Does a national curriculum make sense? *Teachers College Record, 95*(2), 222–241.

Apple, M. (1999). *Power, meaning, and identity: Essays in critical educational studies.* New York, NY: Peter Lang.

Bracy, G. (1997). Public education and its discontents. *America tomorrow* [Online]. Retrieved from http://www.kidware.com/ati/gb71221.htm

Bredo, E. (1994). Cognitivism, situated cognition, and Deweyan pragmatism. *Philosophy of Education Society yearbook* [Online]. Retrieved from http://www.ed.uiuc.edu/eps/pes-yearbook/94_docs/bredo.htm

Bruner, J. (1996). *The culture of education.* Cambridge, MA: Harvard University Press.

Cary, R. (2004). Howard Gardner's theory of visual-spatial intelligence: A critical retheorizing. In J. Kincheloe (Ed.), *Multiple intelligences reconsidered.* New York, NY: Peter Lang.

Cherednichenko, B. (2005). Teacher thinking for democratic learning. In J. Kincheloe & R. Horn (Eds.), *Educational psychology: An encyclopedia.* Westport, CT: Greenwood.

Covaleskie, J. (2004). Philosophical instruction. In J. Kincheloe & D. Weil (Eds.), *Critical thinking and learning: An encyclopedia.* Westport, CT: Greenwood.

Dei, G., & Doyle-Wood, S. (2005). Knowledge or multiple knowings: Challenges and possibilities of indigenous knowledges in the academy. In J. Kincheloe & R. Horn (Eds.), *Educational psychology: An encyclopedia.* Westport, CT: Greenwood.

Emdin, C. (2016). *For White Folks who teach in the hood … and the rest of y'all too: Reality pedagogy and urban education.* New York, NY: Beacon Press.

Emdin, C., & Adjapong, E. (Eds.). (2018). *Hip-hop as education, philosophy, and practice.* Leiden/Boston, MA: Brill Sense Publishers.

Freire, P. (1970). *Pedagogy of the oppressed.* New York, NY: Continuum Press.

Giroux, H. A. (2015). *Education and the crisis of public values: Challenging the assault on teachers, students, and public education.* New York, NY: Peter Lang.

Goodson, I. (1999). The educational researcher as public intellectual. *British Educational Research Journal, 25*(3), 277–297.

Gresson, A. (1995). *The recovery of race in America.* Minneapolis, MN: University of Minnesota Press.

Gresson, A. (2004). *America's atonement.* New York, NY: Peter Lang.

Henke, S. (2000). *Representations of secondary urban education: Infusing cultural studies into teacher education* (Dissertation). Miami University, Ohio. Retrieved from http://www.units.muohio.edu/eduleadership/dissertations/henke-dis/henke_ch6.pdf

Herrnstein, R., & Murray, C. (1994). *The bell curve: Intelligence and class structure in American life.* New York, NY: The Free Press.

Horn, R. (2000). *Teacher talk: A postformal inquiry into educational change.* New York, NY: Peter Lang.

Kincheloe, J. (2001). Describing the bricolage: Conceptualizing a new rigor in qualitative research. *Qualitative Inquiry, 7*(6), 679–692.

Kincheloe, J. (Ed.). (2004). *Multiple intelligences reconsidered.* New York, NY: Peter Lang.

Kincheloe, J. (2005). Introduction: Educational psychology—Traversing a treacherous terrain. In J. Kincheloe & R. Horn (Eds.), *Educational psychology: An Encyclopedia.* Westport, CT: Greenwood.

Kincheloe, J., & Berry, K. (2004). *Rigour and complexity in educational research: Conceptualizing the bricolage.* London: Open University Press.

Kincheloe, J., McLaren, P., & Steinberg, S. R. (2012). Critical pedagogy and qualitative research: Moving to the bricolage. In N. Denzin & Y. Lincoln (Eds.), *Sage handbook of qualitative research.* Thousand Oaks, CA: Sage Publishing.

Kincheloe, J., & Steinberg, S. (1993). A tentative description of post-formal thinking: The critical confrontation with cognitive theory. *Harvard Educational Review, 63*(3), 296–320.

Kincheloe, J., & Steinberg, S. (2004). *The miseducation of the west: How the schools and the media distort our understanding of the Islamic world.* Westport, CT: Praeger.

Kincheloe, J., Steinberg, S., & Hinchey, P. (1999). *The postformal reader: Cognition and education.* New York, NY: Falmer Press.

Kincheloe, J., Steinberg, S., Rodriguez, N., & Chennault, R. (1998). *White reign: Deploying whiteness in America.* New York, NY: St. Martin's Press.

Kincheloe, J., Steinberg, S., & Villaverde, L. (Eds.). (1999). *Rethinking intelligence: Confronting psychological assumptions about teaching and learning.* New York, NY: Routledge.

McLaren, P. (2000). *Che Guevara, Paulo Freire, and the pedagogy of revolution.* Lanham, MD: Rowman & Littlefield.

Reason, P., & Bradbury, H. (2000). Introduction: Inquiry and participation in search of a world worthy of human aspiration. In P. Reason & H. Bradbury (Eds.), *Handbook of action research: Participative inquiry and practice.* Thousand Oaks, CA: Sage.

Rodriguez, N., & Villaverde, L. (Eds.). (2000). *Dismantling white privilege.* New York, NY: Peter Lang.

Seidel, J., & Jardine, D. (2013). *Ecological pedagogy, Buddhist pedagogy, Hermeneutic pedagogy: Curriculum for miracles.* New York, NY: Peter Lang.

Shor, I. (1992). *Empowering education: Critical teaching for social change.* Portsmouth, NH: Heinemann.

Shotter, J. (1993). *Cultural politics of everyday life.* Toronto: University of Toronto Press.

Steinberg, S. R. (2010). Power, emancipation, and complexity: Employing critical theory. *Power and Education, 2*(2), 140–151.

Steinberg, S. R. (2011). Employing the bricolage as critical research in science education. In B. Fraser, K. Tobin, & C. McRobbie (Eds.), *Second international handbook of science education.* Dordrecht, NL: Springer Publishing.

Steinberg, S. R. (2015). Proposing a multiplicity of meanings: Research bricolage and cultural pedagogy. In K. Tobin & S. R. Steinberg (Eds.), *Doing educational research.* Rotterdam: Sense Publishing.

Steinberg, S. R. (2018). Politics and the bricolage: How do we make sense of recent events? In *Zeitschrift fur Qualitatie Forschung.* Berlin & Toronto: Verlag. https://doi.org/10.3224/zqf.v18i1.05

Wexler, P. (1997). *Social research in education: Ethnography of being.* Paper presented at the International Conference "The Culture of Schooling." Halle, Germany.

Willinsky, J. (2001). Raising the standards for democratic education: Research and evaluation as public knowledge. In J. Kincheloe & D. Weil (Eds.), *Standards and schooling in the U.S.: An encyclopedia.* Santa Barbara, CA: ABC-Clio.

Wilschut, A. (2001). Historical consciousness as an objective in Dutch history education. Retrieved from http://home.casema.nl/wilschut/consciousness.htm

PART II

How Do We Teach? Why Do We Teach?

CHAPTER 4

Curriculum
Understanding What We Teach and Where We Teach It

Joe L. Kincheloe

We need to nurture a vision of teachers as self-directed scholar-professionals who produce their own knowledges and diagnose the needs of their students. In this empowered vision of the profession teachers are also curriculum developers. Here a central thesis of this book reemerges: the contemporary struggle for teachers to control their profession and engage in meaningful pedagogies in light of efforts to control and standardize every dimension of their work. A key dimension of the effort to become self-directed professionals involves teachers operating as curriculum developers. This chapter focuses on what it might mean to be a teacher as curriculum developer.

What Is the Curriculum?

When you ask diverse individuals around the country to define curriculum, you begin to understand the confusion about the topic. Many people believe that the school curriculum is or should be pretty much the same everywhere and, with minor updates—because "new stuff happens"—has always been the same. This is simply not the case. The goal of education, it is argued, is to take this standardized knowledge and simply insert it into the file-cabinet minds of students. This "common-sense" information-transmission model of curriculum is the one that we see so clearly in the top-down standards-driven schools. The routine is simple: we develop a body of objective and neutral data, transmit it to students who commit it to their Office Depot files, and then test them to see how much they "mastered."

Numerous curriculum scholars over the last four decades have challenged this simplistic story, offering instead a reconceptuaization of the nature of curriculum and the purposes of curriculum development. In light of more complex and critical understandings of all of the complicated dynamics that are involved in curriculum development, senior scholars such as (in alphabetical order) Michael Apple, Lilia Bartolome, Deborah Britzman, George Dei, Paulo Freire, Sharon Friesen, Henry Giroux, Jesus 'Pato' Gomez, Madeleine Grumet, Maxine Greene, Patricia Hill-Collins, David Jardine, Gloria Ladson-Billings, Patti Lather, Carl Leggo, Donldo Macedo, Marla Morris, Edmund O'Sullivan, Jo Anne Pagano, Joao Paraskeva, Bill Reynolds, William Schubert, Yolanda Sealey-Ruiz, David Smith,

William Watkins, John Weaver, John Willinsky, and many others cultivated a revolution in the domain. Look up these names in databases and examine the work they have produced over the last decades. You will find in the work of these scholars that the curriculum involves more than the course of study. Indeed, from the reconceptualized perspective the curriculum involves a more holistic view of a student's experience, the analysis of the individual as she relates to the world, the process of inquiry about the self and world, the insights that are produced in such an activity, and so on. If the curriculum involves the dynamics, then classroom teaching, teacher education, evaluation procedures, and the principles of educational reform will have to be reconceptualized as well.

The perspective I am promoting in this chapter involves preparing teacher-scholars who are researchers and who understand the repressive context in which contemporary education takes place, undertaking a major role in the development of the school curriculum. What do teachers need to know to undertake such a role? Critical teachers in this quest understand

- how knowledge is produced and certified;

- the sociocultural, political, and economic context in which schooling takes place;

- the skills and insights of scholar-teachers operating with a critical cosmological consciousness;

- the ways reductionism undermines the complexity and multiple perspectives which are a part of all curriculum development;

- the ways power wielders subtly shape what is allowed in the curriculum;

- the different purposes that different educational institutions have pursued.

Simply put, these teachers learn to deal with complexity. There is nothing simple about the ways that curricula are forged and hawked to the public as official (Abukhattala, 2004). If teachers can examine only a few factors involved in this process, then they can develop tremendous insight into its complexity.

The Critical Curriculum: Knowledge, the Classroom, and Who We Are

In a repressive, dumbed-down curriculum and top-down standards, certified knowledge is taught to students regardless of where they come from, their personal relationship to the subject matter, or what they need. Pedagogy becomes a process of simple transference: the teacher as a Domino's Pizza delivery person. Why talk about teaching method in this case? All the teacher needs to do is get the data in the students' filing cabinets. Thus, in the cosmos of top-down standards and regulated classrooms, this book is irrelevant: teachers don't need to study these types of issues. They are after all just unskilled laborers who deliver the correct goods to the students, nothing more, nothing less. The curriculum is a body of unconnected "facts" separate from those who learn it or the contexts in which it is learned.

The naïve realism and positivism of standardized education, with its separation of knower and known and its assumption of an objective world "out there," philosophically grounds the standardized curriculum. Advocates of a critical reconceptualized curriculum maintain that if knowledge is the prerequisite for social action and if social action transforms knowledge, then knowledge cannot be conceived as static and certain. We begin to understand the importance of the way both reality and the curriculum is socially, culturally, and politically constructed. What is included in the standardized curriculum of the contemporary era—no matter how much positivists and reductionists may deny it—is always a political process. When many individuals call for educators to keep politics out of the curriculum, critical teachers know that such a move is impossible. Whose knowledge do we teach, mine or his? In what way do we teach it, her way or their way? We have to make a decision.

As with the social construction of what we refer to as "reality," the same dynamic is at work with the curriculum. It is most often a social and political construction and is always the result of a covert and not generally known set of historical and contemporary power struggles. Like all knowledge and all curricula, knowers also belong to a particular, ever-changing historical world. Humans, being part of history, are reflexive subjects: this means that they are entities who are conscious of the constant interaction between themselves and the world around them. This interaction and the consciousness it helps construct recognize that all knowledge, all curricula, are fusions of knowers and what is known, operating in a context shaped by power. We see a curriculum that erases the ways, for example, the power of racism shapes the daily life of all peoples, institutions, and power relations in the United States.

Many White students living lives isolated from the negative effects of racism and operating without a larger racial consciousness are not aware of this curricular neglect of the power of race. In such a context, they see nothing unusual about an education that rarely deals with issues of race. Students of color, Indigenous students, however, often see a very different reality. Their historical role reminds them on a daily basis that in dominant society they are racial beings who must deal with unpleasant situations that arise merely because they are racially marked. The racial curriculum of silence affects them in a manner quite different from most middle-class White students. Reflecting my description of the curriculum as a fusion of knowers and known, they see this racial silence as another manifestation of racism within the culture. Thus, in this example we begin to get a clearer picture that the curriculum is never a simple, objective structure. It is always ideologically inscribed and a product of specific human-made choices. Thus, in a functioning democratic society it can never be developed innocently or without conflict. Only in a totalitarian educational system can a curriculum be developed so smoothly.

These are not the insights teacher education students and teachers obtain unless they have access to a critical professional education program, progressive community groups, a critical union or unless they had developed these insights before entering the profession. Too often contemporary, uncritical teacher education teaches students that the curriculum mandated by standards movements and reforms are the "truth." This is a dangerous proposition in a democratic society. Such a "truth curriculum" operates on the foundation of what the ancient Greeks referred to as the myth of Archimedes. The myth assumes that the human perceiver occupies no space in the known world, that there is a point—the Archimedean point—from which the cosmos can be seen in its entirety. From this point we possess a "God's-eye" view of the world; we see the world totally objectively. The knowledge produced from this point cannot help but be true.

Contemporary advocates of standardized education see their curriculum as emerging from the Archimedean point. The lesson of the myth, of course, is that there is no such point, and thus all of our views of the world are from partial, limited perspectives. Thus, it follows that our knowledge of the world is from somebody's viewpoint and thus partial and limited. Since we can never develop knowledge apart from ourselves and our lives, then our curriculum should understand the ways our lives shape our knowledge of the world and how knowledge in turn shapes the nature of our lives. Here is the complex act of analysis, here is where our cognitive ability is boosted to a higher power, where the critical complex curriculum earns its spurs. Such a curriculum helps us turn out students who possess a much more mature sense of what is known and what is not known about the world.

With this knowledge we are poised to become scholars who understand the way the world works, the way "educated" people get duped by power wielders who construct the knowledges they commit to memory. Knowing this, we work to redefine what it means to be a scholar. Encouraged by our critical curriculum we do not want to be hegemonized scholars who sell our academic skills to the highest-bidding power wielder. Instead, we want to be scholars who work for the social good, smart people who help those who need it most actually benefit from education and in the process keep their souls intact.

Critical classroom teachers operating in this critical zone tell the public, political leaders, and students that the reductionist effort to deny the influence of values, historical circumstances, and political considerations in the construction of the curriculum is a power-produced smoke screen.

The curriculum developers operating in the small conceptual box created by dominant power deny the influence of values, circumstances, and considerations. Knowledge is just knowledge, they contend. The conditions of its production really don't matter. Critical teachers know that the conditions of its production matter just as much, if not more, than the knowledge itself. To ask students to commit such knowledge to memory without examining where it came from is one of the most irresponsible acts in which a teacher can engage. Those who are concerned with only the facts have not yet grasped the notion that every historical era, every culture produces particular rules as to how we produce a fact. Different rules privilege different causes. And whether they know it or not everyone has a cause.

What we call the "facts" we teach about the world are constructed by living and breathing people. They are not just "out there" waiting to be discovered. The critical curriculum's disclosure of this constructed nature of knowledge and curriculum marks the end of the teacher's and the learner's innocence. With this realization, critical classroom teachers enter a new passageway in the maze of reality. We are wizened in this journey as we move to a new intellectual plain. There is no doubt that it can be a lonely position, as many of those teachers who surround us will not understand the complexity we discern. From their perspective, they will sometimes ascribe unsavory motives to our quest for good scholarship, social justice, better understanding of students, and democratic educational goals. We must be emotionally ready to deal with such assertions and move on more adroitly with our pedagogical work.

Killing the Life Force: Ideology and Objectivity

A positivistic curriculum that operates in the name of rigor and a hard-boiled realism insults the very concept of rigor, as it fails to account for the forces that construct self, school purpose, knowledge, and the curriculum itself (Gordon, 2001). Not only is the positivist educator isolated from the forces that shape him or her, but the curriculum produced is also isolated from the conditions that give it meaning to students and teachers. The concept of photosynthesis, for example, in the positivist standardized curriculum becomes simply a disembodied word to be defined in a dictionary-type manner. The miraculous process as it plays itself out in the lived world of the forest, for instance, or in the everyday life of the community is lost in the disembodiment process commonly observed in the top-down imposed standards curriculum.

This reductionist curriculum filters away the very features of photosynthesis that grant it importance. I'm reminded of a botany class I was excited to take in my freshman year at a small college in the mountains of Virginia. The trees that surrounded the science building were some of the most beautiful I had ever seen. I hoped that the botany class would teach me more about them. By the end of the first month of the term, I could hardly make myself attend the class. We memorized endless botanical categories and taxonomies. Not once did we ever look out the window as part of the classroom pedagogy. The life force of botany had been killed in that "rigorous" classroom. I earned a D. The curriculum existed apart from my lived experience. The knowledge that was delivered in the classroom had decayed in its isolation from the world. It smelled like rotten meat.

Such reductionist curricula provide predigested, second-hand, ready-made knowledge. I felt like a baby bird: the professor, the mama bird, was vomiting the data from her mouth into ours. Then we had to keep the previously chewed knowledge intact and spit it back to the professor on the test. The ideological nature of such a curriculum of regurgitation helps us understand not only how curriculum development takes place but also how power works to shape society. Ideology as a social dynamic that shapes the world by making unequal relations appear natural constructs the positivist curriculum as if it could be no other way. It claims, after all, to be a presentation of truth about the world, simply the facts, a reflection of the real world. Understanding the complexity of knowledge and knowledge production, critical teachers appreciate the naivete of such proclamations of neutrality. Thus, such teachers employ their literacy of power and ideology with any curriculum—especially a predesigned one, for example— to rigorous analysis. What are the political interests behind the curriculum proposed (imposed)? If the curriculum is offered simply as a course of study, what political assumptions undergird the subject matter both included and excluded?

Critical teachers as curriculum developers appreciate how these and other questions help us move beyond reductionist knowledge production and the teaching of the "truth." They understand that innovations in the production of knowledge rarely come from a linear accumulation of objective curricular data gleaned from knowledge of previous "discoveries." Major reconceptualization comes out of a meta-analysis, a deeper study of the ideological and epistemological assumptions on which the framework supporting knowledge production and the academic curriculum is grounded. Complex insights and discipline-changing analyses are produced not so much by asking questions *within* the framework as they are by asking questions *about* the framework.

As critical scholars ask questions about the hidden biases within disciplines, the empirical generalizations that lead to universal knowledges, the use of knowledge produced to control the lives of individuals living in the domain being researched, or the effects of knowledge produced by research methods that remove social, cultural, psychological, or educational phenomena from the contexts that give them meaning, they begin to knock down disciplinary houses of cards. Such a process leads to a reconceptualization of the curricula that are built on the knowledges such traditional disciplines produce.

Thus, the limitations of the old disciplines are exposed, and the possibility for revolutionary insight is unleashed. The types of questions delineated here can be described as tools to help scholars reflect ethically on domains of practice that emerge from knowledge production and curriculum development. The epistemological, ethical, and educational malformations that come out of these dynamics produce the need for action. But first we must recognize that the malformations exist. Students who have been subjected to the curriculum of reductionism and standardization, with its refusal to question disciplinary and educational frameworks, are less likely to discern such malformations. Too often they see the reductionist curriculum as just the way things are. Such students have no protection against an often antidemocratic, inegalitarian, and colonialistic knowledges and forms of social organization that are insidiously promoted in schools and the cultural curriculum of the media. In today's society we have a new vocabulary based on the inability to read what is and isn't real. In 2016 *Oxford Dictionary* declared post-truth the word of the year, in a time when what we see with our own eyes is, indeed, challenged as "false news," it is difficult for teachers (and students) to discern what is ethical, honest, and clear. We are told by testmakers and politicians that we "must be objective," without any conversation about the fact that we live in a subjective world.

Surviving the Brave New World of the Standardized Curriculum

Out of this same cult of objectivity, dominant ideology works to mystify our understanding of the way the world operates in order to perpetuate the status quo. The teacher evaluations often designed to make sure teachers teach "official knowledges," the sanctioned curricula constructed to prevent dissent, and the teaching methodologies shaped to subvert particular types of student exploration and analysis are all clothed in the garb of technical expertise. "These educational designs have been produced by leading scientific experts," we are told, "how could they be wrong?" The force field of positivist certainty surrounds them, rendering them impenetrable to the misgivings of those directly affected:

- creative teachers with negative evaluations;

- individuals from low-status cultures and class backgrounds whose experiences and subjugated knowledges are absent from the school curriculum; and

- brilliant students with unique learning styles whose talents are not appreciated by the culture of the schools nor measured by standardized tests.

Contrary to the assumptions of the positivistic cult of certainty that too often shapes schools practice, meanings are never closed but remain forever open to negotiation. This seems to me one of the most important lessons teachers can learn as they enter the classroom. Interpretations are never final because humans are incapable of a final perception. But in the reductionistic standardized curriculum almost all information is presented as a final perception. Knowledge doesn't age well; it often turns to vinegar. New facts come to light, and fresh interpretations uncover new relationships that render traditional accounts out of date (Ellis, 1998; Rose & Kincheloe, 2003). In the 1890s the American Medical Association (AMA) was still proclaiming that women should not go to college because such mental work would take away from their primary role of reproduction—all that thinking would take blood away from the uterus. Albert Einstein the student was viewed as a failure in his German schools; Einstein the scientist was/is viewed as one of the greatest geniuses of all time. Yesterday's certainties are tomorrow's superstitions. "Doctor, is it time to bleed the patient? Should I get the leeches?"

In the world of the standardized fact-based curriculum, there is often an effort to keep teachers and students from considering these issues. In the name of reason, the curriculum is stupidified, as Donaldo Macedo would note, and many come to believe that teaching and knowledge production could take place in no other way. Just as work bureaucratized old factories, content standards devisers and school-district office staffs take apart the curriculum, sequencing knowledge, numbering it, and subnumbering it—for example, objective 1, activity 7. In this context teacher lesson plans are required to match an official format and to fit particular standardized objectives and proficiencies. Subjects such as English with a diverse range of content are reduced to measurable proficiencies involving reading comprehension and grammar. Social studies and science are reconstructed into fragments of facts (factoids) and arbitrary pieces of jargon. Measurability thus takes precedence over substance and significance.

Deeper, more complex, more existentially significant questions are erased in such curricula because we cannot control contextual variables. If the goal of education is to produce a kind of thinking that sees beyond surface appearances and focuses on both solving problems and imagining unthought-of problems to solve, then evaluations centered around standardized test measures do not tell us much about our successes and failures. Such an orientation to evaluation tends to force teachers to direct their attention to isolated skills and quantifiable entities that render the entire process inauthentic and inert. If teachers, students, and schools are assessed on the basis of how much homework is assigned, then teachers will be leaned on to increase homework assignments. It doesn't take an astute observer to figure out that if the homework is repetitive memory work, then students will learn little and feel more alienated, more uninterested in school.

Standardized test-driven evaluations of teaching and curriculum often convey a misleading message with dangerous consequences to teachers and the public at large. A short analogy is in order. When researchers studied airline performance, they asked which airline had the best record for being on time. When such a factor is analyzed outside a variety of contextual factors such as safety, serious consequences may result from airlines scrambling to achieve a better on-time record. Along the same line, researchers who evaluate teachers on the basis of particular outcomes may miss the brilliance of their lessons if they do not take into account particular contextual factors.

Knowing a student's special needs may move a teacher to abandon a particular content objective in order to provide a pupil with a much-needed success experience (Steinberg, 2018). The validation of the student's ability may mean far more to both the long-term emotional and the learning needs of the child than would a short-term factual understanding (Berry, 2001; David, 1988; McNay, 1988; McNeil, 1988; McNeil & Valenzuela, 1998; Wesson & Weaver, 2001). Not only in the standardized curricula of the contemporary era are teachers reduced to pizza deliverers of fragmented data, they are evaluated by how quickly they can get the pizza (factoids) to the student consumers. Such reductionist policies are dangerous to the well-being of teachers, students, and the future of democracy. The authors of this book want you to be ready to deal with such realities when you enter your classrooms.

Teachers as Curriculum Developers

In the middle of the first decade of the twenty-first century, American society does not view elementary, junior high or middle school, and high school teachers as scholars. In the context of the reductionist curriculum, however, why should teachers be scholars if all they do is simply pass along knowledge created by experts and administer preconstructed standardized tests that measure their students' mastery of such data? Indeed, most Americans do not hold an image of teachers that is characterized by individuals engaged in reflection and research, sharing their work with others, constructing their workplace, producing curriculum materials, and publishing their research for other teachers and community members in general. In a reductionistic worldview, these activities for teachers seem like unnecessary complications of what seems like a simple act of knowledge transfer—like that of pizza delivery. Critical teachers must reeducate the public about the role of teachers if we are ever to produce an educational system that moves us to new levels of social, intellectual, democratic, and ethical accomplishment.

Critical teachers are dedicated to the production of scholar-teachers who can recognize and remedy the fragmented irrationality of the reductionist curriculum. The critical scholar-teachers treat students as active agents, render knowledge problematic, utilize dialogical methods of teaching, and seek to make learning a process where self-understanding, self-direction, and learning to teach oneself are possible. Scholar-teachers help students become good citizens with the insight to identify social conditions that harm people and the civic ability to envision and implement alternative forms of social and political organization (Aronowitz & Giroux, 1985; Kincheloe & Steinberg, 1997; Steinberg, 2001). Thus, the scholar-teachers operating in schools shaped by these critical understandings are agents of democracy who understand the relationship between learning and the future existence of a democratic state. There is nothing simple about democratic living; students must understand complex social relationships if they are to comprehend the way power operates to smash the fragile concept of democracy.

As curriculum developers, critical teachers understand the technicalization, rationalization, and bureaucratization of reductionist reforms that quash the democratic vision of what schools can become. Operating with a vision of this possibility, critical scholar-teachers work to integrate the knowledge of academic disciplines, subjugated knowledges of marginalized groups, student experience, popular culture, and the effects of dominant modes of thinking in the larger effort to help students and community members make sense of their relationship to the world. Using knowledge from history, literature, math, physics, biology, chemistry, environmental studies, anthropology, political science, philosophy, and cultural studies, along with a critique of mainstream disciplines, critical teachers examine the processes of identity construction, knowledge production, learning to teach oneself, democratic participation, technological innovation, and social change. A powerful curriculum designed for particular students can be developed with these concepts in mind: a curriculum that changes lives and the world for the better.

As we examine the complex processes, they turn the lenses of analysis upon themselves and their own professional education. As researchers and knowledge workers, they are empowered to reveal deep structures that shape the professional activities of teachers. In the process, they develop a reflective awareness that allows them to discern the ways that teacher perception is shaped by the socioeducational context, with its accompanying linguistic codes, cultural signs, and tacit views of the world. This reflective awareness, this stepping back from the world as we are accustomed to seeing it, requires that the teachers construct their perceptions of the world anew.

What we are talking about in this curricular context is a revolution of consciousness, an exciting prospect that promises an exciting new life of insight. Such reconstruction of perception is conducted not in a random way but in a manner that undermines the forms of teacher thinking that appear natural, that opens to question expert knowledge that has been marked "off limits to inquiry." Reflectively aware teachers as curriculum developers ask where their own ways of seeing and thinking come from, in the process clarifying their own system of meaning as they reconstruct the role of teacher. The ultimate justification for such scholarly activity is an empowerment that provides teachers the skills to overcome the reductionist tendency to discredit their integrity as capable, self-directed professionals. In this new educational context, scholar-teachers can get on with the process of developing a challenging, democratic, complex curriculum.

There is so much more to teaching and curriculum development than meets the reductionist eye, more than is included in technicist teacher education. The purpose of a complex teacher education is not to learn the right answers, the hand-me-down knowledge of the research experts; on the contrary, such a rigorous teacher education consists of making the most of the unanticipated complications of the classroom. Technicist method courses and student teaching do not address the innate uncertainty of the curriculum—indeed, they attempt to deny it. Thus, teacher-educators operating in the critical zone advocated here refuse to provide a generic form of teaching and expert-developed curriculum that are applicable to all students in all contexts. Understanding the complexity of pedagogy demands a humility, an admission that we don't hold all the answers to what one is supposed to do in the confusing complications of everyday practice. We always know that curriculum development takes place in a complex and ambiguous microcosm. A curriculum produced by outsiders who are unfamiliar with this complicated world of the classroom is doomed to failure.

Constructing the Critical, Interconnected Curriculum

The critical curriculum I am proposing here always views human beings, society, the physical world, and the pedagogical process as interconnected features of a broader framework and deeper order. A central component of becoming an educated person involves appreciating and expanding upon the nature of these connections. Each of the component parts of this deeper order gains its meaning(s) as part of this and many other relationships. As such realms of connection are revealed in relation to humans, new evolutionary possibilities for the species are brought into focus. Positivist educators armed with their top-down technical standards have failed to think in terms of this connectedness and the possibilities it raises for human becoming. The notion of embracing new forms of human being and cognition seems never to occur to those involved with reductionist education.

Advocates of such a positivist pedagogy fall into the fragmentation trap, manifesting the scourge of cognitive reductionism as they allow the compartmentalization of knowledge to define its importance. As we compartmentalize the world and knowledge about it, we draw boundaries between what is spoken and what remains unspoken. In this context, many students may graduate from high school never having given a thought to what disciplines exclude from analysis, what has been censored from their curriculum. I don't think it is inaccurate to argue that the greatest artists, writers, inventors, doctors, business and labor leaders, teachers, and researchers who emerge from positivist schooling have to learn how to think in innovative and creative ways outside of their formal educational experiences (Kincheloe, Steinberg, & Tippins, 1999). Such students acquire their cognitive power in spite of—rather than as a result of—schooling. The critical connected curriculum works to repair this fragmented, stupidifying process.

As educational leaders, politicians, and the public begin to understand the nature and limitations of reductionistic fragmentation in education, schooling will begin to change. The weight of history is on the side of a critical education and the curriculum it supports. To avoid reductionism in curriculum and cognitive development, teachers and students must learn to derive meaning from direct experience. Learning from and extending the knowledge derived from direct experience, as in primary research, we move into a realm of connectedness where new awareness carries us beyond the boundaries of conventional ways of thinking. As we pursue this connectivity in these relationships among data, context, experience, and the complexity of perception, Western education may overcome its scholarly retreat and move toward higher dimensions of human experience.

Critical teachers as curriculum developers understand that knowledge does not exist in isolation. Knowledge conceived in the zone of complexity is always in process: it comes from somewhere and is going somewhere. From this perspective, those who view knowledge as an "end product" to be consumed fail to understand the very nature of knowledge. The critical curriculum is grounded on this process-based, interconnected understanding: knowledge can never be viewed outside its genesis, the process of its production; it can never be conceptualized outside of its relationship to other information and other contexts. Whenever we attempt to view knowledge outside of these boundaries, we make a logical mistake that holds serious consequences and produces a chain of reductionistic ramifications. In the most basic curricular sense, the knowledge taught in reductionist curriculum is isolated in the preceding ways from the life experiences of students. Such a degraded view of knowledge, of course, sets off a flood of reductionistic ramifications such as teaching to tests, the loss of meaning, student and teacher boredom, regimentation of learning, diminished creativity, cognitive reductionism, and ignorance of the forces that shape our identities and worldviews.

As the reductionist curriculum presents absolute truth, students gain the notion that there is no need for pursuing alternative ways of knowing. Such alternative or, from the perspective of positivism, deviant ways of seeing are dismissed as irrelevant for the reductionist, fragmented curriculum. Such information is not viewed as an important source of new insight or socioeducational innovation. As we study these reductionistic ramifications of the fragmented curriculum, we understand the fear generated among reductionists by the diverse conceptual frameworks brought to school by philosophical diversity and the analysis of the knowledge production strategies of diverse cultures (Race, 2018). The critical connected curriculum is fascinated by, and dedicated to, diversified conceptual frameworks and knowledge-production strategies. As teachers and students gain familiarity with such diversity, social, political, psychological, cultural, and educational innovation is catalyzed.

The reductionist, disconnected positivist belief in an underlying natural order characterized by universal regularity in human action exerts a profound impact on knowledge production and curriculum development. These regularities, or social laws, positivists maintain, are best expressed through quantitative analysis and the language of mathematics. The assumptions of social regularity and certainty behind this disconnected, decontextualized, positivist tradition dramatically influence social and educational practice and curriculum development. What begins as a research method evolves into a view of the world that includes descriptions of what humans should know, exactly what such knowledge means, and how they should behave as a result of knowing it. Curriculum that is grounded in positivism assumes that the laws of society and the knowledge of human existence are verified and are ready to be inserted into the minds of children.

There is no limit to what education can become when empowered teachers as curriculum developers, understanding the forces that oppress our consciousness and shackle our intellects, engage students in analyzing and producing diverse knowledges. I have a thousand stories of teachers and students who when released from the hitching post of a standardized curriculum created their own knowledge. In the process they changed not only the communities in which they lived but also their schools and themselves. Over and over again they tell me: I had never engaged in such a powerful learning experience, now I know what education could be. In this context the authors of this volume ask you to keep exploring this topic, to join with us in an effort to make education something more than a Marvel Comics film for the status quo, for an inequitable world, and classrooms as boring rituals that we all must endure. I could never have become a teacher if teaching meant merely conforming to this dark reality.

References

Abukhattala, I. (2004). The new bogeyman under the bed: Image formation of Islam in the western school curriculum and media. In J. Kincheloe & S. Steinberg (Eds.), *The miseducation of the west: How schools and the media distort our understanding of the Islamic world.* Westport, CT: Praeger.

Aronowitz, S., & Giroux, H. (1985). *Education under siege.* South Hadley, MA: Bergin and Garvey.

Berry, K. (2001). Standards of complexity in a postmodern democracy. In J. Kincheloe & D. Weil (Eds.), *Standards and schooling in the United States: An encyclopedia.* 3 vols. Santa Barbara, CA: ABC-Clio.

Bogdan, R., & Biklen, S. (1982). *Qualitative research for education: An introduction to theory and methods.* Boston, MA: Allyn and Bacon.

David, J. (1988). The use of indicators by school districts: Aid or threat to improvement? *Phi Delta Kappan, 69*(7), 499–503.

Ellis, J. (1998). Interpretive inquiry as student research. In S. Steinberg & J. Kincheloe (Eds.), *Students and researchers: Creating classrooms that matter.* London: Falmer.

Fenimore-Smith, K., & Pailliotet, A. (2001). Teaching standards of complexity in preservice education. In J. Kincheloe & D. Weil (Eds.), *Standards and schooling in the United States: An encyclopedia.* 3 vols. Santa Barbara, CA: ABC-Clio.

Gordon, M. (2001). Philosophical analysis and standards—Philosophical and analytical standards. In J. Kincheloe & D. Weil (Eds.), *Standards and schooling in the United States: An encyclopedia.* 3 vols. Santa Barbara, CA: ABC-Clio.

Janesick, V. (2004). Standards and critical thinking. In J. Kincheloe & D. Weil (Eds.), *Standards and schooling in the United States: An encyclopedia.* Santa Barbara, CA: ABC-Clio.

Kincheloe, J. L. (2001). *Getting beyond the facts: Teaching social studies/social sciences in the twenty-first century.* New York, NY: Peter Lang.

Kincheloe, J. L. (2002). *The sign of the burger: McDonald's and the culture of power.* Philadelphia, PA: Temple University Press.

Kincheloe, J. L. (2004). *Critical pedagogy.* New York, NY: Peter Lang.

Kincheloe, J., Slattery, P., & Steinberg, S. R. (2000). *Contextualizing teaching.* New York, NY: Longman.

Kincheloe, J. L., & Steinberg, S. R. (1997). *Changing multiculturalism.* London: Open University Press.

Kincheloe, J. L., & Steinberg, S. R. (2004). *The miseducation of the west: How schools and media distort our understanding of the Islamic world.* Westport, CT: Greenwood.

Kincheloe, J., Steinberg, S., & Tippins, D. (1999). *The stigma of genius: Einstein, consciousness, and education.* New York, NY: Peter Lang.

Linne, R. (2001). Teacher perspectives on standards and high-stakes testing: From the urban to the suburban. In J. Kincheloe & D. Weil (Eds.), *Standards and schooling in the United States: An encyclopedia.* 3 vols. Santa Barbara, CA: ABC-Clio.

McLaren, P. (2000). *Che Guevara, Paulo Freire, and the pedagogy of revolution.* Lanham, MD: Rowman & Littlefield.

McNay, M. (1988). Educational research and the nature of science. *Educational Forum, 52*(4), 353–362.

McNeil, L. (1988). Contradictions of reform. *Phi Delta Kappan, 69*(7), 478–486.

McNeil, L., & Valenzuela, A. (1998). The harmful impact of the TAAS system of testing in Texas: Beneath the accountability rhetoric [Online]. Retrieved from http://www.law.harvard.edu/civilright/conferences/testing98/drafts/mneil_valenzuela.html

Novick, R. (1996). Actual schools, possible practices: New directions in professional development. *Education Policy Analysis Archives, 4*(14). Retrieved from http://epaa.asu.edu/epaa/v4n14.html

Ohanian, S. (1999). *One size fits few: The folly of educational standards.* Portsmouth, NH: Heinemann.

Oxford Dictionary. (2016). [Online]. Retrieved from https://en.oxforddictionaries.com/word-of-the-year/word-of-the-year-2016

Pinar, W., Reynolds, W., Slattery, P., & Taubman, P. (1995). *Understanding curriculum.* New York, NY: Peter Lang.

Race, R. (Ed.). (2018). *Advancing multicultural dialogues in education.* London: Palgrave Macmillan.

Rose, K., & Kincheloe, J. L. (2003). *Art, culture, and education: Artful teaching in a fractured landscape.* New York, NY: Peter Lang.

Steinberg, S. R. (2001). *Multi/intercultural conversations.* New York, NY: Peter Lang.

Steinberg, S. R. (2018). Bringin' it. In C. Emdin & E. Adjapong (Eds.), *Hip-hop as education, philosophy, and practice.* Leiden/Boston: Brill Sense Publishers.

Wesson, L., & Weaver, J. (2001). Educational standards: Using the lens of postmodern thinking to examine the role of the school administrator. In J. Kincheloe & D. Weil (Eds.), *Standards and schooling in the United States: An encyclopedia.* 3 vols. Santa Barbara, CA: ABC-Clio.

CHAPTER 5

Indigenous Knowledge and the Challenge for Rethinking Conventional Educational Philosophy

A Ghanaian Case Study

George J. Sefa Dei and Marlon Simmons

Just what exactly is this thing called philosophy? Where does philosophy reside? How do we come to know philosophy? And which body is accorded the title of philosopher? These are some of the burgeoning questions with which we engage in this piece. With this chapter, we choose to move beyond legitimized geographies of knowledge which constitute themselves as geography. Moreover, we locate philosophy as a hegemonic discursive framework that privilege a particular way of knowing. Of course, we recognize philosophy as a canon, one that has, and, continues to make meaningful contributions to ways of knowing and to the different educational systems. We do have a gripe with the dominant epistemic location of philosophy, as it resides within the hallways of academe. We offer a counterinsurgency of knowledge through an Indigenous episteme.

Much of the ongoing intellectual discussion on "education" is located in the dominant paradigms of Western thinking. Alternative visions and counter/theoretical perspectives of education struggle to disentangle from the dominance of the Eurocentric paradigm are not encouraged. For example, how much of local cultural resource knowledge base is taught to learners in schools? (see Dei & Asgharzadeh, 2006a; Dei, 2004; Semali & Kincheloe, 1999). This chapter will address the issue of schooling and education in African contexts with a particular focus on the pedagogic and instructional relevance of local cultural resource knowings such as proverbs and folktales. Using Ghanaian (and to some extent Nigerian case studies/material) case studies, this chapter examines how such local cultural resource knowings (as Indigenous knowledge and philosophies) inform education and socialization of youth and point to ways for rethinking knowledge, schooling, and education in contemporary times. We argue that contemporary education is mired in the reproduction of colonial hierarchies of power and knowledge and a struggle for local relevance. Such education is cut in the web of reproducing dominant knowledges and not necessarily imagining new possibilities for knowledge production in an academy. Today Indigenous and local communities continue to struggle to carve out education that paves the way for new cultural, economic, and political imaginings and imaginaries.

In this burgeoning epoch of globalization and advanced capitalism, schooling and education as populated through the Western body have come to promote a particular ordering of society, one in which the socializing processes for youth today come to be imbued in and through the ebb and flow of compliance and control (see McLaren & Farahmandpur, 2005). From curricula, to pedagogies, epistemologies have been localized to some governing Eurocentric paradigm, well steeped within colonial specificities. But contrapuntal to such standardized knowledge is Indigenous epistemes, which have been positioned as operating tangential to the conventional classroom text (see Dei, 2008; Battiste & Youngblood, 2000; Kincheloe & Steinberg, 2008). Yet, education for all must include the multiple ways we come to know and understand our social environment. Education for all must include the local everyday philosophies of students and all learners alike. We cannot continue to buy into the governing neo-liberal ideologies, which profess to be emancipatory and inclusive for all. Education for all must meet the needs of our local communities. Historically, education has produced/reproduced colonial relations within the institutionalized and social settings. Moreover, schooling and education have emerged as commodities of Enlightenment and at the same time proclaimed a particular humanism of Euromodernity, whereby the immanent cultural expressions, attitudes, and ways of behaving help to form the material conditions of the Eurosubject, as reified through the Western text. Education must consider the social environment, the local communities, and the cultural aesthetic; education is not simply out there as some theorized commodity, as positioned by the state, waiting to be consumed by the contemporary subject. Education ought to be conversant with a holistic conceptualization of the living social beings. School and education are not neutral events, by no means are they apolitical moments as being circumscribed through some ontological neutrality. At the same time we cannot continue to shout *revolution, revolution* and wait for the powers that be, to proceed with haste, to meet the educational needs of the local peoples. If are thinking transformation then, we need to move beyond the shout of resistance and rebellion. We need more to think of a philosophy of education through decolonisation and speak about subversive pedagogies. We need to dialogue with counterinsurgent knowledges that embody the civic will of local peoples and that embody questions of local citizenry, community and environment needs. What does it mean for educational philosophy to reside within conventional classrooms and as being devoid of the lived experiences of the learner? We bring this seemingly simple question to broach some of the limitations and possibilities for schooling and education. Today, immanent within schooling and education all learners alike come to know and understand through a particular mode of alienation. If then we are thinking, dis-alienation, subversive pedagogies, decolonization as oriented dialectically, as particular counterhegemonic processes, then we ought to speak about Indigenous philosophies and the link to schooling and education. Indigenous philosophies reside outside the conventional classroom and inculcate different ways of knowing through multiple methods that come to be well-steeped in the social environment through particular moments of self-determination, survival, development, recovery, mobilization, healing, transformation, and decolonization (Smith, 1999, p. 116; Maurial, 1999).

Educational philosophies for social justice ought to embody activist scholarship. Notably, liberation, decolonization, and emancipatory pedagogies have come to be ontologically absent from Enlightenment epistemologies. We are also constantly reminded that philosophy as dwelling within academic corridors reveals itself in a manner that wittingly proclaims an ahistorical phenomenology of racism. Racism in a sense becomes psychologized onto the particular individual body, as differentiated from any historic systemic lineage. Educational philosophy for emancipatory praxis must work with the ontological primacy immanent to the different geo-bodies. With the globalization of education, we ask education for whom and at what cost? What are the perils when we think of "development" through conventional educational philosophies that centre the will of capitalism as its ontological mantra? From global exploitative relations, to the continued production of underdevelopment in the Southern context, to the continued destabilization of racialized geographies, conventional educational philosophies continue to bring sustainability to the Western metropolis. Southern peoples continue to cry for help; in fact, economic inequality has become a way of life for the peoples of the South. Moreover, schooling and education as residing within dominant knowledging produce a set of social practices, in which the organizing principles are steeped within Euro-Enlightenment philosophies (see Abdi, Puplampu, & Dei, 2006; Abdi & Cleghorn, 2006). Pedagogical procedures experienced here engender banking (Freire, 1970) modalities of learning, in which, the expectation being for all learners alike is to reproduce dominant paradigms of knowledge, which then promulgates contemporary schooling. Such educational philosophies often appear as neutral and objective, as not having a politic, as not being biased, as not being racialised, and also, often enough these educational philosophies speak from the location of education for all learners (see Marcuse, 2009a, 2009b). Also ensuing from these philosophies is a particular curriculum that becomes discursively contoured to meet the needs of "development" and modernization from the context of Euromodernity. Today "underdevelopment" is actively deployed through specific measures of governance by overdeveloped countries. From Structural Adjustment Policies (SAPS) to the World Bank to the IMF, Western governments work collectively to ensure the present control of destabilizing relations with Southern geographies are here today and tomorrow (see Langdon, 2009; Dei & Simmons, 2009). If we profess social change, then we ought to seek a critical educational philosophy that ultimately seeks transformation of Western/colonial educational systems through subversive pedagogies. Social change means decolonization. Decolonization is all interwoven with dialectical ways of knowing. So in the African context, educational philosophies for decolonization must consider relevant knowledge that local peoples come to know as their own. At the very least decolonization cannot only be interpreted as another epistemology to be theorized within academic institutions. No, certainly not, if we are talking about decolonization and educational philosophies in the African context then we must speak about the lived experience of Africans on the continent and beyond its boundaries, we must consider the history of Africa in relation to other histories, keeping in mind that all forms of knowledging is political and not independent of consequences and implications, keeping in mind that which is colonial is not simply foreign or alien forces, but also dominating and imposing forces, which might also reside in the local context from within (see Dei, 2006b).

Concerning educational philosophies, the issue of the production and positionality of the different epistemes and how they come to be accorded with power, privilege, and discursive authority within academia need some attention here. In what way do these different moments of power, privilege, and discursive authority come to constitute epistemic violence? (Spivak, 1988) What are the academic perils when an educator speaks through an integrative Indigenous discursive framework? What then are the consequences for the different voices of the oppressed when the politics of identification, the politics of representation, the politics of knowledge legitimation, work to dissipate the collective oppressed voice of colonial histories within academic spaces? Many have spoken about Africa before. Many have talked about what Africa is doing and what Africa ought to do. But if we are speaking about "the ought" and Africa, then we have to consider colonial histories, historic specificities and knowledge "for whom." If we are speaking about "the ought" and Africa then we ask: Development/modernization for whom and on whose terms? How long will Africa continue to be represented through the imagination of the colonizer? And what about when the African body his/herself take on this colonial imagination as her/his own? If one of our goals is to counter such colonial imaginations, then schooling and education for Africa must dialogue with educational philosophies imbued through African-centered epistemologies and anti-colonial discursive frameworks (see Asante, 1988, 1991, 2010). But there has to be some type of bridge, that is, to engage with an integrative Indigenous discursive framework, which centers the African episteme and at the same time come to broach or to dialogue with conventional forms of knowledging. Today in our classrooms we are saturated with particular Euro-Enlightenment paradigms that work to organize and inscribe classroom curricula, which in turn promote hyper-scientific forms of what it means to be human; put another way it promotes hyper-scientific forms of what it means to be "developed." Hence, all learners alike engage in a form of education where the body engages in certain types of self-regulating practices, beliefs, behavioral patterns and attitudes, and particular expressions, which have historically been cryptically codified through particular colonial Enlightenment moral codes. So the learner comes to be informed through certain permutations of dehumanizing modalities in which the self comes to be known.

We need to conceptualize education *beyond the boundaries* of academic institutions and classrooms and importantly consider the material embodiment of this learning process. With all the *high theorizing* about education, we might forget that education is about doing, education is a lived moment, education is a human experience. By no means is education some empty space. The fact of the matter is that education is filled with bodies as lived through myriad historic-socio-cultural communities. We also need to keep in mind that historically, educational research proclaimed the concept of empiricism as being governed though the humanism of particular geo-bodies as being normate. We are left continually thinking of the ever-shifting consequences for contemporary schooling. Continuously thinking of the implications for learning, continuously thinking of the permutated complexity ongoing for different bodies to come to know, to learn, of coming to make meaning through educational philosophies, which through Euro-Enlightenment beliefs come to be permanently anchored within ethnocentric forms of empiricism, the methodological limitation ensuing here, being EuroEnlightenment epistemologies as providing the sense for a universalized way of knowing. But knowledge resides with the different Indigenous bodies as they come to be grounded through their local histories (see Roberts, 1998). The problem here is that Indigenous knowledges have been demarcated and located tangentially to Western philosophy. The challenge for the Indigene is to participate in educational research without compromise. If we are speaking here about integrating multiple educational systems of thought, if we are speaking about the different geo-subjects working together in some form of harmony, then the archetype conception of education ought to be re-conceptualized to include these subversive Indigenous pedagogies (see Dei, 2000). In a sense then, the task for educational research is to move beyond the positivistic tropes of education and instead genuinely engage in dialogue with holistic, communal forms of knowing and understanding (see Denzin, Lincoln, & Smith, 2008). Yet, as the Indigene broach the present lacuna residing within contemporaneous educational philosophies, the caution is to co-exist and not to co-opt Indigenous beliefs and historical value systems. On another note concerning the integration of different knowledge systems, that importantly here we are amplifying that with integration while we are concerned about how the resources come to be shared, we feel the need to say we are more concerned with emphasizing which geo-body has the power, the material sense of entitlement to distribute and relocate resources. So, again we return to the ubiquitous question, that, on whose terms do Indigenous peoples negotiate their humanism? How long Indigenous peoples will have to continue to say, "yes, we too are human and we have the right to live through our ancestral beliefs, customs, language, traditions, spiritual ways of knowing and cultural practices?" And what about the expropriation of Indigenous land and raw resources through legitimized juridical procedures of the state? Must this expropriation continue in the name of "development" and globalization despite the constant warnings of the detriment of climate change and global warming?

We know that particularly in the African context, the imposition of European philosophies and theories of knowledge was accompanied by the devaluation of Indigenous ways of knowing. This imperial project contributed in no small measure to the epistemological colonization of African Indigenous systems of thought. We also know that this imperial project did not go unanswered, in fact a number of Indigenous voices have come to the fore with some critical questions (see also Abdi, 2005). Among the current questions being broached are: How do we recover, reclaim and recuperate our Indigenous ways of knowing to give full sense of our lives? What are the sites that make such political and intellectual processes for reclamation of local knowledge possible? How do we lay claim to our local/Indigenous cultural resource base from an understanding of how rural communities continually reference local proverbs, fables, and tales as part of everyday living and conversations? What are some of the specific teachings highlighted by these Indigenous philosophies? And, what are the implications for rethinking philosophy and the philosophy of education? While we do not presume to have answers to all the questions we nonetheless want to draw attention to the various possibilities and challenges of understanding African Indigenous philosophies through the study of some of the teachings of local proverbs.

Case Study: Context, Method and Study Findings

Beginning in the 2007–2008 academic year, one of the authors (George Dei) has worked with a team of graduate researchers to examine African proverbs and folktales for the pedagogic and instructional relevance for youth education in the specific areas of character and moral development of the young learner. A major learning objective has been to understand how local cultural resource teachings constitute important knowledge for educating youth in the development of strong character, moral, and civic responsibilities. The study has a specific pedagogic interest in understanding how African proverbs as local Indigenous knowings can facilitate school teachings and learning in the academy. In the sociology of knowledge production we believe local cultural resource as Indigenous philosophies can serve as important sources of information and/or tool for educational delivery. Throughout the entire research period, 2007–2009, at least a dozen focus group discussions have been organized together with workshop sessions with student-educators, field practitioners, and educationists. There has been a total of over 85 individual interviews conducted with 25 educators, 20 elders/parents, and 40 students drawn from the local universities, secondary schools, and community colleges as well as local communities in Ghana and a college community in Nigeria. The focus on the interviews was understanding the use and meanings of local proverbs and African Indigenous philosophies, as well as the instructional, pedagogic, and communicative values and challenges in local teachings using proverbs, fables, folktales, myths, etc. about (in)discipline, and respect for self, peers and authority. The research period has also been a time for George Dei as Principal Investigator (PI) to network with Canadian educators and academic researchers on current directions of undertaking critical investigations concerning research and moral and character education.

In this chapter we highlight local voices as they attest to a particular source of Indigenous knowledge and their pedagogic and instructional lessons for learners. We highlight some themes emerging from analysis of the subject voices that not only point to the pedagogic and instructional relevance of African proverbs and folktales but also highlight ways Indigenous philosophies can inform the knowledge production and the sociology and philosophy of knowledge.

Proverbs as Indigenous Philosophies: Limits and Possibilities of Knowing

Local communities see proverbs as part of their Indigenous philosophies that speak about worldviews and the relations of society, culture, and nature. Proverbs are conceptualized as part of everyday experience. Within cultures proverbs are common but have sophisticated sayings. Nana Bodine is the current assistant headmaster for academics in a local senior high school, and is well known for his use of proverbs in teaching youth. He sees a central place of proverbs in the school system and doubts whether the schools have done enough to promote proverbs in teaching. Teaching local Indigenous languages is seen as critical. But while Nana Bodine is enthusiastic about teaching such Indigenous knowledges as proverbs in schools, he laments on the question of language and the local contexts for instructing on proverbs:

> No, the schools have not done much. Especially, these days when the local languages are being removed from the schools. You see, just as I said you cannot speak the proverbs in English language to get the impact. [File 09: Text Units 202–220]

Nana Bodine insists proverbs must be about social change and improvement in human lives and asserts there can be some problems attached to some proverbs, which do not instill in youth affirmative solution oriented teachings:

Yeah, some proverbs that will diminish progress. That will discourage especially the youth. You must avoid them. In our traditional society, they have been using them and do not think about the repercussions but we know that when you say this and you say that you just pull the youth away from being progressive. So if you sit down and you sample some of these things you will know that these ones are not very suitable and appropriate for this time. So you have to do that.

To Nana Bodine there is a responsibility that comes with the knowledge and wisdom that he has on proverbs. He has to ensure that such knowledge is passed on, especially, since he has been made a family head and he sees his role as helping make the person whole in all their knowings. The African learner who has been educated holistically will know about proverbs and their value in society as a powerful medium of communication.

Proverbs have meanings in the languages within which they are uttered. Mastery of local knowledge facilitates an understanding of local proverbs. Lasi, a teacher of Ghanaian languages with a diploma in Akan, discusses his understandings of proverbs and how he came to know about these cultural sayings. When asked how these cultural teachings can be brought back into schools to help educate youth, particularly what exactly needs to be done, Lasi replies:

What is required is the training of personnel who will handle the subject in the schools. Because during those days, I am talking about something like the Ghanaian language very, very … was well taught. Every Ghanaian language was well taught depending upon the society. In the Volta region, they were teaching their Ewe language very effectively. So, if you go to the Akan area too, the same thing. So, by the time the teacher leaves the training college he or she must be well vested in the language and the proverbs. But, these days it is not so. So, if you want to bring back the proverbs then the teaching and learning of Ghanaian language in our training colleges must be reintroduced. [File 22: Text Units 148–149]

Interviewer: Yeah … [and]. … beyond the level of comprehension of the proverbs. … There is also the question about … can some children or some youth say certain kinds of proverbs and at what times or what stage are they considered appropriate or inappropriate?

Eh proverbs are proverbs. And there are some proverbs whether they are being said by children or adults need caution. That is why we have what we normally say or we have the phrase "sebi ta fra kye." Sebi is more or less the eraser that cleans the dirty aspect of the language. So, if you are a child and you happen to meet up with adults, and it is necessary for you to use a particular proverb there is no limit. You only have to be cautious and use the "sebi" and "Ta fra kye." [File 22: Text Units 236–253]

In the above exchange Lasi recognizes teaching local proverbs in schools call for professional training and local expertise. This is because of the deep meanings often embedded in proverbs. There is also a recognition that proverbs have to be uttered in their appropriate contexts. Some proverbs are said to be for adult usage, in other words, to be appropriately uttered by an adult not a child. While proverbs can become part of everyday conversation in schools, nonetheless, it requires training educators on how to use and teach proverbs to youth. He laments the fact that such training of educators seems to have been lost in the current school system. Lasi notes the culture specificity of proverbs and argues that we have to look at the context in which a proverb is used. When asked if proverbs can "also move from place to place" and prompted with the example of whether a proverb said in the Volta region of Ghana, can have similar meanings in the eastern region, he reasons:

Oh yes, a lot of them. A lot of them, because there are some proverbs. … No, they cut across because what pertains here also happens there. There are some few examples where what we do here is not done there and therefore proverbs here will not work somewhere else. Generally proverbs cut across but you see there are some proverbs for instance in English, if they are translated word for word may mean nothing to us Akans here. I remember, I was once teaching a class and "Once bitten twice shy." And then a student interpreted it in a very, very … and "let sleeping dogs lie." Then he said "ma nkraman a wade da ntwa atoro." (laughs). Look at that. So, you see we have the equivalent here but they may not be in the same wording. [File 22: Text Units 308–340]

He recognizes the wide applicability of proverbs in their pedagogic and instructional value and relevance. But he admits the local contextuality of proverbs and the challenge for the education is to be able to mesh such specificities with the broad lessons for social responsibility, community building, and moral ethic and conduct that proverbs offer learners.

Culture, Schooling, and Indigenous Knowledge

Reclaiming proverbs as Indigenous philosophies also is about acknowledging the role of culture in schooling, knowledge production, and education. In a focus group discussion with finalyear student teachers specializing in social studies at the University of Education in Ghana the students offered poignant critiques of colonial education and its impact on local culture. The student narratives spoke about the way in which culture, values, and traditions are significant in the schooling of young adults.

| Interviewer: | I want to come back to the point about the culture and you said we have lost it, right? Could you speak a bit about it? |
| Student: | We were talking about our culture respect for the elderly is totally not there anymore. When we were kids in the recent past we were told that when you meet an elderly person in a vehicle and you are sitting, you stand up for the elderly person but nowadays it is not there like that. You will be in the vehicle with an old person and this. [File 20: Text Units 2093–2122] |

It is interesting that in the foregoing discussion the students highlight respect for the elderly, authority, and school leadership as critical for moulding one's character and perseverance. They point to cultural sanctions that can be applied in local communities to help cultivate in youth, a sense of respect and responsibility to themselves, peers, and authority figures. Teaching African culture is teaching about respect and social responsibility. Respect and culture can be context-bound. They are both part of the socialization process for youth. Socializing a learner is also teaching about respecting oneself, peers and authority. Teaching respect and local culture is also an integrated practice. If one knows about his or her local culture and its values such knowledge cannot be separated from everyday educational practice. Such knowledge is grounded in everything one does. Local cultural knowings can be infused in school/classroom teachings as educators go about their everyday teaching. If socialization and education is to proceed the way African communities have impacted knowledge then it will be seen that local cultural knowings are infused in the various processes of knowledge production, validation, and dissemination. When asked how we bring culture back in education or in school, the finalyear student teachers specializing in social studies at the University of Education in Ghana are adamant about noting and understanding the empowering and disempowering aspects of culture and tradition:

| Female student: | All of us agree that our culture has been gone and we have integrated … but we have forgotten one question. There are some aspects of the culture which was very bad and was very inhuman like the "female genital mutilation,". … Trokosi. … and other things which has gone. So as for that I think it is good. But there are some too which we could have retained but those one too are gone. Now looking at our culture as maybe when an older person comes in a bus you stand up and greet; I think that if the bus could have been partitioned. |

No culture is immune to criticism. Every culture should be interrogated. The point that is made is very important, because there is a tendency to throw away a lot of an Indigenous culture and just adopt some things. So on the question, "how do you bring back culture into the schools?" a student in the focus group responds:

| Student: | I said that formerly they had something in school called culture studies. This in particular teaches about culture in the Ghanaian society and teaches both the good aspect and the bad and tells to show the bad and tells us to maintain the good aspect but as time goes on culture studies has been taken away from the syllabus and has been replaced by other European. … which we are being forced to learn. Because they said the world has become a global village and by so doing we neglect our own culture, so the generations coming forth, their minds are being polluted with the Western European style so they don't normally conform again to that part of the society that we are in. By so doing our culture is lost because it is the youthful generation that replaces the older generation. So until we are able to find that part of culture of our society and inculcate it in the curriculum, from the junior stages so that we can have people to teach and bring resource people from the society to really give examples, then if we do that then it means that we can bring our culture. [File 20: Text Units 1443–1513] |

No doubt, the students are lamenting about "lost culture." They also recognize that there are sites of empowerment as well as disempowerment in local cultures and cultural traditions. The students do not bring an unquestioned faith to the reclamation of culture. Every culture is dynamic and culture moves with the times. Their call to "bring back local culture" is grounded in a firm belief that some aspects of traditional cultures have been helpful in socializing learners into responsible adults. No particular culture is an island unto itself. Cultures influence each other but one cannot discard their culture and traditions simply in favor of an alien culture. What learners can be assisted to do is to integrate values and ideas that have proven to work effectively in the socialization and education of youth in their own culture and cultural practices. The critical teaching of culture and cultural studies may be a good starting point. On the relevance of gender and gender values in such discussions concerning schooling, culture and society, final-year student teachers at the local University of Education noted issues of gender bias, disparity and the absence of critical gender analysis in school curriculum:

Female student:	It is also very common … specially seeing the female being highly marginalized in terms of curriculum in the performance of leadership roles. That is the topic on which I am writing on now. You see them as being sidelined when it comes to the performance of leadership roles in the classroom. Always women are somewhere and that trend has continued.
Female student:	When you get out to the field in politics; in all the executive sectors of the economy. We find men throughout. At times too most of them are being ridiculed and the few ones who will like to fight boot to boot with their men counterparts are nicknamed devil, witches and whatnots. I went somewhere and the lady was a carpenter roofing and thousand and one people were gathered looking at her and some calling her names. "Beyiefoo wei" [witches] and what nots … all nasty names.
Female student:	It all boils down to the values. In our society it is said that even if the woman buys a gun it is the man who is supposed to keep it. It boils down to what the society perceives the woman to be. [File 20: Text Units 755–776]

In reclaiming culture, the place of gender in society must be taken seriously to interrogate social and political structures that marginalize women in society. Schools contribute to the problem by the lack of any critical focus on gender issues to allow learners complete grasp of the complexity of social interactions. If culture is to be claimed then the sites of empowerment as well as disempowerment for certain groups (e.g., women, children and religious, ethnic and sexual minorities) must also be exposed and addressed. Educators must be able to tease out the gender tropes of proverbs in order to teach proverbs critically about gender relations in society. Some proverbs because they are heavily embedded in cultural traditions can be reproducing gender stereotypes of the subordination of women in society. In a patriarchal society proverbs can affirm masculine views and power relations, and the responsibility of an educator is to help learners understand such gender dimensions and to begin to ask critical question about why, how, and when such patriarchal ideologies in society get reproduced in proverbial sayings. Unfortunately not many learners openly acknowledge the problematic aspects of proverbs.

The Question of Language

As already noted one cannot teach proverbs as Indigenous knowledge/philosophies without understanding the local language. The connections between language and Indigenity are clear. M.Phil. human rights student, Abana, at the university and currently working with the local ministry of management affairs, agrees that language is important in such discussion about proverbs:

> Yeah language is very important because it means that we actually communicate and in communicating language as a tool helps a lot. And, you should be able to understand the language that you are using to convey your message. And, so language is important. [File 07: Text Units 248–253]

Language facilitates communication in local proverbs. Abana's colleague, Amobi expands on the role of language in the teaching of proverbs calling for the integration of local languages and English in the instructing of young learners:

> I think it plays a very important role because language is part of our culture and we can learn best through our own local language. And, if we use our local language in addressing such issues, I think it will have a very good impact on the children. Yes, even though we can still use English language, it is also very important anyway but how they will understand it better is the main thing. So, the local language should be used and we should also add the English language and I think it will help them to move ahead. [File 14: Text Units 165–213]

Arts Design educator Fiifi also argues that language is central or significant to a discussion of proverbs:

> Well, in terms of the language, what I know about language in relation to proverbs; now for instance, the teacher teaching students as I said with the language reference; language you use to teach. Now supposing you are using English in teaching and you have some proverbs to put across, now if you don't have enough to elaborate more on the various tribes because you have different kinds of peoples or students in your class. The best thing a teacher does is if you say a proverb and you think it will be very difficult to explain you just literally translate it in English to make it easier, at least, for every student to understand because that is the language you are noted for to teach with. I think that is far better than to go as being partial to others, I mean to develop hatred between you the teacher and students. [File 15: Text Units 234–278]

Fiifi, however, conversant of the diversity of linguistic groups in the school system would appreciate a more modest approach of using the English language as a starting point to begin conversations around such local cultural knowings as proverbs. Master of Arts in Library studies student who hails from the Upper West region, Danny also links language and proverbs. He points out that to understand the proverbs of the community you must first understand the language of the community:

> The language is necessary because you have to understand the language so that if it is even changed in a certain way, you will be able to know that though this is the direct meaning of this word but in this context it means this. So, it is necessary to understand the language. [File 18: Text Units 123–128]

Focus group discussions with final-year student teachers graduating in social studies at a local Ghanaian university revealed some additional perspectives on Indigenous knowledge. In discussing what educators see as their role in the schools, the broader issues of language, culture and Indigenous knowledge surfaced:

Interviewer:	… The whole issue about indigenous knowledge; what role do you see the teaching of indigenous knowledge?
Student:	In the school?
Interviewer:	Well, in the school, at the college or at the university?
Male student:	The teaching of indigenous knowledge, just recently, was the medium of instruction for the lower level of … for the lower primary but recently it has changed for the medium of instruction to be the English language. I have a problem with that because … if English should be used as the medium of instruction it means that some of the things that we want to teach the children; we cannot do because basically some of these things; you have to say it in the local language for the child to know exactly what you are speaking about. But now we are being told to use the English language to do that and I think it will have a great effect on the students.
Female student:	Teaching of indigenous knowledge; to me, I would say to some extent we are doing good in Ghana because we have the teaching of the Ghanaian language in our various schools, through primary school to university level. Even in this university we have a department of Ghanaian languages, where various languages are studied. It is through the study of these languages that other things about our culture will be studied. So for me, to some extent we are doing well in our schools regarding the teaching of indigenous languages. [File 20: Text Units 1551–1593]

The tensions in using the dominant language to convey Indigenous perspectives is highlighted in these discussions. Local language is critical to the survival of Indigenous ways of knowing. Indigenous language needs to be kept alive in local communities, and schooling and education in Africa has a role to play in such undertaking. Teaching local language then ensures the survival of local Indigenous knowledge systems. Language conveys powerful meanings. Language and culture are interconnected. When used inappropriately (as for example outside an appropriate cultural context) such meaning is lost. The language of other peoples cannot be used to teach or convey the full thoughts and ideas as expressed or embedded in such local cultural knowings as proverbs. Mathematics teacher Bafoah speaks about the relevance of teaching proverbs and the question of responsibility. He stresses the importance of meaning and how language is critical to fully comprehending what is contained in the local cultural sayings. He points to some of the things we need to be careful of, when we talk about proverbs, particular how the dominant language (i.e., English) can misrepresent what is being said in a local context:

… I think eh … sometimes when we use eh … sometimes, the language barrier because sometimes when you want to translate; because sometimes one thing I see is that for the benefit of other students who do not understand the Akan language, it tries to translate it directly into the English language. And, sometimes me being an Akan when he says it in English it does not have the same impulse as it is in the local language. Yeah so that is one of the things. [File 04: Text Units 148–156]

Forty-six-year-old Patiah is a professional teacher with a bachelor's degree in education. He majored in English language and is currently studying to be a human rights advocate at the local university. In his view there is a sense that we need to keep these local proverbs going otherwise they are going to be lost. He sees teaching proverbs also as a way to keep local Indigenous languages alive:

There is the tendency. Even with the present Ministry of Education policy teaching indigenous language at the basic cycle. … Yeah, it is a hot argument. Others are of the view that you start with English language, you know foreign language, even at the nursery. So that, the children will pick on, very early. Other scholars also hold on to the fact that, we should give them, first, the native language so that when they pick the proverbs, other elements and the traditional roles, from that language then they can build upon it when they are in the primary school with the English language. Well, we allow the two things to go on. But I personally feel that the usage of the native language, at the commencement of education, that is the basic level, will help them a lot to imbibe such proverbs. Otherwise, they will get lost. They will die a natural death, so we need to look at that. [File 16: Text Units 166–180]

Patiah's narrative suggests the important place of Indigenous language in any attempt to rethink schooling and education to serve local needs and purposes. If we believe proverbs have important pedagogic and instructional relevance when it comes to the education and socialization of the contemporary learner then it is important we cultivate the medium and mode of communication that allows such Indigenous cultural knowings be sustained. In fact, Patiah sees the teaching of proverbs as a form of Indigenous knowledge and expands on his conception of the term:

> Yes. I see it to be a sequence to uphold the originality of the language. That is the beauty of the language. If you are able to use proverbs they bring about variation. They bring about beauty and it even leads to deep thinking; critical analysis and all those things. So we have to encourage them. There is the necessity that we maintain them. I will even suggest that those who are reading the native languages in the university; they should write more and those on the field should also encourage it so that it remains. [File 16: Text Units 211–220]

Indigenous language, like all languages, is complex and dynamic. Schooling and education must engage in practices that uphold the centrality of Indigenous languages. Tamipiah, in speaking about the power and efficacy of traditional knowledge, also points to the dangers, perils and/or limitations in bringing this knowledge into the school system:

> Yes. The ... challenge that I will still hammer is our indigenous language, our indigenous language that is not being used in schools. Because nowadays it is quite often that we see that teachers use English which is not our mother tongue more often than our local dialect. And, sometimes it is difficult you know to express or give proverbs in English. Sometimes even if you do the literal translation it would not sound as it is. So, it is about time if we want to promote the use of proverbs then it means that our local dialect must also be promoted where students must be made to learn. It will form part of the curriculum to be fixed in there. So, that, when these things are learnt; in delivering it in our local tongues it won't be a problem. But once that thing has not been done, I see it to be a block or impediment for the teaching of the proverbs. And, eh another thing is also understanding the local culture and other things. Now we are looking at somebody who did not stay in the area. He or she went somewhere to stay and is now coming back. Sometimes it will take them more time to be able to let the person know or understand the culture of the area because these proverbs as they are when we say it or when you use it in relation to an expression that you want to say. They try to explain or shorten certain expressions that we want to do. [File 17: Text Units 190–213]

He reiterates that we cannot hope to promote the teaching of proverbs in schools without first ensuring the survival and vitality of our Indigenous language system. We cannot also understand local proverbs without a full grounding of local culture. Proverbs are part of the cultural values system. A complete "stranger" cannot teach or fully comprehend local proverbs because she/he hardly knows the Indigenous language and culture. They may have an appreciation of such knowledge system but hardly grasp its intellectual intricacies.

Conclusion

Today, one of the challenges facing the academy and Indigenous philosophies alike is that Indigenous philosophies co-exist through interrelated and interdependent spaces, spaces that might not materialize into some readily available legible text, resulting in a sense, a type of academic gripe for Indigenous representation; so, working in tandem with the racial snub from the academy, there exists this epistemological classification, which within conventional knowledge spaces, determines the conditions whereby Indigenous oral epistemologies come into being a sum legitimate philosophy. Historically, educational philosophy emerged through the material presence of the written text, consequently forming hegemonic relations with Indigenous ways of knowing. Concerning here is the form, the material body of Indigenous language, the oral of Indigeneity, the flux, the fluidity and the capacity, to come to co-exist in some way with conventional schooling and education. The operative term here being capacity and not compatibility. For as a subversive pedagogy, Indigenous philosophy is not seeking some romanticized union with conventional philosophy. At the same time we wish to share with the power resources, so at the same time we are not seeking some segregated space, but to work with conventional knowledging on Indigenous terms, acknowledging the multiple ways we learn. Part and parcel of Indigenous knowledge, is resistance, survival; it is about operating counter-hegemonic to colonial Western forms of knowledging. Historically, EuroEnlightenment interpretations of Indigenous culture negated personal narratives, life histories, stories, and local proverbs. But these personal accounts were not some narrative to be quickly disposed of by the colonizer, to be deemed suspect knowledge, to be labeled as superstitious, these personal narratives held Indigenous culture together.

Educational philosophy ought to be about socializing the learner to be a whole, complete person, a learner who is well aware of her or his surroundings and strives to meet the mutual obligations that go with membership in a thriving community. Proverbs teach about understanding, conduct, and moral behavior. Proverbs motivate one to do healthy deeds. Proverbs offer a course of action to follow in life. The elderly can teach the young. So too can students teach their educators. The critical teacher is not only a listener but someone (who) is prepared to let her or his students teach him/her. In the same vein a critical educator can learn a lot from a traditional elder or cultural custodian well versed in the culture, traditions, and cultural resource knowings of the community. The connection of moral and civic education is significant as it highlights some of the teachings of proverbs that stress social responsibility and the importance of education and socialization in bringing out the community of learners to civic responsibility. To local educators morals address the accepted values of society. It is through education that one begins to learn about the accepted morality and the expectation to govern one's life and experiences accordingly. Values are long-held rules, expectations and codes of conduct of a community. Some values are highly regarded and cherished by all members of the community. Any disrespect for such values is frowned upon and may elicit heavy community sanctions. Children are socialized and educated into the societal values, and it is important for educators to be conversant with a variety of pedagogic and instructional ways to impart societal values to young learners. In other words, values are a way of life. Teaching values is teaching about society in general—culture, traditions, perspectives, expectations, moral standards as well as social relations among groups. Societal values can be found or be expressive in Indigenous proverbial sayings.

Acknowledgments

The fieldwork component of the study was funded by the Ontario Literacy and Numeracy Secretariat (LNS). George Dei would like to acknowledge the assistance of Dr. Meredith Lordan, Munya Kabba, Jaggiet Gill, Camille Logan, Rosina Agyepong, Paul Adjei, Dr. Anthony KolaOlusanya, and Marlon Simmons all of OISE/UT who at various times worked as graduate researchers on various aspects of the project. Thanks also to Professor Kola Raheem and the staff of the Centre for School and Community Science and Technology Studies (SACOST), University of Education, Winneba, as well as Mr. Paul Akom, former Dean of Students at the University of Education at Winneba for their invaluable assistance on the field research project. Similar thanks to Mr. Tola Olujuwon and the provost, faculty, staff and students of the Adeniran Ogunsanya College of Education, Otto/Ijanikin, Lagos State, Nigeria, where George Dei was a visiting scholar for a short period in the fall of 2007. Special mention to Messrs. Ebenezer Aggrey, Alfred Agyarko, Isaac Owusu-Agyarko, Martin Duodo, Kwaku Nii, Stephen Asenso, and Dickson K. Darko, all who participated as local research assistants. Finally, Marlon Simmons would also like to thank George Dei for the invitation to co-author.

Note

1.   All local names used here are pseudonyms.

References

Abdi, A. A. (2005). African philosophies of education: Counter-colonial criticisms. In A. Abdi & A. Cleghorn (eds.), *Issues in African education: Sociological perspectives* (pp. 25–42). New York: Palgrave Macmillan.

Abdi, A., & Cleghorn, A. (eds.) (2006). *Issues in African education: Sociological perspectives.* New York: Palgrave Macmillan.

Abdi, A. Puplampu, K., & Dei, G. (eds.) (2006). *African education and globalization: Critical perspectives.* Lanham, MD: Lexington.

Asante, M. K. (1988). *Afrocentricity.* Trenton, NJ: Africa World Press.

Asante, M. K. (1991). The Afrocentric idea in education. *Journal of Negro Education 60*(2): 170–180. Asante, M. K. (2010). *Maulana Karenga: An intellectual portrait.* Cambridge: Polity.

Battiste, M. & Youngblood, H. J. (2000). "What is indigenous knowledge?" In *Protecting indigenous knowledge and heritage* (pp. 35–56). Saskatoon: Purich.

Cajete, G. (2008). Seven orientations for the development of indigenous science education. In N. Denzin, Y. Lincoln, & L. T. Smith (eds.). *Handbook of critical and indigenous methodologies* (pp. 487–496). Los Angeles, CA: Sage.

Dei, G. J. S. (2000). African development: The relevance and implications of indigenousness. In G. J. S. Dei, B. L. Hall, & G. Rosenberg (eds.). *Indigenous knowledges in global contexts: Multiple readings of our world* (pp. 70–86). Toronto: University of Toronto Press.

Dei, G. J. S. (2004). *Schooling and education in Africa: The case of Ghana.* Trenton, NJ: Africa World Press.

Dei, G. J. S. (2006b). Introduction: Mapping the terrain—towards a new politics of resistance. In G. J. S. Dei & A. Kempf (eds.). *Anti-colonialism and education: The politics of resistance* (pp. 1–23). Rotterdam: Sense.

Dei, G. J. S. (2008). Indigenous knowledge studies and the next generation: Pedagogical possibilities for anticolonial education. *Australian Journal of indigenous Education* 37, Supplement: 5–13

Dei, G. J. S. (2011). Introduction: indigenous philosophies and critical education. In Dei, G. J. S. (ed.). *Indigenous philosophies and critical education.* New York: Peter Lang Publishing.

Dei, G. J. S. & Asgharzadeh, A. (2006a). Indigenous knowledges and globalization: An African perspective. In A. Abdi, K. Puplampu, & G. Dei (eds.). *African education and globalization: Critical perspectives* (pp. 53–78). Lanham, M.D: Lexington.

Dei, G. J. S. & Simmons, M. (2009). The indigenous as a site of decolonizing knowledge about conventional development and the link with education: The African case. In Jonathan L. (ed.). *Indigenous knowledge, development and education* (pp. 15–36). Rotterdam: Sense Publishers.

Denzin, N., Lincoln, Y. & Smith, L. T. (2008) (eds.). *Handbook of critical and indigenous methodologies.* Los Angeles: Sage.

Freire, P. (1970). *Pedagogy of the oppressed.* New York: Continuum.

Kincheloe, J. L., & Steinberg, S. (2008). Indigenous knowledges in education: Complexities, dangers and profound benefits. In N. Denzin, Y. Lincoln, & L. T. Smith (eds.), *Handbook of critical and indigenous methodologies* (pp. 135–156). Los Angeles: Sage.

Langdon, J. (2009). Indigenous knowledges, development and education. In J. Langdon (ed.), *Indigenous knowledge, development and education* (pp 1–13). Rotterdam: Sense.

Marcuse, H. (2009a). Lecture on education, Brooklyn College, 1968. In D. Kellner, T. Lewis, C. Pierce, & K. Daniel Cho (eds.), *Marcuse's challenge to education.* New York: Rowman & Littlefield.

Marcuse, H. (2009b). Lecture on higher education and politics, Berkeley, 1975. In D. Kellner, T. Lewis, C. Pierce, & K. Daniel Cho (eds.), *Marcuse's challenge to education.* New York: Rowman & Littlefield.

Maurial, M. (1999). Indigenous knowledge and schooling: A continuum between conflict and dialogue. In L. Semali. & J. Kincheloe (eds.), *What is indigenous knowledge? Voices from the academy* (pp. 59–77). New York: Falmer.

McLaren, P., & Farahmandpur, R. (2005). *Teaching against global capitalism and the New Imperialism.* New York: Rowman & Littlefield.

Richard R. (1989). *Contingency, irony, and solidarity.* Cambridge: Cambridge University Press.

Roberts, H. (1998). Indigenous knowledges and Western science: Perspectives from the Pacific. In D. Hodson (ed.), *Science and technology education and ethnicity: An Aotearoa/New Zealand perspective.* Proceedings of a conference held at the Royal Society of New Zealand, Thorndon, Wellington, May 7–8, 1996. The Royal Society of New Zealand Miscellaneous series #50.

Semali, M. L. & Kincheloe, L. J. (1999). Introduction: What is indigenous knowledge and why should we study it. In M. L. Semali & J. L. Kinchloe (eds.), *What is indigenous knowledge? Voices from the academy* (pp. 3–57). New York: Falmer.

Smith, L. (1999). *Decolonizing methodologies.* London: Zed.

Spivak, G. C. (1988). Can the subaltern speak? In, C. Nelson & L. Grossberg (eds.), *Marxism and the interpretation of culture* (pp. 271–313). Chicago, Urbana: University of Illinois Press.

CHAPTER 6

The Teacher as Mediator between Schools and Students

Tricia Kress

You see a lot doctor, but are you strong enough to point that highpowered perception at yourself? Or maybe you're afraid to. (Utt, Saxon, Bozman, & Demme, 1991)

On the first morning of a high school English class, Hannibal Lecter[1] tested my understanding of what it means to be an educator. I had gone through my normal first day "get to know you" routine where I attempted to give my students a bit about my background and myself in order to help them begin to get comfortable with me as their teacher. My goal was to try to establish a measure of common ground and then over time ease into the role of not only a teacher but also a mediator between my students and the institution. I always like to reveal a little of who I am outside of school, so that my students will know that I am more than just an employee of the institution. During this morning I shamelessly admitted that I'm a movie junkie, and one of my favorite films is *The Silence of the Lambs*. One of my students quickly admitted that it was his favorite, too. In fact, he had a copy of Thomas Harris's newly released *Hannibal* (sequel to *Silence*) on his desk.

So there I sat, sweaty-palmed with twenty-five pairs of eyes challenging me. At that moment I felt as if I might have been sitting in front of Dr. Lecter himself. They were sizing me up and trying to determine exactly what I was all about. I had made it clear that I wanted my students to be involved in determining what we would be studying to give them a sense of ownership over the curriculum, and now I had to make a decision: go back on what I said and lose trust, which would classify me as no different than any other authority figure in the school, or entertain the idea and possibly wind up using material that my experiences as a student and educator told me was inappropriate for the classroom.

What was I supposed to do? What would my colleagues think? *Hannibal* certainly isn't considered a classic. How would other teachers or administrators respond to a pop-culture, serial-killer novel being used in class? Yet, I didn't want to say no. I had already read the book myself, and I knew that it was rich in literary elements and devices we could study. So I took a gamble, and we put it to a class vote, *Hannibal* or *Fahrenheit 451* and *A Clockwork Orange*. Surprise, surprise, they chose *Hannibal*. I'm not sure if my students' decision was based on their comfort with studying a text they had already been exposed to in cinematic form, or if it was a way for them to buck the system and go outside the realm of a traditional curriculum. Either way, to them, the cannibalistic main character was less frightening than the prospects of tackling "modern classics." I, on the other hand, was terrified. I was sure I would lose my job, but at least I had earned my students' trust by showing that I could follow through on my word.

I didn't think much then (or want to) about why I had the reservations I did when teaching the novel, or why I would hide that I was using it in the classroom. When socializing with colleagues, I would remain silent while everyone else exchanged curriculum stories and ideas. I felt guilty, like I was harboring a dirty secret, yet at the same time I loved going to class every day because I knew my students would be there on time, waiting to discuss the horrors and plot twists of their weekly reading assignments. They would eagerly tackle concepts like symbolism, characterization, metaphor, allegory, and foreshadowing. As nerve-wracking as it was to hide my guilty pleasure, it was also the best class I've taught thus far.

My students and I had become co-conspirators in our exploration of the taboo realm of popular culture and how it reflects society at large. We would discuss in small groups, as a whole class, and individually not only *Hannibal* in isolation but how we could relate it to other works and look at the text as something bigger than just a story. What could this tell us about the world in general? How did this relate to our lives (or not) on a grander scale? Together we navigated critically through complex literary, social, and psychological issues that my students would surely need to understand and negotiate in order to be successful in school and life. Over the term, our conversations spilled out into the hallway in whispered excitement, and the afterschool hours suddenly were a time for my students to find each other or me just to ask a quick question or make an observation that they would then explore at home. During that experience, I learned as much from them about what it meant to be a teacher/mediator as they did from me about literature.

Now, years later, I can look back and understand that at the moment when my students asked me to choose between what they wanted and what the institution declared was appropriate, I was forced to question everything I knew to be true about classroom practice. The effects of a lifetime of traditional, conservative, teacher-centered instruction became painfully apparent, and I was introduced to a new reality—the way I knew of teaching was not the only way, nor was it the best way. Up until that point, I hadn't yet understood the full meaning of what it meant to serve as a mediator between my students and the institution they were compelled to attend. As Bruner says in *The Culture of Education,* "an educational enterprise that fails to take the risks involved becomes stagnant and eventually alienating" (Bruner, 1996, 15). And that was where I found myself. At the time, I hadn't been exposed to ideas like this before, but I was very aware that if I didn't roll the dice, anything I did from then on would amount to nothing. I would have lost my students' respect before the term even started. Without taking that chance, I would have failed them from the start and set a bad example. How could I expect them to believe in themselves and have faith in the strengths and assets they brought to the classroom if I couldn't do it myself?

As a team, my students and I had made a decision to use the text in class, and after a lengthy discussion about why other staff and administrators might frown upon our using the text, my students and I made a pact—this book was just for us, we would keep it to ourselves. But this also meant at times we would do double the work, because we'd have to link this to other things that needed to be covered throughout the term. We had found a way to include not only what the institution wanted but also what we as a class wanted. I knew what we were doing was risky, but if I had simply dismissed their plea to include something they thought was relevant to them in the curriculum, I would have in no way differed from the administrators and reformers who implement one-size-fits-all curricula and standardized testing. My students and I would not have been working together in education; we would have been working as opponents. I would have shown them that talk about democratic education means nothing, and it's the way of the institution or no way at all. Unintentionally, I would have been acting as a conduit of the institution and not as a mediator between my students and the institution as I had hoped to be.

> "Have your supervisors demonstrated any values, Clarice? How about your parents, did they demonstrate any? If so are these values the same? Look into the honest iron and tell me." (Harris, 1999, 32)

In the classroom managed by a teacher whose goal is to mediate between the demands of the institution and the needs of the students, students can no longer be mere passive receivers of information. Uniform and packaged curricula ask that students absorb and regurgitate knowledge provided to them by their teacher. The teacher-as-mediator asks that students learn to view the role of student as critical knowledge producer, not just an empty vessel to be filled. Students carry experiences and knowledges to be shared and built upon. These knowledges are valuable assets the teacher can use to educate them to be democratic citizens. Simply pushing abstract facts on students is not just insufficient for educating students to participate in a democracy but is also dangerous. The institution insists on the type of superficial education that ignores the political nature of schooling and how it can replicate the status quo depending on the types of pedagogical approaches that are taken and the knowledges that are given primacy. It is the teacher-as-mediator who is aware of this and can help prevent students from being limited to this type of schooling.

The teacher who is unable to mediate between the needs of the students and the institution merely relies on a curriculum that does not leave room for student contribution. This silently enforces the institution's goal that "[s]tudents become 'fact collectors,' not knowledge workers who can conduct research and interpret data. Intelligence is defined in a narrow way that excludes those qualities that make individuals agents of positive social change. The use of such a limited definition may leave students with unique characteristics unrewarded and unaware of their potential achievements" (Kincheloe, 2001, 50). However, when teachers get students involved in the creation of the curriculum, the things they study will be meaningful to them and will reflect their lived realities. Students will not be limited to the canned education forced upon them by an institution that continues to disenfranchise so many of those situated within it.

As Chomsky (2003) rightly states,

> Real education is about getting people involved in thinking for themselves—and that's a tricky business to know how to do well, but clearly, it requires that whatever it is you're looking at has to somehow catch people's interest and make them *want* to think, and make them *want* to pursue and explore. And just regurgitating "Good Books" is absolutely the worst way to do it—that's just a way of turning people into automata. You may call it an education if you'd like, but it's really the opposite of an education. (p. 27)

Thus, lessons in school should grow out of students' "own past doings, thinkings, and sufferings … [which then] grows into application in further achievements and receptivities, then no device or trick of method has to be resorted to in order to enlist 'interest'" (Dewey, 1902, 27). They can engage in the subject matter, and they can begin to develop dialogues with themselves and each other. "All students, not just those from marginalized groups seem eager to enter energetically into classroom discussion when they see it as pertaining directly to them" (hooks, 1994, 87). From here they can begin to question their lived realities and what they have come to accept as truth. This is not to say that basic skills are unimportant. On the contrary, basic skills are essential, but rather than just drilling students with information and procedures, the teacher-as-mediator emphasizes that basic skills be mastered and internalized, so they can then be built upon within a larger social practice rather than just requiring students to memorize a standardized curriculum (Dewey, 1902; Dewey, 1938; Kincheloe, 2001; Lave & Wenger, 1991).

I don't think that many people would argue that students should learn literacy, basic math, the location of different continents, and the like without cluttering their minds with Britney Spears and the

WB; but in teaching, I have learned that education doesn't need to take the form of mental discipline either. Rather, students should be able to explore subjects at their individual pace, bringing with them their own knowledges and experiences. They should be exposed to a myriad of ideas and disciplines in an interesting and engaging way that allows them to develop a dialogue between the classroom material, themselves, their peers, their lives outside of school, and their teacher. In the current push for standardized curricula and high-stakes tests, this is often forsaken.

Thus, the teacher-as-mediator will attempt to include students in the process of creating a curriculum that meets the needs of all participants involved. In this way, the teacher can help students to negotiate between what is essential knowledge to them and what is essential to the institution. As Freire states,

> The role of an educator who is pedagogically and critically radical is to avoid being indifferent. ... On the contrary, a better way to proceed is to assume the authority as a teacher whose direction of education includes helping learners get involved in planning education, helping them create the critical capacity to consider and participate in the direction and dreams of education, rather than merely following blindly. (Freire as cited in Giroux, 2000, 148)

In this respect, authority and legitimacy are then given to the students and the knowledges they already possess. Students become teachers as well as learners as they share their knowledges and experiences with teachers and other students (Delpit, 1995; Dewey, 1902; Dewey, 1938; Lave & Wenger, 1991). It is then the responsibility of the teacher-as-mediator to guide students toward recognizing which bodies of knowledge are given legitimacy within their educational institution. From there, they can work together to determine how these things can be addressed in the curriculum without compromising what is important to the students.

By acknowledging the contradictions present between the demands of the institution and the needs of the students, teacher and students can develop their own discourse. It should be honest, inclusive, and able to openly critique power relations and social dynamics in the larger society, in the institution, and within the classroom itself. This requires "the significance of shifting the analytic focus from the individual as learner to learning as participation in the social world, and from the concept of cognitive process to the more encompassing view of social practice" (Lave & Wenger, 1991, 43). Within this, teachers and students can

> discuss openly the injustices of allowing certain people to succeed, based not upon merit but upon which family they were born into, upon which discourse they had access to as children. ... Only after acknowledging the inequity of the system can the teacher's stance then be "Let me show you how to cheat!" And of course, to cheat is to learn the discourse which would otherwise be used to exclude them from participating in and transforming the mainstream. (Delpit, 1995, 165)

Teacher and students can work together to understand the codes of society in order to maneuver through the institution and then change it. And at the same time, they must still "acknowledge and validate students' home language without using it to limit students' potential. Students' home discourses are vital to their perception of self and sense of community connectedness" (Delpit, 1995, 163). It is essential that the teacher-as-mediator recognize this and know that each student needs to see herself as part of a whole, a member of a collective and not just one of many miniscule faces in a large and alienating institution.

By addressing issues of "inequalities in race and gender, and the abuse of privilege and power" we can raise "a new generation equipped to deal effectively with those abuses" (Kliebard, 1995, 24). Curriculum makers often don't take into account how different children and educators perceive things differently. One person's understanding of abuse may be very different from another's, and how exactly do we effectively deal with these issues? Educational reforms are all very easy to propose, but the monstrous task of trying to implement them is quite daunting. It's not as simple as flipping a switch, but repositioning one's self this way, as not just a teacher but also a mediator, is at least a beginning.

"The doctors managed to set her jaw more or less, saved one of her eyes. His pulse never got above eighty-five, even when he ate her tongue." (Utt, Saxon, Bozman, & Demme, 1991)

In order to fully appreciate the importance of the teacher-as-mediator in the classroom and to begin conceptualizing what it means to reposition one's self as such, I think it is essential that we take a step back for a few moments and examine the traditional reform processes and ideologies of educational institutions. Historically, reforms in education have almost always been started by people who were not actually involved in teaching. By understanding this, it is easy to grasp why public education institutions work the way they do.

The politicians and reformers of the institution tend to model public education after business, and they always want to see precise statistics and instant results when they implement reforms. However, there is no such thing as a quick fix when it comes to education. They often fail to acknowledge that any change is going to take a lot of hard work, a lot of patience and persistence, and a lot of time. Merely measuring children and teachers as you would chemicals in an experiment is counterproductive, but this is what seems to have happened in the last twenty years of neo-conservativism. No one listened to what the teachers and students thought about much of this stuff. But why should they have felt obligated to? Historically, teachers and students hadn't really been an integral part of any reform movements. With the exception of John Dewey and a very few others, most reformers were rarely in the classroom, so just as subjects in school are taught in isolation from each other, schools are treated as isolated institutions out of touch with the rest of society (Kincheloe, 2001). All too often, though, reformers and politicians don't recognize this as a flaw but rather as a necessity because it is so historically ingrained. It is this that causes a great problem in contemporary education, because "education does not stand alone, and it cannot be designed as if it did. It exists in a culture. And culture, whatever else it is, is also about power, distinctions and rewards" (Bruner, 1996, 28).

The rhetoric of the institution's policymakers tells us that through the right educational model we can create an efficient and competitive society that is infused with equal opportunity, good values, and happy children. How lovely and utopian it sounds, and Lecter's small-toothed, charming smile is so alluring, too. What many people fail to see is, underneath all this charisma, charm, and refinement lies a predator, and in the policymakers' defense, they probably don't even realize it or have the slightest idea how to control it. Like a serial killer, they can't help themselves, because they've got a real taste for this. So many movements throughout history have propelled us toward where we are now: a place where children are stifled by learning and squashed under the thumbs of politicians who think they know what's best for the children while only doing what's best for themselves. As Lecter did with his victims, they first consume the sweetbreads, and then they dispose of the remains.

Now after metaphorically consuming our children's minds, we aren't that much better off than we were a century ago when public schooling meant assimilating—or "Americanizing"—a growing immigrant population that politicians thought would spread urban and moral decay. Only now instead of forcing students to learn about proper hygiene and good "American" values, we cram facts down kids' throats hoping they'll regurgitate enough of them to pass exams, so teachers can secure their jobs and kids can go off to college whether they want to or not. The romantic vision of the one-room schoolhouse is far behind us and barely recognizable, yet policymakers show no remorse. There is no time for children to learn from each other anymore, which disrupts children's understanding of what it means to live as members of a larger society. Instead there is a smothering sense of competition, which keenly reflects the temper of a free market enterprise. "As we envision them, schools in a democratic society should exist to help students locate themselves in history, to help them obtain the ability to direct their own lives, and to empower each of them as active agents of democracy" (Kincheloe, 2001, 50). But children are too young and parents are too optimistic to see the slight distortion of the glass ceiling hovering above them and boxing them in, so competition in a free-market society often becomes a primary goal of education.

We are thus fed standards and codes under the guise that they will make us better as a society. Supposedly, if children can live up to the new standards they will be successful. If they can just play the game, they will go to college, get white-collar jobs, and earn six-figure salaries as adults. Or so we are led to believe. Policymakers entice us like a rider dangling a carrot in front of a horse's nose, in the same way Hannibal Lecter entices Clarice Starling with an opportunity to further her career and rise up from the hauntings of a White-trash childhood. But unlike Lecter, what standard-hungry policymakers and administrators fail to see is that by trying to force children into a mold that not everyone can fit into, they are damaging what it is they say they are trying to preserve: democracy and freedom of choice. Jump through these hoops and we'll give you a cookie, they say, but they fail to acknowledge that not everyone is capable of jumping—or desires to jump—through these hoops (Ohanian, 1999). In a time where government turns a deaf ear to demands for equality and the pursuit of happiness for all (because supposedly this has already been established), how do we explain the limited opportunity for upward mobility?

"I'll give you a chance for what you crave most—advancement." (Utt, Saxon, Bozman, & Demme, 1991)

In an educational system that only offers one ostensibly "neutral" worldview and only one set of knowledge that is deemed to be true, as in the case of current institutions, we can be sure that what is being taught is a curriculum designed by the dominant group (Delpit, 1995; Fine, 1991; Villanueva, 1993). In traditional education, students are taught that people are due life, liberty, and the pursuit of happiness though in the lived realities of many students, they are not always given basic necessities such as food or health care. They are told there is social mobility, and they can live the "American Dream," yet the average CEO earns a wage that is 400 times greater than his (not her) lowest-level worker, whose chances of climbing the corporate ladder are slim to none. They are told all men (not men and women) are created equal, and yet the color below the poverty line is often Black or brown as are the majority of inmates in prisons around the country (Apple, 1982, 2001; Dreier, Mollenkopf, & Swanstrom, 2001; Giroux, 2000). The traditional educational institution requires all people to be the same. It does not leave room for difference in race, culture, religion, or gender—it is exclusive.

This is dangerous for public education because of the very nature of the system upon which these beliefs rest. Too often people do not ask themselves whether "[i]n the reality of industrial society, can the school environment [as it is] promote either human development or social equality?" (Bowles & Gintis, 1976, 25). "Common sense" supports that the school environment can promote human development and social equality; however, "common sense" is socially constructed. These ideas—the ideas of the privileged and the institution—are the rhetoric of hegemony, which says that in our current society equality means social mobility and financial gain. When education is seen as a forum for equal opportunity, poverty, and inequality become "the consequences of individual choice or personal inadequacies, not the normal outgrowths of our economic institutions. The problem, clearly, is to fix up the people, not to change the economic structures which regulate their lives" (Bowles & Gintis, 1976, 26). This doesn't leave room for discussion about inequalities that have been historically perpetuated in schools, nor does it provide awareness about overt and tacit race, class, and gender discriminations that exist in our society. It also ignores how quite often financial inequality tends to fall across race and gender lines (Bowles & Gintis, 1976; Dreier et al., 2001). In addition, this undermines the potential for schools to challenge the myth that everyone can climb to the top if they only work hard enough and to create spaces for diverse knowledges to be brought into the classroom (Apple, 2001; Bowles & Gintis, 1976).

The rhetoric of the institution leads people to believe that education is directly linked to the market economy and social mobility. Therefore, the goal for students is to acquire as much education as they can with as little effort as possible in order to exchange their human capital for financial capital. As Gabbard—in the tradition of Marx—so neatly explains, in a capitalist society people feel they are

> born as a raw [material] without immediate use-value to the market. This condition poses a threat to [them] in a market society, for in a market society [they] need use-value to exchange on the market in order to meet all of [their] other needs. In a market society, [their] survival depends on this exchange. Therefore, [people] learn to need use-value. Learning this need disguises the fact that the state *compels* [people] to attend school. Instead of learning that the state compels [them] to attend school, [people] learn to *need* school for [their] acquisition of use-value. (Gabbard, 2003, 67)

Basically, people learn that credentials can be traded for, at the very least, survival but more preferably for social mobility.

This then creates a demand for standards, packaged curriculum, tracking, promotion, and credentials, which further deskills teachers and puts students in direct competition with each other (Labaree, 1997). As a result, "the consumer perspective on schools asks the question, 'What can school do for me, regardless of what it does for others?' The benefits of education are understood to be selective and differential rather than collective and equal" (Labaree, 1997, 27). Consequently, the American educational system is one that reproduces society and reinforces inequalities and power relations. It also makes the task of teachers-as-mediators that much more important, because they must expose the dominant ideology as a myth. This will help students to openly discuss how this type of institution divides communities of people by making competition between middle and lower classes seem natural and necessary, thereby ensuring that the privileged few can maintain their power and status. The teacher-as-mediator will bring these types of issues to the foreground and help students to understand that this type of competitive schooling is detrimental, particularly to lower- and working-class children. Therefore, the healthier classroom environment is cooperative and inclusive, not divisive and exclusive.

"I will show you a quality you have that will help you: you have the onions to read on." (Harris, 1999, 31)

Still, the process of fulfilling one's goal of teaching a class with a discourse that is politically charged, inclusive, and relevant to the students' lives—while desirable—is also difficult and can be alienating. As traditional education excludes teachers from curriculum development, it deskills and disempowers them while removing them and their students from their contexts. It does not regard them or their students as critical and situated beings. It offers no vision of teachers having expertise or students' classes having diversity. It does not recognize that teachers have been deprofessionalized by the bureaucratic system in which they work as a way of efficiently managing a large and diverse population of students. It does not care that teachers have been scapegoated as the prime reason for student failure although often the failure lies in the one-size-fits-all curriculum. "This becomes more obvious in light of the major assumption underlying management pedagogy: that the behavior of teachers needs to be controlled and made consistent and predictable for different schools and student populations" (Aronowitz & Giroux, 1994, 37). Management pedagogy further stereotypes teachers as being incompetent and uneducated, as if their knowledge and experience were insufficient for classroom use. Administrators do not trust teachers to do their jobs, and teachers then become resistant because they do not trust that administrators' beliefs lie in their or their students' best interests. This causes a self-sustaining cycle of mistrust between teachers and administration (Aronowitz & Giroux, 1994), which can slowly affect the teachers' daily classroom practices.

Reducing the status of the teacher in this way prevents teachers from creating learning environments that meet the needs of their diverse students and encouraging dialogue about the larger purpose of schooling: educating informed and critical citizens. It is important to recognize that the presence of the teacher in the classroom "has a total effect on the development of the student, not just an intellectual effect but an effect on how that student perceives reality beyond the classroom" (hooks, 1994, 137). Therefore, when a teacher attempts to be a mediator, it is crucial that she have the necessary autonomy and critical consciousness to be aware of just what type of perceptions students are forming in their classrooms. Then she must consider how this might affect the students' perceptions of social dynamics such as race, class, gender, and the power relations that involve these dynamics.

Deprofessionalized and disempowered teachers cannot be mediators; they cannot promote democratic education and honest dialogues that address the lived realities of their students. Instead, they

> are more likely to move toward silencing. Disempowered teachers are unlikely to view the "personal problems" of students (and dropouts) as their professional responsibility, but are more likely to render them outside the domain of education. And disempowered teachers are unlikely to create academic contexts of possibility and transformation, but are more likely to want to go home at 2:00 and to retire in the year 2004. (Fine, 1991, 140)

This further marginalizes those students whose needs are already not being met by the school environment. Thus many students drop out, are forced out, or simply refuse to participate as a means of resistance. Teachers committed to transforming their role into that of not only teacher but also mediator should be able to "develop the ability to differentiate pathology from acts of resistance, which are responses (though not always conscious) to domination. ... Resistance is used to help individuals or groups deal with oppressive social conditions and injustice and needs to be rerouted so that it is connected to positive political projects of change" (Leistyna, 2003, 122). The teacher-as-mediator will recognize resistance and work with students to try to understand and alter the circumstances that are causing the students to respond in this way. "Instead of blaming youth for the world that they are caught up in, but that they did not create, educators and other cultural workers desperately need to forge critical partnerships with them in order to analyze and confront the oppressive conditions and social formations that have inevitably manufactured and imposed a history of despair" (Leistyna, 2003, 121). Including students in dialogue and decision-making may help in understanding and preventing this type of resistance.

> "The most stable elements, Clarice, appear in the middle of the periodic table roughly between iron and silver. Between iron and silver. I think that is appropriate for you." (Harris, 1999, 32)

That term my students and I worked together to analyze *Hannibal* and determine how this macabre work could illuminate issues we encountered in our everyday lives. We came to realize that unlike the film adaptations of Harris's works, his novels deal with not merely the grotesque but the grotesquely misunderstood and the grotesquely marginalized. Harris seemed to try to point out that people in the mainstream of our society—especially people who have some measure of power—tend to categorize other people and make decisions that will affect the lives of others without ever really knowing them.

On the other hand, Harris's serial killers—while never glorified—are always multifaceted and somehow sympathetic. In *Red Dragon* it is the disfigured man who was once an abused boy and developed an alter ego to help him cope (Harris, 1990). In *The Silence of the Lambs* it is the transvestite uncomfortable in his own skin, who then felt the need to wear the skin of others. And in *Hannibal* it is the small boy orphaned in a war-torn country, his parents murdered, and his sister eaten by soldiers, who grows into a cannibal with a taste for feeding on those he considers "free-range rude." These characters not only are not accepted by the mainstream but also have been somehow damaged by the society that now shuns them and declares them monsters. The real villains in his works, the truly grotesque characters, are the ones who pass judgment on the "monsters," the ones who fail to try to understand, the ones who see only one way of viewing reality. They are the ones who do not feel remorse or sorrow, and they are unapologetic for their views of others. Most often they represent the dominant groups: the smug know-it-all psychiatrist; the homophobic, misogynistic, crass government agent who steps on anyone in order to move up in the ranks; the self-righteous socialite who uses the power of his wealth and status to prey on those beneath him. Together, my students and I were able to examine these issues and then make the jump from the text to our own experiences.

As an educator, what struck me most was one particular part of *Hannibal* that I felt worked very well to summarize the teacher in the classroom and the institution as whole. In a letter to Clarice, Hannibal asks her to look into her mother's iron skillet and recall her working-class childhood. "The most stable elements, Clarice," he writes, "appear in the middle of the periodic table roughly between iron and silver" (Harris, 1999, 32). Clarice, with her working-class upbringing, has one foot in the world of the victims (both victims of the system and victims of the killers). On the other hand, with her prestigious job at the FBI she also has one foot planted within the judgmental "system." Clarice—the more stable, reliable, predictable of the two—stood somewhere between iron and silver.

The urban teacher, trying to negotiate between the needs of her students and the demands of an institution that so often alienates, marginalizes, victimizes, and criminalizes those students, also stands somewhere between iron and silver. With one foot in the iron world of students, the teacher celebrates the practical, sturdy, heavy, honest, and yet unrefined knowledges that are so often declared undesirable by those in power. With the other foot in the silver world of the institution, the teacher understands that educational reform is flashy and desirable; credentials are of market worth and serve as a status symbol. Yet, reforms are often impractical, and empty credentials are much softer than a solid understanding of what it means to be a critical thinker from just one point of many on the web of reality.

It's ironic that during this precarious dance is when the teacher becomes the most stable element in the very unstable world of education. Like Clarice, the teacher understands, protects and serves, guides and is guided, and aims to prevent or put right that which is unjust. She does not buy into the rhetoric of the institution and does not allow herself to be a mere cog in the machine. She aims to not only stop the screaming of the lambs (like Clarice), but also prevent it by enabling the creation of safe spaces where critical dialogue can occur and students can feel confident and celebrate the diversity they share. Thus the teacher-as-mediator situates herself somewhere there in the middle, shifting her weight from one foot to the other, wobbling under the clumsy contradictions of society, negotiating through the painful realities of both sides. It's a scary place to be, balancing there between iron and silver. I think that is appropriate for you.[2]

Notes

1. Hannibal Lecter is the chilling character from Thomas Harris's novel, *The Silence of the Lambs*. The book was made into a movie of the same name in 1991 with Anthony Hopkins playing the Lecter role. Hopkins also portrayed the psychiatrist turned killer in two sequels: *Hannibal* in 2001 and *Red Dragon* in 2003. The Lecter character is based on a real serial killer in the 1930s who ate his victims—thus, the nickname, Hannibal the Cannibal. When it came time to decide which books we would study that term, I brought out my selections for the students to choose from, and my fellow Lecter-lover quickly suggested that we read *Hannibal* as part of our curriculum. It was just as much an attempt at forcing me to earn the class's trust, as it was an honest attempt at participating in what I had told them would be a "democratic" classroom.

2. Two years after my students and I studied *Hannibal,* my sister, nine years my junior, read Harris's novel in order to fulfill an assignment for an English class. With a little prompting from me, the portion of the text she analyzed was the letter in which this quote appears. Her analysis involved understanding diversity by looking at people as you would elements on a periodic table—each is different, but all are equally important in our world. She was a senior in high school at the time. Now in college with another writing assignment, she recently revisited that experience as having been the first time she understood that reading should be a critical process. This assignment of hers happened to align with my writing this article. Her work led me to my overarching metaphor. It inspired me to draw the connection between the teacher as mediator and the most stable elements on the periodic table. Thank you, Christina, for your youthful wisdom. You also fall between iron and silver.

References

Apple, M. (1982). *Education and power.* Boston: Routledge.

Apple, M. (2001). *Educating the "right" way: Markets, standards, God, and inequality.* New York: Routledge Falmer.

Aronowitz, S., & Giroux, H. (1994). *Education still under siege.* Westport, CT: Bergin & Garvey.

Bowles, S., & Gintis, H. (1976). *Schooling in capitalist America: Educational reform and the contradictions of economic life.* New York: Basic.

Bruner, J. (1996). *The Culture of education.* Cambridge, MA: Harvard University Press.

Chomsky, N. (2003). The function of schools: Subtler and cruder methods of control. In K. Saltman & D. Gabbard (Eds.), *Education as enforcement.* New York: Routledge.

Delpit, L. (1995). *Other people's children: Cultural conflict in the classroom.* New York: The New Press.

Dewey, J. (1902). *The child and the curriculum, The school and society.* Chicago: University of Chicago Press.

Dewey, J. (1938). *Experience and education.* New York: Simon & Schuster.

Dreier, P., Mollenkopf, J., & Swanstrom, T. (2001). *Place matters: Metropolitics for the twenty-first century.* Lawrence: University Press of Kansas.

Fine, M. (1991). *Framing dropouts.* Albany: State University of New York Press.

Gabbard, D. (2003). Education is enforcement! In K. Saltman & D. Gabbard (Eds.), *Education as enforcement.* New York: Routledge.

Giroux, H. (2000). *Stealing innocence: Corporate culture's war on children.* New York: Palgrave.

Harris, T. (1990). *Red Dragon.* New York: Dell.

Harris, T. (1999). *Hannibal.* New York: Delacorte.

hooks, b. (1994). *Teaching to transgress: Education as the practice of freedom.* New York: Routledge.

Kincheloe, J. (2001). *Getting beyond the facts: Teaching social studies/social sciences in the twenty-first century* (2nd *Ed.*). New York: Peter Lang.

Kliebard, H. (1995). *The struggle for the American curriculum: 1893–1958.* New York: Routledge.

Labaree, D. (1997). *How to succeed in school without really learning: The credentials race in American education.* New Haven: Yale University Press.

Lave, J., & Wenger, E. (1991). *Situated learning: Legitimate peripheral participation.* New York: Cambridge University Press.

Leistyna, P. (2003). Facing oppression: Youth voices from the front. In K. Saltman & D. Gabbard (Eds.), *Education as enforcement.* New York: Routledge.

Ohanian, S. (1999). *One size fits few.* Portsmouth, NH: Heinemann.

Utt, K., Saxon, E., Bozman, R. (Producers), & Demme, J. (Director) (1991). *The silence of the lambs* [Motion Picture]. USA: MGM Entertainment.

Villanueva, V. (1993). *Bootstraps: From an American academic of color.* Urbana, IL: NCTE.

CHAPTER 7

The "Social" Dimensions of Classroom Teaching

Elizabeth E. Heilman

Finally, after a busy morning of paperwork and meetings, Jessica was alone in the room that was to be her fourth grade classroom. The bright summer sun reflected silver off of the chairs that were stacked upside down on top of student desks. The room had a new coat of bright white paint; the walls and bulletin boards were empty, and Jessica was reminded of the feeling of heightened possibility and anticipation she experienced every time she started a new journal and confronted the first clean page. This classroom seemed to be a blank page and she would write inspiration, self-confidence, critical thinking, a love of literature, good citizenship and scientific inquiry, and so much more into this space. For a moment, Jessica's reverie was interrupted by a pealing police siren, a common sound in this urban neighborhood. But this is my place, my oasis, removed from the complicated world outside of the classroom, she thought to herself.

Four months later Jessica sat alone at her desk in the thin light of a December morning, but she felt crowded, surrounded, and a little bit vulnerable. She wistfully recalled that first image of her classroom, and that sense of blankness, insulation, and possibility. Her uneasiness increased as she looked around her classroom and saw evidence all around that her classroom was and is full; the world outside permeates the classroom and the people outside are here as well. Britney Spears and Eminem are on her bulletin board featuring essays with the opening line, "When I grow up, I want to be like. …" Her father is here saying, "Just do it because I say so" and tying her tongue when she wants to protest a recent edict from her principal about having students practice for standardized tests. Jessica's boyfriend, Jason, is here; he is a high school chemistry teacher, and he helped her create lessons on metals and the elements and brought her the elements poster that hangs on her wall. He is here, too, on days when Jessica feels so well loved that she has patience for every answer to questions already answered, and for every student complaint. She realizes with unease that Jason is also here when she feels less patient, when she comes to school moody and wonders if Jason is really committed to their relationship.

Other teachers are in the room as well. Jessica has a "hot lunch or cold lunch?" magnet board near her door. As students come in, they place a magnet on one side or the other. She thinks this sort of thing is fine for younger students but is a waste of time and space in her classroom. But Jessica has it because the other upper-grade teachers insisted, asserting: "This-Is-How-We-Do-It-Here." Jessica couldn't resist their pressure. The big local automobile assembly plant is here on the "Good-bye" poster. Two students, whose parents were just laid off from the plant, were moving. All sorts of social problems are here as well. Racism was here when Madison called Shante a "n-----" last week. Poverty is here. Madison has elevated levels of lead in her blood from the substandard housing she has always lived in, and Kayla can't participate on the soccer team she longs to join because her parents are working at 4:30 p.m., when the practices are held and they can't afford sports equipment and playing fees. Instead of playing soccer, Kayla is home alone watching television.

Crack is here in the classroom in the prenatal brain damage that still affects Alexis. War is here at Jacob's desk where a photo of his cousin, a soldier in the Middle East, is taped to his desk. Jacob was new to the school this year, and he was already moving again. Classism is here with Emma, a student from one of the middle-class neighborhoods areas that feed into this school. Emma's mother, Jennifer, is the room mother, and Jessica's jaw often aches from clenching it so often as Jennifer makes snide remarks about "kids like this. ..." Jessica thought today of different words, written for her into the space of her classroom, like poverty, racism, classism, illness, tragedy, despair, conflict, testing, stress, standards ... yet there is hope too. One wall features their civic action project work. The class is working on a school project to pass legislation that will force landlords to promptly decontaminate houses that have tested positively for lead.

What Jessica is coming to more fully realize is that her work as a teacher is profoundly influenced by the social. It is influenced by social roles, social interactions and groupings, the school as a social institution, social problems, and social messages. Education also inevitably teaches social visions and values. Teachers, administrators, students, and their parents all live and work within multiple, interrelated spheres of social influence and hope. When teachers are aware of the many dimensions of the social in education, they are better prepared to navigate the more challenging and even discouraging social influences. They're also better able to reflectively enact social roles and develop social visions, positive social interactions, and social commitments to inspire their work with students and to improve the worlds we live in now and in the future.

Social Roles

In ways that she is both aware of and unaware of, Jessica's work is shaped by the social roles she enacts. Social roles and stories help us define what is salient about our lives, what differentiates us from others, and how we should make choices. We use narratives to develop and sustain a sense of personal unity and purpose from the diverse experiences of our lives. Everyone has more than one narrative story of self, and these sometimes accompany specific social roles. Jessica's identity as a teacher is influenced by her roles as daughter, sister, girlfriend, athlete, student, worker, and hero-teacher, and also by her gender, social class, religion, and ethnicity. In some ways, we each feel like we are unique creations and unique individuals. We are. And yet our identities are also shaped from cultural stories and in accord with social types, roles, and patterns. Though identity stories and ideas of narrative itself are changing, there are still recognizable narrative identity types such as "hero-teacher" or "good daughter" that are taught to us at home, in school, and by a wide range of cultural media, both fiction and nonfiction.

In Jessica's work as a teacher such social roles influence her in different ways at different times. For example, Jessica's school has been considering ways to improve students' scores on standardized tests. The principal, a man of her father's age, proposed spending a full day each quarter to simulate testing. Jessica disapproved of this idea but she didn't say so in a recent meeting. In these kinds of situations, she sometimes finds herself responding as a dutiful daughter who won't disobey the grown-up or responding as a good worker who is paid to follow the rules established by her superiors. Like many teachers,

Jessica was also a good student who liked school, and this "good student" identity also sometimes makes it hard for her to challenge an educational authority figure.

Jessica also has some very specific teacher roles that she tries to emulate. Two of the social role models for Jessica's teaching are Dr. Morris, an education professor Jessica took a class with in her senior year, and Mrs. Kellogg, a sweet, loving teacher whom Jessica had in second grade. Jessica sometimes thinks of these role models and asks herself, "How would Mrs. Kellogg respond to this? What would Dr. Morris do?" The images of these mentors guide her choices. Yet, she can't really imagine Mrs. Kellogg wrestling with the implications of high-stakes testing or Dr. Morris being intimidated by the principal. On the other hand, Jessica also has a concept of herself as hero-teacher. She thinks about feisty LuAnn Johnson from *Dangerous Minds* and stubborn Jaime Escalante from *Stand and Deliver*. In some situations, Jessica enacts this more powerful role of the hero-teacher who sticks to her guns. In a recent meeting with all of the upper-grade teachers, after months of discussion everyone finally agreed to include civic social action projects in the fourth and fifth grade curriculum. This was Jessica's idea and it was a hard-won battle. Her colleagues had many concerns for her to listen to and to address. In this work with her fellow teachers, another social identity, her identity as a sister, helped her. As a sister, Jessica learned to listen to different points of view and to respond constructively. In their many disagreements, Jessica's mother used to make her and her sisters repeat and consider the other's opinions before they were allowed to state theirs, and this family experience of listening and negotiating with her sisters helped when she needed to speak calmly and persuasively to her colleagues. While convincing colleagues to change the social studies curriculum, Jessica had also been persistent, bringing in many resource materials and showing the other teachers how this type of civic project would develop both critical thinking and self-esteem in students and also help fulfill required social studies and language arts standards. During this three-month process, Jessica had the feeling of hanging in there and finding strength when you don't have strength that came from her experience as an athlete in cross-country running. When they agreed, she felt like a hero.

As we can see in Jessica's case, the development of a teacher's identity relies on all sorts of social and cultural sources and is a dynamic and lifelong process. Eisenhart (1989) suggests that "individuals fashion meaningful ways of being in the world from the various material and symbolic resources that are available to them in different settings, with diverse people, and for different purposes" (p. 20). Dorinne Kondo (1990) points out that people "forge their lives in the midst of ambivalences and contradictions, using the idioms at their disposal" (p. 302). Instead of being solid or singular, "identity is constantly recreated, coming forward or retreating to the background in response to the politics and relations that characterize changing social situations" (Davidson, 1996, p. 4). As Cooper and Olson (1996) describe, teacher identity is continually created and recreated as teachers reflect on their life and work and as they interact with others. These theoretical perspectives help us understand Jessica's experience in which her identity is hybrid and complex and involves multiple social roles and role models. Jessica's identity also shifts as she has different experiences in different contexts. These descriptions remind us that everyone has multiple identities and that being aware of our social constructs can help us locate autobiographical and cultural sources of inspiration. This awareness can also help us identify the social sources of some of our conflicts in teaching. For example, how can a teacher be both a good daughter/worker and also a hero who challenges any rules that interfere with her vision of fairness and good teaching? How do our experiences as family members influence the ways we react to students and to colleagues? How can we become aware of the multiple social roles that influence us? How can we actively choose among these and direct our efforts creatively as teachers?

As Britzman (1991) explains "learning to teach constitutes a time of biographical crisis as it simultaneously invokes one's autobiography" (p. 8). Research on teachers tells us that teaching involves both professional and personal experiences, and it makes reference to the past as we reflect on present challenges and keep in mind our future hopes and expectations (Clandinin & Connelly, 1995;

Holt-Reynolds, 1992; Knowles, 1992; Knowles & Holt-Reynolds, 1991; Miller Marsh, 2002; Van Manen, 1991; Vinz, 1996). Multiple influences shape teacher choices and identity, including media images, school experiences, life experiences and beliefs about teaching that come from pre-service teacher education. Knowles (1992) for example, finds four sources of teacher identity to be especially important: (1) role models, especially positive ones; (2) previous teaching experiences; (3) significantly positive or negative education classes; and (4) remembered childhood experiences about learning and family activities. Good teachers learn how to reflect on these social roles and identity influences and make the best of them.

Social Interactions and Groupings

Being able to understand and respond well to dynamic social interactions and groupings within the classroom and among school colleagues is also an essential aspect of good teaching. It wasn't Jessica alone who led to the adoption of the civic action curriculum. The curriculum change relied on her understanding of social interaction in the social groups of her school, and the social studies curriculum change was ultimately a social group choice. Jessica had been surprised to find that the teachers in her school were loosely organized into peer groups. Jessica had a set of friends that she met during her teacher education program (including her boyfriend Jason) with whom she discussed teaching, and these peers were a very important social support. They even talked about teacher groups and student groups!

In Central Elementary, the new teachers, Amanda and Jessica, decided that recognizable teacher groups included what they called the clock punchers, the pumpkin sweater teachers, the old yellers, the Black teachers, and the circle time teachers. Clock punchers were uninspired teachers, just there for a paycheck, who went along with everything and anything while their students completed work-sheet after worksheet. The old yellers were old and yelled a lot at students. The Black teachers often ate lunch together in the small teachers' lounge on the second floor where copies of *Ebony* magazine and the *Essence by Mail* and *BET Shop* catalogues were on the counter. The pumpkin sweater teachers wore spider-web earrings and pumpkin sweaters at Halloween and did curriculum units on things like teddy bears that Jessica and Amanda thought lacked conceptual substance. According to Amanda and Jessica's definition, circle time teachers were progressive teachers who built curriculum with students' interests in mind and developed critical thinking.

Still, as they talked about it, Jessica and Amanda thought their categories weren't exactly right. Linda Harris wore pumpkin sweaters and was progressive as was Yvonne Jackson, a Black teacher. Donald Lewis, was old and yelled but did a rainforest inquiry project that all of the students loved. These groups were fluid and changing and boundaries were hard to draw. But still, there were social groupings and this was part of actual life in their school. In order for the fourth and fifth grades at Central Elementary to agree to include the civic action in the formal curriculum, Jessica had to face and triumph over what she thought of as "the tyranny of the pumpkin sweater teachers." As studies by Carew and Lightfoot (1979) and Metz (1978) have shown, several diverse teacher cultures can exist even in a single school, and teachers often face conflicting pressures by colleagues. As John Dewey (1966/1916) explained, "Unless an individual acts in the way current in his group, he is literally out of it" (p. 34). Nobody wants to be isolated. Even though teachers spend a lot of time alone in their classrooms, the social influence of colleagues needs to be taken into account. Good teachers try to understand the ways they balance a need to belong with a need to have an independent view. They reflect on the social aspects of their choices and on their feelings about the social environments of where they work.

Teachers are social creatures who have social and emotional needs. They can sometimes have the sense that they are victims in their own lives, victims of other teachers and of policies, institutions, and school cultures if they perceive others as having power over them. Sometimes teachers yield to social power and conform, which sometimes happened to Jessica. When it happens, others don't even necessarily know. For example, Jessica never told anyone that she thought the "hot or cold lunch" magnet board was dumb. There is often a tension between how a person or a group understands why it is doing what it is doing and what meaning others attach to the person's behavior. When meanings are unread or misunderstood there is often a corresponding unrecognized desire to have an impact on another, to speak and be heard, to make a difference to the other. The ability for all members of a community to have voice in decisions is a key aspect of successful social groups. When a teacher consistently lacks voice and power and a chance to be herself, that teacher is likely to leave teaching. It is crucial, however, for teachers to understand that they are never without choices, they are never powerless. Ideally, teachers should think about the ways in which various social groups among both teachers and students influence their sense of power and how they can have both positive and negative effects.

Teachers also need to think collectively about social groups, rituals, routines, and school values and about how to promote friendship and mutuality. It is not enough that a single teacher is caring or has a vision. As Jessica discovered, she felt most effective when there were interlocking social networks of caring, commitment, knowledge, and vision. Ideally teachers in a building can promote friendship and cooperation, both for their own benefit and to serve as positive role models to students. As well, it is best if students also care about each other and about the teacher. When either colleagues or students seem to have "bad" behavior, a real challenge for good teachers is to try to understand that these can be expressions of underlying unmet needs to express their identity, have power, belong, to be cared about, and to feel competent. As Peterson (1992) observes:

> A human being and social situations are not without life, mere objects to be manipulated and judged from a distance. All people are dependent on tacit knowing, emotional knowing, intuitive knowing, body knowing, and not merely rational knowing. Teaching that is intended to enhance the intellect is strengthened by recognizing this, not weakened. We are social in every aspect of our existence. The place, the learning community, is of greatest importance for it is within the group that we come to value who we are and what we can do. Students in residence, confident in themselves and trusting of others, are in a position to take charge of their learning. (p. 44)

The School as a Social Institution

In Jason's efforts to foster positive social relations in his secondary science classrooms, he had to address both student social groupings and the grouping imposed by his school as an institution. Jason thought that recognizable groups of high school kids included the popular kids, the jocks, the band kids, the intellectuals, the drama kids, the skaters, the goths, the druggie burnouts, and the nerds. In spite of the various social groupings structured by society and by the school as an institution, teachers have a lot to do with the kind of society that they foster in their classrooms. In his chemistry and earth science classrooms, important goals for Jason are to create independent thinkers and cooperative inquirers. He feels that a safe and supportive classroom community provides the anchor for his students' academic work and for their social and emotional well-being in school. As part of constructing a democratic classroom, Jason's students have to set classroom rules and make choices about how to work together. When conflicts occur, Jason talks with students about being sensitive to people inside and outside of peer groups as well as being sensitive to culture, race and gender differences. In these discussions, Jason's students had changed his ideas about student groups, pointing out that there were intellectual jocks, druggie band kids and even popular goths, and that gender and ethnicity effected groups in different ways. The students also thought that many kids defied grouping and that their memberships changed over time. Like teacher identity, student identity is fluid and dynamic. Still, groups existed and both Jason and his students observed ways in which the school contributed to divisions among students.

Jason finds that the institutional structures of his high school don't always reinforce his social values and vision. His science classes are divided through tracking, and peer group prejudices are hard for him to influence in just one class per day. Tracking assumes that students differ greatly in academic potential and that separation is necessary to manage the difference. Peer group tensions and social, cultural and economic grouping can be particularly detrimental when they are reinforced by the tracking of students into groups like remedial, average, and Advanced Placement. Prominent researchers have found that education that leads to knowledge, power and position in society is generally available to advantaged classes and often withheld from the working classes (Anyon, 1980; Apple, 1979; Bowles & Gintis, 1976; Oakes, 1993). Tracking "places the greatest obstacles to achievement in the paths of those students least advantaged in American society" (Oakes, 1993, p. 276). Jeannie Oakes' research on tracking indicates that tracking doesn't merely reflect students' social difference and peer groups; it can contribute to or cause them. Further, her research showed that students in high-tracked groups had access to "considerably different types of knowledge and had opportunities to develop quite different intellectual skills" while students in low-tracked classes were generally restricted to memorization or low-level comprehension (p. 281). Also, instructional time, teaching quality, and classroom environment were found to be far superior in high-tracked classes. The net effect is differentiated education according to social class, which violates a fundamental precept of the purpose of education in a democracy, as asserted by Thomas Jefferson, "that talent and virtue needed in a free society should be educated regardless of wealth, birth, or other accidental condition, and … the students of the poor must be educated to a common experience" (Padover, 1970, p. 43).

In addition to experiencing differential treatment in the tracked courses of the formal curriculum, teachers who are interested in creating positive and democratic school environments can be frustrated by the ways in which extracurricular activities can further reinforce social divisions rather than contribute to a sense of community or camaraderie. In many schools like Jason's, high-status extracurricular activities, such as soccer and cheerleading, are enjoyed by a privileged sub-group of students. Catherine Cornbleth's research (2001) identified five aspects of school climate that can have a negative impact on social relations and can discourage important social goals of meaningful learning, democratic cooperation and critical thinking.

1   a bureaucratic climate with an administrative emphasis on law and order;

2   a conservative climate intent on maintaining the status quo;

3   a threatening climate of external curriculum challenges and self-censorship;

4   a climate of perceived pupil pathologies and pedagogical pessimism; and

5   a competitive climate dominated by student testing and public school ranking.

There are also issues that have to do with forces outside schools. Teachers are influenced by the school as an institution, by local, state and federal policies, and also by the economic and cultural structures in which the school is seated (Apple, 1979, 1982; Bowles & Gintis, 1976; Foucault, 1980, 1983; McNeil, 1988; Rosenholtz, 1989). Even though some of Jason's students were obviously tracked into less challenging and less academic courses, his school was generally middle class and had a different climate from Jessica's working-class school. A state law had recently been passed to make sure that the same amount of money was spent to educate each child in the state. In the recent past, nearly half of school funding depended on what could be raised through local property taxes. It had not been unusual for schools in impoverished rural and urban areas to have half as much money as the wealthiest areas. But there were still effects of social class and income inequality. The new law couldn't change the condition of the buildings. Facilities were drastically worse in poorer areas like Central Elementary. Also, for many years, teacher salaries had been significantly higher in suburban areas, and talented teachers tended to leave for higher pay and easier conditions in the suburbs. Jason believed that the most of the "old yellers" in Jessica's school were just teachers who were not good enough to get jobs in the suburban areas back when they used to pay much more. In the nearby suburban area where Jason taught, the PTA raised over $17, 000 to improve the library, while Jessica's PTA proudly raised $2,300 for extra teacher supplies. Jason school had four times as many students, but there was still a clear discrepancy. Like all teachers, Jessica and Jason are influenced by a wide range of policies and institutional forces.

Social Problems

As Jessica sits at her desk on this December morning, her students are on their way to Central Elementary. Madison starts the six-block walk from her apartment to Central Elementary with her brother and three other students from her building. The students stay close together because the walk has what they call "scary parts and nice parts." The scary parts are a house where gang members gather, a corner where a friend's brother was shot, and an apartment from which they often hear the sounds of domestic violence. The nice parts include a neighbor and her dogs which often greet them from a porch, and the colorful ladies and spicy cooking smells from a house with several Cambodian families.

Madison's mom, Melissa, thinks about leaving the city every day. It now has one of the highest murder rates in the country, and the quality of many of the schools is low. Blood tests have shown that both of her children have worrisome levels of lead, yet Melissa's landlord won't even make the bathroom sink work, let alone test and repaint the house because of lead. Melissa used her own money to paint every room and even one of the floors to make sure that any lead paint was covered. Melissa earns $8.60 an hour, working thirty-five hours a week at a factory plus weekend sales clerk work in the mall for $7.50 an hour, yet she can't save for the down payment and two months rent needed to move. Her son Michael's recent emergency room visit for a bad asthma attack took the last of her savings. But over the past few months Melissa has been feeling better about Central Elementary School. Madison loves school this year.

The lives of Jessica's students and their experiences in Central Elementary are influenced by a wide range of social problems and institutions. Socioeconomic conditions are a clear influence on Jessica's classroom. Social and economic conditions can vary a great deal from community to community or even from one school district to the next, and specific trends and problems will have more relevance for some teachers than for others. Yet a number of social, economic, and demographic trends continue to influence students and the teachers who educate them. Understanding the social contexts of students' lives is crucial for teachers. For example, 37% of all students in the United States live in low-income families—that is, these families earn only up to $37,700, which is twice the income considered poverty level ($18,850). Like many new teachers, Jessica's first job was in a low-income school.

Living without enough family income places students at risk for a wide range of social and educational problems. The basic needs for food, shelter, and clothing of low-income students can be inadequately or inconsistently met. A child who is hungry or sleepy cannot perform at her best. The need for self-mastery diminishes when more basic needs dominate the child's awareness. Similarly, the safety needs of disadvantaged students may be threatened by domestic or neighborhood violence, as in the case of Madison, whose six-block walk from home to school each day passes a house frequented by gang members, a corner where a friend's brother was shot, and an apartment that emits sounds of domestic violence. If the child's microsystem is unsafe, the basic human need for protection may pre-empt curiosity, creativity, and other growth needs, as the child's energies are consumed by fear. Needs for belonging, affection, and love may be jeopardized in households where parents are stressed out from struggling day in and day out to make ends meet. If students perceive parents to be distant, angry, and depressed, they may wonder whether they are really loved. This makes them more likely to be insecure and even to attack others. When Madison called Shante a "n-----," she may have been acting out her own fears and low self-esteem. When families are compelled to move frequently, as in the case of Jacob, they may not have an opportunity to develop friendships, satisfy the need to develop a sense of belonging, and learn how to work well with others.

The increase in economic stress and a decline of family life has been well documented by sociologists and is often discussed in the media. Since half of all marriages now end in divorce, three quarters of parents with school-aged students are in the work force, and moonlighting is on the rise, parents have less time and energy for parenting. A number of researchers have documented a relationship between financial strain and insensitive parenting behaviors that result in decreased emotional and practical support for students (Harter, 1993; Mayhew & Lempers, 1998; Patterson, 1982; Wills, 1990). Many families have less money than in previous decades, as real wages have declined for the average family since 1973. Researchers also have discovered that when parents are under financial strain, students are also likely to experience social self-consciousness and rejection (Simons, Whitbeck, & Wu, 1994). Students have fewer hours with parents, and like Kayla, an estimated seven million students are home alone after school and are far more likely to use drugs and alcohol, receive poor grades, and miss out on recreational and educational activities. Students are more often exposed to parents' financial worries, and relocate and change schools more frequently than in recent decades. More than forty-three million Americans move every year, and American has the highest level of mobility of any population in the world (Hodgkinson, 2002). For example, one study indicates that "parental contact hours with the average American child dropped by an estimated 43 percent between 1965 and the late 1980's"—a trend that has continued (Gill, 1997, p. 238). It is also currently estimated that "before they reach eighteen, more than half of all children in the nation will live apart from their fathers for at least a significant portion of their childhoods" (Gill, p. 25). Understanding the stress that many children and families experience helps teachers understand classroom behavior and offer support to students.

Social Messages and Social Visions

Teachers must address these social contexts and work to provide positive social visions, social interactions, and social commitments. Jessica's most dearly held educational goals are to help students feel good about themselves and to help them become curious, critical, autonomous, lifelong inquirers, who act confidently and effectively in the world. In her teaching, she tries to identify and understand her students' social, cultural, and economic contexts in order to best support their growth and development. In her classroom, Mexican tapestries and African artwork cover the walls along with posters reading: "There is no alternative to being yourself" "The more you know the less you need" "Imagine what you can be" "Dream the impossible dream" and "Don't put up with put-downs." Books from a wide range of cultures on a wide range of topics fill shelves that line one side of the room. Student work is displayed on the front wall and outside of the classroom. As part of the fourth grade civics curriculum that Jessica argued for she is teaching students about the functions of citizens and of local and state government. Her class has decided upon a social issue of concern that they will take civic action to change. Based on Madison's family's experience, the class is working in support of legislation that will require landlords to remove all lead within three months when real estate they own poses a health hazard.

Yet as Jessica tries to develop positive attitudes in her students and also teach civics, she is sometimes frustrated by the social messages that students bring into the classroom. Most of them have a belief that "you can't fight city hall" and that they have no power at all. Keisha thought that some people were born to be in charge and others are were born bad. As an example, she described the film *The Lion King* and Simba, the dynastic heir to the throne. The hyenas were Keisha's example of how some people are born bad. Keisha was Black, and Jessica was bothered by the fact the hyenas had vernacular accents just like Keisha herself. Was Keisha learning that she was bad and was not born to be in charge? The hyena characters were voiced by Whoopi Goldberg and Cheech Marin. Goldberg's character had an African American accent and Marin's character spoke with a Hispanic accent.

Jessica often had to discover what students had learned from culture and popular culture and then teach with or against social messages. Social messages are the wide array of information, values, lifestyle, ideals, and habits that are conveyed by family, schools, culture, and popular culture. Yet, Jessica didn't think her students were passive victims of media, and she was aware that her students often had very different responses to the same media. Some of the students seemed to think scientists were wacky older White men with wild hair and lab coats and that chemistry would involve substances bubbling over or blowing up. Others thought Indians lived in teepees and wore feathered headdresses. Ashley drew a Mexican to look like a Chihuahua dog, and Mohammed thought that the astronauts could visit all of the planets like in the TV show *Magic School Bus*. Disturbingly, Alex thought activists like Martin Luther King and Rosa Parks were "extinct people from the past." The students seemed to have little sense of who they might become in the world and little understanding of on-going, contemporary efforts to create a more just and democratic society. As Jessica pondered this, she couldn't think of any portrayals of social action on television or in films that the students would see.

As Jessica's assignments asked "In a democracy, the government isn't them ... it is us. What's important to us? How do we want to live? What does government do? What should we change?" Over a couple of months students created a long list of public institutions and functions that affected them: schools, health clinics, immunizations, taxes, clean water, police, jails, parks, libraries, garbage control, inspection of restaurants and stores, adoptions, food stamps, W.I.C., dog pounds, stop signs, license plates, child protection, community centers, courts, child support, roads, fire departments, movie ratings, historic preservation, and homework centers. A large bulletin board titled "People who changed the course of history" showcased pictures of Dr. Martin Luther King, Jr., Albert Einstein, Marie Curie, Malcolm X, Harriet Tubman, Frida Kahlo, Sojourner Truth, Jackie Robinson, Rosa Parks, and other important thinkers, cultural figures, and activists. They had just begun to add people they knew. First, the children thought Jessica should be on the bulletin board. But just last week they had decided that each one of them should be on that bulletin board, too.

References

Anyon. J. (1980). Social class and the hidden curriculum of work. *Journal of Education, 162*(1), 67–92.

Apple, M. (1979). *Ideology and curriculum.* Boston: Routledge & Kegan Paul.

Apple, M. (1982). *Cultural and economic reproduction in education.* Boston: Routledge & Kegan Paul.

Bowles, S., & Gintis, H. (1976). *Schooling in capitalist America.* New York: Basic Books.

Britzman, D. (1991). *Practice makes practice: A critical study of learning to teach.* Albany, NY: State University of New York Press.

Carew, J., & Lightfoot, S. L. (1979). *Beyond bias: Perspectives on classrooms.* Cambridge, MA: Harvard University Press.

Claire, H. (1996). Museum education departments and initial teacher training: A developing partnership. *Journal of Education in Museums, 17,* 20–22.

Clandinin, J. D., & Connelly, M. F. (1995). *Teachers' professional knowledge landscapes.* New York and London: Teachers College Press.

Cornbleth, C. (2001). Climates of constraint/restraint of teachers and teaching. In W. B. Stanley (Ed.), *Critical issues in social studies research for the 21 century.* Greenwich, CT: Information Age Publishing.

Cooper, K., & Olson, M. (1996). The multiple "I's" of teacher identity. In M. Kompf, D. Dworet, & R. Boak (Eds.), *Changing research and practice* (pp. 78–89). London: Falmer Press.

Cox, L. H., & Barrow, J. H. (2000). On display: Pre-service teachers in the museum. Retrieved November 1, 2002, from: http://beliot.edu/~newb/ed281sp02/Work/Challenges/cox_barrow.html.

Danielewicz, J. (2001). *Teaching selves–Identity, pedagogy, and teacher education.* New York: SUNY Press.

Davidson, A. (1996). *Making and molding identity in schools.* Albany, NY: SUNY Press.

Dewey, J. (1966/1916). *Democracy and education.* New York: Free Press.

Eisenhart, M. (1989). Reconsidering cultural differences in American schools. *Educational Foundations, 3*(2), 51–68.

Foucault, M. (1980). *Power/knowledge: Selected interviews & other writings, 1972–77* (C. Gordon, Ed.). New York: Pantheon.

Foucault, M. (1983). *This is not a pipe.* Berkeley, CA: University of California Press.

Gill, R. (1997). *Posterity lost: Progress, ideology and the decline of the American family.* New York: Rowman & Littlefield.

Harter, S. (1993). Causes and consequences of low self-esteem in children and adolescents. In R. F. Baumeister (Ed.), *Self-esteem: The puzzle of low self-regard* (pp. 87–116). New York: Plenum.

Hodgkinson, H. (2002). Demographics of diversity. *Principal, 82*(2), 14–18.

Holt-Reynolds, D. (1992). Personal history-based beliefs as relevant prior knowledge in course work. *American Educational Research Journal, 29*(2), 325–349.

Kagan, D. M. (1992). Implications of research on teacher belief. *Educational Psychologist, 27*(1), 65–90.

Knowles, J. G. (1992). *Models for understanding preservice and beginning teachers' biographies: Illustrations from case studies.* In I. Goodson (Ed.), *Studying teachers' lives* (pp. 99–153). New York: Teachers College Press.

Knowles, J. G., & Holt-Reynolds, D. (1991). Shaping pedagogies through personal histories in preservice teacher education. *Teachers College Record, 93*(1), 87–113.

Kondo, D. (1990). *Crafting selves: Power, gender, and discourses in identity in a Japanese workplace.* Chicago: University of Chicago Press.

Mayhew, K. P., & Lempers, J. (1998). The relation among financial strain, parenting, parent self-esteem and adolescent self-esteem. *Journal of Early Adolescence, 18,* 145–172.

McNeil, L. M. (1988). *Contradictions of control: School structure and school* knowledge. New York: Routledge.

Metz, M. (1978). *Classrooms and corridors.* Berkeley, CA: University of California Press.

Miller Marsh, M. (2002). Examining the discourses that shape our teacher identities. *Curriculum Inquiry, 32*(4), 453–469.

Oakes, J. (1993). Tracking, inequality, and the rhetoric of reform: Why schools don't change. In H. S. Shapiro & D. E. Purple (Eds.), *Critical social issues in American education: Toward the 21st century.* New York: Longman.

Padover, S. (1970). *Jefferson.* New York: Mentor Books.

Patterson, G. R. (1982). *Coercive family process.* Eugene, OR: Castalia.

Peterson, R. (1992). *Life in a crowded place.* Richmond Hill, Ontario: Scholastic.

Rosenholtz, S. J. (1989). *Teachers' workplace.* New York: Longman.

Simons, R. L., Whitbeck, L. B., & Wu, C. I. (1994). Resilient and vulnerable adolescents. In R. D. Conger & G. H. Elder, Jr. (Eds.), *Families in troubled times: Adapting to change in rural America* (pp. 223–234). New York: Aldine de Gruyter.

Van Manen, M. (1991). *The tact of teaching: the meaning of pedagogical thoughtfulness.* Albany, NY: State University of New York Press.

Vinz, R. (1996). *Composing a teaching life.* Portsmouth, NH: Boynton/Cook.

Wills, T. A. (1990). Social support and the family. In E. Blechman (Ed.), *Emotions and the family* (pp. 75–98). Hillsdale, NJ: Erlbaum.

CHAPTER 8

Including Families in the Teaching and Learning Process

Nina Zaragoza

As I think back on raising my three boys, I realize that it wasn't until my last son that I began to deeply understand the importance of forming real bonds with the families of my students. Of course I understood that I needed to communicate consistently and clearly about my expectations for their children and about the curriculum—I wrote a letter once a month and even called homes with good news about their students. I also understood that it was important to involve families by inviting them to special school and class events, and I even realized I should begin my letters with "Dear Families" since many of our children come from diverse homes. I understood all this and thought I actually did a great job connecting with my families. And I guess I did at a certain level. But it was not until I traveled across the world to live in a small town in Russia and became an immigrant parent myself that I could feel true compassion for families with children in the public schools of the United States.

My stomach twisted into a knot and my knees shook. I was called to Derek's school again. Ugh! I was terrified. Could I manage this myself? No, definitely not! I couldn't even buy milk at a store yet: how could I talk to this teacher? Could I get someone to help translate at such short notice? Where was Julia now? Oh, she wouldn't be out of work until past three. Who could I find to help me through this? Who would have thought this would be so difficult for me? I'm a teacher! I'm a professor of education! How hard could it be? But, of course, not speaking the language of the school, I was reduced to an uneducated basket case!

Actually, in the United States I became pretty skilled at teacher conferences since I have had extensive experience dealing with Derek's teachers since kindergarten. Unlike his older brothers, he was definitely one to challenge teachers and provide me with the lessons needed to be a more sensitive teacher toward my students' families. For example, whenever I picked up Derek from kindergarten his teacher seemed to have a negative comment virtually every single day. It got to the point where at 3:00 every afternoon a knot in my stomach would form and I would pray, "Oh God, please don't let her say anything today!" It got so bad that I finally decided not to pick up Derek at all. I sent my son Michael instead! While that provided some relief, for me at least, it didn't really remedy the situation, so I finally had to be honest with the teacher. I gathered my courage and with my head held high, I walked toward the dismissal area:

Mrs. L.:	You know, Dr. Zaragoza, after the pledge to the flag during the minute of silent meditation Derek disrupted the entire class.
Me:	(Feeling sick to my stomach, as usual) Oh, I'm so sorry. What did he do?
Mrs. L.:	He decided to teach the children how to chant "om." He actually got them all to do it.
Me:	(Trying not to burst out laughing) Really? I guess he learned that from the yoga classes I used to take.
Mrs. L.:	He is very disruptive you know. Please talk to him.
Me:	I will Mrs. L. Let me ask you something. Do you ever have anything positive to say about my son?
Mrs. L.:	What do you mean?
Me:	Well you know that almost every time I pick him up you have negative remarks. Does he ever do anything that you approve of?
Mrs. L.:	Well. …
Me:	I'm a little tired of only hearing bad reports. It makes me afraid to talk to you about anything.
Mrs. L.:	Oh, it's just that I thought you'd like to know.
Me:	Of course I want to know how I can help my son, but I'd also like to know that you appreciate some of his strengths. I hope that next time I pick him up you will tell me something positive.

From that conversation on, Mrs. L. never bothered me again with every little incident that Derek was involved in. For a while she was silent, but as time passed she actually shared some of Derek's strengths and even laughed at some of his clowning around.

Similar kinds of things happened in second grade (Mrs. L. was also Derek's first grade teacher so I had a reprieve), third grade, and fourth grade. Derek was a child who needed to test his teachers, and until about November when the power struggles were settled it was a rocky road. It seemed that I was the one who always needed to encourage the teachers to look at Derek's strengths and then work on some of his needs. It all usually ended up okay, and, in fact, some of his teachers became my friends.

So then I took Derek to Russia for his fifth and sixth year of school, and I thought, "How could Derek get into trouble? He doesn't even know the language!" Little did I realize that he would learn to speak Russian in two months—lucky child! So began my journey as an immigrant parent—one who needed to depend on her ten-year-old for basic street survival. Derek needed to ask for directions, ask about trolley bus stops, deal with the post office, and most stressful for him, help me in the grocery store. In the Russian town where we lived you couldn't just pick up things from the shelf, throw them into your cart, pay, and leave. All of the products were behind counters on display, and you needed to ask a Russian-only speaker for every item. I never realized that asking for things when his mother was right beside him was embarrassing for Derek until he finally pleaded with me, "Mom, can't you try and ask? You're the adult."

Yes, I was the adult, and now the adult was being called into school to speak to the teacher. But because of the language barrier, I did not feel like an adult at all. I felt like a frightened child unable to express myself and unable to meet my needs and responsibilities in the society I lived in. I felt powerless and alone especially in institutional-type places like schools, libraries, post offices, and train stations. Thank God for translators. Thank God for those patient people who spoke slowly or showed with their eyes and nonverbal kindness that they understood my struggle. Thank God for those who understood that I was still an adult filled with knowledge and experiences and who treated me as such even though I didn't speak Russian.

It took a while for me to feel at home being an adult on the street again. During the first few months of our return to the United States, I still automatically looked to Derek for help with acquiring goods and services. Once walking in Manhattan, Derek wanted a hot dog from a street vendor so we stood on line. When we got to the front I glanced at Derek and signaled him with a nod of my head to order. He looked at me and said, "Mom! We're in the United States. You can order. You speak English!"

I do speak English (and finally some Russian!) in my own country and now totally understand how my immigrant families feel facing their child's American teacher. And I know now that I will be the teacher who eases their pain as they try to do the best they can in a new and foreign world. Some of the principles I will share with you have also come from my experiences dealing with Derek's teachers in the United States and from my experiences as a teacher in the United States and Russia.

No matter who your families are or where they come from, they deserve to be treated with dignity and respect. Because the language of a place is the tool for power, those who don't speak the language obviously feel less powerful if not totally powerless. I have often seen non-English-speaking family members being treated like idiots even though they might be quite educated in their home country. Raised voices, contorted expressions, and exasperated sighs permeate these conversations, so that what is engendered is frustration and not comfortable communication.

So what do we as teachers do when we meet a Chinese mother who speaks no English for the first time? I think at this point it's less a matter of doing and more a matter of what we are thinking and for many of us changing our thinking. We need to begin to understand that we are interacting with an adult who is living a full life filled with joy, pain, success, and failure. This person comes with unique stories but also has the same needs we all have. What do we all need in our lives? I think some of the things we all yearn for include respect, love, a sense of connection/belonging, a sense of purpose, and a feeling of power. When we keep these needs uppermost in our mind, satisfying interactions are almost guaranteed.

I'll share with you some of the artifacts (family letters, transcripts of phone calls, face-to-face meetings) that try to address these needs, but, of course, relationships are complex and cannot be easily broken down into organized boxes of concrete materials. There is no one recipe I can pass on to you because part of my success with families is because I am who I am. You cannot be who I am, but you can examine your own heart and make the decision to treat your families and their children the way you would want to be treated—with respect. No matter what language your families speak, there is no way you can fake respect. I'm sure you know this through your own experiences with people. Caregivers will know immediately if your smile is false and if your comments about their children are contrived. Therefore, some of you might need to drastically work on changing your heart and your thinking about families that are unlike you in language, background, and education. You must truly look at each of your families through eyes of respect. If this is difficult for you, perhaps you need to find ways outside of the classroom to work on feelings of empathy and compassion. I went to Russia and lived the experience of an immigrant parent. My experiences with my child here in the United States also helped me develop empathy for other parents. Without this kind of identity with others, a foundation of respect will be impossible to build. Unless there is mutual respect between teacher and the family, attempts to include families in the teaching learning process will fail.

First Meeting with Nengyuan's Mother

Okay, let's return to the Chinese mother. What are the things we can do and say that enable us to help this mother feel respected, cared for, connected, purposeful, and in power? Here's my first interaction with her:

Me:	(as I bow slightly and smile) Hello!
Mother:	(bows back and smiles)
Me:	(patting Nengyuan on the shoulder and smiling) Nengyuan had a very good day!
Mother:	(bowing and smiling also pats her son and bows again)
Me:	Nengyuan, show your mother your homework.

Nengyuan:	Look, Ma, homework.
Mom:	(smiling, looking at homework)
Me:	(smiling) This is Nengyuan's homework. He needs to finish it for tomorrow. (smiling)
Mother:	(smiling, bows, pats me on the shoulder)
Me:	Thank you. See you tomorrow. Nengyuan, don't forget your homework! (I smile and bow).

Yes, there is definitely a lot of bowing and smiling in this first meeting, but why not? What do we usually do when we first meet a person? Do we bombard them with tons of information, or do we smile and say, "Glad to meet you"? Think about how this first interaction begins to lay a respectful foundation. Have I helped Nengyuan's mother feel comfortable? Yes, because I know she understands the genuineness of my good feelings toward her and her son through my smile. While this might sound trite, a smile really is a powerful way to connect—especially if it is genuine.

Notice, too, that I begin to engage Nengyuan's mother in our work together by showing her his homework. In this way I am communicating that she is a part of our work, will be informed of all classroom happenings, and will have an opportunity to be an active participant throughout the year. Without any real communication, this mother has been able to feel respected and cared for. She also is beginning to feel a sense of purpose and power in her child's education. This is, of course, crucial to including our families in the teaching and learning process.

What to Speak, What Not to Speak

As you remember, I asked Derek's kindergarten teacher to speak to me positively about Derek once in a while. I wondered if when you read this, you thought, "Well, what if nothing positive occurred? What if the child behaved absolutely horribly in the classroom?" In connection to these questions, I ask you to reflect on the following:

- Do we need to think of some report each time we see a family member?

- Do we need to inform the family about every little incident in the classroom?

- Do we need only to talk to parents when a problem occurs?

- Can you find something positive in what might be seen on the surface as an absolutely horrible situation?

I have come to realize that many times teachers almost automatically report incidents because they think it is part of their job. If they see a family member they quickly review the day and find at least one thing to report even if it basically carries no importance. I remember being upset with Derek's third grade teacher because she would report every petty little thing whenever she saw me: "Oh, Derek didn't put his pencil down when I told him to" or "Derek called out today." It seems that this teacher felt she was doing a good job with this type of interaction, and when I began to understand this, that she just needed to say something, her words carried little weight for me.

So you see what this teacher inadvertently did here to herself and her authority as a teacher? Because she bombarded me with so much unimportant information, she weakened her own voice. Because she spoke so many words, these words became empty and worthless. This is similar to teachers who send a child to the principal for every minor infraction and basically send the message to their students and the principal that they cannot handle the responsibility of maintaining a positive classroom. These teachers are seen as ineffective, unskilled, and bothersome. The responses of families and principals alike are: "They're the teacher! Can't they do their job? Why do I need to deal with this?"

Teachers do need to do their job, and while there is a time to communicate with families there is also a time to remain silent. There are so many things that can be handled by teachers and students themselves. If I told Matthew's mother everything I needed to do to help Matthew be successful, she would be overwhelmed and discouraged. There is absolutely no positive purpose for this. There are times when I just smile and wave goodbye when she picks up her son and that's okay. Remember, so much can be said without words. When we speak we need to choose our words carefully, and we must also feel comfortable with saying nothing at all.

Phone Calls

When I interact with my families, I make sure that I always have some positive comments. If I cannot make a positive comment, I wait until I can. One of the first times I speak to a family member is during the first or second week of school in person or over the phone. Whether the child threw a chair the first day of school or not, I make sure that this first connection is positive:

Me:	Hi, this is Dr. Zaragoza. I'm Leann's teacher this year. Is this her mom?
Aunt:	No, it's her aunt. Did she do something bad already?
Me:	No, not at all. I just called to say hello.
Aunt:	Okay, I'll get my sister.
Mom:	Hello?
Me:	Hi, this is Nina Zaragoza. I'm Leann's teacher this year.
Mom:	Is she okay in school?
Me:	Oh, yes! I am so happy to have her in my class. She really loves to talk.
Mom:	I know. Her last year teacher always complained about that.
Me:	Oh, but she's doing fine. I can tell she is going to have a lot of story ideas.
Mom:	Oh, I never had a teacher call me to say something good.
Me:	Oh, don't worry about when I call. Most of the time it will be to tell you how she is improving and to let you know how we can both help Leann.

The reactions I get from the family with this first phone call are usually similar to that of Leann's mother and aunt. First, they are concerned when they are called to the phone with, "It's Adrian's teacher on the phone." They know it is not an emergency because I call when the children are home, but they usually figure it is something not too positive. After a while, though, because my calls are consistent throughout the school year, they are not surprised by good reports. In fact, they soon await them:

Me:	Hi, Mrs. Ramirez, it's Dr. Zaragoza. How are you?
Mom:	Fine. Crystal told me you were going to call.
Me:	Yes, I wanted to call because she had such a great day. She was so helpful with Emil today, and she shared the book she was reading with the class.
Mom:	Oh, how great! Thank you for helping her.
Me:	Thank you for working with her each night. She is doing very well! Bye. I'll talk to you soon.

This conversation actually took place in Spanish, and I know that Crystal's mom felt very comfortable with me because I spoke to her in her native language, but even if I had spoken in English, the positive tone of the phone call would have emerged anyway. The conversations vary in length, and while this one was particularly short others are longer and cover many more topics both personal and academic. As Crystal's mother mentioned, I usually do tell my students when I will call their families, and often they know I will pass on some good news:

Me:	Jason, you are having a fantastic day! Do you want me to call your mother and tell them about it?
Jason:	Yes!
Me:	What do you want me to tell her?
Jason:	Everything!
Me:	Okay. I'll tell her about how well you did in Math and how you're almost finished editing your story and—what else?

| Jason: | That I did good independent reading. |
| Me: | Oh, yes you did. Tell her I'll call about 6:00. Oh, unless you want her to be surprised! |

The children love when I call their families in this way. Just imagine how nice it is to end the school day with the knowledge that your teacher will call to say something nice about you and your work. It's a switch, I know, but worth it. Can you see how I am building a positive relationship with my families? They come to understand that I care about their children and see them as precious. They are touched by the amount of time I devote to staying in contact, and I know they are confident that their children are with someone who will keep them safe and help them to excel.

Are you wondering about how much time I spend on these phone calls? Actually, they don't take as long as you might think. I call three or four families a night during the first and second week, and these phone calls last about a minute or two. I actually hang my class list on the refrigerator door and make calls while cooking or washing the dishes. The rewards of this little sacrifice are priceless. Because I have begun a positive relationship with my families, I know that when I do have to talk about a negative incident, I will be heard within a context of love. The families know that I love their children and that I am dedicated to meeting their needs both emotionally and academically. Indeed, I am setting the stage on which we can together help their children have a successful year.

Oh, another thing I do with phone calls is allow the children themselves to call their families. Before the onslaught of cell phones I use to take a student to the office to call right after some amazing work:

| Me: | Hi, Ms. Brown. Everything is fine. Tiffany just wanted to tell you something. |
| Tiff: | Hi, Mom. I wanted to tell you I'm having a great day and that I published my story! |

Now with a cell phone it is easier than ever!

Horrible Situations

Can you look at a seemingly horrible situation in a positive light? Can you find a strength in a person you have a really difficult time with? Try these things. It's good practice and it might even change your heart about a child and his family. Let's take the time when Derek taught his whole class to chant "om." How can you change this from a negative to a positive? What are some of the strengths that Derek exhibits here? Well, the first thing that comes to my mind is leadership. He definitely illustrates an ability to get others to follow him! Do you see that this points to Derek also having a wide range of knowledge and experience? Look at how I turned around Leann's talkativeness. Instead of complaining about it as previous teachers had done, I looked at it in a positive way: "I can tell she is going to have a lot of story ideas."

I have had children in my classrooms who have thrown temper tantrums all day, have been aggressive, resistant, and angry. Even within these kinds of behavior I look for a positive. Maybe the child smiled one more time than yesterday. Or maybe for the first time he/she said "Good morning"—that is a positive! Here is a conversation I would have if I needed to report such an incident:

	(At dismissal)
Me:	Hello, Mary. How are you?
Mary:	Pretty good. How's Melissa doing?
Me:	Well, I want to thank you for making sure Melissa completes her homework.
Mary:	Yes, I make sure she does it the minute she gets home now.
Me:	I can tell you're also helping her with reading. She did an excellent job sharing her book today. What she does need to work on is not distracting the others around her when they are trying to concentrate on individual work.
Mary:	What exactly is she doing?

Me:	Well things like kicking German under the table, making noises with her mouth, grabbing Christian's pencil. I could seat her somewhere else, but I want her to act appropriately no matter where she sits. I told Melissa I was going to share this with you. I'd like you to talk to her about this.
Mary:	We will definitely talk to her. Thanks for your help.
Me:	Thank you! See you tomorrow.

Because Mary already knows that I care about her daughter she doesn't become defensive when I mention Melissa's inappropriate behavior. Some families who do not know the teacher well or who have only heard negative things about their child might come back with "Well, what did German do to her? Did Christian take something of hers?" Mary takes my words seriously because she respects me. She figures I checked out the situation before I decided to report it to her. She knows, too, that I expect her to help me with Melissa just as she expects my help. She understands that we are partners in the endeavor, and I will seek her help when I feel it's necessary. Remember, though, that I haven't bombarded Mary with every little detail of Melissa's behavior each day so when I do need help my words carry weight. How do Mary and the other families know all this about me?

Well besides my phone calls and regularly positive greetings at dismissal, all my families receive detailed monthly letters. Because many of my children come from homes where English isn't spoken, my letters and conversations need to be translated. For languages I don't know, I seek help from others. I think you will soon understand that the time it takes to find a translator is well worth it. Let's look at a few of these letters.

Letters to the Families

Through my letters I empower my families with the knowledge of the structure and curriculum of the classroom. In this way, they are continually connected and included in our community. My first letter, given on the first day of school, is a letter of introduction and expectations:

September

Dear Families,

I am looking forward to working with you and your child. It will be a year of learning and high achievement. I am an experienced educator and have had 15 years experience at both elementary school and university levels. I strongly believe in the importance of including the family in all aspects of your child's educational program.

You can expect me to provide for your child:
- *a safe, accepting, and structured learning environment;*
- *high expectations for learning and behavior;*
- *a classroom that values independence and cooperation among children and adults; and*
- *a program that will encourage your child to express him/herself through writing, reading, and performing poetry, drama, and other literature forms.*

I expect that your child will:
- *do all his/her work to the best of their his/her ability;*
- *behave in a friendly and cooperative manner toward classmates and adults;*
- *return completed homework on the day that it is assigned; and*
- *come to school with a cheerful and enthusiastic attitude.*

I expect that your family will:
- *make sure that your child is in school every day, on time, and ready to work;*
- *provide your child with sufficient supplies needed to complete work appropriately;*

- *provide enough time and space for your child to complete daily homework; and*
- *feel welcome to communicate and participate freely in all classroom activities.*

Again, welcome! It is an honor to serve you and your child. Please feel free to contact me if you have any questions or suggestions.
Nina Zaragoza (305) 555–3699 home; (305) 555–9633 work

Notice that the messages I am sending with this letter are not only the ones written on the page but also, perhaps even more importantly, the ones that are understood without words. What are these unsaid messages? Well, they definitely relate to some of the major needs I mentioned in the beginning of the chapter, don't they? Informing the parents of my expectations clearly lets them know that I respect them by including them immediately in the teaching and learning process. This letter helps set up a three-way partnership almost immediately. It is clearly communicated that the children, their families, and I, will all work together to reach common goals. While these goals are not specifically stated in this letter they will emerge as our relationships grow.

As you can see, I ask my families immediately for comments and suggestions. Some teachers might do this as a formality but I really do want their comments and suggestions. I respect the knowledge they have of their children, and I know that there are times I will need to ask them for help. Many times part of my conversation will include: "Do you have any suggestions on how I can help Samuel understand the addition process? I have tried a number of ways but he is still having some difficulty. Can you think of anything that might help?" With these types of genuine requests my families understand that they do have shared control over what is happening in the classroom. They are, in fact, empowered to be a major influence in the teaching and learning process.

October

Dear Families,

We have had a busy month! You should be very proud of your children. They are doing well and learning every day. I want to thank you for all your help with making sure your children do their homework and return their homework books. Please continue reading with them every night. I'm sure you can tell that they are already beginning to read!

During the next few weeks I will be sending home a script of the play we have written together. Your children have worked very hard on learning their lines, and we hope to present the play to you and the rest of the school at the end of October or the beginning of November. Please help them with their lines as you encourage them to speak loudly and clearly.

We have also learned some new poems during this past month. Ask your children to recite "Dreams" by Langston Hughes; "The Giggles" by Martin Gardner; "Hope" by Langston Hughes; "Rudolph Is Tired of the City" by Gwendolyn Brooks; and "Two Friends" by Nikki Giovanni.

Please continue helping your children with their first and last names. I will send home lined paper so that they can practice writing within the lines. We are also practicing to write the letters Mm, Tt, Pp, Aa, Ss, and Nn. Ask them about words that begin with these letter sounds. For example, "What sound does Mommy begin with?" "What other words begin with the same sound that 'Mommy' does?"

In Math your children are learning to recognize numbers 0–10 and to draw sets for each number. For example, 1 = 0; 2 = 00; 3 = 000; etc. Please help them with this up to the number 10. We are also doing simple addition and learning our right hand from our left.

In Science and Social Studies we are talking and reading about living things and community helpers. Ask them to categorize what is living and not living. In connection to this we are reading Charlotte's Web *aloud. Ask your children about Charlotte and Wilbur!*

As you can see, your children are getting many types of learning experiences. Please make sure they are in school every day and on time (8:15). We start our learning immediately and learn straight through the entire day. When your children miss a day of school they miss a lot!

Let me share our daily schedule:

8:15–8:30	*Get silent reading books, write diary entry*
8:30–8:40	*School announcements*
8:40–9:20	*Good morning song, collecting homework, schedule*
9:00–9:20	*Circle discussion time: attendance/reading aloud/Sci/SS*
9:20–9:30	*Writing process including sharing*
9:30–10:15	*Choral poetry/Sci/SS*
10:15–10:20	*Prepare for lunch*
10:20–10:50	*Lunch*
10:50–11:20	*Silent reading*
11:20–11:50	*Reading discussion*
11:50–11:55	*Put silent reading books away, choose homework book*
11:55–12:00	*Reading aloud*
12:00–12:25	*Outside play*
12:30–1:15	*Math*
1:15–1:45	*Individual learning time*
1:45–2:00	*Review assigned homework; ending discussion; poetry; reading aloud; goodbye song*

Remember, you are always invited to come and learn with us!
Sincerely,
Nina Zaragoza

Let's talk about the greeting *Dear Families* for a moment. As I mentioned earlier, all my letters open like this because I think that the use of the word families respects various family structures since it is more inclusive than the word *parents*. Many of our students do not live with their parents but with grandparents, aunts, uncles, or even older siblings, so using "families" shows respect to these different family situations. I urge you to consider using this more inclusive term. The words we use are so important to building a foundation of respect.

The body of this October letter clearly elucidates the structure and curriculum of our classroom and enables family members to participate in every aspect. The information and suggestions I provide empowers them to actively assist their children and move them toward further progress. And families really do get involved as they roll up their sleeves and make sure that their children are reading, adding, completing their homework, memorizing poetry/drama, and internalizing science and social studies concepts. In fact, they become invested in the work along with their children because they are provided with the knowledge they need to be a partner in the education of their children. Knowledge is power, and I help my families become powerful contributors to the teaching and learning process.

Did you notice my closing line of invitation? Well, my families don't take this invitation lightly! They do come and learn with us when they can; they often bring younger siblings or send older siblings, cousins, uncles, aunts, and grandparents. Most work during the day, but they come in full force whenever we have evening drama presentation, poetry recital, or reading/writing celebrations. It makes sense, doesn't it? They want to see all their work come to fruition, too!

November

Dear Families,

As you know, we have had a fantastic month! Your children are doing so well and progressing rapidly! Thank you for all your help. Almost every child brings in homework each day. Thank you for helping with this important responsibility. Our play practice is going very well. We have started practicing on stage and will be ready to perform for you soon! We are already talking about our next play. We have also learned some new poems during this past month. The newest include "My Little Sister" by William Wise, "Sun Song" by Langston Hughes, and "My People" by Langston Hughes. I know they would love to recite them for you! Ask!

Please continue to help your children with reading as you allow them to read their homework books and their word list each night. Please let me know if you do not have the word list I sent home.

As you know, in Math your children are learning addition up to the number 10. Please continue to help them as you allow them to count on their fingers or draw corresponding circles for each number. Most children recognize their numbers, but make sure if your child needs practice that you work on this at home. We have also started counting with pennies and measuring with rulers. Next month we will begin working on telling time.

In Science and Social Studies we are talking about the body and keeping ourselves healthy. We are also growing our very own flowers and talking about taking care of our trees. We finished reading Charlotte's Web *and have already started a new book called* James and the Giant Peach. *Ask your children to tell you about James' two aunts.*

As always, please make sure your child is in school every day and on time (8:15). Your children are a pleasure to work with! Thank you!

Sincerely,
Nina Zaragoza

I'm sure you can tell how much I love to write these family letters. I know that the families appreciate them and these letters help me to regularly connect as we strengthen our collaborative relationship. They also help me to review what we've done and to decide on what we will do in the future. In fact, they allow me to monitor my curriculum and make sure that important academic connections are created and continued. Of course, the relationships I have with my families are maintained, and our ease with each other deepens as we carry on our work together. It really helps to know that I am not in this alone and that I can depend on families for their help. I'm sure they feel secure in this process as well.

You have a good idea about the monthly letters and how they help families feel comfortable and empowered to enter as full participants in our classroom community. Let me just share with you an example of a final letter of the year. I continue to ask for help, and as you will see I encourage them to strong advocates for their children in the coming grade:

May

Dear Families,

Can you believe it's almost June? We have come such a long way. I know you are proud of your children's accomplishments. I am! Our class has excelled in reading, writing, and math. Most children are already reading at a first-grade level. Our math skills are very advanced as well! For kindergartners to be able to add and subtract as quickly as your children is quite amazing. Thank you for all your help with moving them along. All that math homework really did make a difference!

As we close off the year I am focusing on making sure all the children successfully read all of the red books. Most of them are almost there. Please continue to help them every night with these books. Please help them, too, with the new word list I sent home last week. When they master these books and word lists they will have a strong head start in first grade.

I thank you all for working so well with me. We, together, have really made a positive influence in your child's life. Each child already understands the importance of education, being responsible, and working hard to achieve goals. Most important, though, each leaves kindergarten with a true love of learning. Congratulations on a job well done. I urge you to continue to monitor your child's education closely so that they grow to their fullest potential.

I wish you and your family the best. Your children will always be in my heart and prayers,

Nina Zaragoza

Final Wishes

I also wish you the best as you make the decision and take the actions necessary to build a respectful working relationship with your students and their families. I hope that you realize that it is this type of relationship that is the basis for successful teaching and learning. I wish you words of life. I wish you words of hope that will encourage, empower, and enable you and your families to feel cared for, purpose filled, and powerful.

PART III
Different Kids, Different Classrooms

CHAPTER 9

Unmasking Whiteness in the Teacher Education College Classroom
Critical and Creative Multicultural Practice

Virginia Lea

WE

I am the white guy you see
who wishes to be seen for what I am a potential
friend.
You curse my privilege;
I am inclined to agree. After all I made it here in
spite of me.
You suspect narrow mindedness; it's not
true. The opinion I seek belongs to you.
You judge that I don't care,
but you don't know. I seek the other because I
yearn to grow.
My color erects a wall that hides the true me.
To you I am only that color that you see.
We're both white so you share a joke
about ghetto life. I guess you've yet to meet
my wife?
My children won't be white like me. Their
un-whiteness is all that society will see.

The above "I-Poem" was written by a twenty-something, White, male student-teacher as part of the cultural portfolio I assign to the student-teachers in my Multicultural Pedagogy course. The "I-Poem" assignment, like the other assignments that make up the portfolio, is designed to help students identify the discourses/cultural scripts—the ways of thinking, feeling, believing and acting—they embody. In this way they become more critically conscious of the often unconscious discourses that shape their actions in the classroom. At the end of a recent semester, another of my students expressed her enhanced consciousness as follows:

Before taking this class, I always tried to convince myself that I treat everyone equally and that I did not give into society's petty stereotypes. Perhaps this hardening of my heart and inability to be truthful and humble derives from growing up in a school system that tried to ignore these stereotypes for so long. However, I quickly realized just how much I have let society influence my perception of different cultures, races, classes, and gender. I first came to this realization when doing my *culture shock exercise*.

I shall return to the culture shock exercise later in this chapter.

For the past ten years, I have been teaching two educational foundations courses for the multiple subjects credential program at a California State University. The population of my classrooms is almost entirely made up of students of European American and Jewish/Middle-Eastern origin, categorized in this society as "White." As a person who also falls into this category, I try earnestly to work on the same assignments I give my students. I recognize that my partial Arab ethnicity in no way disrupts the White privilege I gain daily because of my physical appearance as a woman socially classified as White. It does nothing to interrupt the advantage I gain from speaking English with an English accent, or from my knowledge of the norms and values of the corridors of power, both in the United States and in Western Europe. While I am aware of the reality that "race" is socially constructed, I am also aware that race is "real in its consequences" (Thomas, 1923). It will take a long time and a considerable conscious commitment from large numbers of people before race no longer defines in important ways the lives of U.S. citizens. One cannot easily abolish race (Ignatiev & Garvey, 1996; Roediger, 1991), or the ways in which it continues to influence our lives in the United States, Western Europe, and beyond. Claiming color blindness will not abolish this impact (Bonilla-Silva, 2006).

In what follows, I explore how Whiteness as hegemony operates in the field of education, particularly in the United States. More specifically, I offer answers to the following questions of critical importance to educators working in the field of critical multicultural, anti-racist, post-colonial education, interspersing my answers with reflections on some of the course assignments that have empowered my student-teachers to interrupt their own Whiteness en route to becoming critical multicultural educators:

- What is Whiteness?

- What is hegemony?

- How does Whiteness as hegemony prevent most schools from empowering their students to become critically, creatively, and multiculturally literate?

- How can Whiteness be unmasked and rendered visible? How can college students be empowered to develop the critical and creative multicultural practice denied to so many students in K–12 and college classrooms?

What Is Whiteness?

Whiteness involves what we look like—the color of our skin, the texture of our hair, the breadth of our noses, the shape of our backsides, all codes for race in the United States. However, Whiteness is not only about race. It concerns more than our symbolic capital (Bourdieu, 1993):

Whiteness is a complex, hegemonic, and dynamic set of mainstream socioeconomic processes, and ways of thinking, feeling, believing, and acting (cultural scripts) that function to obscure the power, privilege, and practices of the dominant social elite. Whiteness drives oppressive individual, group, and corporate practices that adversely impact schools, the wider U.S. society and, indeed, societies worldwide. At the same time, whiteness reproduces inequities, injustices, and inequalities within the educational system and wider society. We use the term whiteness rather than hegemony alone to signal these processes because a disproportionate number of white people have benefited, to greater or lesser extent, from whiteness. However, it is not our intention to continue to center whiteness. As a set of processes, whiteness recenters itself, and as such needs to be identified and transformed. (Lea & Sims, 2008, pp. 2–3)

The White male student-teacher who wrote the poem above was rare in his desire to cross race, class, and cultural borders and understand the process of Whiteness that kept him from doing so. He was also rare in that he was married to a woman of color and thus, his motivation for understanding Whiteness was deeply personal and emotional. Within the field of critical multicultural education, Ladson-Billings (1994), Nieto and Bode (2007), and Valenzuela (1999) among many researchers have shown that cultural, linguistic, and personal relevance are necessary to engage students in a curriculum. This was certainly true for this student. His poem, written at the end of the semester, suggests that fifteen weeks of the Multicultural Pedagogy course helped him relate to his own experience in gaining a greater understanding of his own White privilege. In his final reflection on the course, he wrote:

> This class has forced me to work outside my comfort zone more than any other class with the exception of speech class. I feel that I have come away with a better understanding of the place I occupy within society. I see that I am part of the dominant portion of society that gets to set the rules. As I made my mask I found that there were many things that would work for the side depicting how others see me. But when I tried to find images representing how I see myself I had a hard time. Part of the problem is that I feel unique and I feel that the mainstream media tends to dehumanize its subjects. I should not have been surprised that I have trouble finding images of "me" in glossy magazines.

The Mask is another course assignment that makes up the cultural portfolio. It is based on the theoretical idea that those of us who find meaning and support in our social groups do not question the authenticity of our identities. However, our identities are far from fixed. They are constituted by the discourses within which we live, work and play (Rabinow, 1984). As Stuart Hall (1993) told us:

> identity is not only a story, a narrative which we tell ourselves about ourselves, it is stories which change with historical circumstances. And identity shifts with the way in which we think and hear and experience them. Far from coming from the still small point of truth inside us, identities actually come from the outside, they are the way in which we are recognized and then come to step into the place of the recognitions which others give us. Without the others there is no self, there is not self-recognition. (p. 8)

In addition, our identities are complex. When we leave home to attend college, we often develop new identities, constituted by the new discourses we encounter at school. Returning home, we may find that old identities feel like badly fitting coats, hanging uncomfortably on the outside of new clothes. In my case, resisting the identity I was expected to inhabit as a child and young adult meant traveling six thousand miles from home to live freely with the new sense of who I was. Nevertheless, shedding the skins of old identities is never complete. "Our new skins always bear the marks of their predecessors" (Sumara & Davis, 1998).

The Mask assignment is designed to help students recognize the extent to which we are "designed" by the discourses/cultural scripts within which we are socialized. If teachers are to be able to develop their own voices in the service of educational social justice, they need to become aware of the ways in which public hegemonic discourses have shaped their identities. They need to recognize the extent to which they are seen by others in terms of these discourses and to which they actually identify with these discourses. This awareness is gained through the process of constructing their masks.

Students decorate the outside of their masks with images reflecting how they think others see them; they decorate the inside with images that reflect how they see their complex selves. The assignment helps student-teachers discuss whether, given the opportunity to step outside the discourses that define us, they would express more diverse selves. Creating their masks helps students recognize the ways in which they differ from the stereotypes others associate with their physical appearance—a process many low-income students, especially those of color, find particularly meaningful. Students also like the fact that the juxtaposition of their private and public selves opens up a space in which they can reflect critically on the discourses/cultural scripts that have impacted their lives. This is difficult when one is immersed in these discourses. As Clyde Kluckhorn wrote, "The fish would be the last creature to discover water" (Maxwell, 2004, p. 153).

Exercises like the Mask help us to see the water and explore the suggestion that nothing can be done to interrupt the deterministic power of cultural history. The dialogical act of juxtaposing our public and private selves allows us to step out of the water onto the banks from where we may gain a better view of the discourses that tell us what these selves are all about. Strengthened by this critical consciousness, we can better understand how the discourses of Whiteness are embedded in our private as well as our public selves. As yet another of my students wrote in her end of semester reflection:

> My two favorite activities were the *Mask* and *I-Am Poem*. I believe these were my favorite and the most effective for me because I tend to express myself artistically. While writing my poem, I was astonished to find that I predominately related myself to the ocean. In the process of relating myself to the ocean, I found myself referring back to myself being caught in the waters of whiteness (a concept which I remember most from the readings). I began to realize how much this class has helped reshape my perception of culture and has taught me the importance of stepping outside the waters of whiteness in order to discard my former prejudices and stereotypes. Lastly, the mask allowed me to think critically about how I believe other people see me from the outside versus how I see myself on the inside. Doing this activity forced me to examine the ways in which my prejudices and stereotypes have outwardly affected the people I come in contact with on a daily basis. Doing this activity made me more aware of how people view me and made me want to change some of those things so that I, as an individual, can create a better, more culturally accepting, and peaceful society to live in. I definitely believe that the things which I have learned in this class as well as the tools I have been given have instilled a passion and desire inside of me to promote a multicultural education and in turn, touch the lives of all the children I come in contact with. *(White, female)*

Once critically aware of the ways in which Whiteness has constituted us as subjects who are complicit in reproducing the increasingly hierarchical, capitalistic, neo-liberal state in which we live, we will be better able to see how Whiteness works through us as a set of systematizing, normalizing, and disciplinary technologies that we impose on students in the classroom. In fact, over the last 500 hundred years, so-called Western states, including the United States, have been developing ever more effective technologies to shape their citizens who will work and live most effectively within evolving and increasingly corporatized socio-economic structures (Rabinow, 1984). Yet this process by which we are made in the image desired by the state is not wholly deterministic. Michel Foucault wrote: "Nothing is fundamental. … There are only reciprocal relations and the perpetual gaps between intentions in relation to one another." (Foucault, in During, 1993, p. 164.). We can unmask and interrupt this reciprocity and its function as Whiteness, by recognizing the nature of our different relations and intentions and stepping into the gaps between them.

Unmasking Whites and interrupting his reciprocal relations with other White people in his life was exactly what my White, male student was exploring in his poem. In the poem, he sees that his "*color erects a wall that hides the true me.*" He recognizes that other Whites only see his persona of Whiteness. He is able to engage in a racist joke, secure in the knowledge that he must reciprocate their assumptions about people of color: "*To you I am only that color that you see. We're both white so you share a joke about ghetto life.*" Then, he points out that the presence of his wife would interrupt this reciprocity, this mutual acceptance of the process of Whiteness—"*I guess you've yet to meet my wife?*" He is fully aware that racism and Whiteness will mean that his children will not be able to experience this reciprocity based on mutual Whiteness. His children will experience life on the downside of White privilege: "*My children won't be white like me. Their un-whiteness is all that society will see.*"

Liberation from the Whiteness discourses that most of us learn as part of our discursive communities from birth to death is a painful process. In fact, we do not usually have a chance to question this Whiteness from alternative perspectives. Yet, engaging in a questioning process is essential if student-teachers are to become reflective educators, conscious of the lenses of Whiteness through which they view the world—lenses that may potentially oppress their students. In dialogue, a few of my students tell me that they feel that their White privilege came at a price. While it continues to give White people—even poor Whites—a social advantage, it locks them into a stereotypical box that limits how they are seen and expected to think, feel, believe, and act. It also confines them in a hierarchical dualistic relationship with people of color that precludes their working together to interrupt the laws and policies that have oppressive socio-economic consequences on the lives of all low-income people. It should be noted that rigid cultural expectations are also associated with gender, sexual orientation, linguistic, age, ability, and other complex socio-cultural discourses.

Some Whites perceive that their privilege comes at a cost. They give up their diversity—ethnic and socio-economic class—in order to gain the advantage of Whiteness. Some people of color also give up, at least publicly, their ethnic diversity and assume the cultural trappings of Whiteness in order to be successful in the social hierarchy. However, the trade-off made by people of color has a more serious impact on them as a group. If Whites want to remain within the mainstream of Whiteness, they are limiting the discourses/cultural scripts available to them; their self-perception, their relationships with people of color, and the categories of knowledge they are likely to explore (Foucault, in Rabinow, 1984). However, given their numbers and relative power, they are not limiting their access to other Whites. On the other hand, people of color, while limiting their self-perception, and the categories of knowledge they are likely to explore, are also limiting their relationships with a majority of people of color who do not embrace an upwardly mobile frame of reference (Ogbu, 1995). Even facing these trade-offs, it is understandable that people of color as well as Whites would embrace many of the cultural norms and values of Whiteness in order to be successful within the existing socioeconomic structure. It is hard to escape Whiteness; it is the "best game" in town. In spite of this possibility for human agency and resistance, (we should) "not deny that (people) are often duped by culture" (Grossberg, in Giroux & McLaren, 1994, p. 6)—in this case the cultural process of Whiteness as hegemony.

What Is Hegemony?

Hegemony is the process through which this duping takes place. As a social process, hegemony is a broader concept that includes ideology in terms of its impact on society. Ideology has been defined as "shared ideas or beliefs which serve to justify the interests of dominant groups" (Giddens, 1997, p. 583). Ideology is disseminated through all of the major institutions in the United States. Those in positions of corporate and/or political power disseminate ideology in order to have a conservative and/or self-serving impact on relations of power. People who manipulate ideology aim to reproduce their own interests.

> Hegemony combines ideological power with the consent of the people. Gramsci meant the permeation *throughout* society of an entire system of values, attitudes, beliefs and morality that has the effect of supporting the status quo in power relations. Hegemony in this sense might be defined as an "organising principle" that is diffused by the process of socialisation into every area of daily life. To the extent that this prevailing consciousness is internalised by the population it becomes part of what is generally called 'common sense' so that the philosophy, culture and morality of the ruling elite come to appear as the natural order of things. (Boggs, 1976, p. 39)

While members of dominant groups may be very sincere in their beliefs or ideas, they may be seen by those of us occupying alternative ideological territory as manipulating common sense public narratives or blatantly distorting reality to achieve their ends. By its nature, hegemony masks the origins of the ideological discourses it represents. It "bamboozles" us into thinking its processes are grounded in truth and are natural and normal. For example, the 2002 Elementary and Secondary Education Act, was dubbed "No Child Left Behind" (NCLB). Yet it is my contention, whether they were all aware of it or not, the authors of NCLB never intended to "leave no child behind." Public schools today are pursuing the same agenda as those of the common school in the nineteenth century. Joel Spring (2008) has clearly articulated that the main agenda of the common school when it was developed in the United States in the nineteenth century was to domesticate those students who met citizenship requirements into acquiring the cultural norms and values that would enable them to serve the nascent corporate, capitalist, "Christian" political economy. Spring and others (Kumashiro, 2008; Emery & Ohanian, 2004) argue that the public school agenda was, and remains, to prepare these students to fill the positions required by an increasingly hierarchical economy, requiring, in order to be functional, a significant redundant prison worker population. Thus, schools may be seen as functional when they *do* produce high school dropouts.

In *American Education* (2007), Spring asks the following questions and offers a significant response:

> How did educating workers for a global economy get translated into core high school curriculum of only four years of English and four years of math consisting of algebra I and II, geometry, and data analysis and statistics? Why aren't other subjects included in the core curriculum such as history, civics, art, physical education, and science? The answer is that communication skills and math, along with a good work ethic, are the main concern of employers filling entry-level jobs.

In spite of its proclaimed goal of improving educational achievement and reducing the "achievement gap"—or the "wealth gap" as Kitty Kelly Epstein calls it (Epstein, in Pollick, 2008)—between White and Asian students on the one hand, and students from African American, Latino, and Indigenous backgrounds and children from low-income backgrounds on the other,

> after six years, there is overwhelming evidence that the deeply flawed "No Child Left Behind" law (NCLB) is doing more harm than good in our nation's public schools. NCLB's test-and-punish approach to school reform relies on limited, one-size-fits-all tools that reduce education to little more than test prep. It produces unfair decisions and requires unproven, often irrational "solutions" to complex problems. NCLB is clearly underfunded, but fully funding a bad law is not a solution.
>
> Public recognition of the law's ill effects has produced a growing consensus in favor of a fundamental overhaul. It's time for a new conception of the federal role in education—beyond standards, tests and punishments—in order to strengthen schools and truly leave no child behind. (Pytel, 2007)

Hegemony also plays out in teachers' responses to NCLB. While the act has restricted the practices of teachers in elementary and secondary schools, turning them into technicians, obliged to teach to a script associated with high stakes tests (FairTest, 2008; Sleeter, 2004), the vast majority of educators go along with the increasingly standardized teaching practices that NCLB mandates (Pytel, 2007).

How does Whiteness as hegemony prevent most schools from empowering their students to become critically, creatively, and multiculturally literate?

Whiteness, as hegemony, works in powerful ways to curtail genuine educational opportunities for low-income students, who are disproportionately of color. Research indicates that among the most economically challenged social classes, socio-economic and cultural factors, particularly family and neighborhood influences—not genetics—are strongly associated with academic performance (Berliner & Nichols, 2007; Steinberg & Kincheloe, 2007; Bowles & Gintis, 1976). However, the current reductive curriculum and the hierarchical evaluation system by which California schools and students are being assessed provide modern-day deficit theorists with a great deal of hegemonic ammunition for their classist, racist, and sexist explanations of why some children fail to meet the standards of "hyper-accountability" in public schools (Epstein, 2006; Mansell, 2007; See Ryan, 1971, for a critique of deficit theory.) Given the longevity of hegemonic racism and classism in the United States, punctuated by pseudo-scientific race theory constructed to legitimize the socio-economic system of slavery and legal segregation, we should not be surprised that White people, who have not been encouraged to engage in assignments designed to unmask Whiteness, still hold deficit views about people of color. Nor should we be surprised at the tenacity of internalized racism experienced by students of color who live in a discursive system in which Whiteness, as hegemony, conceals the awful details of slavery, and the genocide of native people, and uses school to gain the consent of citizens to a kinder version of "American history." In her excellent analysis of "post traumatic slave syndrome," Dr. Joy DeGruy Leary (2008) "traces the history of African Americans from slavery through their virtual re-enslavement by Peonage, Black Codes, Convict Lease and Jim Crow segregation to contemporary problems facing African Americans today." In spite of their extraordinary resiliency, African Americans, Indigenous people, Latinos/as and others whom John Ogbu (1995) termed "caste minorities," have experienced officially sanctioned oppression and genocide, the details of which are still missing from most text books (Loewen, 1995). Howard Zinn's and Rebecca Stefoff's (2007) new *Young Peoples' History of the United States* redresses this issue and is a timely addition to available historical texts for children.

In pursuing their analysis, deficit theorists, then, harness historical U.S. hegemonic mechanisms. Consciously or unconsciously, or what Joyce King called "dysconsciously" (1991)—when we seek to avoid discomfort by relegating a matter to a place just below consciousness—deficit theorists do not recognize and/or they personally benefit from the oppressive bias in their analysis and practice. They have been successful over the years in colonizing public educational space with Eurocentric, competitive, and rationalistic values and cognitive processes that define the assessment measures by which students and schools are judged. For example, Ruby Payne's (1995), *A Framework for Understanding Poverty,* is a deficit prescription for ameliorating the limited school achievement and success of poor students within the rules of a cultural game, designed in the nineteenth century to domesticate those students who met citizenship requirements into acquiring the cultural norms and values that would enable them to serve the nascent corporate, capitalist, "Christian" political economy (Spring, 2008; 2007; Kumashiro, 2008; Emery & Ohanian, 2004).

Payne herself has little or no idea that her own "Whiteness" is driving the prescription she is advocating for the schooling of generationally poor students (Payne, 2006). She validates, without question, the cultural space that is typically considered to be normal in school. She describes poor students in terms of deficit stereotypes instead of framing the reality faced by generationally low-income students as one of being in a vulnerable, powerless position in relation to the privileged school culture, with which they are often unfamiliar. She argues that these students need to reject the "hidden rules" associated with the norms, values, and relationships familiar in their class and/or ethnic backgrounds in order to be successful in school (Payne, 1995). Unlike Igoa (1995), who told us that her newcomer students needed to have their home cultures integrated into and validated by the classroom culture in order to feel "alive and whole in the world," Payne's message is clear: the mainstream, White, middle-class school culture is the only one of value.

The pedagogical space considered valid by Payne is colonized by the hegemony of Whiteness. As Dyer told us many years ago, Whiteness has "colonized the definition of normal" (Dyer, 1988). Unless our student-teachers, who are disproportionately White, have interrogated their own Whiteness (Lea & Helfand, 2004; McIntosh, 1989) and are able to engage in praxis—reflecting on their own Whiteness in the classroom as it emerges and acting to transform it—they are likely to continue to reproduce the status quo in which Whites and some Asians are most successful in school. Moreover, as suggested, this transformation is not just about teachers working on their own Whiteness. Whiteness is encoded in how and what we teach. As we have learned from Michel Foucault (Rabinow, 1984), controlling ideas and relations of domination inform most of our present-day patterns of social, economic and political organization, social policies, and dominant ideological positions. These same patterns are present and may be unveiled in the field of education:

> [These] "dividing practices" are clearly central to the organizational processes of education in our society. These divisions and objectifications are achieved either within the subject or between the subject and others. The use of testing, examining, profiling, and streaming in education, the use of entry criteria for different types of schooling, and the formation of different types of intelligence, ability, and scholastic identity in the processes of schooling are all examples of such dividing practices. In these ways, using these techniques and forms of organization, and the creation of separate and different curricula, pedagogies, forms of teacher-student relationships, identities and subjectivities are formed, learned and carried. Through the creation of remedial and advanced groups, and the separation of the educationally subnormal or those with special educational needs, abilities are stigmatized and normalized. (Ball, 1990, p. 4)

How can Whiteness be unmasked and rendered visible? How can pre-service teachers be empowered to develop the critical and creative multicultural practice denied to so many students in K–12 and college classrooms?

> We need to provide [student-teachers] with opportunities to identify the hegemonic practices that divide us and that constitute us as ideal subjects that reproduce the status quo. We need to help [student-teachers] to question the dominant categories of knowledge that those in positions of corporate and political power consider acceptable and appropriate. The dam that prevents counter-hegemonic knowledge from reaching the mainstream could theoretically burst if more of us joined the already growing number of individual and group activists to plan, organize, and work in solidarity to publicly challenge the whiteness hegemony that is being practiced in our names—from the standardized testing and tracking practices in schools to the imperialist policies abroad. (Lea & Sims, 2008, pp. 191–192)

The I-Poem and the Mask are both assignments that have helped my student-teachers to "identify the hegemonic practices that divide us and that constitute us as ideal subjects that reproduce the status quo" (Ibid). Through these and other assignments, some of which are outlined below, my student-teachers develop critical, multicultural, and creative consciousness that will theoretically serve them well in the quest to facilitate critical, multicultural, and creative consciousness in their own students. I am currently undertaking research to find out how new teachers fare once they leave college in terms of implementing a critical social justice curriculum in which Whiteness is unmasked in an ongoing basis. Data suggest that many new teachers struggle to maintain the teaching agenda to which they appeared committed while they were in my class—one that includes developing critical, multicultural, and creative consciousness in their own students from a young age. Most new teachers find themselves in school cultures that validate the hegemonic mainstream. They find themselves swimming upstream. As a result, while we need to continue to develop assignments that help student-teachers (and ourselves) to unmask Whiteness and empower critical and creative multicultural practice, we must also work with and connect communities and institutions outside of the college to support and further our students' goals.

In my teacher education courses, I strive to present *education* as the process by which we develop critical consciousness and understanding, from multiple perspectives, of how our world and society work, and of how we think, feel believe and act in that society and world. To be educated is to become more and more liberated. "Liberation is a praxis: the action and reflection of men (and women) upon their world in order to transform it" (Freire, 1993/1970, p. 62). To be educated requires that we reject the idea that education is a one-way street in which the teacher chooses and deposits knowledge in his/her students, controlling their behavior and responses, treating his/her students as appropriately meek objects of her authority.

> Throughout much of my educational years, I have suffered under what we call the "banking concept of education" (Freire, 1993/1970). Teachers and former professors would continuously pour out various facts and dates that I was expected to memorize and regurgitate in the form of a written test. Overtime,

I began to see this method as ineffective and unbeneficial not only to my education, but to my overall development of an individual of society. While reflecting back upon this whole process (of the Multicultural Pedagogy course), I have come to realize how much richer and beneficial my education could have been had my teachers and professors put more emphasis on a multicultural education. *(White, female student-teacher)*

In traditional hegemonic terms, the good student is a "docile body" (Foucault, in Rabinow, 1984). In critical multicultural terms, the good teacher engages in "problem-posing education" in which content scripted by a state increasingly interwoven with corporate interests is replaced with "the problems of men (and woman) in their relations with the world" (Freire, 1993/1970, p. 63). Problem-posing education is the development of critical, emotional, and spiritual literacy through dialogue. It is the process by which we construct our own knowledge in response to the contradictions and tensions of our everyday experiences. It is meta-consciousness. It is the development of critical, emotional, and spiritual literacy through dialogue. It is the process by which we construct our own knowledge in response to the contradictions and tensions of our everyday experiences. It is, as we learned from the insights of Paulo Freire (1993/1970), the ability to be able to "read the word and the world," and act on it justly and humanely.

While my students in the Educational Foundations and the Social Studies methods courses that I teach gain insights into how Whiteness, as hegemony, operates through school through, for example, role plays, critiques of official texts, videos and DVDs, the following represents the main assignments in the Multicultural Pedagogy course:

1. **The Cultural Portfolio (including narratives (Lea, 2004), I-Poem (Lea & Sims, 2008), Mask, and Imaging Whiteness (Lea & Sims, 2008) assignments:** This assignment is designed to help student-teachers become more aware of how public discourses or cultural scripts shape their private behavior toward and ways of thinking, feeling, believing about students, their families, and communities and about what should go on in the classroom. The I-Poem and Mask have been discussed earlier in this chapter. The other two assignments, *Cultural Narratives* and *Imaging Whiteness,* are discussed in Lea (2004) and Lea and Sims (2008), respectively.

2. **The Culture Shock:** This assignment is designed to help student-teachers address the stereotypes and anxieties they hold with respect to social and cultural groups about which they have had little and/or negative contact. Student-teachers seek out and experience culture shock in a "safe" situation, with a group of people about whom they hold deficit assumptions. They learn how to navigate their own culture shock. They apply what they have learned from their own experience to developing ways of helping students who are not part of the mainstream school culture to navigate culture shock in the classroom. They consider how to develop a classroom climate that meets all of their students' needs. (Igoa, 1995)

3. **The Funds of Knowledge:** This assignment is designed to help candidates cross cultural borders, recognize the rich cultural resources that exist in cultural communities that they hitherto saw in deficit terms. Through local schools or other relationships, students identify families from ethnic and socio-economic class backgrounds about whom they have little knowledge or hold deficit assumptions. They ask permission of these families to interview them in their homes as a ways of learning more about their strong cultural knowledge and networks. They then identify the cultural resources located in the homes and communities and list them as the bases for rich, inviting, cultural responsive learning plans. (Moll et al., 1992)

4. **Multicultural Teaching Strategies:** This assignment is designed to help candidates *begin* to develop critical and culturally relevant learning plans that teach students about social justice, equity, and caring, and meet students' needs by incorporating critical multicultural teaching strategies and building on students' "funds of knowledge."

While my students have found all of the assignments important to the development of their critical consciousness, the Culture Shock is the assignment that students cited as having first jolted them out of the discursive water they have been swimming in. The assignment involves students going by themselves into a community about which they honestly recognize that they have deficit and/or stereotypical cognitive and emotional assumptions. They spend about four hours in this environment, identify their emotions and assumptions, and write about these responses to the experience. The goal of the assignment is for students to experience and observe their reactions to the discomforting feelings of disorientation to a cultural world that is strange to them (i.e., many of the familiar cultural markers have moved or are absent). It is an experience familiar to many of their students as they enter the school world colonized by Whiteness.

This activity is based on two widely recognized premises: (1) Culture shock is endemic—If we are to move in an unsegregated world, we cannot inoculate ourselves against it. We can, however, improve our recovery mechanisms, minimize discomfort, and maximize our understandings of the unfamiliar cultural world; and (2) Our not-OK feelings, once recognized, have a tendency to dissipate if not disappear all together (Neves, 1998).

One of my students reflected on her culture shock experience as follows:

> For my culture shock exercise, I wanted to go somewhere where I would experience a culture that I have had little to no contact with. I decided to go to a Korean church in Santa Rosa. I was surprised to find that before I even went to the church, I expected the Korean people to be shy, quiet, and driven (a stereotype that I have obviously collected from society over the years). After doing this assignment, I realized just how much I have been led astray by society's perception of Koreans and I learned that this ethnic group of people can actually be very lively, outgoing, talkative, and friendly. When I returned home, I began to think of previous encounters I have had with Koreans. I realized that there have actually been many opportunities in which I could have embraced the Korean culture but I had chosen not to simply because they were different and I didn't have to engage with them if I chose not to. This is a sad realization, but it is very true. Little did I realize, I would learn a very similar lesson when conducting my Funds-of-Knowledge activity.

However, public education in the United States does not generally offer students a curriculum that allows students to experience and recover from culture shock, leading to critical consciousness, social justice activism, and hope. I include in the notion of "curriculum" more than is usually understood by the student-teachers who enter my *multicultural pedagogy, educational foundations,* and *social studies methods* courses. Curriculum is an "ongoing, if complicated, conversation" (Pinar, 2004, 188). It is co-constructed, whether the parties are aware of it or not, by teacher and students within school and classroom power relations and cultural norms and values. From a critical multicultural perspective, textbooks and scripted assignments are always interpreted through the discourses/cultural scripts that the teacher and students bring into the classroom. These discourses shape, for example, which reading texts are used or, in an age of mandated texts, *how* they are used. The emergent curriculum, even in a scripted classroom, has the potential to be a site of empowerment, as described by McLaren (2003):

> Schools should provide students with a language of criticism and a language of hope. The languages should be used in order to prepare students to conceptualize systematically the relationships among their private dreams and desires and the collective dreams of a larger social order. New generations of students must be capable of analyzing the social and material conditions in which dreams are given birth, and are realized, diminished, or destroyed. More importantly, students need to be able to recognize which dreams and which dreamers are dangerous to the larger society, and why this is the case. Schools need to foster collective dreaming, a dreaming that speaks to the creation of social justice for all groups, and the eventual elimination of classism, racism, sexism, and homophobia. This can occur only if schools are able and committed to help students analyze the ways in which their subjectivities have been ideologically formed within the exploitative forces and relations of globalized, transnational capitalism. (pp. 178–179)

I agree with McLaren's conception of what schools should provide our students. However, it is more often these days the imposition of a one-sided conservative, back-to-basics narrative that sees the classroom as a tool to prepare students for future economic roles in low-skilled jobs and service industries. It is more than 2000 years since Plato described the ideal social system in *Republic* (Rouse, 1956), yet the notion that such a system naturally consists of a hierarchy is alive and well. Many, if not most, of the teachers I encounter, who have been socialized within a society in which the hegemony of Whiteness touches us all, still continue to categorize their students' reading and math levels as "high," "middle," and "low." This categorization is not unlike the classifications Payne (1995) uses in her book—"poverty," "middle class," and "wealth"—which she associated with reductive stereotypes.

Many teachers demonstrate no critical awareness of the potential consequences of the labels high, middle, and low on their own expectations of their students (and on their students' expectation of themselves if they recognize, as they often do, what these labels mean). In Platonic metaphors, most teachers apparently still see students as belonging to groups made of differentially valued metals. They use official classifications of students as unproblematic—English language learners, special education, at-risk, for example—and their pedagogy derives from these classifications.

We are loathe to live in the state of cognitive dissonance that accompanies the process of change (Festinger, 1957). It is not easy to come to different views about the nature of students, people, school, and society than those of our significant others. Such a departure would lead to open conflict with those with whom we crave harmony, company, and support. So we avoid deep personal change. Those among us who have been socialized at an early age into believing that race is a material condition that ranks us hierarchically in society, usually continue to believe in this distortion of reality as we experience it as common sense. The alternative view was, at its inception, that race was a myth whose authors concealed their intentions, perhaps even from themselves, to legitimize slavery, indentureship, and colonialism. They managed to encode this myth in law and public policy and persuade the public of its veracity and common sense. Some of my students have a hard time taking this latter interpretation seriously. They have been raised on a diet of patriotism, saluting the flag in their infancy, spoon fed at least one line from U.S. President Abraham Lincoln's Gettysburg Address of 1863 in which he succinctly explained that "all men are created equal" (Lincoln, 1863). It is hard to unmask the hegemonic nature of what seems like the normal and natural foundation of their lives.

However, as humans and, thus, cultural beings, we are potentially dynamic and open to change. With awareness of our tendency to follow the hegemonic tide down river, we can thrust out towards a tributary and change the direction of our practice. Like the vast majority of students in schools in the United States, my youngest daughter had her own version of what was normal and natural. At age five, she saw the film *Jaws* on television, fell in love with sharks, and dreamed of saving them from human predators. At age fourteen, closely guarding her dream of becoming a marine biologist, she attended the reception for new high school students at our local ethnically diverse, working-class public school in northern California. During the reception, she was approached by a White male counselor, who asked her what she wanted to become when she left school. My daughter told him about her dream of becoming a marine biologist. The counselor was clearly impressed. He asked her where she was thinking of going to school. "UC Santa Cruz," my daughter replied. The counselor was less impressed. He told her to try California State University, Humboldt, or even better to begin her university career at the local junior college.

As an associate professor at a California State University (CSU), I have enormous respect for the public higher education system that the CSU represents, as I do for the California community college system. In spite of the current shortsighted budget proposal that many of us who work in the CSU and Community College systems are currently challenging, these higher education systems have played an important historical role in offering students, whose K–12 experiences were not educationally empowering, the opportunity to pursue higher education. The cuts would disproportionately impact low-income students and students of color.

However, if my child chose to dream of going to a university that was harder to enter—one of the universities that made up the University of California (UC) system—I would not have this counselor, a person who had no knowledge of my child, dampen her dreams. I was standing behind my daughter, and edged forward. My daughter sensed my presence and said to the counselor, "This is my mother." The counselor looked at me and then turned back to my daughter. Momentarily he said, "Maybe you can get into a UC."

The significance of this story is lost unless the reader is aware that my daughter's father is African American. She is a child of African, Cherokee, and European (multiple ethnicities) descent. The counselor took one look at my coloring and features and categorized me as someone whose presence in my daughter's life would give her a better chance of going to a UC. He may have been unaware of his racist assumptions, but, over time, this man could have exerted considerable negative influence over my daughter if my own Whiteness had not interceded—unspoken—and reframed the lens through which he saw my daughter. How many students of color in the United States can draw on unearned White privilege to disrupt the nightmare of racism and Whiteness that they all too often encounter in public school in the United States?

My youngest daughter went through high school six years ago. She was very successful in terms of her schooling and was able to fulfill her dream of going to UC Santa Cruz. She is now pursuing a Masters degree at a California State University. However, in my view, my daughter's *education* in her public high school had more to do with the critical and creative spaces that she and her friends—who called themselves "the AP chicas"—constructed within the confines of their schooling than with the official school curriculum. Early on in their high school careers, these seven friends, from African American, Mexican American, Chicano, European American, Japanese American, Indian American, and African backgrounds, developed an understanding that if they were going to be able to navigate the contradictory cultures of school, they would need to do so as a collective. There was strength in their numbers. They could avoid the potential tension that existed because of their friendships with the students in "honors" classes who had decided not to participate fully in what they perceived to be the irrelevant curriculum of school (Kohl, 1991). They did not dream of higher education, perhaps because of what Claude Steele terms "stereotype threat." According to Steele, "when a person's social identity is attached to a negative stereotype, that person will tend to underperform in a manner consistent with the stereotype" (Steele, 2004). Responding to the ubiquitous racist and classist stereotypes, which abounded in my daughter's school, these students did not aspire to enroll in the few AP classes available at the school that would help them get into a UC. To survive in these contradictory waters, the girls decided to study together, hang out together on weekends, and support each other when some of their "friends" called them names for working hard to get the grades that would allow them access to a UC. These seven girls, from diverse ethnic backgrounds, all fulfilled their UC dreams.

Conclusion

As my daughter's stories illustrate, below the surface of change in the United States, Whiteness is still playing a role in propping up the hierarchical edifice of capitalism (McLaren, 2005). While we do see some change in the color of the faces of those in the passageways of the mainstream, the underlying socio-economic structures remain intact. Indeed, there is an increasing concentration of wealth in the hands of the few and increasing poverty for the many.

According to Anyon (2005),

a full 38% of American children are identified as poor—27 million who lived in families with income up to 200% of the official poverty line. These children live in poverty as well—although official statistics do not designate them as such ... This revised measure reveals a national scandal (which) is that the majority of Black and Latino children still suffer poverty ... a full 57% of African American, 64% of Latino children, and 34% of White children were poor in the U.S. in 2001. (Lu, 2003, p. 2)

A few token people of color and women make it to the top of the hierarchy, a greater number make it into the mainstream, and a man of mixed-race descent, Barack Obama, has been chosen by the Democratic voters to run for the presidency of the United States—although not without facing a highly racialized campaign manipulating many of the nation's hegemonic race, socio-economic, and gender commonsense discourses (Dowd, 2008). Yet, people of color and women are still more likely to find themselves at the bottom of the socioeconomic scale. This is how race and socio-economic class are interwoven—people of color are still disproportionately poor and experience the consequences of poverty.

Yet, formal education offers us the space in which to unmask the hegemony of Whiteness and empower critical and creative multicultural practice. It is not neutral. In the last book he wrote before his death, Paulo Freire, the well-known Brazilian educator wrote: "Nobody can be in the world, with the world, and with others in a neutral manner" (Freire, 2004, p. 60). Freire sees human beings as "a presence in the world." This presence involves taking risks; "education also involves risk and change." Our purpose is not to adapt to the world, but to transform it. Freire also notes that when we feel we have to adapt to the world, we should see this as a temporary phase on the road toward intervening and transforming the world. This is because "being in the world" means recognizing our responsibilities and commitments toward the other human beings in it (Farahmandpur, 2006).

Although the forces of history shape our past and present, we can change the course of history and in the process make history. As Freire puts it, "The future does not make us, we make ourselves in the struggle to make it" (2004, p. 34). We can break away from the chains of history passed down to us from previous generations and make our own history. In other words, while we as human beings are conditioned by history, we can, like Freire, refuse to accept that we are determined by it. For us, as for Freire, history can be possibility.

At the end of the semester, I tell my student-teachers to continue to critically read the official texts they are asked to use in their classrooms and to learn to critically read their world. I ask them to embrace a *Pedagogy of Indignation* as well as a *Pedagogy of Hope* (Freire, 1994). I ask them to look closely at themselves every day to recognize how they contribute to both reproducing and changing the inequities they see around them. I ask them to take whatever risks they can to challenge the existing oppressions and injustices in the world. At the same time, I encourage them, where possible, to stand in solidarity with others in a space that promises the possibility of action in the service of greater humanity and social justice.

By the end of a semester in my Multicultural Pedagogy class, a majority of my White, middle-class students wrote reflections that indicated the effect that some of their experiences in the class had on their ability to unmask Whiteness—institutional, cultural and in themselves:

Throughout this semester I have learned many things about myself that I never thought I would have to examine, I have been forced into seemingly uncomfortable situations in order to get a view from the other side, I have learned to think critically about my culture/background, my ethnicity, my religion, and other values I hold, and most importantly I have learned to be open and accepting of other opinions put forth by my peers. This process has been both familiar, and at times unfamiliar in its workings. All my life I have tried to convince myself that I am not one to judge, or base my thinking about people off of stereotypes, but in making my way through the course of this class I have discovered that most of these stereotypes I encounter are unconscious. In other words, I have no idea that I am even using judgments in any of my thought processes! I have been able to see the prejudgments I make unconsciously on a regular basis and change my thought processes so that I am able to avoid making stereotypes before learning more about an individual. *(White female student)*

In this chapter, I have shared some small but, I believe, significant and hopeful steps in the form of critical and creative classroom practice in teacher education college classrooms towards unmasking Whiteness.

Note

A very significant event has just overtaken this chapter. In 2008, the United States elected its first Black president, Barack Obama, a reality many of us did not believe possible in our lifetimes. Listening and participating to the joy of so many African Americans, from ordinary citizens to Civil Rights leaders like Jesse Jackson and John Lewis, the enormity of what had happened swept over me. At the time of writing, 52% of the population has voted for Obama, a number that includes 60% of the White vote, and an overwhelming number of voters under twenty-five. The demographic map of Obama's victory looks much more like the United States than that of his opponent. I heard accolades from Kenya, the country from which his father hailed, from Japan, from England and the European Union. Only the president of Russia seemed to offer a less than positive response.

I cried tears of joy for the potential empowerment Obama's election offered my own children, who, like the president elect, were born of a White mother and Black father. Someone "like them" had achieved the highest office in the land. I cried tears of joy that my two-year-old grandbaby, also descended in part from enslaved Africans, would grow up knowing that one drop of African blood would no longer, de jure or de facto, determine what one could achieve in the United States. I cried tears of joy for all of the children who pass through our schools for whom Obama's success might be motivational in their own journeys. I saw the joy of people of color and White allies, at home and abroad, celebrating the possibility of a new future. All of them had hoped and worked long and hard for this day.

I also saw many people whose interest in electing Obama had more to do with his proposed solutions to the economy in crisis than his ethnic background. They chose Obama for the "content of his character"—his policies at a time of economic crisis at home and war abroad—rather than "the color of his skin." Journalists were asking if Obama's election signaled the end of racism. In his concession speech, John McCain said, "I have always believed that America offers opportunity to all who have the industry and will to achieve it."

And herein lies the concern of Bonilla-Silva (2006) and others, a concern I share, with respect to "the new racism" in the United States. We *did* witness last evening a revolution of American values and ideas, but those who voted for Obama constituted barely more than half the electorate. We *have* witnessed a transformation of American politics. However, the rhetoric from the liberal media never once addressed the enormous cultural and structural inequities, represented in law and public and educational policy, that will not be dissipated by this election. Obama's election does not mean that the playing field of United States society is suddenly equitable. The public sphere has not suddenly become an unbiased, objective space in which all comers compete fairly for resources. Structural and cultural racism, classism, the hegemony of Whiteness, and other interlocking oppressions continue to shape our lives.

On the other hand, hegemonic forces are already "spinning" this election into a cloth it cannot possibly become. Manning Marable, interviewed by Amy Goodman on the radio/television show, *Democracy Now*, clearly described the reality. African American expectations cannot be realized by the election of one man. The apparatus of American society was not designed to liberate Black people. Indeed, Obama in his acceptance speech warned against outrageous expectations and described a difficult road ahead that requires much work. The majority of the electorate may have moved beyond personal racism in electing Obama, but institutional and cultural racism still colonize the public arena, including school. Our unconscious hegemonic assumptions are, in large measure, still associated with Whiteness.

To work towards dismantling hegemony we must feel comfortable in our dissent. Yet, in his concession speech, John McCain also said that there was no reason now why anyone should not cherish his or her citizenship of the United States. In my view, this was a warning to those of us who would continue to critique the socio-economic and political structure of the United States and the way those in power are able to manipulate the public media, education, and other cultural tools to reproduce their power. It was a continuation of the Bush Administration's McCarthyesque warning against dissent after the events of 9/11—a discourse that characterized the McCain campaign. In many parts of the country and in many schools, it will continue to be hard to voice a challenge to the "common sense" (Kumashiro, 2008) hegemonic view that the United States is a meritocracy. It will continue to be difficult to convince people that many corporate and governmental policymakers and administrators see students as "human resources," rather than human beings, competing for existing jobs under a system of "equal opportunity" (Spring, 2007). Some amongst us who are managing to live quality lives will continue to see poor people, who are disproportionately of color, as deficient in some way if they do not make it out of poverty. Moreover, arguments legitimizing the hurdles that punctuate this hierarchical social system and make access to higher education, highly paid jobs, and professional work difficult will continue to be made. Some will use Obama's election as evidence that these hurdles are not so high and that anyone can surmount them with determination and effort.

So, while we must take heart and energy from Obama's victory for the work ahead, we must recognize that Whiteness, racism, classism, sexism, homophobia, ableism, and other interlocking oppressions still exist in the light of day in the United States. These realities will have to be brought to the willing consciousness of a critical mass of the people and then systematically dismantled. As Dr. Robert Franklin, president of Morehouse College in Atlanta, overjoyed as he was with the result, said after the election: "Race continues to be an issue but we have bounded forward in an extraordinary way." We have forward momentum that we can harness to continue to interrogate and challenge the Whiteness that so many of us embody to a greater of lesser degree. We will need to engage in a vigilant praxis to make sure that we interrupt the Whiteness that will otherwise continue to play out in the everyday details of our private and public lives, including school. We will have to work on all fronts to reframe and transform the socio-economic infrastructure that supports the socio-economic, cultural and political inequities that now characterize the landscape of the United States.

Those who are concerned about hegemony as Whiteness acknowledge this reality and see this election as a platform from which we should launch an even greater effort to institute critical multicultural education in our schools. Much work is needed to unmask Whiteness in the teacher education college classroom and beyond, and engage in critical and creative practice. Indeed, we must work together to bring about greater social justice and caring in our professional and interpersonal lives.

References

Anyon, J. (2005). *Radical possibilities: Public policy, urban education, and a new social movement.* New York: Routledge. Ball, S. (1990). *Foucault and education.* New York: Routledge.

Berliner, D. & Nichols, S. L. (2007, March 12). High-stakes testing is putting the nation at risk. *Education Week.* Boggs, C. (1976). *Gramsci's Marxism.* London: Pluto Press.

Bonilla-Silva, E. (2006). *Racism without racists: Color-blind racism and the persistence of racial inequality in the United States.* Lanham, MI: Rowman & Littlefield.

Bourdieu, P. (1993). *Language and symbolic power.* Cambridge, MA: Polity Press.

Bowles & Gintis (1976). *Schooling in capitalist America: Educational reform and the contradictions of economic life.* New York: Routledge.

Dowd, M. (2008, March 2). A wake-up call for Hillary. *The New York Times.* Retrieved May 20, 2008: http://www. nytimes. com/2008/03/02/opinion/02dowd.html?scp=6&sq=Michelle+Obama%2C+Patriotism&st=nyt

During, S. (1993). *Cultural studies: A critical introduction.* New York: Routledge. Dyer, R. (1988). White. *Screen,* 29 (4).

Emery, K. & Ohanian, S. (2004). *Why is corporate America bashing our public schools?* Portsmouth, NH: Heinemann. Epstein, K. K. (2006). *A different view of urban schools: Civil rights, critical race theory, and unexplored realities.* New York: Peter Lang.

FairTest (2008, January 25). "Child Left Behind" After six years: an escalating track record of failure. Retrieved April 11, 2008 from the FairTest website: http://www.fairtest.org/NCLB-After-Six-Years

Farahmandpur, F. (2006, January 11). Freire, Paulo. (2004). *Pedagogy of Indignation.* Boulder, CO: Paradigm Publishers. Retrieved May 20, 2008 from The Education Review: A Journal of Book Reviews website: http://edrev. asu.edu/reviews/rev454.htm

Festinger, L. A. (1957). *A theory of cognitive dissonance.* Evanston, IL: Ron Peterson. Freire, P. (1993/1970). *Pedagogy of the oppressed.* New York: Continuum.

Freire, P. (1994). *Pedagogy of hope: Reliving pedagogy of the oppressed.* New York: Continuum. Freire, P. (2004). *Pedagogy of indignation.* Boulder, CO: Paradigm Publishers.

Giddens, A. (1997). *Sociology.* 3rd ed. Cambridge: Polity Press.

Grossberg, L. (1994). Introduction: Bringin' it all back home: Pedagogy and cultural studies. In H. A. Giroux & P. McLaren (Eds.), *Between borders: Pedagogy and the politics of cultural studies.* New York: Routledge.

Hall, S. (1993). Negotiating Caribbean Identities. *Walter Rodney Memorial Lecture.* Centre for Caribbean Studies, University of Warwick.

Ignatiev, N., & Garvey, J. (1996). *Race traitor.* New York: Routledge.

Igoa, C. (1995). *The inner world of the immigrant child.* Mahwah, NJ: Lawrence Erlbaum Associates.

King, J. (1991). Dysconscious racism: Ideology, identity, and the miseducation of teachers. *Journal of Negro Education,* 60 (2), 1–14.

Kohl, H. (1991). *I won't learn from you!* Minneapolis, MN: Milkweed Editions.

Kumashiro, K. (2008). *The seduction of common sense: How the right has framed the debate on America's schools.* New York: Teachers College Press.

Ladson-Billings, G. (1994). *The Dreamkeepers: Successful teachers of African American children.* San Francisco: JosseyBass.

Lea, V. (2004, March/April). The reflective cultural portfolio: Identifying public scripts in the private voices of white student-teachers. *Journal of Teacher Education,* 55 (2), 116–127.

Lea, V., & Helfand, J. (2004). *Identifying race and transforming whiteness in the classroom.* New York: Peter Lang.

Lea, V., & Sims, E. J. (2008). *Undoing whiteness in the classroom: Critical educultural teaching approaches for social justice activism.* New York: Peter Lang.

Leary, J. D. (2008). Post traumatic slave syndrome: America's legacy of enduring injury and healing. Retrieved May 23, 2008: http://www.joyleary.com/store.html

Lincoln, A. (1863). http://showcase.netins.net/web/creative/lincoln/speeches/gettysburg.htm.

Loewen, J. (1995). *Lies my teacher told me: Everything your high school history textbook got wrong.* New York: The New Press.

Lu, H. H. (2003). *Low-income children in the United States.* National Center for Children in Poverty. New York: Columbia University, Mailman School of Public Health.

Mansell, W. (2007). *Education by numbers: The tyranny of testing.* London: Politico's Publishing.

Maxwell, K. E. (2004). Deconstructing whiteness: Discovering the water. In V. Lea & J. Helfand (Eds.), *Identifying race and transforming whiteness in the classroom.* New York: Peter Lang.

McIntosh, P. (1989, July/August). White privilege: Unpacking the invisible knapsack. *Peace and Freedom.*

McLaren, P. (2003). Critical pedagogy: A look at the major concepts. In A. Darder, M. Baltodano, & R. Torres, R. (Eds.), *The critical pedagogy reader.* New York: RoutledgeFalmer.

McLaren, P. (2005). *Capitalists and conquerors: A critical pedagogy against empire.* Lanham, MD: Rowman & Littlefield.

Moll, L. C., Amanti, C., Neff, D., Gonzales, N. (1992, Spring), Funds of knowledge for teachers: Using a qualitative approach to connect homes and classrooms. *Theory into Practice,* XXXI (2).

Neves, A. (1998). *Multicultural education and the social studies syllabus.* Sonoma State University, CA.

Nieto, S. & Bode, P. (2007). *Affirming diversity: The sociopolitical context of multicultural education.* New York: Allyn & Bacon.

Ogbu, J. (1995). Cultural problems in minority education: Their interpretations and consequences—Part one: Theoretical background. *The Urban Review,* 27 (3).

Payne, R. (1995). *A framework for understanding poverty.* Highlands, TX: aha! Process.

Payne, R. K. (2006, January). Personal communication.

Pinar, W. F. (2004). *What is curriculum theory?* Mahwah, NJ: Lawrence Erlbaum Associates.

Pollick, M. (2008). Hidden curriculum. Retrieved May 23, 2008: http://hiddencurriculum.pnn.com/5726-the- front-page

Pytel, B. (2007, March 16). NCLB: It's all about the test. Good teaching vs. test scores. Retrieved April 11, 2008 from Suite 101 website: http://educationalissues.suite101.com/blog.cfm/nclb_its_all_about_the_test

Rabinow, P. (Ed.) (1984). *The Foucault reader.* New York: Pantheon books.

Roediger, D. R. (1991). *The wages of whiteness: Race and the making of the American working class.* London: Verso. Rouse, W. H. D. (1956). *Great dialogues of Plato,* translation. Denver, CO: Mentor Books.

Ryan, W. (1971). *Blaming the victim.* New York: Vintage.

Sleeter, C. E. (2004, May). *Critical multicultural curriculum and the standards movement.* Paper presented at the meeting of the California Council on Teacher Education, San Jose, CA.

Spring, J. (2007). *American education.* New York: McGraw-Hill.

Spring, J. (2008). *The American school: From the puritans to No Child Left Behind.* New York: McGraw Hill.

Steele, C. (2004, September 24). Steele Discusses "Stereotype Threat." Retrieved April 11, 2008 from *College Street Journal,* Mount Holyoke College website: http://www.mtholyoke.edu/offices/comm/csj/092404/steele. shtml.

Steinberg, S., & Kincheloe, J. (Eds.) (2007). *19 urban questions: Teaching in the city.* New York: Peter Lang.

Sumara, D. J., and Davis, B. (1998). Unskinning curriculum. In W. F. Pinar (Ed.) *Curriculum: Toward new identities.* New York: Garland Publishing.

Thomas, W. I. (1923). *The unadjusted girl.* Boston: Little, Brown, and Co.

Valenzuela, A. (1999). *Subtractive schooling: U.S. Mexican youth and the politics of caring.* Albany, NY: State University of New York.

Zinn, H., & Stefoff, R. (2007). *A young people's history of the United States: Vol. I & II.* Seven Stories Press.

CHAPTER 10

(Still) Making Whiteness Visible
Implications for (Teacher) Education

Nelson M. Rodriguez

Working with predominantly White, middle-class, pre-service student-teachers around the issue of racism, in particular White racism and White privilege, can be frustrating, disheartening, and tiresome, on the one hand; it can be meaningful, positive and hopeful, on the other. Yet, whatever the emotion attached to this project, examining White privilege and racism with White pre-service student-teachers is a necessity. This necessity arises out of several important social-psychological conditions.

First, although public school demographics nationally show a major increase in the number of students of color, still the majority of public classroom teachers, over 80%, are White. This fact raises important questions, especially around so-called multicultural education. For instance, without an awareness of systemic White racism and White privilege, in what *direction* will White teachers *perform* their antiracist education? Will they see racism, for example, as a "person of color problem" and thereby experience their response only in terms of what they can do to "help" that person? This important yet limited approach to antiracist education can perpetuate White racism in educational and societal settings by not enabling White teachers to understand their own complicity in the problem. Indeed, by only examining racism as something that is a "problem" for people of color, coupled with only seeing one's antiracist (approach to) education in the form of helping the Other, this way of thinking and acting "allows White people to remove themselves from complicity in the problem while thinking that they are doing something about it" (Derman-Sparks & Brunson-Phillips, 1997, p. 16).

The necessity of examining White privilege and racism with White students also stems from a lack of discursive exposure to a more comprehensive understanding of racism and the reasons for its persistence. That is, White students typically have a limited sense of what racism *means*. This lack of knowledge is in large measure the result of a limited range of available discourses in our society for White folks to think through a broader understanding of racism. Indeed, White students often tend to think of racism only as racial prejudice, thereby not confronting systemic White racism and White privilege. One implicit suggestion, then, of this chapter is to urge teacher educators to provide a critical pedagogy that challenges the way most (White) students have arrived at their understanding of the concept of racism.

Finally, the necessity of examining White privilege with White students has to do with the issue of "loss of one's humanity." That is, many Whites have not been taught to see their privilege, to understand its significance both personally and socially. To be sure, quite the opposite is the case: They have been carefully taught not to see it. As Peggy McIntosh noted two decades ago in her essay, "White Privilege and Male Privilege: A Personal Account of Coming to See Correspondences through Work in Women's Studies": "As a White person, I realized I had been taught about racism as something which puts others at a disadvantage, but had not been taught one of its corollary aspects, White privilege, which puts me at an advantage" (1997, p. 291). Although McIntosh made this latter statement back in 1990, I would argue that, for the majority of White students, their lack of awareness of and thinking through about White privilege still very much hold true today. The result of this lack of awareness, then, provides fertile ground unfortunately for White students to lose their humanity in their White privilege, that is, to lose sight of the fact that White privilege is typically had at the expense of subaltern racial groups. Cultivating a critical consciousness around White privilege, then, is a responsibility that we educators must "impose" on our students if we want them to become aware of the privileges of the White skin and how they might use such privileges not only for the betterment of people of color but also to prevent themselves from losing their moral consciousness to the abyss of white racism.

This important concern with addressing White privilege with White students raises several important questions that have been debated within the field of critical White studies. These include: Do White students think much about their Whiteness? If they do, how do they understand it? For example, do they "see" and construct their White identity around the idea that Whiteness is now under attack? Indeed, as Charles Gallagher (1994, p. 168) asks, is it accurate that "Whiteness is no longer invisible or transparent as a racial category because it is in crisis?" Other important questions include: For White students who do think about their Whiteness, is this understanding "situational and fleeting, or is it more akin to a dull constant pain?" (Gallagher, 1994, p. 166) Do White students ever think about their Whiteness in terms of White privilege? Or, is it more the case that White students see racism as "unfortunate" but not something in which they are implicated? What about those students who rarely, if ever, think about their Whiteness in any aspect?

Based on my personal experiences and critical work with White pre-service student-teachers that draws its data from interviews, researcher-facilitated group discussions, and content analysis of students' responses to several texts, this chapter seeks to informally "test" (i.e., theoretically explore) the erosion of the White-invisibility thesis put forward by sociologist Charles A. Gallagher (1994) in his essay titled, "White Reconstruction in the University," a seminal and continuously, cited essay in the literature on critical White studies.

An examination of White identity formation among a group of White students at a large urban university, Gallagher's essay is significant on a number of registers, not the least of which is his assertion that Whiteness is no longer invisible to White students. Gallagher's "discursive disruption" to the "invisibility thesis" so pervasive (still) in the field of critical Whiteness studies today has positively pushed the conversation in this academic area in a new and healthy direction. In much of the literature, Whiteness as an *invisible* racial marker or norm has become the typical approach to talking about and analyzing Whiteness. As Mike Hill (1998) remarks: "The fact that the 'invisibility thesis' is evoked and remarked on these days with such regularity, indeed, itself so visible an hypothesis as to appear unimpeachable, would seem once again to return Whiteness to the ordinary" (p. 230). Because of its centrality in the field, let me take a few moments to discuss the pervasive "invisibility thesis" within critical White studies.

Although it might appear that the examination of Whiteness is a recent undertaking, it should be noted at the outset that the study of Whiteness is nothing new. As an object of study, Whiteness has been undergoing scrutiny for centuries. As an example, historian David Roediger, who, arguably, is a pioneer in contemporary critical White studies, has exhumed a past tradition of thinking and writing by Blacks about Whites in his edited publication (1998) titled, *Black on White: Black Writers on What It Means to Be White.* So, if the study of Whiteness is not new, what, then, gives contemporary critical Whiteness studies their freshness or originality or even their importance? The answer lies in the argument that Whiteness is a social construction. From the perspective of inquiry and research, to say that Whiteness is a social construct is to want to examine the "social mechanisms that falsely legitimate Whiteness as normative or superior" (Thompson, 1999, n.p.).

Implicit, then, in the argument that Whiteness is a social construction is the notion that Whiteness is invisible and, therefore, needs to be interrogated and made problematic. "The project of Whiteness theorists [in other words] is to problematize the normalization of Whiteness as racelessness, to make 'visible [that is] what was previously unseen'" (Thompson, 1999, n.p.). This notion of making Whiteness visible at the individual, institutional, and/or cultural levels has come to be understood within the literature as the "invisibility thesis," and it is this thesis that still animates, albeit in a variety of forms, the majority of theorizing within the field of contemporary critical White studies. Indeed, whether one takes a psychological, materialist, and/or discursive approach to analyzing Whiteness, each paradigm in general is concerned with marking or making visible the "pervasive non-presence" of Whiteness. For example, materialist approaches to Whiteness are often concerned with making visible the "multiple material forms that White privilege may take, especially in such arenas as access to equal education, housing, bank loans, and police protection" (Thompson, 1999, n.p.).

Interestingly, however, even though the invisibility thesis is the pervasive and dominant idea circulating within contemporary critical White studies, this thesis itself has been recently contested. Arguing that Whiteness is no longer invisible, some theorists within the field believe that U.S. society and culture in the late twentieth and early twenty-first centuries are characterized by a widespread and aggressive "new politicization of Whiteness," thus rendering "the explanatory powers of the invisibility thesis simplistic and anachronistic" (Gallagher, 1994, p. 173). While I most certainly agree that Whiteness has been politicized in the post-civil rights era, I am concerned nevertheless with the argument that this politicization has somehow made Whiteness visible, especially to White, pre-service student-teachers and to other students as well. I will explain my position here in a moment when I turn to a series of narratives I've garnered while working with White student-teachers. These narratives serve as a particular structure of explanation that helps give insight into the way such students "think about" their Whiteness.

The overriding project, then, within critical Whiteness studies has been one of deconstructing Whiteness, of making visible the various forms of mechanisms of Whiteness, and of showing how Whiteness is related to racism. As philosopher of education, Audrey Thompson, notes: "For the most part [the emphasis of critical white studies] is not on Whiteness as an announced value but Whiteness as a suppressed, invisible privilege" (Thompson, 1999, n.p.). Challenging, then, the regularity of the invisibility thesis, Gallagher has opened up the necessary discursive space for thinking through how we talk about Whiteness in the twenty-first century.

Having said that, I'm still somewhat puzzled. I have been working over the past four to five years now with undergraduate pre-service student-teachers, most of whom are White. In particular, I've been teaching courses that take up the issue of "education and cultural diversity," in which most of the students enrolled in these courses identify racially as White. When I first started teaching these courses, I conceptualized them around teaching about the "Other." I have always been committed to having my students encounter so-called difference and always within the framework of analyzing social injustice, and how the institution of schooling might be used to challenge such injustice. Also, because these courses encourage, by their very titles, an examination of a range of diversity issues, in addition to teaching units on racial injustice, especially in relation to African American and Native American struggles for racial justice, I have spent much time in these courses on an examination of gender oppression and homophobia and heterosexism. I have come to believe that these courses are rewarding for students in sensitizing them to the struggles, past and present, many subordinate groups have waged for their own liberation, and how these particular struggles have been linked by their commitment to a broader politics of social justice.

Yet, at the same time, I have come to feel that cultural diversity courses, especially those with a mostly White audience, are lacking in their potential transformative politics if they do not critically take up the issue of Whiteness. It was in this context that I came (and have returned) to Gallagher's study, which has helped me to think more deeply about the role of a critical Whiteness discourse in the diversity classroom. But what Gallagher was expressing in his essay seemed to be at odds with my experience working with students who seemed not to think much about their Whiteness. That is, given that Gallagher's study was conducted at a university located in a large urban center in the Northeast, I wondered, based on my experiences, if his argument that Whiteness is no longer invisible would bear out with my White students at colleges located in suburban settings. He seems to suggest that it would. Indeed, Gallagher winds down his essay with the following general claim: "No doubt many whites do not think about their Whiteness, but I would argue they are increasingly in the minority" (1994, p. 184). I do not argue here that Gallagher has got it wrong; in fact, I would assert the opposite. Instead, I want to put into dialogue his arguments about the reasons and significance about how White students "get raced" with informal data that I have garnered from working with White pre-service student-teachers who not only attend a college that is predominately White but also have grown up in predominately White communities. Where do these students stand on the issue of Whiteness? What similarities are there between them and White students located in urban centers around the country? What differences exist? By putting in dialogue, then, Gallagher's arguments with my data, I hope to provide another layer to Gallagher's crucial discursive disruption.

As I mentioned earlier, in his essay, Gallagher discusses the implications of an ethnographic study he conducted with White undergraduate students at an urban university in the Northeast. Based on his study, Gallagher arrives at the argument that, because of contemporary racial politics and the effects of the media, whites increasingly see themselves as White and further, have come to see or make sense of their Whiteness as a disadvantage. As Gallagher (1994) explains: "Race matters for these [white] students because they have been weaned on a brand of racial politics and media exposure that has made White-ness visible as a racial category while simultaneously transforming Whiteness into a social disadvantage" (p. 166). Gallagher concludes his essay with the argument that, based on seeing their Whiteness as a liability, the next generation of White adults just might respond to "the political and cultural mobiliza-tion of racially defined minorities" (p. 167) in a reactionary way. How? By "develop[ing] solidarity in their Whiteness," thus removing themselves from the project of racial equality and social justice (p. 185).

I want to reiterate that Gallagher's essay is important for a number of reasons. First, from the per-spective of internal debates within the field, he has challenged the *regularity* of the invisibility thesis within contemporary critical White studies. In addition, Gallagher's argument that Whiteness is being redefined as a liability or disadvantage is absolutely on the mark, and his worry that White students may, as a result, develop solidarity in their Whiteness should be taken seriously, especially by educators. My bone of contention, then, with Gallagher's argument is one of *degree*. That is, I am not as convinced as he is that *most* White students today think about their Whiteness.

As I mentioned earlier, then, my current work wishes to explore Gallagher's thesis that most White students today think about their Whiteness. Locating Gallagher's thesis within the specific context of teacher education, I wish to demonstrate that White pre-service student-teachers do not consider the issue of Whiteness and White privilege. Such a defining absence, I argue, raises important concerns for how to conceptualize cultural diversity courses that enable White student-teachers to recognize that "everyone [occupies] a place in the relations of racism" (Frankenberg, 1993, p. 6). This chapter, then, represents one example of my ongoing work of connecting critical White studies to the field of educa-tion, and in particular, to teacher education.

Racism, Whiteness, and Education for Critical Consciousness

In her essay, "Transformative Pedagogy and Multiculturalism," bell hooks (1993) discusses the importance of an education for critical consciousness. By such an approach, hooks is arguing for getting students to recognize and change societal inequities and injustices and to use the terrain of the classroom for such thinking and action. In short, hooks is calling for a critical pedagogy. However, when educating for critical consciousness, hooks is sensitive that such critical consciousness-raising is often quite painful for many students. This pain arises in part because of how students experience major paradigm shifts in their thinking as a result of being brought to "criticality." As hooks (1993) notes, "Students have taught me that it is necessary to practice compassion in new learning settings where individuals may be confronting shifts in paradigms that seem to them completely and utterly threatening. I saw for the first time that there can be, and usually is, some degree of pain involved in giving up old ways of thinking and knowing and learning new approaches. I respect that pain. And include recognition of it now when I teach, that is to say [when] I teach about shifting paradigms and talk about the discomfort it can cause" (pp. 95–96).

Recently, I witnessed this pain in my students when we discussed the distinction between racial prejudice and racism. More specifically, I had my students read a chapter titled, "Defining Racism," from Beverly Daniel Tatum's (1997) book, *Why Are All the Black Kids Sitting Together in the Cafeteria? And Other Conversations about Race*. Drawing on David Wellman's (1993) publication, *Portraits of White Racism*, Tatum draws a distinction between racial prejudice and "racism." Racial prejudice would include thoughts and behaviors that most people would think of as racist. These include racial slurs, violence committed against people of color, and "preconceived judgment and opinion, usually based on limited information" (Tatum, 1997, p. 5). Racism, on the other hand, is defined by Tatum as a system of advantage based on race. To fine-tune this distinction, Tatum goes on to make a distinction between active and passive racism so as to point out that one need not be a hate-monger to be complicit in the spread of racism. The point of exposing students to Tatum's definition of racism was not only to engage them in that paradigm shift to which hooks refers, but also to begin the process of gaining insight into how they think about Whiteness. Thus, in this phase of my work, I was concerned with the following question: In what way can students' understanding of the concept of racism shed light on the degree to which they think about their Whiteness? This is the question with which I initiated my attempts to understand how and whether my students were thinking critically about Whiteness.

As mentioned earlier, under the terms of mainstream U.S. ideology, racism is typically defined as personal prejudice, hatred, or violence committed against people of color. From this perspective, racism, while utterly horrible, is viewed as a person of color's problem and not something that implicates mainstream, liberal White society. Defining racism in this way limits it to be seen as a "fringe ideology" and dissociates it from questions of Whiteness and White privilege. I believe that most White, preservice student-teachers arrive at their cultural diversity classes thinking that racism is only about racial bigotry. To see how my students think about racism and, as a result, what this says about the degree to which they think about their Whiteness, I had them grapple with Tatum's definition of racism. Below I introduce the data from this portion of my work.

During interviews and group discussions following their reading of Tatum's definition of racism, most of my students' comments betrayed their lack of understanding of racism as above and beyond racial prejudice. The following statements by three different students were typical of most students' comments. One student, Gretchen, put it succinctly, when she said: "I have always equated 'racism' with 'prejudice' and 'discrimination' and never thought twice about these terms having unique meanings." Another student, Jason, responded to his encounter with Tatum's definition of racism in the following way: "I have always known about racism and knew it still existed, but I never saw it the way I do now. For example, I knew about the Civil Rights movement and their fight for equal rights,

I knew about the Klan and the types of behaviors they participated in, and I knew that some people didn't like Black people. However, I didn't know about passive racism. I never really thought about the idea I guess." Finally, Nichole expressed her thoughts about racism as a system of advantage as follows: "Before reading this essay I had never thought of myself as racist, because I don't believe any race to be superior to another, but that is not the definition of racism the author uses. [The definition of racism as] a system of advantage based on race sheds new light on an old concept."

These comments reveal just how ingrained the notion of "racism-as-bigotry" is in the minds of these students. Indeed, before coming across Tatum's definition of racism, and being challenged by it, these students (and so many others) had not conceived of racism in ways other than personal prejudice. More important, from the perspective of critically thinking about Whiteness, these students had not thought about Whiteness in terms of associating it with racism. Some students did make the association between Whiteness and racism before reading Tatum; however, their association was not a critical but reactionary one. That is, several students commented that whites are experiencing what they called, "reverse-discrimination," especially in such areas as college admissions and scholarship programs. From this perspective, these students did link racism to Whiteness prior to reading Tatum but, as with Gallagher's students, they associated Whiteness with disadvantage. To repeat, though, most important to this phase of my work was recognizing that the students' limited understanding of racism prevented them from critically thinking about their Whiteness as a system of advantage based on race. Not making the association between racism and Whiteness can misdirect how White teachers engage in antiracist education.

To illustrate racism as defined above, Tatum (1997) provides the following concrete example:

> In very concrete terms, it means that if a person of color is the victim of housing discrimination, the apartment that would otherwise have been rented to that person of color is still available for a White person. The White tenant is, knowingly or unknowingly, the beneficiary of racism, a system of advantage based on race. The unsuspecting tenant is not to blame for the prior discrimination, but she benefits from it anyway. (p. 9)

In this example, Tatum powerfully shows that one need not be an active racist to be complicit in the perpetuation of racism, a notion that many of my students had not considered. Indeed, by simply being part of a society that is deeply entrenched in racism, all one has to do to perpetuate it is to go about one's life in a usual fashion. As Tatum highlights:

> For many white people, the image of a racist is a hood-wearing Klan member or a name-calling Archie Bunker figure. These images represent what might be called active racism, blatant, intentional acts of racial bigotry and discrimination. Passive racism is more subtle and can be seen in the collusion of laughter when a racist joke is told, of letting hiring practices go unchallenged, of accepting as appropriate the omissions of people of color from the curriculum, and of avoiding difficult race-related issues. Because racism is so ingrained in the fabric of American institutions, it is easily self-perpetuating. All that is required to maintain it is business as usual. (p. 11)

By defining racism, then, as a system of advantage based on race, students painfully recognize that they can no longer remove themselves from the structures of racism. This causes great angst for before encountering the conceptual distinction between racial prejudice and racism, white students could easily point the finger elsewhere and recognize with assurance "a racist." Indeed, there was some comfort in knowing that what they pointed to they certainly did not see in themselves. However, with this newfound sense of the meaning of racism, White students painfully recognize that their own involvement in keeping racism going is much deeper than they had previously thought. This is both painful and irritating. As one student asked in class soon after thinking through the distinction, "Will this be the definition of racism that we will continue to use all semester?" This comment reflects uneasiness, a painful feeling if you will, in thinking about racism as a system of advantage based on race. Indeed, racism defined in this way is like experiencing an irritating thorn in one's side. There were similar comments that in fact were blunter, as when another student remarked, "I understand this distinction, but it makes me uncomfortable, really uncomfortable." What both of these comments demonstrate, especially the second, is that on a conceptual level, students understand and, to a certain extent, can embrace this distinction. On an emotional or affective level, however, the students were struggling to keep their emotions at bay in knowing not only that they are potentially complicit in the spread of racism but also in knowing that being complicit meant that they, too, were "racists." No longer could the finger be pointed simply in one direction.

Indeed, if understanding that they perpetuate racism in ways unknown to them was painful, it was even more painful to be called a racist within this context. Almost all the students I interviewed and worked with in group-facilitated discussions resisted being called a racist. This label was just too painful and for most students would not be accepted. Many students wondered if another word could be used instead. This is interesting because, again, many of the students understood and could accept the distinction, but would not allow themselves to be called a racist. Many students argued that that was an unfair label to use for whites who unknowingly perpetuate racism. Others argued that using such a word would turn off many whites and thereby undermine one's project in getting whites to join in the quest for racial justice. As one student, Melissa, commented:

> I believe that Tatum's definition of racism is valid, yet I am still not giving it my full support. It definitely would not be accepted by our society as a whole. Again I agree with Tatum that the reason for this rejection is how the definition offends people, especially Whites. Not everyone is fortunate enough to have a detailed discussion of this definition and its implications after reading the article, so they may not be able to truly understand what is being said. Until we discussed this topic, I was one of the offended.

Whether the argument is that using the label "racist" is unfair or that it will turn off whites, both arguments do raise the broader pedagogical problem of how to get across these important but touchy subjects. Indeed, as Melissa made clear, most whites do not have the luxury of being able to "unpack" these issues in an intellectual environment.

Yet, I also wonder if their resistance to being called racist stems from other sources, most notably as a defense mechanism. That is, by resisting the label racism, perhaps students are, to a certain degree, resisting the new definition of racism that they seem to understand and embrace on a conceptual level. Indeed, the word "racist" hovers, constantly reminding students of this newfound definition and most important, of their involvement in the spread of racism. In other words, calling oneself a racist in this context is a constant reminder that racism is a *White* problem. Removing the label racist, to put it another way, is a way to, in some way, distance oneself from being complicit in the spread of racism. A coping mechanism no doubt, but a rather effective one indeed. But perhaps there is a way to turn this around so that students see the importance of keeping the label. In my own pedagogical struggle, I responded to another student as follows:

> Perhaps using the word racist might actually be a way to get people to work toward eradicating the system of advantage so that they no longer have to consider themselves racists. From this perspective, calling oneself a racist is done not to make one feel guilty; rather, it is done to keep one outraged about racism as a system of advantage as well as keep one committed to eradicating such a system. Eradicating racism as a system of advantage, in other words, can be the motivation for no longer having to consider oneself a racist.

Whether the pain involved stems from being called a racist or from encountering a definition of racism that one had not previously considered, exposing students to a definition of racism as a system of advantage based on race has raised the consciousness of White students about the meaning and function of racism in the twenty-first century. This critical pedagogy, however, more important to the argument set forth in this chapter, has also illuminated how students understand or think through their Whiteness. *Or perhaps it might be more appropriate to say that the distinction the students grappled over revealed how much they do not think in critical terms about their Whiteness.* It is to this discussion to which I now turn.

Whiteness, Multicultural Education, and Critical Pedagogy

It would be absurd to argue today that whites have not been affected by identity politics. Indeed, living in the post-civil rights era, whites have some sense of their Whiteness. They feel it to a certain extent. With White students, this fact is perhaps most evident in their discussions about affirmative action. As Howard Winant (1997) astutely notes:

> Assaults on these policies, which have been developing since their introduction as tentative and quite limited efforts at racial redistribution, are currently at hysterical levels. These attacks are clearly designed to effect ideological shifts, rather than to shift resources in a meaningful way. They represent Whiteness as a disadvantage, something which has few precedents in U. S. racial history. This imaginary white disadvantage—for which there is almost no evidence at the empirical level—has achieved widespread popular credence, and provides the cultural and political "glue" that holds together a wide variety of reactionary racial politics. (p. 42)

It is in the sense that no one escapes their Whiteness in the post-civil rights era that I agree with Gallagher when he argues that, generally speaking, White students see their Whiteness. But there is an issue of degree that is missing from Gallagher's analysis. While, yes, I would argue that most whites in the post-civil rights era have some sense of their Whiteness, I think for many White students, the issue of seeing their Whiteness is more a question of *degree,* not fact. That is, for most of my White students, their Whiteness is something about which they think very little. From this perspective, the questions as an educator that I'm concerned with are: How do I enable them to (1) think about Whiteness, (2) think about it in a *sustained* way, and (3) think about it in a *meaningfully transformative* way? With these three points in mind, I conclude by turning to Howard Winant's (1997) discussion of the concept of "white racial dualism."

Having just begun to establish, through Tatum's work, a critical association between racism and Whiteness, the second phase of my critical pedagogy focused on involving the students in a more explicit discussion of Whiteness. From the perspective of my work and research, the importance of such an explicit discussion was to once again demonstrate that most White pre-service student-teachers either do not think about Whiteness at all or do not think about it in *critical* terms. From the perspective of my students, the value of such an explicit discussion was to have them grapple with a set of critical discourses that would raise their consciousness about social positionality, that is, about how their Whiteness positions them at an advantage within the web of racial reality.

Engaging in an explicit discussion of Whiteness within the context of multicultural education was important for two reasons. First, such a discussion connected the issues of race and racism *directly* to their lives. Second, such a discussion enabled the students to critique forms of multicultural curricula that take up "cultural difference outside of a historical, power-literate context" (Kincheloe and Steinberg, 1997, p. 18). One of my students, Leanne, had this to say about explicitly discussing Whiteness in a cultural diversity course: "I have had another education class at this college, which taught us about multicultural education but there was no mention of the injustices and human suffering which are the result of White supremacy within our country. Nor was there any mention about 'Whiteness' and what advantages White people receive due to their race. I realize now that my previous education classes have endorsed 'cultural tourism.'"

Underlying theoretically my explicit discussion of Whiteness with my students is a concept known as "white racial dualism," an idea that I borrowed from the work of Howard Winant. Drawing from

W. E. B. Du Bois, Winant coined this phrase to describe how identity politics in the post-civil rights era has caused whites to experience a kind of double consciousness. As Winant (1997) explains: "[White racial dualism] is an extension to whites of the Du Boisian idea that in a racist society the 'color line' fractures the self which forces [whites] to see themselves simultaneously from within and without" (p. 40). From the perspective of pedagogy, I find Winant's term to be highly useful. That is, because I believe most White pre-service student-teachers do not think about Whiteness, I drew upon Winant's concept of white racial dualism to help guide me in selecting materials that would enable my students to begin the critical work of both seeing their Whiteness "from within and without." The question I asked myself was, "How can I create within my pedagogy the conditions for cultivating in a meaningful way the experience of white racial dualism among my students?" Winant's concept led me to several texts including Lee MunWah's (1994) film, *The Color of Fear*, and Peggy McIntosh's essay, "White Privilege and Male Privilege." I will end this chapter with a discussion of the implications of McIntosh's article for cultivating the experience of white racial dualism among White student-teachers. I will also demonstrate how my students' responses to such an experience corroborate my thesis that most White pre-service student-teachers do not think about their Whiteness.

Although McIntosh is white, I believe that, because of the critical work she has done on herself in the area of Whiteness, her voice represents, to the extent that it can, an outsider's view on Whiteness. That is, given that most whites do not think critically about Whiteness, McIntosh's voice is outside of how the majority of whites think about Whiteness. In this sense, McIntosh is an "outsider-within." Indeed, as Alison Bailey (1998) notes, McIntosh represents a small number of "privilege-cognizant whites who refuse to animate expected whitely scripts, and who are unfaithful to worldviews whites are expected to hold" (p. 27). From this perspective, McIntosh's work enables White pre-service student-teachers to awaken to their Whiteness from within by virtue of encountering an "outsider's" critical account of Whiteness.

Through work that has been done in women's studies in analyzing how men are often asleep to our systemic male privilege, McIntosh then turns the critical gaze back on herself to analyze how she, as a White woman, is privileged by her Whiteness. As McIntosh (1997) notes: "I think whites are carefully taught not to recognize white privilege, as males are taught not to recognize male privilege. So I have begun to ask what it is like to have white privilege" (p. 291). To critically explore her Whiteness, McIntosh creates a forty-six item list of the daily effects of White privilege in her life. For example, one item on her list reads, "I can if I wish arrange to be in the company of people of my race most of the time." In another item, she notes, "I am never asked to speak for all the people of my racial group." Finally, in another example, she explains that, "I can turn on the television or open the front page of the newspaper and see people of my race widely represented."

The strength of this list in awakening in my students a critical sense of their Whiteness cannot be overstated. Two students' comments, Sara's and Carrie's, provide insight into the impact an explicit discussion of Whiteness can have in moving White pre-service student-teachers to new levels of consciousness. In a response paper to McIntosh's essay, Sara, for example, wrote: "Gender topics have always been discussed in my classes so I am always conscious of how my gender affects how I am treated (good or bad). However, I have never, until reading McIntosh's [essay], really considered how my color affects how I am treated." In Carrie's comment, she responded similarly to the shift in consciousness she experienced as a result of engaging in an explicit and critical discussion of Whiteness:

> I enjoyed this article because of the list that she provided of the effects of privilege in her daily life. It really made me open my eyes and see all the advantages I have just by being a white individual. This is something I have never thought of, and even more amazingly something that has never been pointed out to me. Personally, when talking about racism I think about people of color, prejudices, and discrimination. Never did I think of racism as involving whites and even more ironically advantages, which is really sad.

Sara's and Carrie's comments demonstrate not only that the students I worked with were not thinking about Whiteness but also confirm the importance of engaging students in a pedagogy of Whiteness committed to making Whiteness visible in critical ways. From this perspective, these students' narratives help demonstrate the political and social urgency of a critical pedagogy of Whiteness as integral to the overall discourse on cultural diversity and teacher education. Still, making Whiteness visible continues to be central to such a pedagogy.

References

Bailey, A. (1998). Locating traitorous identities: Toward a view of privilege-cognizant white character. *Hypatia*, 13(3), 27–42.

Derman-Sparks, L. & Brunson-Phillips, C. (1997). *Teaching/learning anti-racism: A developmental approach*. New York: Teachers College Press.

Frankenberg, R. (1993). *White women, race matters: The social construction of Whiteness*. Minneapolis: University of Minnesota Press.

Gallagher, C. (1994). White reconstruction in the university. *Socialist Review*, 94(1&2), 165–187.

Hill, M. (1998). Souls undressed: The rise and fall of the new Whiteness studies. *The Review of Education/Pedagogy/Cultural Studies*, 20(3), 229–239.

hooks, b. (1993). Transformative pedagogy and multiculturalism. In T. Perry & J. Fraser (Eds.), *Freedom's plow: Teaching in the multicultural classroom*. New York: Routledge.

Kincheloe, J. & Steinberg, S. (1997). *Changing multiculturalism*. Philadelphia: Open University Press.

McIntosh, P. (1997). White privilege and male privilege: A personal account of coming to see correspondences through work in women's studies. In R. Delgado & J. Stefancic (Eds.), *Critical white studies: Looking behind the mirror*. Philadelphia: Temple University Press.

McIntosh, P. (1990). White privilege: Unpacking the invisible knapsack. *Independent School*, 49(2), 31–35.

Roediger, D. (1998). *Black on white: Black writers on what it means to be white*. New York: Schocken Books.

Tatum, B. T. (1997). *Why are all the black kids sitting together in the cafeteria? And other conversations about race*. New York: Basic Books.

Thompson, A. (1999). Book review of *Off white*. Available: http://coe.asu.edu/edrev/reviews/rev76.thm. Wellman, D. (1993). *Portraits of white racism*. New York and Cambridge: Cambridge University Press.

Winant, H. (1997). Behind blue eyes: Whiteness and contemporary U.S. racial politics. In M. Fine, L. Weis, L. C. Powell, & L. M. Wong (Eds.), *Off white: Readings on race, power, and society*. New York: Routledge.

CHAPTER 11

Creating a Third Wave Islamophobia
Formulating Prejudices Through Media

Shirley R. Steinberg

I received an alarming phone call on September 13, 2001. My student called to say she could not attend that evening's class. An observant Muslim, she wore a modest veil to school. As she attempted to shop on September 12 in her predominantly Muslim part of Flatbush, she was spat upon and called names. She realized that she was in danger, and she should not travel to school that week. We saw several instances that echoed this student's experience. My partner called the CNN news desk and asked to speak to a researcher. He related the student's story and suggested that CNN investigate and cover the anti-Muslim incidents in Brooklyn during this period. The reporter laughed and told him that they had more important events to cover, and that, indeed, these incidents should happen more often—*maybe his student got what she deserved.*

After September 11, I watched each breaking news story, in every venue. I knew I had to write about what I saw, heard, and felt. Moreover, I was curious to see how others responded to the barrage of media stemming from that fall day. What emerged in my media-saturated brain? What was it that kept my attention? Romping through the construction of my consciousness dealing with Muslims and Arabic-speaking people, I realized how very easy it was to hate Arabs, to hate Muslims. As soon as those two planes had hit the Twin Towers, the American public was spewing volatile observations about all Arabs, all Muslims. It really took no time at all for an entire country to explode into rampant Islamophobia. And media became our interpreters. Indeed, the constant television and radio coverage served to facilitate and control our perceptions, our knowledges, our conclusions, and our psyches. As a media theorist, I recognized that this horrendous event was going to become curated by media. It was clear to me that the narrative produced by networks would facilitate the narrative viewers would retain (Steinberg, 2007).

How long had I been aware of Muslims? Of Arabs? As a Jewish woman, I have always been aware of my sister religion. In early religious classes I learned that a slave woman, Hagar, had borne Ishmael from Abraham and this lineage begat those considered Arabic. The children of Sarah and Abraham became the Jews. Religious mythology followed me throughout my life—stories of how Arabs became dark-skinned, versions of nomadic existence, and exotic tales from *The Arabian Nights*. I remember watching many early films with Arabs as grand fighters, usually brandishing swords, fighting the White man. I recall veils, belly dancing, tents, camels, large-toothed men with rifles and dirty robes.

My Media Autobiography

When did popular culture collide with my religious stories? In 1962, I sat through *Lawrence of Arabia* (Spiegel, Lean, Lawrence, & Lean, 1962). It did not take long to get the point, and the remainder of the show was tedious: a minor officer from England was sent to visit Prince Faisal and ended up leading an army of Arabic tribes to fight the Turks—he was a hero. I guess that was my earliest media exposure to Arabs.

Sometime around 1968, *Time Magazine* featured a cover story on the plight of the Arab refugees. I recall giving a speech based on the issue; my 16-year-old brain could not understand why the Arabic countries surrounding Israel would not let their Muslim brothers and sisters into their homelands. I understood why the Israelis did not make room—the country was too small and had been given to Jews. My social studies teacher didn't know anything about it.

In June 1968, just down the freeway from my school, Robert Kennedy was shot by Sirhan Sirhan, defined in the news as "a man of Jordanian descent." Many readers may remember the dark and swarthy photos of the murderer, who quickly disappeared from the limelight. A lot of Americans thought all hopes of social equity and freedom died with Bobby that day, at the hand of the Arab.

Four years later, when I began a new college semester, the news hit that Israeli athletes had been kidnapped at the Munich Olympics by Arab terrorists, a group known as Black September. We were glued to the television as we watched cameras cover the occupied residences; we saw shadowy figures identified as the kidnappers on the phone negotiating with authorities. Then we saw the German police shoot and kill the terrorists and athletes on the tarmac of the Munich airport. I have flown to Munich once, and I assumed the tarmac was still there. No one was able to show me where it was. Almost a quarter of a century later, Steven Spielberg produced *Munich* (Kennedy, Mendel, Spielberg, Wilson, & Spielberg, 2005). Ironically, the film did not deal with the city or with much of the terrorists and athletes. It was typical Spielberg-stylized rehistorization, a story of the supposed retaliation of the kidnappings by the Israelis. The film followed the murders of many of the Muslim suspects and was problematic on almost every level: the justification of the revenge killings; the fact that the German authorities were never implicated in the shootout at the airport, and the image of the Twin Towers on the horizon at the end of the film. What knowledge did this loosely historical/fictional film give to the viewers? Many people with whom I spoke had never heard of the Munich massacre, and now Spielberg has given them their history.

I had not visited New York City after the Twin Towers had been built. When the World Trade Center was bombed in 1993 it was shocking, but very removed from my life. I had never seen the buildings. Few were killed, but lots of expensive cars were destroyed. The news reported it was the work of Arabic terrorists. In 1994 we went to New York and scanned the World Trade Center to see where the bomb had hit. We were astounded at how huge the buildings were and how small the bomb damage had been. The buildings were obviously indestructible.

In 1996, I was watching CNN in a hotel in San Francisco—a bomb had destroyed a federal building in Oklahoma City. All of the first reports from the radio, TV, and newspapers indicated that Arabic terrorist groups had planned the mass attack. Hours later, a White man was in custody. No apology was offered to the previously identified, supposed perpetrators. Some Arab Americans complained about the erroneous accusation, but the news quickly moved on to the unfolding Timothy McVeigh story. Upon reflection, I do not recall any attempts by American citizens to spit upon Irish Catholics (McVeigh's background), attack McVeigh's hometown, or pull over White men of 30 who resembled the lanky terrorist.

A network break-in to regular programming in 1997 revealed the headline that Princess Diana had been killed in an auto accident along with her boyfriend, Dodi Fayed. Fayed was a Muslim, an Egyptian, whose wealthy father had been denied British citizenship by the Queen—the elder Fayed owned Harrods of London. Continued tabloid coverage over the years has claimed that Diana could have been murdered in order to keep her from humiliating the royal family by her relationship with an undesirable man.

By the time the first plane hit in lower Manhattan that Tuesday in September, many Americans' cultural curricula had been imprinted and validated. I believe that was why it was so easy to hate Arabs and Muslims. Naturally, we would be able to hate terrorists, but McVeigh was a terrorist, and our hatred and outrage were limited only to him, not his entire culture, religion, state, or community. Media literacy being my field of study, it was obvious that I would analyze the cultural pedagogy of Hollywood—How had Muslims and Arabs been depicted by Hollywood?

I maintain that if pedagogy involves issues of knowledge production and transmission, the shaping of values, and the construction of subjectivity, then popular culture is the most powerful pedagogical force in contemporary America. The pedagogy of popular culture is ideological, of course, in its production of commonsense assumptions about the world, its influence on our affective lives, and its role in the production of our identities and experiences (Grossberg, 1995). Movies help individuals articulate their feelings and moods that ultimately shape their behavior. Audiences employ particular images to help define their own taste, image, style, and identity—indeed, they are students of media and film pedagogy.

Audiences often allow popular culture vis-à-vis films, to speak for them, to provide narrative structures that help them make sense of their lives. This emotional investment by the audience can often be organized in emotional/ideological/affective alliances with other individuals, texts, and consciousness formations. Thus, this effect mobilized by the popular culture of film provides viewers with a sense of belonging, an identification with like-minded individuals—this feeling becomes progressively more important in our fragmented society (Grossberg, 1995). Keeping in mind the complexity of the effects of film popular culture, the effect produced is different in varying historical and social contexts. With these notions in mind, I went in search of the assumptions that may have been made in the viewing of films having Arab or Muslim characters. I did have a couple of research questions in mind: Why is it so easy for many North Americans to hate Muslims? Why are they so easy to fear and blame? With these questions, I hoped the films I viewed would shed some tentative answers, and, more importantly to my own scholarship, provoke more questions.

I selected movies when my viewing signaled that there was sufficient depiction of Arabs and/or Muslims to discuss. I asked others if they recalled any films that I should be viewing. Consequently, these films were culled out of our combined cultural collective. I did not consult written research in order to gather my films; I wanted to know what stood out in our minds from films that depicted Arabs and Islam. I viewed 17 films and scripted scenes and/or dialog that needed reexamination. After I had gathered these data, I revisited my notes in order to identify themes, archetypes, and authorship in the films.

Film and Islam

Most of the films I viewed dealt with Muslim Arabs. However, *Not Without My Daughter* (Ufland, Ufland, & Gilbert, 1990) and *East Is East* (Udwin, Khan-Din, & O'Donnell, 1998) are films about Muslims, not Arabs (those from the Arabian Peninsula). Sally Field's compelling, yet whining performance in *Not Without My Daughter* (based on a true story of one woman's experience) dealt with an American woman married to an Iranian doctor who deceitfully brought his wife and daughter to his home in Iran. Sally did not want to go: "We can't go to Iran—it's much too violent." Swearing on the Qur'an, "Moody" promises they will be safe. After reaching Iran, greeted by a slain goat (in their honor), Sally is horrified. Cultural analysis is attempted by Sally and her spouse: "It just seems so primitive." "Beliefs seem primitive when they aren't your own." Mother and daughter become prisoners as the husband reverts to Ayatollah-generated fundamentalism. "Islam is the greatest gift I can give," assured Moody. Persian women (in full black *burqas*) are yammering, scheming, whispering, and occasionally beaten by their husbands or other available men—this was a dark, frightening, and smothering world to the former Sister Bertrille. Field's character is starkly White in comparison to the darkness that cinematographically depicts the Muslims in the film. Women peering out of slits in their *burqas* are routinely belittled, demeaned, and marginalized by their husbands. There are occasions when Field's character attempts to bond with women and ask for their help. Alas, everyone turns against her, shuns her, or turns her in to her husband. Islam is depicted as unreasonable, and Moody is equally unreasonable, as he immediately becomes a tribalized tyrant to his wife and little girl. When Field reminds Moody of his promise made on the Qur'an and tells a holy man of this breach of faith, she is met with verbal attacks by everyone within earshot. A message is sent to the viewer that Islamic vows on holy books are not kept, and holy men are indeed as evil as everyone else. *Not Without My Daughter* is based on a true story. Obviously, I am in sympathy with anyone whose child is stolen and who is abused by a spouse. However, the film does not center on the marital issues as much as it is an indictment of the entire community in Tehran.

East Is East is BBC-produced and deals with a lower-middle-class Pakistani man who marries a British woman. He insists on being a traditional Muslim, and his wife respects that—as long as her husband does not catch the children carrying the statue of Jesus during the Easter Parade. As the children are proudly marching in the parade, someone warns them that their father is approaching. They toss the religious statues to other people, peel off their costumes, and dash home to be there before their father opens the door. The father is depicted as stupid for not catching on, and the family continues the ruse, being Muslim to their father, but really being Christians. Dad is devastated by his older son bailing out of his own arranged wedding. He tries to match-make the other sons: "I'm not marrying a fucking Paki." As a father he is overbearing in his desire to see his children as happy Muslims—he adds insult to injury as he insists on giving his gift of an Arabic watch to each child. He had saved the watches for a special time and ceremoniously presents each of them with the watch. They explode with anger and disgust imagining that they would actually wear a watch with strange symbols.

They are furious when he insists they go to a school to learn the Qur'an. After various defeats, a broken man, he begins to beat his wife and children. Once again, cinematography plays an important role as the camera angles began to change; as the father gets meaner, his character is filmed from below the nostrils of his huge, sweating, bulbous nose—he also had yellowed, crooked teeth. Within an hour of the film, he transforms from a princely, kindly father and husband (in both appearance and context) to an evil fool. Frustrated, he bemoans that neighbors think he is a barbarian. When interviewed about *East Is East*, the actors (most of whom were South Asian) agreed that the film was an important document of immigration and acculturation into British society. None of them even alluded to the racist, Islamophobic depictions of Pakistanis and Muslims.

Tontos and Sancho Panzas: Hollywood Sidekicks

The other films I viewed were about Arabs—those from Arabia (or countries divided from Arabia). With the exception of *Lawrence of Arabia* (Spiegel et al., 1962), all movies were filmed in the West. *Lawrence of Arabia* is a dramatic (and long) saga about a blond, blue-eyed Englishman who, caught up in the myth of Arabia and the desert, convinces marauding rival Bedouin bands of "barbarians" to unite in their fight against the equally barbaric Turks. Peter O'Toole's character is a prototype to Sean Connery and Mel Gibson and is accompanied by Omar Sharif, once an enemy—now a converted sidekick. Angering the British; "Has he gone native?" Lawrence eventually leaves Arabia—naturally, in better condition than he found it: "I did it." "Arabia is for the Arabs now."

Sharif, as a desert sheikh, begins as a proud, brilliant warrior. However, as he is tamed by O'Toole, he becomes his bodyguard, brother-in-arms, and gives his life for O'Toole. He is reduced in the film from a man of stature to a colonized camel rider. Sharif's character is the example for others to follow. It is obvious to all who watch that the Arabs in tribal form could never survive and that the British and Lawrence were sent as divine leaders to organize and unite the different groups. Interestingly, even as Lawrence exoticizes the natives—wears their clothing, rides camels, and imitates their lives—he never forgets that he is an Englishman and that they are barbarians: "Any time spent in a bed would be a waste—they are a nation of sheepskins." "They (the Arabs) are dirty savages." "Arabs are a barbarous people."

As with Sharif in *Lawrence of Arabia*, many of the films introduce a sidekick character for the White male lead. Loyal and faithful to death, the Tonto-ized friend is simpler, devoutly Muslim, full of Islamic platitudes and premonitions, and is frightened easily. In two of the Indiana Jones films, *Indiana Jones and the Raiders of the Lost Ark* (Lucas, Kazanjian, Kasdan, & Spielberg, 1981) and *Indiana Jones and the Last Crusade* (Lucas, Marshall, Boam, & Spielberg, 1989), both of which are set in the Middle East, Indy is accompanied by his Egyptian pal who fears that Indy's ideas are dangerous and will create anger from Allah. He attempts to convince Indiana that he is not stupid: "even in this part of the world we are not entirely uncivilized." Endangered at times, this minstrelized sidekick puts his hands in the air, opens his eyes widely, and shouts for safety. Tonto is a Spanish word for stupid or idiot.

Filling in the Scene with Arabs

Ironically, films that were Arabic in context and content had little to do with Arabs. *Abbott and Costello Meet the Mummy* (Christie, Grant, & Lamont, 1955), *Casablanca* (Wallis, Philip, Epstein, & Curtiz, 1943), *The Mummy* (Daniel, Jacks, & Sommers, 1999), *The Mummy Returns* (Jacks, Daniel, Sommers & Underwood, 2001), *Ishtar* (May, 1987), and *The Jewel of the Nile* (Douglas, Rosenthal, Konner, & Teague, 1985) contain plots directly concerned with Arabic/Islamic themes. Actors with dialog, though, are Western. Depending on the film, extras appeared to be Arabic. Action shots with Arabic peoples are almost exclusively shot in loud marketplaces. No heads are left uncovered; the fez is an accessory of choice for comical extras. The militaristic extras (sword carrying) most often wore a *kaffiyeh* (couture Arafat), and several Arabs sported turbans. What struck me about the extras was the "clumping" in which they would always appear. Let me borrow from Joe Kincheloe as he describes the French Fry Guys of McDonaldland: "The most compelling manifestation of conformity in McDonaldland involves the portrayal of the French Fry Guys. As the only group of citizens depicted in the Hamburger Patch, these faceless commoners are numerous but seldom seen" (Kincheloe, 2004). They intend to look, act, and think pretty much alike. Parent French Fry Guys are indistinguishable from children, and vice versa. They are so much alike that, so far, no individual French Fry Guy has emerged as a personality identifiable from the others. They resemble little mops with legs and eyes and speak in squeaky, high-pitched voices, usually in unison. They always move quickly, scurrying around in fits and starts (McDonald's Customer Relations Center, 1994). Kincheloe goes on: "As inhabitants of a McDonaldized McWorld, the French Fry Guys are content to remove themselves from the public space, emerging only for brief and frenetic acts of standardized consumption—their only act of personal assertion." In these films, Hollywood's French-frying of Arabs leaves them to stand in clumps, to surround the action, to yell loudly in the background, and to run the market. They are incompetent in keeping their shop area organized as someone is always running through it, knocking the wares down, and leaving a fist-flinging *kaffiyeh*-clad merchant screaming from behind.

White Boy Saviors and Dirty, Smelly Arabs

Included in my content/discourse analysis of these films was woven the weft of the White, male leader: sent to save citizens or artifacts from unscrupulous individuals. Lawrence and Indiana serve as perfect

Aryan messiahs to these dark, mysterious Muslims. The word barbaric (or barbarous, barbarian) was used in each film. *Aladdin* (Disney Studios, 1992–1996) opens with an overture and opening song that describes the mysterious, dark, barbaric East. Indeed, after the first release of *Aladdin*, American Muslims were irate that the opening song talked about cutting off an ear. … The music was changed; however, references to "it's barbaric, but, hey … it's home" were kept.

Physical characteristics of the Arabs generally show bad teeth, large hooked noses, and unclean tunics and caftans, and headgear that are just a tad too exaggerated. Once again, *Aladdin* does not run more than five minutes without describing one of the Arabic characters as "pungent." The films I viewed metaphorically included aroma vision, as one could vividly smell the camel-dirt-smeared, sweat-clinging clothing of Muslim characters. The market scenes imply that Islamic countries center their cities and livelihoods on the marketplace. The Shylockization of these people is obvious in their attempts to barter and cheat consumers. Indeed, once again, in *Aladdin*, the fat, toothless, dirty Arab "businessman" flings out his tablecloth and "for-sale" sign and indicates that anything can be bought for a price. As I take in his hooked nose and sales pitch, the Semite in his character reminds me vividly that both Jews and Arabs share many of the same stereotypes: they lie, cheat, and steal.

Prototypes for Hatred

Islamic characters are not only compared to other Semites through an analysis, but also to other marginalized groups. There were many, many visible comparisons to Hollywood depictions and assumptions about African Americans. Many times I was sure that the negrofication of these characters served to show that any hated group can be exchanged with another. Exemplifying this is the language that served to incant slurs to African Americans: sand nigger and dune coon were among the nastiest I heard in the films. Negative characteristics of Arabs and Muslims are not compared to those of White people.

While Indiana Jones deals with Nazis in *Raiders*, their characters adhere to the traditional expectations of viewers. The Nazis are anal, obsessive (anal-obsessed?), cruel—but clean and human. The characterization of Arabs always has an underlying implication that puts them on the borderline between human and animal. In each film, Whiteness is the standard to which all Arabs and Muslims are measured. In addition to the racism that Whiteness nurtures, the categories, the lexicon, the otherization, all become stenciled from one race and ethnicity to the other. When a group of people has been defined and depicted with such singular definition, it seems apparent that viewers can become complicit in fear and racism.

24 Ways to Stereotype on Television

When I first published a version of this article in our book, *The Miseducation of the West: How Schools and the Media Distort Our Understanding of the Islamic World* (Kincheloe & Steinberg, 2004), I concentrated on the images of both Arabic peoples and Muslims in films. 9/11 had just happened, and the public was quick to make connections to the stereotypes of Arabs and Muslims seen in the cinema. Television had, for the most part, ignored, avoided, or just didn't bother with much in the way of Islamic or Arabic themes, characters, or even plots. The short-lived *Whoopi* (2004–2004) sitcom did include Whoopi Goldberg's sidekick, Nasim Khatenjami, played by London-born Iranian comedian, Omid Djalili. The interplay of the two characters was indeed refreshing, and Djalili's character asides were insightful and addressed issues that were at play in anti-Arabic sentiments (naturally, the show was canceled within a year). Other than *Whoopi*, Arabic and Islamic characters had seldom been part of American TV landscape.

When the 24-hour-a-day broadcasts of 9/11 had become yesterday's news, there was a period in which television seemed to have declared a silence on all things Arab. Occasionally a show would mention September 11, and a few dramas would bring in racist behaviors against Muslims. *Law & Order*, *NYPD Blue*, and other dramas were some of the first TV shows based on racism against Arabs. A common scenario included a store or restaurant owner, and a terrorized and tortured family, victims of those who blamed 9/11 on them. The Islamic families were portrayed as hardworking and honest, and the show was well received. Thematic shows grew around the issue of White/American hatred and fear of Arabs and Muslims. It began to appear on television that different shows were willing to tackle the notion of Islamophobia by association to 9/11. Possibly television would be a medium which would equalize the overt racism associated with cinematic Muslims and Arabs. My hopes were brief, the warm vibes that television had begun to radiate cooled off, and Arabic and Muslim-bad-guy-themed shows emerged. Kiefer Sutherland's blockbusting hit, *24*, was supposed to debut in September 2001. After the World Trade Center attacks, Fox network and Sutherland determined it would be prudent and politically sensitive to delay the show until late fall. Based on a fictional American Counterterrorist Unit, Sutherland's *Jack Bauer* would save the day each season fighting world-threatening terrorist threats. Due to the nature of the show, producers felt it would touch nerves. So close to September 11, it would be in bad taste. The show finally began late in 2001, ranking between 29th and 74th for the first three seasons. Jack Bauer saved the world three years in a row, having fought biological weapons, South American terrorism, and a manipulative and sociopathic First Lady.

In 2004, the Season 4 of *24* featured a Muslim family: mother, father, and teenaged son engaged in a deadly day. An upstanding, middle-class, suburban family, Navi, Dina, and Berooz Araz are thrown into chaos by Turkish Muslim terrorist Habib Marwan's desire to destroy the United States. Navi and Dina had been planted in Los Angeles as part of a small cell whose existence was based on waiting for Marwan's signal to join the jihad. Sixteen-year-old Berooz had not been aware of his parents' other life, and faced his own father's attempt to kill him when Berooz tried to stop the terrorists. Familial love was replaced by Navi's barbaric allegiance to Marwan's evil goals. As I began to view that new season of *24*, I watched the first episodes waiting for the foil—the twist, one that would take us away from the plot that was starting to develop. My media-viewing mind was begging Sutherland to not *go there*. I started to see that Hollywood's détente with Arabs and Muslims was over. They became fair game for directors and producers, and a support system for American governmental policies in the Middle East. The only twist was the tension produced in a new narrative: the evil terrorist Muslims were counterbalanced by the good Muslims. Young Berooz rebelled against his terrorist inheritance, never wavering from his commitment to goodness and the United States. Dina reluctantly worked with Jack Bauer to bring down Habib Marwan, and Navi, the evil father, was killed. The season ended with Jack victorious, and viewers were torn between the terrorist threat of the Turkish Muslim cell and the innate goodness of young Berooz. A polarized view of the Muslims was left with the audience; for every bad Muslim there was a good Muslim.

Other than the depiction of the terrorists as evil, dark-skinned, and determined fundamentalists, Fox could claim plausible deniability as to anti-Muslim sentiments. Themes were established that:

- Muslims are in our midst, hiding among us, they can be upscale; can be our next-door neighbors.

- They would do anything; even kill their own child for the cause.

- Occasionally there are good Muslims who step up to serve the greater good of America.

Season 4 brought *24* into the top 25 shows of the year. I certainly never expected an Islamic-themed *24* again, Fox had pushed it as far as it could go and was lucky to get away with it. Smartly peppering the bad guys with the redeemable Muslims, they had made it through a highly rated season.

Season 5 returned Jack Bauer to a terrorist plot that dealt with internal political terror. Before the premiere of Season 6, the United States was going through political changes. The Bush Administration suffered an overwhelming loss to the Democrats in the November election and the American public was ostensibly becoming antiwar in regard to the occupation of Iraq. Television news was a hotly contested venue between the far-right via Fox news and conservative talking heads and the newly vocal "liberal" reports. After losing Republican seats and acknowledging that Iraq was not working out as planned, the Bush regime began to repeat their worries of losing to not only the angry Iraqi people, but to the terrorists who wanted to take away our freedom and occupy our own country. There became a need to revilify Muslims.

An unprecedented media campaign on major news programs highlighted the January 2007 return of Jack Bauer. As in previous seasons, no one was privy to the plot of the new year, and since Jack had conquered Latin American, Russian, Turkish, and presidential terrorists, Fox would have to come up with something new. The first four episodes of the show were aired back-to-back, indicating that again the show was relying on Muslim-themed terrorists.

The premiere of Season 6 of 24 begins with Jack Bauer's realization of urban unrest. Terrorist attacks are taking place all over the United States; the entire country is in a state of panic and alert. The man who is blamed for the attacks is Assad, and the audience is quickly aware that the plot will again be Muslim terrorists in 2007: "These people are in the Stone Age," a government agent explains. This time Fox had not anticipated the public and media uproar created by the first six episodes. Within the first two nights, Islamic terrorists had exploded the first of the five nuclear bombs in urban Los Angeles. (As the story was told, I was convinced that someone in production had read my work on Hollywood stereotypes and made a point of planting them in every frame possible.)

Jack Bauer joins reformed terrorist Assad, to apprehend Abu Fayed, the author of the domestic chaos and death. Fayed has been running a cell out of Los Angeles. Scene switches to a Los Angeles upscale suburb, and we see two large White men beating the teenaged Muslim Ahmed. He is saved by his best friend's father and brought to the safety of their home. The father and his son are astonished at the unreasonable racism demonstrated toward an innocent family. Ahmed's father was not home, and they insist he stay with them. Very quickly Ahmed's demeanor changes and he is an irrational Islamicist who is indeed part of Fayed's cell. Somehow Fayed has recruited this young American Muslim into his plot, unbeknownst to even his father. Ahmed holds the family hostage and threatens to kill them. We learn again that suburban, upscale "nice" Muslim families can, indeed, be sleeper cells.

Meanwhile, in Washington, the president's sister, who heads the Islamic American Alliance, has been arrested along with her colleague, Walid. They have been unlawfully held against their will, she calls her brother who reminds her that these are terrible times and there is no protection from unreasonable search and seizure, and that the terrorist activities demand that war measures be taken. The two are taken to a holding camp full of Muslims. Quickly, the sister is released, leaving Walid in the prison yard. Walid overhears men discussing terrorist activities and quickly realizes they are involved in the attacks all over the country. The viewer is given a second lesson, there is a reason for unlawful arrest, because chances are that bad guys will be included in the sweep. The shell-shocked Jack Bauer had planned to quit CTU; however, after realizing what the Muslim terrorists had done, he remarks that "he is back, he [is not quitting], not after this."

Again, themes are established:

- They can be anywhere, hiding in our best neighborhoods.

- Even the youth are involved in terrorist endeavors; they will kill you, even a best friend who has saved your life.

- Suspension of habeas corpus is justified because in the twenty-first-century world of jihad, it works to identify Muslims and Arabs, thus possibly stopping the terrorists and thwarting their actions.

- Even if some innocents are involved, it is indeed, for the greater good.

24 is Dick Cheney's favorite show.

Terrorists are Everywhere

Cable TV's *Sleeper Cell* reinforces the fears that *24* has begun but takes them miles further. *Sleeper Cell* first aired in December of 2005 on Showtime; its first two seasons went unchallenged and flew far below any entertainment news or network news radar. Created by writing partners, Ethan Reiff and Cyrus Voris, the show features the first American Muslim protagonist, Darwyn, played by African American Michael Ealy. The show taglines delineate important points:

> Friends. Neighbors. Husbands. Terrorists.
> The enemy is here.
> Know your enemy.
>   (2005; www.http//indb.com/title/H0465353/taglines)

Sleeper Cell: American Terrorist uses different opening credits. One of the most significant openings played in Season 1: the music was distinctly soft, a cello playing an Arabic tune, a map appears, it shows the boundaries of Iraq on the top and Arabia as the "country" on the bottom of the map; as the credits flash faster, the music picks up, becomes louder, and has women wailing indistinguishable Arabic sounds. Quick vignettes of White children in swimming pools, White people shopping, flashes of the American flag, dark Arabic-type men, flash back to American flag, White kids playing in a park—music gets louder, long shot of a GPS centering in on a neighborhood, then a large, suburban home, the GPS locks on the home, close-up, show begins.

To eliminate long summaries, I will bullet some of the episodes from the first two seasons:

Season 1: *Sleeper Cell: American Terror*

- Episode 1: American Muslim Darwyn goes undercover for FBI to uncover sleeper cells. He is recruited at a synagogue by a Holy Warrior. Taken to the desert, Darwyn is encouraged to stone a traitor to the group, he shoots him instead.

- Episode 2: Anthrax becomes the threat, probably for a shopping mall. Darwyn makes more connections.

- Episode 3: Mexican money is to come through the border to finance the plot.

- Episode 4: The Mexican money dries up, so it will come through Canada.

- Episode 7: A young Afghani boy approaches the terrorists to become a jihadist.

- Episode 8: White supremacists cooperate with the Holy Warriors in order to get explosives.

- Episode 9: A truck is hijacked; it is disguised as a LA Airport Mobile Emergency Command Vehicle. Two more cells in the United States have been discovered.

- Episode 10: The cell escapes FBI surveillance.

Season 2: *Sleeper Cell: American Terror*

- Episode 1: Darwyn tries to leave FBI and cell, but his FBI contact, a woman, is beheaded in Sudan by terrorists.

- Episode 2: The leader of the cell, Farik, played by Israeli Oded Fehr, seems impossible to break under questioning.

- Episode 3: Farik is deported to Saudi Arabia in hopes that he can be tortured legally there and give up the cell. Cell orders Darwyn to get a weapon.

- Episode 4: Darwyn saves the life of an Islamic televangelist. One of the terrorists watches the evangelist on TV as he runs on a treadmill between two blonde women. Farik escapes Al-Qaeda prison in Saudi Arabia.

- Episode 5: Nukes become the next threat to Los Angeles.

And so it goes. A search of the Showtime website allows the surfer to play a game in which he or she becomes the member of a sleeper cell. An Islamic dictionary is featured:

Learn the definition and history behind some of the Islamic phrases used during the show. Study now!

At the end of a particularly violent episode, Farik is in a palace in Saudi Arabia, dressed in traditional clothing, he is considering Darwyn becoming the leader of the cell in Los Angeles. The closing credits roll, and a rap song is played loudly. I could not find the artist or all of the lyrics on line or on the episode, so forgive my not crediting the lyrics. Here are some of the phrases from the song:

"Tell me what you think at this."
"You can never understand till we do what we do."
"I can prove what we do given a situation."
"I can come up with a plan."
"Never be ashamed, always be proud."
"So go and do what you do, keep watching the news."
"I got a question for y'all,"
"You think we goin' to let another building fall?"
"Never Again."
"Fuck that. … Send me back to Iraq."

Using a type of affective ideology (see Kincheloe & Steinberg, 1997), the audience is given no reason or argument in a scenario or storyline; instead, the music behind the credits goes directly to our primal affect. It bypasses any filters within the brain that may use logic or rationale and leaves us with a visceral impression. One does not expect the listener to politically deconstruct these lyrics, the affective part of the mind draws the connection between a falling building and Iraq and consequently, the invasion and occupation of Iraq are justified by patriots.

Sleeper Cell may be the very best of the worst in the genre. Each episode is produced with cinematic mastery, every hour with the quality of a fine Hollywood film. The writers and actors are not Arabic, neither are the creators. While Jewish names appear in the credit, distinctly Arabic or Middle Eastern names do not appear. Showtime is a network which has always run edgy and topical shows; however, it has usually leaned to the liberal or left in its ideology. The cell is extremely threatening to viewers; sites chosen for detonation or exposure to deadly chemicals are baseball parks, shopping malls, places in which the normal middle American exists. The cell is insidious and impossible to break; even with Darwyn planted as a mole, the threat is never extinguished. Ending a season with Darwyn "saving the day," he is handed back his pocket copy of the Qur'an; he then finds a lost little blond boy, and the mother thanks him with deep appreciation. He is the Muslim Jack Bauer; he saves the day but is always aware that the cells grow and that he must stay with the job. Any bad guys that are caught, under the laws of war, are "nonprivileged" combatants; they are not put in jail, will not go to trial, and will be placed in holding by the Defense Department. Darwyn's conflicted self is always close to the surface, and when he finishes saving his day, he often retreats to the mosque to receive spiritual solace.

The themes are repeated and added upon:

- They are everywhere, they have penetrated to every part of our society.

- Even vehicles are suspect; an official vehicle can easily masquerade as an emergency vehicle.

- There may be good Muslims, but there always will be bad Muslims.

- We are in Iraq for a purpose, to avenge the 9/11 attacks, and to keep Middle Eastern terrorists from American soil.

Again, this content analysis demands that we recognize the advent of *Sleeper Cell* and the seasons of *24* that correspond with the loss of faith in Republican leadership and the demand to leave Iraq from the American public. Media does matter; it speaks to us, and it can be a better tool than any other to reach viewing citizens.

Everyone Is a Bad Guy

An episode of *Law & Order* (Makris, 2006) opened with an American flag covered by a poster: UNITED AMERICANS FOR ONE AMERICA: ARABS GO HOME. We hear an Anglo voice yelling: "Get up, get up, you Arab pig." A masked man in camouflage pushes a man hooded in black in front of the flag. The entire scene is being videotaped. Another man joins the assailant and they both stand with the victim on his knees flanked by the stars and stripes. The first man speaks: "Lolliyops, towelheads, camel jockeys, you are not Americans, you are parasites living off our citizens, you cheer when our GIs die in Iraq. Why do you live in our country if you hate our way of life?" His partner speaks: "You think we're scared of your jihad? After today, be scared of us, this is our jihad." He takes a knife to the throat of the now-unhooded, crying Arabic man, "God bless America!" he slices the throat of the young man. Cut to the law examining the scene. Following the discovery of the videotape, the investigators spend a great deal of time looking for this White supremacist group which is targeting Arabs and Muslims. Going from one dead end to another, the case resolves itself when a cousin of the dead Muslim is found to be guilty. He had created the scenario of supremacists to keep suspicion from falling upon him. Justice is served; the Arabs are the bad guys, and any White supremacists are relieved from suspicion.

In January 2007, an episode of *Law & Order: Criminal Intent* (Shill, 2007) revolves around the brutal murder of a young Pakistani woman, Meena, who films a group of White and Jewish men beating Latino immigrant workers. The men are seen chasing the woman, trying to take her camera; her film leaves evidence of these White assailants. Hearing a news story of a Jewish woman hit by a car filled with Mexican immigrants on her way to synagogue, the detectives surmise: "this has got to be payback." Discussing the case with a Jewish man (wearing a blue yarmulke with stars of David surrounding it) who admitted being at the beating, he queries: "Some illegal alien runs over a mother and her baby and you arrest me? … We didn't hurt the Mexicans, or that Arab girl. We just want these people out of our neighborhood, before they kill any more of our children." Turns out he was telling the truth; his group merely chased her, scared her, and then he went to the synagogue to teach Hebrew. His rabbi backs him up.

The investigators view a film that Meena had made about her family living in New York. Affluent restaurant owners, Meena's parents had lost everything after patrons stopped coming to dine post-9/11. The detectives are emotionally touched as they view this family's experiences as they are punished for being Muslim. After investigation, the men who had been filmed beating the men were exonerated. The plot leads detectives to find the Pakistani woman had been in love with an Italian, and indeed, it seems obvious that he killed her. She was pregnant with his child. The Pakistani parents mourn the death of their daughter and her sexual violation. The father shows his fury by lashing out at the Italian boyfriend. Her brother watches silently as his family disintegrates. A *Romeo and Juliet* story emerges. The families are intent on blaming one another. A marriage had been arranged with a man who has just come to the States from Pakistan. He is gruff and swarthy and much older than the young murdered victim. He is a suspect for a few days but makes it clear he would have never hurt her as he had no emotional ties to her. Her pregnancy ruled her unfit to be his wife, and he intended to return to Pakistan.

After Chris Noth's (Detective Logan's) crackerjack psychological cop intervention, Meena's brother breaks down and admits he murdered his own sister to protect the good name of his family: she had humiliated them all. It had been an honor killing.

Both these *Law & Order* episodes promote themes:

- Even when you think all the Arabs and/or Muslims are not guilty, one of them is guilty.

- Mexican or Arab, immigrants are not welcome in our country.

- Familial honor is more important than love and loyalty; killing one's sister is honorable.

- Arabic and Muslim peoples create White scenarios to deflect attention from their own criminal activities.

Understanding First, Second, and Now Third Wave Islamophobia

Critical media literacy allows us to understand damaging stereotypes. The early films I watched related to viewers a centuries-long depiction of how Arabs and/or Muslims. While incredibly problematic, I acknowledge that these caricatures are not exclusive. Indeed, critical media viewing will reveal misogyny, racism, homophobia, multiple hatreds, all promoted through film and television. As our culture becomes more aware of notions of antiracism, equity, and social justice, these stereotypes become contested and slowly are adjusted to respect and acknowledge those who have been otherized. I suggest that the stereotypes presented pre-9/11 represent a wave of Islamophobia I will call the First Wave. This refers to stereotypes and hatreds presented through ignorance and a desire to incite, but also to sell.

The Second Wave of Islamophobia was created by noon on September 11, 2001. That day ushered in a new Islamphobia through fear exacerbated by the horror of that day. Driven by fear and anger, it began within the news reports, over media, and quickly became a societal drive. It is important to understand that this Second Wave was based on the incredible helplessness many felt while watching and rewatching thousands of innocents die due to the actions of 19 men, all of whom were Muslim. These responses were human and to be expected, what was not expected was the violent outcry and reaction to many Black or Brown people, and hatred of an ancient, global religion and culture. While human behavior can be understood, what was/is alarming is the sustained hatred and fear of *all* Muslims and Arabs. Almost two decades later, we are not seeing a healthy change or reduction of Islamophobia; indeed, I suggest that again, the procedures and sentiments of Islamophobia have not only increased, but have morphed into a Third Wave.

While certainly not condoned, but somewhat understandable, Second Wave Islamophobia dealt with the fear of reprisal, the shock of a surprise attack, and the notion that North Americans were no longer as safe as perhaps they thought they were. Bringing a type of war, a violent attack across oceans alerted citizens that no country was safe from an attack, by any organized group. This lack of security, of safety, and loss of confidence was replicated after 9/11 in media in every form.

In the second decade following the attacks on September 11, 2001, we have seen a change in the enacting of Islamophobia on media. I would offer this as the Third Wave of Islamophobia. The first being classic, the second a reaction directly related to 9/11, and the third being an institutionalized, political initiative to target one particular ethnic/religious group.

I moved from New York City in 2006 to Montreal, Canada. In 2007, the Bouchard-Taylor hearings began, visiting cities and towns in the Canadian Province of Quebec. Basically, the hearings were questioning the right of different sects to wear certain items of clothing. The question(s) directly responsible for the hearings dealt with asking how *reasonable* should accommodation for different clothing be? Should women be allowed to cover their faces due to religious requirements? The interest in this issue stemmed from attention brought from a conflict with Sikh men wearing a kirpan (small ceremonial knife/sword) under clothing. In 2006, the Canadian Supreme Court ruled that the kirpan was legal, it should be covered and hidden under clothes. However, this question advanced into reactions which become xenophobic in many ways. I would assert that these actions and future production in the media were a direct and politicized result of the post-11 Second Wave; however, it differed in many ways.

Discussed in the Quebec hearings were the rights of other religious people to wear clothing appropriate to their beliefs, and led by groups who insisted they were feminist and acting on the behalf of all Muslim women. Immediately, Muslim women in Quebec began to be harassed for wearing veils or burqas in public places. Arguments from the groups were that Muslim women were oppressed and forced to wear coverings; however, the hearings centered on what was considered appropriate and *safe* to wear in Quebec society. Muslim women became the target of the conversation, veiled women being sent from class unless they uncovered, harassment at the airport, different instances were reported. This became an enormous feminist issue in that it begged for a conversation as to *just who* determines what any woman desires to wear. Again, this brings in the question of power. Who speaks for whom? In this case, non-Muslim women led the charge to oppress and define Muslim women. Eventually, the hearings ended, and in this case, no changes were legislated about Muslim or other religious clothing. This should stand as an embarrassment to the Province of Quebec and to those who insist on speaking for others, assuming they know best.

As a media scholar, I have observed more than a passing Islamophobic craze, but a concerted effort to repress and change an existing society. Conversations about women's veils quickly become about security, and intimating that *any* woman wearing a veil or burqa could be a terrorist. However, in 2017 Quebec passed a bill banning Muslim women to wear a niqab or full-veiled clothing in schools, hospitals, or public transportation. This topic is continually under debate, emulating similar legislated attempts in Belgium, France, and other EU countries, we see that Third Wave Islamophobia is gaining attention and strength.

In 2006, a group of youth in Toronto were arrested for allegedly being an al-Qaeda cell. What is important about this arrest is that the assumption of large amounts of cells, comprised of Muslim youth in both the United States and Canada, became a central focus for police and governments; however, to this date, almost 20 years after 9/11, no evidence has been found of any organized attempts to infiltrate either Canada or the United States by any organized group of youth or citizens of either North American country. By using isolated incidents like the arrest of youth, and the hatred and fear instigated by the 2006 hearings, Muslims and Arabs, in a kind of wholesale assumption, became the direct objects of government suspicion and, in turn, the "stars" of fear and loathing on media. Not to minimize any type of death by killing, it is important for us to understand that while death by terrorism from 2006–2016 was approximately 3600 people worldwide (Statistics Portal, 2018), the death toll by guns in the United States alone in 2016 was over 38,000 (*Time,* 2017). Media however, has created a terrorist obsession about Muslims and Arabs and emphasis on gun violence in the US is largely ignored. The power of media to skew *truths*, create fear, and change the story is evident.

The sophistication of Third Wave Islamophobia goes far beyond the ranting and raving of the father in *East Is East* or the silly depictions of Arabic warriors in *Indiana Jones* films. Avoiding the accusation of being Islamophobic, recent film and television producers have learned how to maintain Islamophobia, but avoid being called out for its use. *Homeland* was in its seventh season (2018) on Fox, starring Claire Danes as an imperfect CIA operative; it is sophisticated in its production and scope, indeed, with Danes and Mandy Patinkin, both liberal in their politics, it presents complex plots and topics, often questioning who, exactly, *them or us*, are the bad guys [*sic*]. It took me several seasons of analysis to attempt to find any institutionalized and overt Islamophobia, and in the fifth season, it was not the plot, but the season promotional posters that came to light. In promoting Season 6 of *Homeland*, only one poster was released. It was a picture of Claire Danes, a blonde woman, clothed in a red cloak and hood. She had her head turned to face the viewer, her exposed, her blue eyes. Danes was surrounded by hordes of faceless, niqab-clad women, all in black, they appeared as anonymous threats in the shape of black lumps of cloth, pushing in on Danes, surrounding her, threatening her. The poster was alarming. It appeared as if this Anglo woman was being crushed by the sheer weight and pressure of all of these unidentified, incognito women. Connecting this with the original hearings in Quebec, the new legislation against women in niqabs, the legislations in Belgium and France, and the rising degree of crimes *against* Muslims and Arabs, I realized that the new Islamophobia was about symbols, figures, and creating a culture of fear of everything Muslim and Arab. No longer connecting it to 9/11, this Islamophobia has appeared from presidents and prime ministers, offering no explanation as to *why* Muslims and Arabs cannot enter countries, immigrate, and why they are systematically expelled.

Third Wave Islamophobia is about power and media. It is about maintaining political power, which insists that a populous must have an enemy (Steinberg, 2009), and it is about media control and propaganda. All terrorism must be condemned, however, by depicting all Muslims and Arabs as enemies, those in power are able to control not only citizenry, but legislate military action, take natural resources (oil and gas), and create an enemy. When a government has an enemy, control of the people is done by what Antonio Gramsci (see Chapter 1) refers to as *hegemony*: the ability to win consent of the citizenry without war or violence, but by suggestion and symbolism. The ability to analyze media, which is the strongest tool to use in the world today, is an ability to read between the lines. Understanding media is essential for our students to become empowered, asking students, *In whose interest is this news story? How are stereotypes used in this show? What is the hidden message behind how this ethnic group is being treated?*

Teaching against Islamophobia: Critical Media Literacy

There is no doubt that we have seen and experienced mass murder, destruction, terror, and horror. Often, the media rushes to define and recreate the story to sell. No longer is the news considered unbiased or historical; indeed, the media is another part of capital, created to sell and for us to buy. As a journalism student I was taught the first day of class, that we chase the story: *if it bleeds, lead*. Media has been conditioned to report what sells, not necessarily what is accurate or responsible. It is essential for us to understand that we must interrogate media and not assume that it is *truth*. Islamophobia is a sign of the power of media to create fear. This is not to say that 9/11 did not happen, but to say that the event created a pandemic which has led to a societal hatred that has no merit. Using a critical media literacy lens to understand the sources of this hatred and fear is essential to continue our attempt to be a democratic society (Kincheloe, Steinberg, & Stonebanks, 2010).

Do we ask why it is easy for many North Americans to hate Muslims? Why are they so easy to fear and blame? We have had concrete reasons to deplore the actions of any terrorists. Islamic terrorism has been tapped as a vehicle to move the causes of many different organizations all over the globe. As a Jew I have always been conflicted as to who has rights over Jerusalem, over the Temple Mount, over Israel. However, my own research has allowed me to reconsider how the construction of my own consciousness has been formed, in a large part, by media. Through my own content analysis of a few TV shows and films, I believe I have isolated dangerous themes which are potent enough to infuse the minds of both children and adult viewers. We offer little or no way to read these themes, to learn how to safely and intelligently view media. Many believe that if it is on TV or placed on film by a legitimate source, then the text is accurate and correct. That text directly feeds our emotional and intellectual selves into making political decisions, personal decisions. If we are able to work with students and parents to learn how to "read" film, the news, the papers, perhaps conversation involving injustice could surround the actions of those that do wrong, not their nationality or religion. We must create a curriculum that enables students to read the media, not to eliminate or censor, but to read. I maintain my contention that indeed popular culture is a curriculum—an overt, influential curriculum that feeds our need to consume entertainment. This Hollywood diet is not innocent: It is constructed on obsession, stereotype, fear, and, most importantly, on what sells. As teachers, it is our social responsibility to facilitate our students when reading the menu.

References

Grossberg, L. (1995, Spring). What's in a name? (one more time). *Taboo: The Journal of Culture and Education,* 1–37.

Kincheloe, J. L. (2004). McDonald's, power, and children: Ronald McDonald (aka Ray Kroc) does it all for you. In S. R. Steinberg & J. L. Kincheloe (Eds.), *Kinderculture: The corporate control of childhood.* Boulder, CO: Westview Press.

Kincheloe, J. L., & Steinberg, S. R. (1997). *Changing multiculturalism: New times, new curriculum.* London: Open University Press.

Kincheloe, J. L., & Steinberg, S. R. (2004). *The miseducation of the West: How schools and the media distort our understanding of the Islamic world.* Westport, CT: Praeger Press.

Kincheloe, J. L., Steinberg, S. R., & Stonebanks, C. D. (2010). *Teaching against Islamophobia.* New York, NY: Peter Lang.

Macedo, D., & Steinberg, S. R. (Eds.). (2007). *Media literacy: A reader.* New York, NY: Peter Lang.

Steinberg, S. R. (2007). Islamophobia: The viewers and the viewed. In D. Macedo & S. R. Steinberg (Eds.), *Media literacy: A reader.* New York, NY: Peter Lang.

Steinberg, S. R. (Ed.). (2009). *Diversity and multiculturalism: A reader.* New York, NY: Peter Lang.

Filmography

Christie, H. (Producer), Grant, J. (Writer), & Lamont, C. (Director). (1955). *Abbott and Costello meet the mummy.* United States: Universal Studios.

Daniel, S., & Jacks, J. (Producers), & Sommers, S. (Writer/Director). (1999). *The mummy.* United States: Universal Studios.

Disney Studios (Producer). (1992–1996). *Aladdin.* United States: Disney Studios.

Douglas, M. (Producer), Rosenthal, M., & Konner, L. (Writers), & Teague, L. (Director). (1985). *The jewel of the Nile.* United States: Twentieth Century Fox.

Gordon, H., & Gansa, A. (Developers). (2011). *Homeland.* United States: Fox21.

Jacks, J., & Daniel, S. (Producers), Sommers, S. (Writer), & Underwood, R. (Director). (2001). *The mummy returns.* United States: Universal Studios.

Kennedy, K., Mendel, B., Spielberg, S., & Wilson, C. (Producers), & Spielberg, S. (Director). (2005). *Munich.* United States: Universal Studios.

Lucas, G., & Kazanjian, H. (Producers), Kasdan, L. (Writer), & Spielberg, S. (Director). (1981). *Indiana Jones and the raiders of the lost ark.* United States: Paramount.

Lucas, G., & Marshall, F. (Producers), Boam, J. (Writer), & Spielberg, S. (Director). (1989). *Indiana Jones and the last crusade.* United States: Paramount.

Makris, C. (Director), Nathan, R., & Postiglione, S. (Writers). (2006). *NBC: Law & order.* Season 17, Episode 17006, "Fear America." Airdate: 13 October 2006.

May, E. (Director). (1987). *Ishtar.* United States: Columbia Pictures.

Shill, S. (Director), & Reingold, J. (Writer). (2007). *NBC: Law & order: Criminal intent.* Season 6, Episode 06012, "World's Fair." Airdate: January 2, 2007.

Spiegel, S., & Lean, D. (Producers), Lawrence, T. E. (Writer), & Lean, D. (Director). (1962). *Lawrence of Arabia.* United States: Republic Pictures.

Statistics Portal (2018). https://www.statista.com/statistics/202871/number-of-fatalities-by-terrorist-attacks-worldwide/. Retrieved May 24, 2018.

Time Magazine. (2017). http://time.com/5011599/gun-deaths-rate-america-cdc-data/. Retrieved May 24, 2018.

Udwin, L. (Producer), Khan-Din, A. (Writer), & O'Donnell, D. (Director). (1998). *East is East.* United Kingdom: Miramax.

Ufland, H., & Ufland, M. (Producers), & Gilbert, B. (Director). (1990). *Not without my daughter.* United States: Metro-Goldwyn-Mayer.

Wallis, H. (Producer), Philip, J., & Epstein, G. (Writers), & Curtiz, M. (Director). (1943). *Casablanca.* United States: Warner Bros.

CHAPTER 12

Creating Schools That Value Sexual Diversity

Elizabeth J. Meyer

Sexuality. It's a hot topic, sure to spark controversy in any school community. Most teachers and administrators avoid the issue at all costs. Many parents also tend to avoid the issue. This absence of adult support leaves many young people without guidance and accurate information about relationships, physical development, sexual health, and important aspects of their identities. It also creates a hostile school environment for students who do not conform to its heterosexual social hierarchies. There can be a wide variety of reasons for this nonconformity: clothes, hairstyle, body size, makeup and accessories (too much, not enough, the "wrong" kind), and extra-curricular interests. These behaviors are often connected to perceptions of a student's masculinity, femininity, or sexual orientation and often results in a student being excluded and/or targeted for bullying and harassment (California Safe Schools Coalition, 2004; Kosciw & Diaz, 2006; Meyer, 2006).

One of the most important things to remember when talking about sexuality is that everybody has one. Heterosexual, bisexual, gay, lesbian, queer, and asexual are some of the descriptors used for talking about sexuality and sexual diversity. Although some may argue that the absence of sexual attraction, or asexuality, is not a sexuality, there are advocacy groups and researchers who recognize it as a category of identity and orientation (see www.asexuality.org). A person's sexuality and associated sexual identity intersect and interact with other identities we may have, such as gender, ethnic, class, dis/ability, racial,1 and linguistic. These various identities are important to all discussions and educational initiatives that address diversity.

This chapter will discuss important factors related to sexual diversity in schools. The first section will define sexual diversity and several related terms that are important for education professionals to understand. The second section will give a brief history of the stigma around sexualities in Western cultures and how this has been reflected in educational institutions. The third section will explore contemporary youth sexualities and some of the various identities embraced by youth today. The fourth section will provide an overview of some of the legal issues that are important to be aware of when talking about sexuality in schools. The last section will conclude with specific recommendations for teachers, counselors, and administrators on how to make their schools more inclusive and supportive of all forms of sexual diversity.

What Is "Sexual Diversity"?

Sexual diversity is a term that is used to refer to the wide variety of sexual identities and orientations that exist in modern society. It can also be used to describe the wide variety of sexual behaviors that humans choose to engage in, but that is not the focus of this chapter. Since this chapter is written for the current or future professional educator, it will focus on the everyday issues that are already present in schools. As many multicultural educators have argued, it can be unhealthy and alienating to ignore parts of our identities when we enter a school or a classroom (Delpit, 1993; Nieto, 1999; Paley, 1979). These identities, particularly in terms of gender and sexuality, are influenced by deeply embedded orientations. The distinctions between identity, orientation, and behavior are important to make, since most controversies surrounding school efforts to be more supportive of sexual diversity result from opponents' mistakenly believing that explicit details on sexual behavior will be taught and discussed. This is generally not true. With the exception of some officially approved sexuality education programs, most initiatives on sexual diversity specifically address issues related to identity and orientation—not sexual behavior. Topics such as respect, physical and emotional safety, friendships, family dynamics, and the harmful impact of inaccurate myths, stereotypes, and discriminatory attitudes and behaviors are the main focus. There are four important terms that must be carefully explained to help educators understand the various elements related to sexual diversity: sexuality, sexual orientation, sexual behavior, and sexual identity.

Sexuality is a term that has different meanings depending on the context in which it is used. As mentioned, every person has a sexuality, which is often used to describe a range of internal identities and external behaviors. Many individuals struggle with their sexuality during and after puberty. However, individuals who are pan-/omni-/bior homosexual may experience more stress and anxiety during this time as a result of the lack of adult role models and accessible information and support (Cass, 1979; Troiden, 1988). As a result, these students may be more aware of their sexualities. They may also experience social exclusion or discrimination as a result of the way their tendencies, predispositions, and desires (orientation) impact their sense of themselves (identity) and their interactions with others (behavior) (Blumenfeld, 1994; Savin-Williams, 1990). Each of these terms is explained in more detail.

Sexual orientation describes whom we are sexually attracted to and is generally determined at a very young age. The following are the four main categories of sexual orientation:

1. Asexuals—not sexually attracted to anyone

2. Pan-/omni-/bisexuals—attracted to some members of all/both sexes to varying degrees[2]

3. Heterosexuals—primarily attracted to some members of a different sex

4. Homosexuals—primarily attracted to some persons of the same sex

Scholars disagree on whether sexual orientation is determined by biology, including genes and hormones, or sociology, that is, mostly influenced by upbringing and environment. However, most researchers acknowledge that it is the result of an interaction of the two (Lipkin, 1999, pp. 25–28). Regardless of which factor exerts a larger force on one's sexual orientation, there is general agreement that sexual orientation is decided early in a child's life and cannot be changed. For example, one study found that gay, lesbian, and bisexual (GLB) youth report first becoming aware of their sexual orientation at age ten (D'Augelli & Hershberger, 1993); another reported that gay adolescents report becoming aware of a distinct feeling of "being different" between the ages of five and seven (Leo & Yoakum,

1992). Although some medical professionals and religious groups claim to be able to change a person's sexual orientation from homosexual to heterosexual, most professional organizations, including The American Academy of Pediatrics, The American Counseling Association, The American Psychiatric Association, The American Psychological Association, and The National Association of Social Workers do not endorse any type of counseling that is a form of "reparative therapy" (Frankfurt et al., 1999). Since there is widespread professional agreement that one's sexual orientation cannot be changed through counseling or religion, those who fear that the homosexual agenda in schools is to "recruit" or "convert" impressionable students may find some comfort in this information.

Sexual behavior is the term used to describe the types of sexual activities in which an individual actually engages. People may engage in a wide array of sexual behaviors, depending on what arouses them physically and emotionally. The sex of one's partner does not limit the types of sexual behaviors one can engage in. One can find as much diversity of sexual behaviors within a group of heterosexuals as among bisexuals and homosexuals. For example, in the late 1940s and early 1950s, Alfred Kinsey and his colleagues conducted a series of interviews with men and women about their sexual desires and behaviors. In this study, they found that the participants engaged in many types of sexual behaviors, regardless of the sex of their partners. He also noted that approximately 37% of adult males and 19% of adult females have had some same-sex erotic experience. In his report, he noted that this reported number was most likely artificially low due to reluctance of participants to report same-sex behaviors (Kinsey, Pomeroy, & Martin, 1948, p. 623; Kinsey, Pomeroy, Martin, & Gebhard, 1953, p. 453).

Sexual behavior is generally informed by one's sexual orientation but not always. Since behavior can be chosen, people may choose to engage in certain behaviors and not others. These can also be influenced by one's culture, social group, and romantic partners. It is not uncommon for people who feel attracted to members of the same sex to engage in heterosexual relationships to avoid the stigma and isolation from friends if they were to "come out" as gay or lesbian, nor is it uncommon for heterosexuals to engage in some same-sex behaviors. Orientation influences our behavior, it does not dictate it. However, when orientation and behavior are in conflict, it is difficult for an individual to develop a cohesive sexual identity, and a healthy sense of self (Cass, 1984; Troiden, 1988).

Sexual identity is how a person chooses to describe him or herself. One's identity can be formed around many aspects of self, including race, culture, religion, language, family, career, and physical or mental dis/ability. The identity-formation process can be long and complex, and many theories exist that use stage-models to describe this process for individuals in Western cultures, including the works of Sigmund Freud, Erik Erikson, and Jean Piaget. More recently, scholars have developed theories of identity development that seek to explain the shared experiences of youth who identify as gay, lesbian, queer, or same-sex attracted (Cass, 1979, 1984; Dube & Savin-Williams, 1999; Kumashiro, 2001; Troiden, 1988). Although these theories explain some of the commonalities individuals may experience, it is important to acknowledge that this process is shaped and influenced by factors such as friends, school, class, race, ethnicity, religion, and gender identity and expression (Rowen & Malcolm, 2002; Waldner-Haugrud & Magruder, 1996). Some of the more widely recognized sexual identities embraced by contemporary youth are discussed at greater length later in this chapter.

Unlearning the Stigmas Attached to Sexual Diversity

Historically, Western cultures have constructed homosexuality as an illness, a deviance, and a sin. This negative bias was created through psychological research, religious ideologies, and the political and financial privileging of heterosexual, monogamous family structures by the state through marriage; this bias has been disrupted and challenged by gay rights activists in movements that gained momentum in the 1960s and 1970s. Many authors have examined the social, historical, and political forces that have worked together to construct the idea of the homosexual and then demonize it (Bem, 1993; Foucault, 1980; Jagose, 1996; Sears, 1998; Weeks, 1985).

Heterosexism, compulsory heterosexuality (Rich, 1978/1993), the heterosexual matrix (Butler, 1990), and gender polarization (Bem, 1993) are all different terms that seek to explain the social construction of opposite-sex attraction and sexual behavior as dominant and "normal." The concept of homosexuality, and subsequently heterosexuality, is just over a century old (Jagose, 1996, p. 17). The resulting prejudice against those who deviate from the heterosexual social script has been carefully developed by institutional heterosexism through organized religion, medicine, sexology, psychiatry, and psychology (Bem, 1993, p. 81). Sandra Bem explains how the cultural lens of *gender polarization* works to reinforce heterosexuality by serving two major functions.

> First, it defines mutually exclusive scripts for being male and female. Second, it defines any person or *behavior* that deviates from these scripts as problematic ... taken together, the effect of these two processes is to construct and naturalize a gender-polarizing link between the sex of one's body and the character of one's psyche and one's sexuality. (81)

These powerful social discourses are generated through various institutions, including schools.

Educational structures wield extraordinary ideological power because of their role in teaching what the culture deems important and valuable to future generations. Ministries of Education, textbook publishers, and teachers determine what lessons are passed on to students and whose knowledge or "truth" is valued (Apple, 1990, 2000). Subsequently, schools are important sites that contribute to the normalization of heterosexual behavior. In Richard Friend's article, "Choices Not Closets," he exposes two processes through which such lessons are passed on in schools: systematic inclusion and systematic exclusion. Systematic inclusion is the way in which negative or false information about homosexuality is introduced into schools as a pathology or deviant behavior. Systematic exclusion is "the process whereby positive role models, messages, and images about lesbian, gay and bisexual people are publicly silenced in schools" (Friend, 1993, p. 215). Ironically, schools make efforts to de-sexualize the experience of students while they simultaneously and subtly, yet clearly, affirm heterosexual behaviors and punish those who appear to deviate from them. Epstein and Johnson explain,

> Schools go to great lengths to forbid expressions of sexuality by both children and teachers. This can be seen in a range of rules, particularly those about self-presentation. On the other hand, and perhaps in consequence, expressions of sexuality provide a major currency and resource in the everyday exchanges of school life. Second, the forms in which sexuality is present in schools and the terms on which sexual identities are produced are heavily determined by power relations between teachers and taught, the dynamics of control and resistance. (1998, p. 108)

These acts of surveillance are rooted in Foucault's (1975) concept of the panopticon—an all-seeing, yet completely invisible, source of power and control. This type of surveillance and control is particularly effective, because we all unknowingly contribute to it, unless we actively work to make it visible by questioning and challenging it. This is one of the most powerful ways that schools reinforce heterosexism. Through the surveillance and policing of bodies and language, school structures mandate hyperheterosexuality using the curriculum and extra-curricular activities.

The heterosexism of the curriculum is invisible to many due to its unquestioned dominance in schools and communities. Some examples include the exclusive study of heterosexual romantic literature, the presentation of the 'nuclear' heterosexual two-parent family as the norm and ideal, and the teaching of only the reproductive aspects of sex or abstinence-only sex education. Other forms of relationships and the concept of desire, or *eros,* are completely omitted from the official curriculum (Britzman, 2000; Fine, 1993; Pinar, 1998). Extra-curricular functions that also teach this compulsory heterosexuality include Valentine's Day gift exchanges, kissing booths at school fairs, and prom rituals that include highly gendered formal attire (tuxedos and gowns) and the election of a "king" and a "queen." This prom ritual has begun to be subverted by alternative proms often organized by gay-straight alliances or community youth groups. At these events, there may be two kings (a male king and female "drag king"), and two queens (a female queen and a male "drag queen").

Art Lipkin's (1999) groundbreaking work, *Understanding Homosexuality, Changing Schools*, provides in-depth accounts of the discrimination experienced by gay, lesbian, and bisexual educators, as well as the painful and enduring stories of students who were emotionally and physically harassed for their perceived or actual non-heterosexual, non-gender conforming performance of identity. In other words, schools are not safe for "guys who aren't as masculine as other guys" or "girls who aren't as feminine as other girls" (California Safe Schools Coalition, 2004). Although the people in control of the school do not directly harass and inflict harm on the non-conforming students (in most cases), it is their lack of effective intervention in cases of homophobic and sexual harassment (California Safe Schools Coalition, 2004; Harris Interactive, 2001; Kosciw & Diaz, 2006; NMHA, 2002) that, along with the invisible scripts that are reinforced by the school through surveillance and discipline, sends the message that these identities are not valued or welcomed.

Heterosexism and its more overt partner, homophobia, are clearly linked to cultural gender boundaries and are informed by sexism and misogyny (Francis & Skelton, 2001; Friend, 1993; Meyer, 2006; Mills, 2004). Misogyny is the hatred or devaluing of all that is female or 'feminine.' For example, the most effective challenge to any boy's masculinity is to call him 'gay,' 'homo,' 'fag,' or 'queer' (Epstein & Johnson, 1998; Macan Ghaill, 1995; Martino & Pallotta-Chiarolli, 2003). What is being challenged is his masculinity—his gender code—but it is being done by accusing him of being gay, which is equated with being 'feminine.' Girls are subject to similar kinds of policing (Brown, 2003; Duncan, 2004), but research shows that it is much more prevalent among male students (Harris Interactive, 2001; California Safe Schools Coalition, 2004). The harmful harassment and violence that result from the policing of heterosexual masculinity and femininity is why some activists and educators are pushing for a deconstruction of gender codes and de-labeling of sexual orientations. As long as we continue to live within the narrow boundaries of language and behavior, the hierarchical binaries of male-female and straight-gay remain unchallenged. This work of dismantling socially invented categories is necessary to create educational spaces that liberate and create opportunities, as opposed to limiting and closing down the diversity of human experiences. We must move towards understanding identities and experiences as falling on a continuum of gender expressions and sexual orientations. Fortunately, many youth are leading the way in exploring diverse sexual identities that break away from the traditional binary of gay and straight and the notion that one's identity is permanent and fixed.

Understanding Diverse Sexual Identities

In conversations about sexual diversity, the realities and experiences of heterosexual-identified, or straight, individuals are often ignored. This is a common error in diversity work where the focus is on the marginalized 'other' rather than on understanding the perspective and experiences of those in the dominant group. It is important to discuss heterosexuality, especially in terms of heterosexual privilege and how it works to make some people's relationships and experiences more valued than others. One valuable pedagogical tool available to help students explore heterosexual privilege is, "The Heterosexual Questionnaire." This activity was created by Martin Rochlin, Ph.D., in 1977 and has been adapted for use in anti-homophobia training around the world. Sample questions from this activity include the following:

1. What do you think caused your heterosexuality?

2. When and how did you first decide you were heterosexual?

3. Is it possible that your heterosexuality is just a phase you may grow out of?

4. If heterosexuality is normal, why are so many mental patients heterosexual?

5. The great majority of child molesters are heterosexual males. Do you consider it safe to expose your children to heterosexual teachers?

6. Would you want your children to be heterosexual, knowing the problems they would face, such as heartbreak, disease, and divorce? (Advocates for Youth, 2005)

These questions are intended to stimulate the reader to reflect on social assumptions about heterosexuality and the related stereotypes and stigmas attached to homosexuality. Although there can be controversy if this tool is not used in the proper context or if the conversations are not well facilitated (Rasmussen, Mitchell, & Harwood, 2007), it often leads to a greater awareness on the part of heterosexuals with regards to how heterosexism and heterosexual privilege function.

The terms 'gay' and 'lesbian' are preferred when speaking about people who identify as homosexual. Although the term 'homosexual' is widely used in the medical and psychological professional communities, it has a very specific history and meaning. When using the term homosexual, these professional organizations generally refer to individuals who engage exclusively in same-sex sexual behaviors. This does not necessarily mean that these individuals choose to *identify* as gay or lesbian. The term 'gay' came into wider use to describe men who engage in homosexual relationships during the gay liberation movement that erupted after the famous police raid at The Stonewall Inn on June 27, 1969, in New York City (Jagose, 1996). Although the word 'gay' can also be used to describe women, many women prefer the term 'lesbian.' This word also has a political history attached to the women's liberation movement of the 1960s and 70s, and is often associated with the concept of lesbian-feminists. Some of these activists considered themselves separatists and chose to live and work independently from men (Jagose, 1996). It is no mistake that these terms both gained wider use during this era of important political changes. The concept of identity politics asserted that "coming out" and publicly identifying as gay or lesbian was an important step towards achieving public visibility, reducing negative stereotypes, and securing greater social equality (Weeks, 1985). Because of the historical specificity and cultural stereotypes that have grown up around these terms, many individuals who engage in same-sex behaviors and relationships may choose to use different words to identify themselves.

For people who do not identify as heterosexual, the terms gay and lesbian are not the only ones they may identify with. Many adolescents and young adults prefer terms such as: bi-curious, fluid, hetero- or homo-flexible, open, omnior pan-sexual, polyamorous, questioning, or queer (Driver, 2007, pp. 42–43; Meyer, 2008). Although the meaning of "queer" changed over the years from "odd or strange" to an insult for gays and lesbians, it is now being reclaimed as a powerful political term by some members of the gay, lesbian, bisexual, and transgender community (Jagose, 1996; Meyer, 2007a). Although there is much debate over the use and meaning of the term "queer" within the LGBTQ community, when used as a source of pride and with a sense of inclusivity, "queer" can be a very empowering term. Some also argue that queer is an exclusively White identifier, whereas Ian Barnard, in his book *Queer Race*, explains that "queer theory already has a racial politics," and that "particular racializations are and can be queer, … [and] queerness can be racialized" (Barnard, 2004, pp. 6, 18). As Driver explains in her book *Queer Girls and Popular Culture*, "queer as a strategically chosen term works against the foreclosure of desires and the imposition of controlling assumptions; it is deployed by girls as a way of enabling possibilities rather than guaranteeing identity or knowledge about identity" (Driver, 2007, p. 43). Even with this postmodern re-appropriation of 'queer,' if it is used to insult and exclude, it still has the power to deeply wound. Even with all these emerging identities, there are many individuals who reject static labels, choosing not to identify their sexuality in any way. This demonstrates a move away from the identity politics of the gay and lesbian rights movement and the tendency for young people to create new identities and communities that more authentically represent their experiences.

The identity categories transgender, transsexual, and two-spirit are often included in conversations of sexual diversity. This is usually because the trans- and two-spirit communities have been active contributors to equality projects taken on by the gay, lesbian, and bisexual community. In the acronym GLBT, the "T" may represent one, two, or all three of these groups. I have chosen to include them here to clarify the links these communities have to the topic of sexual diversity. It is important to understand that transgender, two-spirit, and transsexual people have strong ties to the gay, lesbian, and bisexual community because of shared experiences, discrimination, and exclusion from mainstream culture that are connected to their public challenging of traditional sex and gender role expectations of dress and behavior. However, their experiences are not tied directly to their sexual orientation; rather, they are connected to their gender identity and expression. There is not sufficient room in this chapter to explore these concepts fully, but I have included a brief definition of each of these terms below.

The word transgender entered the English language in the 1980s from the transsexual and transvestite communities (Cromwell, 1997, p. 134) to describe individuals whose gender identity is different from the sex that they were assigned at birth. There are many myths and misconceptions about transgender individuals, and there are as many masculinities and femininities (gender expressions) within the transgender community as there are in non-trans men and women. Some transgender people strongly embrace traditional notions of gender and proudly live as highly feminine or highly masculine people. Other transgender people choose to challenge and disrupt the categories of masculinity and femininity, embracing varying degrees of each (Bornstein, 1998; Feinberg, 1998; Wilchins, 2004). The word transgender is often used as an umbrella term to describe a wide variety of people who challenge traditional notions of sex and gender, including transsexuals, two-spirited people, cross-dressers, and individuals who identify as genderqueer (Nestle, Howell, & Wilchins, 2002).

Transsexuals are individuals who were born as genetic females (XX) or genetic males (XY) and developed the associated physical traits of their genetic sex. However, transsexual people have a gender identity, or an internal sense of themselves, that does not align with their physical characteristics. This conflict between physical and psychological traits has been termed gender dysphoria by the medical profession. Transsexuals are usually assigned the clinical label "gender identity disorder" (GID) from the Diagnostic and Statistical Manual of Mental Disorders (DSM IV) of the American Psychiatric Association, although activists have been trying to get this condition removed from the DSM. As the lead character in the film *Transamerica* so eloquently argued, "If it can be fixed with plastic surgery, is it really a mental disorder?" (Tucker, 2005). Transsexual men and women choose to undergo a series of medical treatments to realign their physical characteristics with their internal identity. These treatments generally include hormone injections and surgery (GIRES, 2006b, p. 29). According to some research, only 23% of children who experience tension between their assigned sex at birth (and thus, their gender of rearing), and their own gender identity, are transsexuals who choose to undergo physical transformations (GIRES, 2006a). Some won't have surgery and hormone treatments because of the expense and challenge in securing approval, and others may not because they are uncomfortable with the risks and limitations of surgery, and still others are happy with their bodies as they are.

Two-spirit or two-spirited are terms used to describe people who are alternatively gendered and are members of Native American (also known as Amerindian, First Nations, Inuit, and Métis) communities. It replaces the earlier term, "berdache," used by anthropologists who studied these cultures (Lang, 1997, p. 100). Early anthropologists often misunderstood the spiritual element of the two-spirited individual and described it as a form of institutionalized male homosexuality. As more recent authors have pointed out, becoming a "berdache" was related more to occupational preferences and social roles than to sexual behavior (p. 101). The term two-spirit is an attempt to create an English-language term to describe a cultural concept of gender that is different from, but refers to, the male/female Western binary. Although the concept of two-spirit emerges from many traditional aboriginal cultures, these communities have been subject to Western colonizing influences and now share many of the heterosex-ist and homophobic beliefs created by Western European ideologies.

All of these identity categories are complicated and formed over an individual's lifetime. Although some people argue that it is inappropriate to discuss sexuality with younger children, their lives are also impacted by sexual diversity. In addition to their own developing sense of themselves, they are shaped by the lives of the adults around them. Many educators who work in early childhood and elementary education believe that discussions of sexual diversity have no place in their schools. How-ever, most families in Western cultures are based on relationships created out of romantic love, thus children's home lives and family structures tend to reflect the sexualities of their parents and caregivers. Recent studies on the experiences of children of gay and lesbian parents indicate that they experience increased harassment at school, and their parents were often excluded from school life (Kosciw & Diaz, 2008; Ray & Gregory, 2001). For these reasons it is important for educators to address diverse family structures and to include sexual diversity when addressing diversity issues with students of all ages. *It's Elementary: Talking About Gay Issues in School* is an excellent film that provides models of how to do this appropriately and effectively with younger students (Chasnoff, 1996). In addition to developing a better understanding of sexual diversity and how it impacts individual lives, it is important for educa-tors to be aware of the various legal issues involved that relate to the topic of sexual diversity in schools.

Sexual Diversity and the Law
USA

There are currently no federal protections that explicitly protect gay, lesbian, and bisexual (glb) people from discrimination in the United States. However, sexual minorities are entitled to the same protec-tion as any other identifiable group. Consequently, a variety of courts across the country have begun holding school districts accountable for violating the rights of students who are being harassed or who have requested the right to form extra-curricular groups that address their needs and interests. The main existing legal protections that are relevant in these cases include: Equal Protection, Title IX, state non-discrimination laws, and The Equal Access Act.

The Equal Protection Clause of the Fourteenth Amendment guarantees equal application of a law to all people in the United States (Macgillivray, 2007). An equal protection claim requires the student to show that school officials (1) did not fairly and consistently apply policies when dealing with the student, (2) were deliberately indifferent to the student's complaints, or (3) that the student was treated in a manner that is clearly unreasonable. The first example of this argument being successfully applied to a case of homophobic harassment in schools was in the case *Nabozny v. Podlesny* in Wisconsin. In this case, Jamie Nabozny was subjected to violent and persistent anti-gay harassment over several years in his school. As a result of this harassment, he had been hospitalized, dropped out of school, and attempted suicide (Lipkin, 1999). The federal appeals court for that region of the United States, the Seventh Circuit, decided in favor of the student. In their decision, the judges wrote that "… we are unable to garner any rational basis for permitting one student to assault another based on the victim's sexual orientation …" and the school district settled with Nabozny for $900,000 (Bochenek & Brown, 2001). More recently in a case in California, *Flores v. Morgan Hill* (2003), the court found sufficient evidence of deliberate indifference to the ongoing sexual orientation harassment of six students in this California School District, which resulted in a $1,100,000 settlement with the students (ACLU, 2004), and the requirement that the school district implement a training and education program for its admin-istrators, faculty, and students (Dignan, 2004).

Title IX is another federal protection that exists to address issues of homophobic harassment in schools. It provides statutory protection for student-on-student sexual harassment under the following conditions: (1) school personnel have actual knowledge of the harassment, (2) school officials demon-strate deliberate indifference or take actions that are clearly unreasonable, and (3) the harassment is so severe, pervasive, and objectively offensive that it can be said to deprive the victim(s) of access to the educational opportunities or benefits provided by the school (*Davis v. Monroe*, 1999). Several cases have successfully made the argument that Title IX protects students from peer sexual orientation harassment. For example, a California Federal District Court concluded,

> the Court finds no material difference between the instance in which a female student is subject to unwelcome sexual comments and advances due to her harasser's perception that she is a sex object, and the instance in which a male student is insulted and abused due to his harasser's perception that he is a homosexual, and therefore a subject of prey. In both instances, the conduct is a heinous response to the harasser's perception of the victim's sexuality, and is not distinguishable to this court. (*Ray v. Antioch Unified School District*, 2006)

In 2000, two important cases were decided that applied Title IX to incidences of homophobic harassment: *Ray v. Antioch Unified School District* (2000), and *Montgomery v. Independent School District* (2000). In both of these cases, separate courts decided that schools could be held liable under Title IX for acting with "deliberate indifference" towards students who have reported persistent and severe homophobic harassment at school. These decisions established important precedents for the cases that followed.

A few years later, a Kansas federal district court considered that the gender stereotyping and related anti-gay harassment of a student who did not identify as gay was actionable under Title IX (*Theno v. Tonganoxie*, 2005). The court wrote that "the plaintiff was harassed because he failed to satisfy his peers' stereotyped expectations for his gender because the primary objective of plaintiff's harassers appears to have been to disparage his perceived lack of masculinity." Therefore, they concluded that the harassment of Dylan Theno was so "severe, pervasive, and objectively offensive that it effectively denied (him) an education in the Tonganoxie school district" (*Theno v. Tonganoxie*, 2005*)*. The district settled with Dylan for a total of $440,000 (Trowbridge, 2005).

One case had a very different outcome. In *Doe v. Bellefonte Area School District* (2004), the court decided for the school district. It determined that campus administrators took Doe's complaints seriously, instituted a series of steps in response to complaints, and escalated punishment when necessary. Therefore, the district was not deliberately indifferent to the harassment of Doe. In addition to federal protections that exist, some states have non-discrimination laws that can offer students some relief. State non-discrimination laws that protect individuals based on sexual orientation, and/or gender identity, only exist in twenty states and the District of Columbia3 (National Gay and Lesbian Task Force, 2007). However, according to a study published in 2006, only nine states (California, Connecticut, Maine, Massachusetts, Minnesota, New Jersey, Vermont, Washington, and Wisconsin) and the District of Columbia have statutes specifically protecting students in schools from discrimination on the basis of sexual orientation and/or gender identity (Kosciw & Diaz, 2006). Students in these states experienced significantly lower rates of verbal harassment than their peers. Since this report, several states (including Nebraska, Iowa, Kentucky, and Wyoming) legislatures have at least considered bills either expanding or limiting the rights of sexual-minority students (Buchanan, 2006). There are also seven states that have legislation that prohibit the positive portrayal of homosexuality (Alabama, Arizona, Mississippi, Oklahoma, South Carolina, Texas, and Utah), and students in these states reported being verbally harassed at a higher frequency than students from states without such legislation (47.6% versus 37.2%) (Kosciw & Diaz, 2006, p. 86).

A recent case in New Jersey extended the protections offered by state anti-discrimination laws to cover students in schools. As a result of the case brought by a student who had suffered persistent homophobic harassment, *L. W. v. Toms River Regional Schools Board of Education* (2007), the New Jersey Supreme Court decided that schools may be held liable under the Law Against Discrimination for permitting student-on-student bias-based harassment (American Civil Liberties Union-New Jersey, 2007). This decision established state-wide protections for students in New Jersey.

The Equal Access Act (EAA) is another legal protection that is being used successfully to advance education around sexual diversity in schools through extra-curricular diversity clubs. Peer support groups, commonly known as gay-straight alliances (GSAs), have become increasingly common in schools (Cloud, 2005; Fischer & Kosciw, 2006). Very little research is available on the efficacy of GSAs, but Fischer and Kosciw (2006) found that the presence of a GSA directly predicted greater school belonging, and indirectly predicted greater academic achievement for sexual-minority youth. Also Szlacha (2003) found in her evaluation of the Massachusetts Safe Schools Program that the presence of a GSA is the aspect "most strongly associated with positive sexual diversity climates" (73). This finding makes intuitive sense when considering the importance of supportive heterosexual peers to a positive experience for sexual-minority youth. However, GSAs are not always met with open-mindedness from students, teachers, administrators, parents, community members, and school boards. Since the late 1990s, there have been several cases of schools trying to exclude these groups from meeting on school grounds. Courts have consistently found that school districts have violated the EAA when banning GSA groups from meeting. *Straights and Gays for Equity v. Osseo Area Schools* (2006) and *White County High School Peers in Diverse Education v. White County School District* (2006) serve as two recent examples. Due to the time and courage put forth by the students who work to initiate these GSAs, there are now over 3,000 such groups in schools, and at least one in every state in the United States (Macgillivray, 2007). Whereas students in the United States have had to search for various forms of protection against discrimination based on sexual orientation, Canada has clearly worded provincial and federal human rights codes that offer such protections.

CANADA

The current progressive political climate in Canada was achieved through a long and slow process of legislative reform that culminated in the adoption of the *Canadian Charter of Rights and Freedoms*. This important document was entrenched into the Canadian constitution by the Constitution Act in 1982 (Watkinson, 1999, p. 22). As part of the supreme law of Canada, this document superseded all existing laws, and for the first time the rights of all persons to be treated equally were given constitutional status. Although public education is governed by provincial statutes, all publicly funded institutions must abide by the spirit and letter of the *Charter* (Watkinson, 1999). This new constitution guaranteed protections for many historically marginalized groups. Sexual orientation, however, was not initially included as a protected class for equality rights under section 15 of the *Canadian Charter of Rights and Freedoms*. The original language of this section reads as follows:

> Every individual is equal before and under the law and has the right to the equal protection and equal benefit of the law without discrimination and, in particular, without discrimination based on race, national or ethnic origin, colour, religion, sex, age or mental or physical disability. (*Canadian Charter of Rights and Freedoms (s. 15)*, 1982)

Although the federal government wasn't willing to explicitly include the phrase, "sexual orientation" in the *Charter*, other provinces had already established human rights codes that included this language. In 1977, the Province of Quebec led the way in the equality movement for sexual minorities by adding "sexual orientation" to its *Charter of Human Rights and Freedoms*. Ontario followed suit nine years later. These were the first legal protections that clearly included sexual orientation as a protected class (Hurley, 2005). Although equality rights supported by the *Charter* were enforced starting in 1985, sexual minorities were not recognized as a protected class until thirteen years later, following a unanimous decision of the Supreme Court of Canada in the landmark case of *Egan v. Canada* (1995). Although this case was not about discrimination in schools, it addressed the issue of access to public services. The ruling provided that discrimination based on sexual orientation was prohibited by s. 15 of the *Charter*, and the justices observed: "*Sexual orientation is a deeply personal characteristic that is either unchangeable or changeable only at unacceptable personal costs, and so falls within the ambit of s. 15 protection as being analogous to the enumerated grounds" (Egan v. Canada, 1995, para. 5)*

This case established the precedent to include sexual orientation as a protected class and had "sexual orientation" read into the *Charter*. Every Canadian was guaranteed equal protection from discrimination based on sexual orientation. Although some provinces were slow to add the term "sexual orientation" to their individual human rights codes, this protection was federally guaranteed as a result of this important ruling.

Since the Supreme Court's 1995 decision in *Egan v. Canada*, various cases have tested the interpretation and application of the equality rights extended in that case. In the first case in an educational institution after Egan was decided (*Vriend v. Alberta*, 1998), a university employee was fired from his position as a lab coordinator, solely because of his homosexuality. He initially brought forward a human rights complaint; however, it was dismissed because the province of Alberta did not have sexual orientation listed as a protected class in its human rights legislation. In this case, the Supreme Court stated that not protecting individuals from discrimination based on sexual orientation was an "unjustified violation of s. 15 of the *Canadian Charter of Rights and Freedoms*," and ordered that the words "sexual orientation" be read into provincial human rights codes as a prohibited ground of discrimination (*Vriend v. Alberta*, 1998, p. 2).

The next test came in May 2001 when the Supreme Court of Canada heard a case from Trinity Western University (TWU), a private, religious institution filed against the British Columbia College of Teachers (BCCT). In this instance, the B.C. professional teachers' organization had responded to a request from TWU to be fully responsible for its teacher training program, which it shared with Simon Fraser University. Trinity Western University wanted more autonomy in the program in order to reflect its Christian worldview. The BCCT chose not to accredit this institution because it believed the institution was discriminating on the basis of sexual orientation in its demands on its students. Trinity Western University required its students to sign a statement that asserted they would "refrain from practices that are biblically condemned," including homosexuality *(Trinity Western University v. British Columbia College of Teachers, 2001, para. 4)*

In its decision, the British Columbia Supreme Court found in favor of TWU, stating that teachers could hold "sexist, racist or homophobic beliefs" (para. 36). However, the Court also made the following distinction:

> Acting on those beliefs, however, is a very different matter. If a teacher in the public school system engages in discriminatory conduct, that teacher can be subject to disciplinary proceedings. Discriminatory conduct by a public school teacher when on duty should always be subject to disciplinary proceedings [and] disciplinary measures can still be taken when discriminatory off-duty conduct poisons the school environment. (*Trinity Western University v. British Columbia College of Teachers*, 2001, at para. 37)

Although this majority opinion sided with TWU and allowed them to continue mandating anti-gay beliefs in their future teachers, the judges made the important distinction between discriminatory behaviors and beliefs, which is common in cases regarding religious freedom. The decision clearly states that teachers may not discriminate overtly against their students but does not address the issue of the subtle and persistent homophobic behaviors that homophobic attitudes engender and the impact they have on a classroom or school community.

This position was reinforced in the case of a teacher who was suspended for making public statements that were understood as anti-gay in nature. In February 2004, a B.C. teacher, Chris Kempling, was suspended for one month for "conduct unbecoming" a teacher because he had published articles that were considered to be defaming of homosexuals in a local newspaper (*Kempling v. British Columbia College of Teachers*, 2004, para.1). The Christian teacher appealed this decision to the B.C. Supreme Court, but the court held that the BCCT was within its jurisdiction to suspend him. The court's rationale for its decision was based on the "wrongful public linking of his professional position to the off-duty expression of personally held discriminatory views in order to lend credibility to those views" (*Kempling v. British Columbia College of Teachers*, 2004, para. 2). These cases have established a clear responsibility on the part of schools in Canada to create learning environments that are free from discrimination. The final case discussed here demonstrates what happened when a school failed to provide such an environment.

Azmi Jubran, a student in Vancouver, was repeatedly called 'gay,' 'faggot,' and 'homo' by his peers in secondary school. In addition to these verbal taunts, he was spit upon, shoved in class and the hallways, and even had his shirt burned. Jubran and his parents made repeated complaints to the school, and, after receiving no satisfactory response, they filed a human rights complaint in November 1996. In April 2002, the Human Rights Tribunal of British Columbia found that the school board in Vancouver had contravened the *Human Rights Code*, "by failing to provide a learning environment free of discriminatory harassment" (*School District No. 44 v. Jubran*, 2005, para. 2). This was an important decision because it affirmed the school's responsibility to protect students from discriminatory behavior and to respond effectively and consistently to incidents of homophobic harassment. After a series of appeals, the fate of this case was decided on October 20, 2005, when the Supreme Court refused to hear a final appeal, and effectively upheld the lower court's decision. This was an important decision. The court acknowledged that the school had made some effort to discipline the students who had targeted Jubran individually but said that it had not done enough. The court stated that the school needed to have communicated its code of conduct to students and provided teachers with resources and training on how to deal with homophobia (CLE Staff, 2005; Meyer, 2007b). This case sent a clear message to educators that they must mobilize multiple resources and be proactive when addressing issues of school climate and student safety that relate directly to human rights protections.

As the above listed cases demonstrate, there are legal precedents that exist to protect students from discriminatory behavior in schools. However, many school boards and educators are ignorant of their legal responsibilities and fail to effectively implement policies, programs, and curricular materials that support full inclusion of sexual diversity in school communities.

Creating Schools That Value Sexual Diversity

While overt acts of discrimination are difficult for schools to ignore, daily acts of covert discrimination persist and impact students' lives in ways that many teachers and administrators fail to acknowledge. When bias against an identifiable social group is present throughout an institution, the entire school is implicated, and the culture must shift. In order to transform ignorance of, and intolerance for, forms of sexual diversity, all stakeholders in the community must be involved in the process: students, families, teachers, administrators, and school board personnel. The tone must be set by the leadership, but everyone must be engaged in changing the culture of the institution. In order to better identify what steps can be taken at each level, recommendations are provided for the following: administrators and school boards, teachers and support staff, students, parents, and community members.

Administrators and School Boards

At the school leadership level, important changes must be made in three areas to set the tone for a positive and supportive school environment. These are policy, education, and resources and support. Without the institutional support provided by the following examples, the isolated efforts of overworked teachers, frustrated parents, and targeted young people will only have a small, short-term impact on the experiences of the students in the school community. In order to have a larger, more lasting effect on the school culture, systemic changes must be made.

Policy. When drafting policies that address issues of bullying and harassment in schools, a whole-school policy that includes clear, definite guidelines on actions against bullying, including response protocols and implementation strategies, is essential (Arora, 1994; Cartwright, 1995; Sharp & Smith, 1991; Whitney & Smith, 1993). Language must also be clear, consistent, and include specific protections against harassment, violence, and discrimination based on sexual orientation and gender identity or expression (Goldstein, Collins, & Halder, 2005).

Education. A policy will not be effective unless those expected to enforce it are made aware of their obligations and community members are informed of the changes. Examples of such efforts include discussing the new policy in staff meetings; inviting a law expert to present a workshop on the definitions of harassment and the school's duty to prevent it; creating study circles with the staff to examine the new policy and discuss implementation strategies; publishing information in school newsletters; and distributing brochures, including information about the new policy.

Resources and Support. The school district needs to allocate resources: time, money, and materials to ensure that these shifts in school climate can occur. Instead of hiring a one-time speaker, some school boards have created full-time positions in order to ensure that the expertise and knowledge will be readily available to support the efforts being made in individual schools. In the state of Massachusetts (Perrotti & Westheimer, 2001) and on the Toronto District School Board, several positions were created that were integral to the success of their programs, such as human-sexuality program workers, equity-department instructional leaders, and student-program workers (Goldstein et al., 2005). The institutional support offered by these various initiatives gives credibility and value to the daily efforts of individuals on the front line.

TEACHERS AND SUPPORT STAFF

Teachers and support staff, such as bus drivers, cafeteria personnel, and lunchroom monitors, have the greatest opportunity to observe and intervene in incidents of discrimination and harassment in schools. Teachers and support staff can focus development in the following areas: understanding of school policies, sharing and practicing intervention tools for incidents of discrimination and harassment, and finding and using appropriate curricular materials and programs that are inclusive of sexual diversity. These expectations mean that teachers and support staff will need to attend workshops and courses, and take some responsibility for their own professional development, in addition to participating in the educational opportunities provided by the school administration. There are many resources available for these pursuits, some of which are listed in the reference list at the end of this chapter. Examples of curricular interventions that can address some of the underlying issues of homophobia and heterosexism include the following:

1. A campaign against name-calling that includes education about what words mean, and why certain insults are inappropriate and discriminatory.

2. Curricular inclusion of contributions by gays, lesbians, bisexuals, and transgendered people to history, art, science, literature, politics, and sports.

3. Providing inclusive and diverse information about sex, gender, and sexual orientation in biology, health, and sexual education classes.

4. Conducting critical media literacy activities that analyze gender stereotypes and heterosexism in popular culture.

Although teachers and support staff have a significant impact on the school climate, without the participation of the student body, a true shift in culture and behavior cannot take place.

STUDENTS

Students make up the largest percentage of a school community and are the trendsetters for what is valued in school. Without the support and investment of student leaders, there will continue to be student-only spaces where incidents of discrimination and harassment take place, such as locker areas, washrooms, and areas on playgrounds and athletics fields. Schools that successfully engage student leaders, such as athletics team captains, student council members, peer mediators and others, can have a much broader and deeper impact on the lives of all students in school. Ways that this can be done include conducting summer leadership retreats, student discussion groups, or weekend workshops that educate students about sexual diversity, and solicit their help and support in challenging homophobia, heterosexism, and other forms of bias in the school. In addition to engaging prominent students in the school population, all students should be informed of the school's policies on harassment and discrimination by posting a code of conduct in each classroom, having students sign a behavior contract, and/or by having home-room discussions about the policy, what it means, and how it might affect them.

FAMILY AND COMMUNITY MEMBERS

Finally, no school community is complete without the input and influence of families and community members. The parents' association and other community groups should be invited and encouraged to become actively involved in developing the school policy and educational strategies. By developing these partnerships early on, schools can anticipate any resistance or potential backlash, and work through these issues before they grow into negative publicity for the school. To be a supportive and inclusive school, it is important to reach out to same-sex parented families to let them know that their input and involvement is welcomed. Gay and lesbian parents may stay closeted or separate from the school community if they are not given any positive indicators that their family is valued and will be included in that community. Most families are deeply invested in the education and development of their children and therefore should be included in such initiatives. Although there may be some resistance to addressing sexual diversity, schools can create a lasting network that will potentially expand their efforts to reduce such bias in the community at large by building strong ties with parent groups and other community organizations,

Sexual diversity is all around us, although it is often invisible and silenced. Schools cannot make the controversies surrounding sexual diversity disappear by ignoring them. In many of the legal cases mentioned earlier, ignoring the issues exacerbated and escalated the problems. As educators who are responsible for supporting and teaching the next generation, it is our responsibility to create schools and classrooms that value and teach about the diversity that is already present in our communities. Teachers and administrators also have the legal obligation to create safe learning environments that are equitable and free of discrimination. By unlearning the harmful messages from old stereotypes and misinformation, educators have the potential to create and teach more contemporary messages of equality, inclusiveness, and diversity.

Notes

1. The use of the term "racial" here is in the critical multicultural sense of acknowledging the social constructedness of race while simultaneously addressing the very real impacts of racism in society. See (Kincheloe & Steinberg, 1997, pp. 215–216) for more on this.
2. There is not sufficient space in this chapter to explore the notion that there more than two sexes. For more information on this assertion please see (Fausto-Sterling, 2000).
3. Minnesota (1993); Rhode Island (1995, 2001); New Mexico (2003); California (1992, 2003); District of Columbia (1997, 2005); Illinois (2005); Maine (2005); Hawaii (1991, 2005, 2006); New Jersey (1992, 2006); Washington (2006); Iowa (2007); Oregon (2007); Vermont (1992, 2007); Colorado (2007); Wisconsin (1982); Massachusetts (1989); Connecticut (1991); New Hampshire (1997); Nevada (1999); Maryland (2001); New York (2002).

References

ACLU. (2004). *Settlement fact sheet: Flores v. Morgan Hill Unified School District.* Retrieved March 28, 2006, from www. aclu. org

Advocates for Youth. (2005). The heterosexual questionnaire. Retrieved March 2, 2008, from http://www.advocatesforyouth. org/lessonplans/heterosexual2.htm

American Civil Liberties Union-New Jersey. (2007). Victory for gay and other students who face harassment. Retrieved October 10, 2007, from http://www.aclu-nj.org/pressroom/victoryforgayandotherstude.htm

Apple, M. (1990). *Ideology and the curriculum.* New York: Routledge.

Apple, M. (2000). *Official knowledge: Democratic education in a conservative age* (2nd ed.). New York: Routledge.

Arora, C. M. J. (1994). Is there any point in trying to reduce bullying in secondary schools? A two year follow-up of a whole-school anti-bullying policy in one school. *Educational Psychology in Practice, 10*(3), 155–162.

Barnard, I. (2004). *Queer race: Cultural interventions in the racial politics of queer theory.* New York: Peter Lang.

Bem, S. (1993). *The lenses of gender: Transforming the debate on sexual inequality.* New Haven: Yale University Press.

Blumenfeld, W. (1994). Science, sexual orientation, and identity: An overview. Unpublished research paper. Gay, Lesbian, and Straight Education Network.

Bochenek, M., & Brown, A. W. (2001). *Hatred in the hallways: Violence and discrimination against lesbian, gay, bisexual, and transgender students in U.S. schools*: Human Rights Watch.

Bornstein, K. (1998). *My gender workbook.* New York: Routledge.

Britzman, D. (2000). Precocious education. In S. Talburt & S. Steinberg (Eds.), *Thinking queer: Sexuality, culture, and education* (pp. 33–60). New York: Peter Lang.

Brown, L. M. (2003). *Girlfighting: Betrayal and rejection among girls.* New York: New York University Press.

Buchanan, W. (2006, April 1). Bills nationwide address gays in schools [Electronic Version]. *SFGate.* Retrieved April 12, 2006 from www.sfgate.com.

Butler, J. (1990). *Gender trouble.* New York: RoutledgeFalmer.

California Safe Schools Coalition. (2004). *Consequences of harassment based on actual or perceived sexual orientation and gender non-conformity and steps for making schools safer.* Davis: University of California.

The Canadian Charter of Rights and Freedoms (s. 15). Part I of the Constitution Act c. 11 (1982).

Cartwright, N. (1995). Combating bullying in a secondary school in the United Kingdom. *Journal for a Just and Caring Education, 1*(3), 345–353.

Cass, V. (1979). Homosexual identity formation: A theoretical model. *Journal of Homosexuality, 4,* 219–235.

Cass, V. (1984). Homosexual identity formation: Testing a theoretical model. *Journal of Sex Research, 20,* 143–167.

Chasnoff, D. (Writer) (1996). *It's elementary: Talking about gay issues in school.* H. S. Cohen & D. Chasnoff (Producer). USA: Ground Spark.

CLE Staff. (2005). BCCA: North Vancouver school board liable for homophobic harassment of student. [Electronic Version]. *Stay current: The continuing legal education society of British Columbia, April 8.* Retrieved April 9, 2005 from www.cle. bc.ca/CLE.

Cloud, J. (2005). The battle over gay teens. *Time, October 10.*

Cromwell, J. (1997). Traditions of gender diversity and sexualities: A female-to-male transgendered perspective. In S.-E. Jacobs, W. Thomas, & S. Lang (Eds.), *Two-spirit people: Native American gender identity, sexuality, and spirituality* (pp. 119–142). Chicago, IL: University of Illinois Press.

D'Augelli, A. R., & Hershberger, S. L. (1993). Lesbian, gay, and bisexual youth in community settings: Personal challenges and mental health problems. *American Journal of Community Psychology, 21,* 421–448.

Delpit, L. (1993). The silenced dialogue: Power and pedagogy in educating other people's children. In L. Weis & M. Fine (Eds.), *Beyond silenced voices: Class, race, and gender in United States schools* (pp. 119–139). Albany, NY: SUNY Press.

Dignan, J. (2004, January 8). Important victory for gay students *Gaycitynews.com* Retrieved October 15, 2007, from http:// www.gaycitynews.com/site/index.cfm?newsid=17008546&BRD=2729&PAG=461&dept_ id=568864&rfi=8

Doe v. Bellefonte Area School District (3rd Cir U. S. App. 2004).

Driver, S. (2007). *Queer girls and popular culture: Reading, resisting, and creating media.* New York: Peter Lang.

Dube, E., & Savin-Williams, R. (1999). Sexual identity development among ethnic sexual-minority male youths. *Developmental Psychology, 35*(6), 1389–1398.

Duncan, N. (2004). It's important to be nice, but it's nicer to be important: Girls, popularity and sexual competition. *Sex Education, 4*(2), 137–152.

Egan v. Canada (2 S.C.R. 513 1995).

Epstein, D., & Johnson, R. (1998). *Schooling sexualities.* Buckingham: Open University Press.

Fausto-Sterling, A. (2000). *Sexing the body: Gender politics and the construction of sexuality.* New York: Basic Books. Feinberg, L. (1998). Allow me to introduce myself. In *Transliberation: Beyond pink or blue.* Boston: Beacon Press.

Fine, M. (1993). Sexuality, schooling, and adolescent females: The missing discourse of desire. In L. Weis & M. Fine (Eds.), *Beyond silenced voices: Class, race, and gender in United States schools* (pp. 75–99). Albany, NY: SUNY Press.

Fischer, S. and Kosciw, J. (2006, April 6). The importance of gay-straight alliances: Associations with teacher and staff response to homophobia. Paper presented at the annual meeting of the American Educational Research Association. San Francisco, CA.

Flores v. Morgan Hill Unified School District, No. 02–15128 (9th Cir. 2003). Foucault, M. (1975). *Surveiller et Punir: Naissance de la Prison*. Paris: Gallimard.

Foucault, M. (1980). *The history of sexuality, Volume I: An introduction*. New York: Random House.

Francis, B., & Skelton, C. (2001). Men teachers and the construction of heterosexual masculinity in the classroom. *Sex Education, 1*(1), 9–21.

Frankfurt, K. et al. (1999). *Just the facts about sexual orientation and youth: A primer for principals, educators, and school personnel*. New York: GLSEN, National Education Association, American Psychological Association, American Federation of Teachers, the National Association of School Psychologists, and the National Association of Social Workers.

Friend, R. (1993). Choices, not closets: Heterosexism and homophobia in schools. In L. Weis & M. Fine (Eds.), *Beyond silenced voices: Class, race, and gender in United States schools* (pp. 209–235). Albany: SUNY Press.

GIRES. (2006a). Atypical gender identity development—A review. *International Journal of Transgenderism, 9*(1), 29–44.

GIRES. (2006b). *Gender dysphoria*. Surrey, UK: Gender Identity Research and Education Society.

Goldstein, T., Collins, A., & Halder, M. (2005). *Challenging homophobia and heterosexism in elementary and high schools: A research report to the Toronto district school board*. Toronto: Ontario Institute for Studies in Education of the University of Toronto.

Harris Interactive. (2001). *Hostile hallways: Bullying, teasing, and sexual harassment in school*. Washington, DC: American Association of University Women Educational Foundation.

Hurley, M. C. (2005). *Sexual orientation and legal rights* (Current Issue Review No. 92–1E). Ottawa: Library of Parliament.

Jagose, A. (1996). *Queer theory: An introduction*. New York: New York University Press.

Kempling v. British Columbia College of Teachers (B.C.D. Civ. 2004).

Kincheloe, J., & Steinberg, S. (1997). *Changing multiculturalism*. Buckingham, UK & Philadelphia, PA: Open University Press.

Kinsey, A., Pomeroy, W., & Martin, C. (1948). *Sexual behavior in the human male*. Philadelphia, PA: W. B. Saunders. Kinsey, A., Pomeroy, W., Martin, C., & Gebhard, P. (1953). *Sexual behavior in the human female*. Philadelphia, PA: W. B. Saunders.

Kosciw, J., & Diaz, E. (2006). *The 2005 national school climate survey: The experiences of lesbian, gay, bisexual and transgender youth in our nation's schools*. New York: Gay, Lesbian, and Straight Education Network.

Kosciw, J., & Diaz, E. (2008). *Involved, invisible, ignored: The experiences of lesbian, gay, bisexual and transgender parents and their children in our nation's K–12 schools*. New York: GLSEN.

Kumashiro, K. K. (Ed.). (2001). *Troubling intersections of race and sexuality: Queer students of color and anti-oppressive education*. Lanham, MD: Rowman & Littlefield.

L. W. v. Toms River Regional Schools Board of Education, A-111–05. (New Jersey Supreme Court 189 N. J. 381, 915 A.2d 535 2007).

Lang, S. (1997). Various kinds of two-spirit people: Gender variance and homosexuality in Native American communities. In S.-E. Jacobs, W. Thomas, & S. Lang (Eds.), *Two-spirit people: Native American gender identity, sexuality, and spirituality* (pp. 100–118). Chicago, IL: University of Illinois Press.

Leo, T., & Yoakum, J. (1992). Creating a safer school environment for lesbian and gay students. *Journal of School Health* (September 1992), 37–41.

Lipkin, A. (1999). *Understanding homosexuality, changing schools*. Boulder, CO: Westview Press.

Macan Ghaill, M. (1995). *The making of men: Masculinities, Sexualities, and Schooling*. Philadelphia: Open University Press.

Macgillivray, I. K. (2007). *Gay-straight alliances: A handbook for students, educators, and parents*. New York: Harrington Park Press.

Martino, W., & Pallotta-Chiarolli, M. (2003). *So what's a boy? Addressing issues of masculinity and schooling*. Buckingham: Open University Press.

Meyer, E. (2006). Gendered harassment in North America: School-based interventions for reducing homophobia and heterosexism. In C. Mitchell & F. Leach (Eds.), *Combating gender violence in and around schools* (pp. 43–50). UK: Trentham Books.

Meyer, E. (2007a). "But I'm not gay": What straight teachers need to know about queer theory. In N. Rodriguez & W. F. Pinar (Eds.), *Queering straight teachers* (pp. 1–17). New York: Peter Lang.

Meyer, E. (2007b). Lessons from *Jubran*: Reducing school board liability in cases of peer harassment. *Proceedings of the 17th Annual Conference of the Canadian Association for the Practical Study of Law in Education*, Vol. 1, pp. 561–576.

Meyer, E. (2008). Lesbians in popular culture. In C. Mitchell & J. Reid-Walsh (Eds.), *Girl culture: An encyclopaedia* (Vol. 2, pp. 392–394). Westport, CT: Greenwood Press.

Mills, M. (2004). Male teachers, homophobia, misogyny and teacher education. *Teaching Education, 15*(1), 27–39.

Montgomery v. Independent School District No. 709, 109 F. Supp. 2d 1081, 1092 (D. Minn. 2000) 2000.

Nabozny v. Podlesny, et al. (7th Cir. (Wis.) 1996).

National Gay and Lesbian Task Force. (2007, September 17). State nondiscrimination laws in the U.S. Retrieved January 3, 2008, from http://www.thetaskforce.org/downloads/reports/issue_maps/non_discrimination_09_07.pdf

Nestle, J., Howell, C., & Wilchins, R. (2002). *Gender queer. Voices from beyond the sexual binary*. New York: Alyson Books.

Nieto, S. (1999). *The light in their eyes: Creating multicultural learning communities*. New York: Teachers College Press. NMHA. (2002). *"What does gay mean?" Teen survey executive summary*. National Mental Health Association.

Paley, V. (1979). *White teacher*. Cambridge, MA: Harvard University Press.

Perrotti, J., & Westheimer, K. (2001). *When the drama club is not enough: Lessons from the safe schools program for gay and lesbian students*. Boston: Beacon Press.

Pinar, W. F. (1998). Understanding curriculum as gender text: Notes on reproduction, resistance, and male-male relations. In William F. Pinar and Mary Aswell Doll (Eds.), *Queer theory in education*. Mahwah, NJ: Lawrence Erlbaum.

Rasmussen, M. L., Mitchell, J., & Harwood, V. (2007). The queer story of "the heterosexual questionnaire." In N. Rodriguez & W. F. Pinar (Eds.), *Queering straight teachers: Discourse and identity in education* (pp. 95–112). New York: Peter Lang.

Ray, V., & Gregory, R. (2001). School experiences of the children of lesbian and gay parents. *Family Matters, 59*, 28–34.

Rich, A. (1978/1993). Compulsory heterosexuality and lesbian existence. In H. Abelove, D. Halperin, & M. A. Barale (Eds.), *The lesbian and gay studies reader* (pp. 227–254). New York: Routledge.

Rowen, C. J., & Malcolm, J. P. (2002). Correlates of internalized homophobia and homosexual identity formation in a sample of gay men. *Journal of Homosexuality, 43*(2), 77–92.

Savin-Williams, R. (1990). *Gay and lesbian youth: Expressions of identity*. New York: Hemisphere.

School District No. 44 (North Vancouver) v. Jubran, 2005 BCCA 201 (BCSC 6 2005).

Sears, J. T. (1998). A generational and theoretical analysis of culture and male (homo)sexuality. In W. F. Pinar (Ed.), *Queer theory in education* (pp. 73–105). Mahwah, NJ: Lawrence Erlbaum.

Sharp, S., & Smith, P. K. (1991). Bullying in UK schools: The DES Sheffield bullying project. *Early Child Development and Care, 77*, 47–55.

Szlacha, L. (2003). Safer sexual diversity climates: Lessons learned from an evaluation of Massachusetts safe schools program for gay and lesbian students. *American Journal of Medicine. 110*(1), 58–88.

Straights and Gays for Equity (SAGE) v. Osseo Area Schools District No. 279. (8th Cir. 2006).

Theno v. Tonganoxie Unified School Dist. No. 464 (2005 WL 3434016 [D. Kan. 2005]).

Trinity Western University v. British Columbia College of Teachers (S.C.R. 772, 2001).

Troiden, R. R. (1988). The formation of homosexual identities. *Journal of Homosexuality, 17*(1/2), 43–74. Trowbridge, C. (2005, December 29). Former student, district settle lawsuit [Electronic Version]. *The Tonganoxie Mirror*. Retrieved March 16, 2006 from www.tonganoxiemirror.com Tucker, D. (Writer). (2005). *Transamerica* [film]. USA: Belladonna Productions. *Vriend v. Alberta* (1 S.C.R. 493 1998).

Waldner-Haugrud, L. & Magruder, B. (1996). Homosexual identity expression among lesbian and gay adolescents: An analysis of perceived structural associations. *Youth and Society, 27*(3), 313–333.

Watkinson, A. (1999). *Education, student rights and the charter*. Saskatoon, SK: Purich. Weeks, J. (1985). *Sexuality and its discontents*. New York: Routledge.

White County High School Peers in Diverse Education v. White County School District (Civil Action No. 2:06-CV-29-WCO (N. D. Georgia, Gainesville Division). 2006).

Whitney, I., & Smith, P. K. (1993). A survey of the nature and extent of bullying in junior/middle and secondary schools. *Educational Research, 35*(1), 3–25.

Wilchins, R. A. (2004). Time for gender rights. *GLQ: A Journal of Lesbian and Gay Studies, 10*(2), 265–267.

CHAPTER 13

(Dis)Embedding Gender Diversity in the Preservice Classroom

sj Miller

What is gender? Why is it important to understand how gender affects classroom flow? What does gender look like in classroom discourse? How do we locate it in and outside of the classroom? What do we draw upon to help conceptualize understandings of gender? How can we prepare our students to remain open to accepting a socially constructed continuum about gender over space and time and in emerging contexts? Even more important, why are such questions about gender necessary? Such questions are timely tipping points for students to discuss as they consider their own positions about their views on the diversity of gender. In this narrative, I explore myriad ways that my undergraduate preservice English students and I have both theoretically and empirically unpacked gender in the classroom and in the context of their teaching lives. Some discussion will focus on describing how students have wrestled with gender in and outside of the classroom space and illuminate how they have been challenged to renegotiate their views about the gender continuum.

What Is Gender?

There are two longstanding arguments about gender. One view holds that gender is something one just *is* such as secondary sex characteristics; the other view portrays gender as something one *has* such as how one is socially positioned as subject. In the first view of gender, one's (biological) sex affects what one does, because of biological characteristics, which include chromosomes, genes, anatomy, gonads, hormones, and so on, and which is typically socially reinforced through a heterosexual model (Wittig, 1983). In the latter argument, feminist research reveals that gender is the social construction of roles, behaviors, and attributes that is considered by the general public to be "appropriate" for one's sex and which is assigned at birth, typically as female or male (Butler, 1990) or as androgyny. In this school of thought, gender roles vary among cultures and along time continuums. de Beauvoir (1973) argues that if gender is constructed, that one becomes a gender and thereby has agency in one's social development as it intersects with culture. She also questions the former argument that the body is not a contested site, that it is quite passive, and already has predetermined social norms attached to it. Irigaray (1985) argues that gender, as social phenomenon, is connected to patriarchy and binds women's bodies to men's control. In other words, women are made or "othered" in men's eyes and so is their sex(uality). Both gender and sex have therefore been socially reproduced to reinforce hegemonic dominance and heteronormativity and to further procreation.

Today, there is a widening divide between notions of gender and sex in society. However, in spite of the gap, teachers often reinforce gender normativity in the classroom. As we educate ourselves on shifting gender norms, we can relocate ourselves as subjects in multiple contexts, and be better equipped to unveil and utilize the shifting discourse. de Beauvoir (1973) argues that the female body should be a site of freedom and a tool of empowerment, and that it is not essentialized. This is highly complex and conflated by a history of male ownership of women through law and religion, and social, economic, and cultural practices. In fact, this institutionalized history, has infused itself into social and cultural practices and by proxy, schooling. Fortunately, the rising waves of feminism and research have sought to place women on equal footing with men both socially and culturally and have been careful not to perpetuate the predated dynamics of subjugating one gender to the other.

Although several theories on gender have been fundamental in shaping dominant perspectives on gender, this discussion is premised on Butler's (1990) notion that gender is performance, which is an outgrowth of prior feminist theories on gender. Butler suggests that the given identity of the individual is illuminated by the gender that one performs. Butler says, "gender is an identity tenuously constituted in time, instituted in an exterior space through a *stylized repetition of acts*" [*sic*] (p. 140). She goes on to suggest that gender is a "surface signification" and that gender "is created through sustained social performances" (p. 141). Butler essentially argues that the individual is a subject, capable of action—not an object to be constructed. Such reasoning infers that people have agency in how they invite and embody an identity. Building from this premise then, by inviting discussion about gender in classrooms, we can begin to see how any identity can take on various gender-performed roles.

An identity is how the core self is illuminated in a given space such as "teacher," "mechanic," "dancer," or "coach." When one leaves one space for another, an identity may be less illuminated in a new space, but it is nonetheless part of what that person performs. Gee (1996) suggests that identities are dialogical and relational, constructed in relation to power and discourse. He also says that individuals have multiple and even hybrid identities, which are intercontextually malleable and consequently ever-changing and readily influenced by space and time. An identity then is something one comes to embody and own as s/he self-defines different aspects of the self and comes into different contexts in space and time (Gee, 1996). An identity is illuminated based on the relationship the individual has within and to the various contexts or social spaces. Social spaces are impacted by political (power) and social ideologies (Foucault 1980, 1986; Lefebvre 1991) and are thereby never totally neutral. Foucault (1986) and Bourdieu (1980) suggest that the effects of power construct identities and that the embodiment of identities is vulnerable as a result of power. Social spaces become central to understanding an identity in terms of "race, ethnicity, social class or gender … those identifications shape engagements in spatial tactics of power and in everyday social, cultural and literate practices" (McCarthey & Moje, 2002, pp. 234–235). Because social spaces are defined in relationship to society, such as a school, café, or bar, identities are highlighted by those social spaces and by the way their identities have been defined in relationship to society. Selves therefore are illuminated by their identities within specific social spaces and yet can be excluded when their identities are not defined by their relationship to that space. Identity can therefore either be stabilized, or affirmed in a given social space, or destabilized when a social space excludes or is unwelcoming of a particular identity. As individuals change and merge with other social spaces, their identities can become hybrids layered with a multitude of subjectivities. Preservice teacher identity co-construction as seen through this premise is thereby sociospatial (Leander, 2002) and teacher identities are discoursed.

Understanding that individuals are subjects within a larger matrix of life is also important in unpacking how gender is performed. Therefore preservice teachers should begin to understand how to co-opt their identities to help them see that they are subjects, capable of acting on and transforming their students' lives, not objects to be constructed. By rupturing the notion that teachers are objects, we shift the status of teachers from subservient clones into transformational agents.

Danielewicz (2001) says that teacher education programs should foster teacher

> identity development to the highest degree possible. In helping preservice teachers recognize their own identity co-constructions, they become more informed about their own subjectivities that can empower them to challenge being co-opted by hegemonic-based discourse and thinking. Recognizing that their own teacher identities are situated within a complex networked matrix of spacetime relationships can help them negotiate their identity co-constructions and help them relocate to spaces that stabilize and affirm their teacher identities. (Miller, 2007b, p.18)

A teacher with agency is a teacher who is better able to challenge the body/mind split.

The body/mind split is important in understanding agency. The dualism of the mind/body split can render a preservice teacher helpless if the individual does not understand the sociopolitical implications of the separation. If a teacher blindly accepts particular curriculum or ideas without completing background research, s/he may be sabotaging her/his agency. Some sociopolitical teaching ideologies are constructed in such a way that teachers may not understand how they divide body from mind and thus, separate one from her/his power to be fully embodied and have agency. If a teacher teaches from this place, s/he passes on the binary of perpetuating status quo ideology that often displaces personal agency. Such thinking sustains dominant culture and binary categorization—meaning that the answer falls into concrete, fixed categories such as Black or White, good or evil, just or unjust.

On the other hand, the empowerment that can arise from the teacher as a whole being, not as object, can lead teachers to be conscientious about their power in constructing their own, as well as students,' identities in the classroom. The importance of such empowerment shifts the binary dynamics and power structures within hegemony and helps individuals become nonbinary agents capable of acting on and transforming the worlds in which they live. On this Bhabha (1994) admonishes us not to simulate the discourse of dominant culture because it reinforces status quo constructs. Nonbinary thinking can liberate and open doors to new possibilities that over time may lead to subvert traditional paradigms once used to keep people silenced and marginalized (Freire, 1970). When we teach preservice teachers to co-opt their own identities, we can liberate them from binary and dominant perceptions that may have once had their time and place in education but which are now antiquated. Rose (1993) advocates for transcending binary constructs and believes that a politics of "difference and identity built on the opening of new spaces" relocates us to a place where counterhegemonic principles can lead to a liberal democracy (Soja, 1996, p. 111). Such a politics lifts us out of binary identifiers and relocates us to a space where ideas can "co-exist concurrently and in contradiction" (Rose, 1993, quoting deLauretis (1987), as in Soja, 1996, p. 112). Teacher education has the power to greatly challenge and subvert dominant paradigms through each of the constituents impacted.

As we move toward nonbinary understandings of gender, it is important to familiarize ourselves with emerging terminology. As we move into the classrooms where we teach, we are likely to meet students who are typically more familiar with these terms than we are because the space and time that youth are living in are more pluralistic. If we hope to support students to adapt to changing times, we can begin to expand our discourse (and our teaching) around gender. Some common ways today that individuals self-identify with regard to gender can be categorized but not essentialized into ag/ aggressive, agendered, androgyne/androgynous, Berdache, bigendered, gender-diverse, genderqueer, intergender, pangender, transandrogyny, transgender, transsexual, and two-spirited (see Appendix A for explanation of terms). Each of these gender categories has sublanguages of its own that are relegated to each of its own cultures. Two other terms are important to define when referring to these emergent gender categories: *gender identity* and *gender expression*. *Gender identity* is one's personal sense of his or her correct gender, which may be reflected as gender expression and *gender expression* is one's choice and/or manipulation of gender cues. Gender expression may or may not be congruent with or influenced by a person's biological sex. If we are to have a true pluralistic understanding about gender, we must begin to inform ourselves about the emerging politics and discourse so we can inform our own students with current and accurate information that will prepare them for real world understandings.

Unfortunately, currently there are only two genders—male and female—that have equal protection under the law. We have gradually seen transgender-identified people receiving more basic human rights than in times past but it is far from equivalent to those who claim to be in the male/female binary. Miller (2007c) writes:

> The transgender movement seeks to have equal protection for transgender people that prohibits discrimination based on "gender identity or expression" and ensures that all transgender and gender nonconforming people are protected by law. This includes jobs, housing, health care, hate crimes legislation, legislative language, antidiscrimination bills, foster care and adoption, marriage, bathrooms, changing birth certificates to reflect the chosen gender, students in school, and being visible in the mainstream eye.[1] (p. 182)

Another way the transgender movement has gained more visibility is through media portrayals, some of which are accurate, some of which are poor. We see these current transgender characters on TV: Alexis Meade on "Ugly Betty," Max on the "L Word," Carmelita on "Dirty Sexy Money," Zarf on "All My Children," Alexis Arquette on "The Surreal Life," and Ava Moore on "Nip/Tuck." In film, we have seen Tina Washington in *The World's Fastest Indian*; Bree in *Transamerica*; Asanee Suwan in *Beautiful Boxer*; Roy in *Norma*; Hedwig in *Hedwig and the Angry Inch*; *Paris is Burning*; Lola in *Kinky Boots*; several characters in *The Adventures of Priscilla, Queen of the Desert*; Noxeema, Vida, and Chi-Chi in *To Wong Foo, Thanks for Everything, Julie Newmar*; Robert Eads in *Southern Comfort*; Brandon Teena in *Boys Don't Cry*; Hank in *The Adventures of Sebastian Cole*; Ludovic in *Ma Vie En Rose*; Dil in *The Crying Game*; Gwen in *A Girl Like Me: The Gwen Araujo Story*; Patrick in *Breakfast on Pluto*; and Luis Molina in *Kiss of the Spider Woman*.

The transgender movement for some has been a way to claim a space or a territory that is connected to the mainstream population but which has its own cultural cues. Common pronouns embraced by some transgender people are "zhe," "hir," and "per" that correlate to he, her, and person. Such as "zhe is going to the bathroom" or "what is hir name?" or "who is that per?" Such a claiming of space means that we must be mindful about speaking in ways that privileges one gender over the other. We have a social and moral responsibility to ask our students what pronouns we should use, what name they want to be called, and if there is anything that we should be made aware of about their gender identity.

Gender Politics in the Classroom

Conjecturing that when we speak about gender in the classroom most students are oblivious to how binary views of gender affect students or their participation because gender is normalized. In fact, criticism is likely to be more about preferential treatment based on gender or appearance. It is not likely that students during this space and time are critical that their teachers are not using inchoate language about gender. However, once we become conscious of change, it is very difficult to go back into binary definitions. As preservice teachers become schooled in emerging gender definitions, the more change can be effected.

Teachers have a social and moral responsibility to update themselves on emerging sociopolitical issues and how they impact the classroom. Likewise, if a teacher lacks particular knowledge and gender performance, s/he may inadvertently marginalize or even destabilize a student who does not fit into the binary. In fact,

> Some students may be hesitant to disclose until they feel safe enough, but unless teachers demonstrate through discourse and behavior that they are an ally, students are likely to assume that they cannot open

up. Along similar lines, we must also be concerned about fostering competitions in classrooms albeit they may appear fun; they reinforce power dynamics and binary roles and beliefs about gender. This means eliminating activities and categories of boys versus girls. It means that we are sensitive with our language all the time and we are deliberate in our actions when designing lessons so we do not marginalize nor reinforce sexism on any level. (Miller, 2007c, p. 183)

Although schools are set up to maintain the status quo (the binary) and to reproduce students who then support the principles under any given democracy, every student deserves a fair and equal education regardless of ethnicity, national origin, national language, appearance, social class, ability, gender, sexual orientation, or gender identity. The consequences, however, may be that if a teacher does not affirm student differences (varying identities) the student may shut down, not complete work, feel separate from the classroom, or be hurt, or in the worst case scenario, attempt or complete a suicide. Teachers can therefore interrupt the cycle of student reproduction (Apple, 2002) as they begin to lead by example and invite social change into the classroom space.

When we begin to discuss gender with our students, there are myriad ways to approach it. Broadening the scope of how our students use gendered discourse must be a deliberate act, and we must therefore also consider our curricular choices, pedagogical stances, and actions so as to reflect the emerging language. Gender is but one aspect within a long continuum of challenging the binary and can and ought to be taught along with ethnicity, national origin, national language, appearance, social class, ability, or sexual orientation. The more inclusive we can be in our teaching, the greater likelihood that it can have a positive efficacy in the lives of students.

The following examples for preservice teachers can be useful in working with their own classroom students.

1. When we speak we must be sure that we explain that all genders should have equal opportunity and that none is privileged over others, although laws are not yet completely equitable or inclusive for all transgender people let alone any of the others. By saying all genders, we mean male, female, transgender, and the other previously referenced genders. The way we also speak about gender, gender identity, and gender expression should be nonbinary because while there are commonly regarded definitions, beliefs, and meanings for gender, there is also a continuum that allows for people to fall outside of what we commonly perceive as binary. As we stay open to a nonbinary understanding of gender, we challenge ourselves to reflect on the changes that occur in our language use every day.

2. Be sure the pedagogy you employ is inclusive, nonbinary, and multidimensional. Examples of such pedagogy include equity pedagogy, critical pedagogy, critical hip-hop pedagogy, liberatory pedagogy, engaging pedagogy, feminist pedagogy, queer pedagogy, and transformative pedagogy.

3. Select texts from all cultures that challenge gender norms and gender identity/expression (see Appendix B).

4. Carefully consider the texts you use and how gender is written about, portrayed, or discussed. Ask questions of your students about texts such as: How is gender portrayed in the text? Describe any variations of gender. What is the gender of the author? How is gender challenged? Affirmed? What do we learn that is new about gender from the text?

5. Use gender-inclusive language in all communications with students, parents, school administrators, and peers. Talk about the broader issues of gender bias, sex-role stereotyping, and discrimination and work to promote gender equity.

6. Create a class library that has a diverse range of texts that embrace differences of culture, class, ethnicity, gender, ability, weight, religion, national origin, sexual orientation, size, gender identity, and gender expression.

7. Place only gender-inclusive posters/placards in the classroom or do not place any at all.

Not all students will be open or receptive to these activities so it is important to assess your classroom students and school environment prior to engaging your students in these gender challenges. In some cases, you may have to solicit parental or principal approval. On the other hand, some students may be ready for this challenge, so you will have to decide how to incorporate these activities based on your assessment. The following are several ways to open discussions about gender.

Activities to use with classroom students (should be modified to suit grade level):

- Discuss new terms about gender and invite discussion and debate.

- Ask students to provide examples of nonbinary portraits of gender in the media.

- Invite discussion and debate about gender norms.

- Ask students to describe where and how they first developed their concept of their own gender identities. Why did they believe that to be true? Who told them? How were those beliefs socialized?

- Ask students to describe how they express their gender. Is that binary/nonbinary?

- Ask students at what age they began to challenge what they learned about themselves? What made them reconsider those beliefs?

- Discuss gender as performance versus gender as fixed.

- Reflect on if there was there ever a time where they thought their answers did not fit the images society had ingrained into them? How did they respond?

- Research former laws related to gender and have them look for bias. Reflect on current change.

- Review antidiscrimination laws.

- Research Title IX, its past, and its future.

- Research which states have nondiscrimination laws and understand how nondiscrimination policies work by state.

- Research which states have laws that privilege homosexuals and transgender people.

- Research which states discriminate against homosexuals and transgender people.

- Research which state laws exclude homosexuals and transgender people.

- Have a critical discourse analysis of a TV show or film on gendered language use.

- Have a discourse analysis of students' use of gendered language.

- Interview people in the local community who challenge the gender binary.

- Invite guest speakers who challenge the gender binary.

- Rewrite a scene or passage from a film (see Appendix B) or text (poem, play, or short story) and shift the use of gendered language so it affirms the characters.

- Deconstruct how mainstream ads reinforce the gender binary.

- Examine what kinds of TV commercials and TV shows are on at particular times and how that sustains the gender binary.

- Examine different genres of musical lyrics and how they affirm or contest the gender binary. (There are hundreds of musical performers who identify outside of the gender binary, see Appendix C.)

- Review clips in the media about how female politicians are compared to male politicians.

- Examine random pay scales in various professions and look for gender equity.

- Review the history of all human rights and all of the major social movements (civil rights, gay/lesbian/bisexual/transgender/two-spirited, women, second-language speakers, bilingual, immigrants, Asian Americans, Native Americans, Latina/o Americans, veterans, war dissenters, disabled, students with disabilities or special needs, and any other nondominant groups).

- Review the "isms" and unpack how prejudice and oppression manifest in students' lives (see chapter 7, Miller, 2007c).

- Talk about what it means to be an ally and how students can become allies for others.

The following activities may be more risky, so first consider discussions with the principal, other teachers, and parents/guardians.

- Challenge students to dress outside of the gender norm (gender expression) for a class period or if successful and it is safe, for an entire school day.

- Invite your students to design a nonbinary gender day for the school with speakers, panelists, and poetry.

- Invite students to attend lectures of community presentations at local universities or colleges to expose them to different perspectives about gender

Keep in mind that students may be quite resistant to challenging the ways that they understand gender so try to be patient, not preachy, and continue to provide opportunities for them to engage in experiences that challenge the binary. Whether or not they agree with the nonbinary idea is not essential; it is more important to expose students to the inevitable changes that are emerging in the world.

It is also important to understand, for both your students as well as yourselves, the consequences of not addressing or challenging the gender binary. By introducing a different way of talking about gender, we can challenge some of the forms of gender oppression that exist. Our students will be better prepared for handling sexism, sexual harassment, bullying, selfinjury, or even hate crimes. Sexism is the systemic oppression of individuals that privileges one gender over the other, and in the United States that is typically men over women (Miller, 2007c, p. 182). Generally stemming from a history of institutional policies and social values defined by men, this system operates to the advantage of men, and more often White men, and to the disadvantage of women. It is vital that we develop a social consciousness with our students around gender bias issues so as not to perpetuate oppressive gender-based hierarchies that are deeply entrenched in society. As we deepen awareness about gender oppression, we ultimately shift gender dynamics in dominant culture and may thwart attacks on individuals who fall outside of the gender binary.

Wrestling with the Gender Binary Inside and Outside the Classroom

This section draws upon empirical examples from my teaching of preservice teachers and illuminates how they have each been challenged to renegotiate their views about the gender continuum. When I consider how to design my syllabus during a particular semester, I take into account what is happening in my students' communities, the nation, and the world at large. I try to choose texts and design lessons that best reflect my students' cultures and values for that particular class or select texts about areas in which we need to enhance our understanding of humanity. When selecting texts, I ask myself what voices I need to have echoed back to my students. The answer often resides in the class itself. As I come to know my students through the dialogic (Freire, 1970) and understand their issues and home lives, I become more informed so I can select authors who resonate with them and their own stories. I often teach works by authors of color and select authors who have been marginalized by dominant society. I also deliberately select texts that have characters or story lines that point to prejudice and that can help point to deeper sociopolitical issues (see examples in chapter 7, Miller, 2007c).

From day one, I raise examples that help students understand how power, privilege, and oppression have been institutionalized and through examples, essentially conduct a historical analysis of groups and individuals that that have been disenfranchised in hegemony. This scaffolding process fosters a larger context for understanding oppression and aptly prepares us to understand how gender is one form among many kinds of institutional oppression. The pedagogy I embrace, employ, and embody is a combination of liberatory and transformative mixed with the theory of critical literacy.

A liberatory pedagogy is one that seeks to educate students to act on and transform their worlds through acts of cognition first, and action second (Freire, 1970). Freire suggests that when we adopt a liberatory pedagogy, two distinct changes will occur: "when the oppressed unveil the world of oppression and through the praxis commit themselves to its transformation," and "in which the reality of oppression has already been transformed, this pedagogy ceases to belong to the oppressed and becomes a pedagogy of all the people in the process of permanent liberation" (p. 54). In so doing, we help free the oppressed from the oppressor, which then activates the oppressed to become agents capable of acting on and transforming their worlds; thus, we emancipate the oppressed. Although our students are not oppressed per se, they certainly are embedded within a matrix that sustains a hegemonic power and that reinforces particular social values and morals. A liberatory pedagogy prepares them to think critically about their worlds and gives them the tools to be informed citizens so that when they need to act, they know how.

Lewinson et al. (2002) suggest that the field of critical literacy is defined by "disrupting the commonplace, interrogating multiple view points, focusing on sociopolitical issues and taking action and promoting social justice" through texts (p. 3). Therefore, critical literacy can be a vehicle through which identity is negotiated as texts bump up against the self. Since critical literacy is "political practice influenced by social, cultural and historical factors"(Barton & Hamilton, 2000; Street, 1995, as in Hagood, 2002, p. 249) and is "committed foremost to the 'alleviation of human suffering and [to] the formation of a more just world through the critique of existing social and political problems and the posing of alternatives'" (Hagood, 2002, p. 249), texts taught through a poststructuralist lens can be a way to help youth negotiate and affirm their identities as they make meaning of the world in which they live. A poststructuralist reading of texts can be a powerful way to assist youth in holding onto their authentic selves while it teaches them to interact with the world so they may act on it in a fashion that does not perpetuate hegemony or the status quo. Youth, with an affirmed authentic self, can seek to transform the world through a subjective self that does not ascribe to the construction that the school system seeks to impose upon them. Consequently, the world/environment becomes vulnerable to a new subjectivity as it transacts with authentic selves, free of construction.

Hagood (2002) contends that critical literacy should assist students in developing an understanding of how texts "produce particular formations of self" (p. 248). Texts are situated within certain social and cultural groups. For all purposes, texts are imbued by larger sociopolitical issues of power that are associated in cultural and social groups. Texts reflect the changes in society, such as in how power may change within particular ethnicities, classes, and/or social patterns. In other words, as perceptions of ethnicities change, and as they may each gain access to positions of power and authority, texts reflect those changes. Our identities are impacted by their transactions with those texts, and when the texts shift along with the changes in society, so too do our identities shift. This means that from a poststructuralist perspective identities are constantly in flux.

An experience of one of my former undergraduate students, Matt, has stayed with me now for a couple of years. It emerged from a unit in an undergraduate humanities literature course in which I was teaching *Herland*, by Charlotte Perkins Gilman. Keep in mind that my students had been schooled in gender-inclusive language so they were quite ready for this activity. The background to the story is as follows. I was teaching a unit about gender normative behavior and doing an activity called the "Gender Box" (see www.glsen.org for more details). Essentially, the words *male* and *female* are placed next to each other in a box that looks like this:

Male	Female
• Breadwinner	• Soft, caring
• Hard working	• Stays home
• Unemotional	• Raises children
• Sports nut	• Committed
• Uncommitted	• Emotional
• Player	• Less educated
• Rugged	• Manipulative

Next, students are asked for words that describe typical gender behaviors or roles played by each. Typically this is quite lively and students tend to challenge each other. Once the box is full, start to have a conversation about what happens to people who don't fit into these behaviors or roles. Generally students spout negative epithets such as "dyke," "fag," "butch," "queer," etc. Then, discuss how the binary has reinforced these negative perceptions and the consequences that may befall anyone who does not fit into the binary. Next, tell students that sometimes we fall within both sides of the box and we transcend gender norms and sometimes we don't fit on either side of the box and we transcend gender norms.

After participating in this activity, Matt raised his hand and said, "Dr. Miller, I have always identified as a male, but now that I see this box, I don't fit into stereotypical categories of male. Therefore, I must be transgendered." I stopped and looked at him and didn't know what to say. After contemplating a supportive answer, I said, "Matt, you can identify however you want."

A preservice student named Samantha I taught in a methods course had an eye-opening experience in the middle school classroom where she was teaching. I had taught a unit in methods on the possible negative effects of bullying on students if left unattended, such as cutting, self-injury, acting out, depression, attempted suicide or successful suicide, risky behavior, and drug use. We examined statistics that revealed which groups of students were at particularly high risk for bullying (see chapter 3, Miller, 2007a). Prior to this students had, once again, been schooled with emerging terminology about gender.

Samantha decided to teach Tolan's *Plague Year*, a story about Molly and Barn who were harassed for their appearances, physical traits, and personalities. Samantha had to be cautious about what to talk about and bring up because she was teaching with a conservative cooperating teacher and was concerned about redress. She put bullying into a larger context that described why some people are bullied while also carefully introducing some of the emerging terms in Appendix A. At the time she taught this, she was very pleased with the outcome because students took it very seriously and even conducted a whole-school survey on who is bullied and for what reasons. Results were published in the school paper. Unbeknownst to her at the time she was teaching, a young woman who identified as male and who did not fit into the binary was ingesting Samantha's teaching. Two years after she left Samantha's course, she ran into her in the local supermarket. The conversation went something like this:

Girl:	"Hi Ms. L. Nice to see you."
Sam:	"Great to see you too. How are you doing?"
Girl:	"Remember the unit you taught on bullying, well it has given me courage to be who I am."
Sam:	"I am very pleased for you—that is so cool."
Girl:	"Yeah, in fact, I started a gay/straight alliance at the high school." Sam: "No way, that's fantastic."

We may not always know the impact we are making in students' lives but we must find the courage in ourselves to open new doors for students to walk through as they struggle to find their sense of place in the world. Samantha, seemed to have a stronger sense of self and even if she has no support in her life, she will always know that a person of credibility validated her sense of belonging. What more can we hope for?

What I realized from both Matt's and Samantha's experiences is that in broadening their awareness about gender norms, depending on where students are in their cognitive, moral, emotional, and psychological development, they will begin to be challenged by or challenge others about gendered offensives. Such awareness can diversify human experience and lead us to places that are still emerging during this and other spaces and times.

(Dis)Embedding Gender: Moving Between Spaces

In our commitment to grow as individuals, we must also stay actively involved in the areas of our lives that can enhance our classroom practice. This could mean staying active by watching all kinds of media, going to popular culture events, attending presentations and lectures, traveling, putting ourselves in situations that challenge our thinking, taking more courses, reading as much as we can (see Appendix D), and conducting research. Not only will we be better informed but so too will the students whom we teach. I still have students who write me and teach me about new terms and ways they self-define, and I look forward to those letters and e-mails as a way to apply change in my own teaching life. Though it may not always be easy to teach about topics that may make us uncomfortable, if we don't, we are cheating our students out of being informed about the emerging contexts during any space and time.

Appendix A: Terms

Ag / Aggressive*: used to describe a female-bodied and identified person who prefers presenting as masculine. This term is most commonly used in urban communities of color.

Agendered*: person who is internally ungendered or does not have a felt sense of gender identity.

Androgyne/Androgynous*: person appearing and/or identifying as neither man nor woman, presenting as either mixed or gender neutral.

Berdache*: used to refer to a third-gender person (woman-living-man). The term berdache is generally rejected as inappropriate and offensive by Native peoples because it is a term that was assigned by European settlers to differently gendered Native peoples. Appropriate terms vary by tribe and include one-spirit, two-spirit, and wintke.

Bigendered*: person whose gender identity is a combination of male/man and female/woman.

Gender: expressions of masculinity, femininity, or androgyny in words, persons, organisms, or characteristics.

Gender Diverse*: person who either by nature or by choice does not conform to gender-based expectations of society (e.g., transgender, transsexual, intersex, genderqueer, cross-dresser, etc.). Also referred to as gender variant because it does not imply a standard normativity.

Genderqueer*: gender diverse person whose gender identity is neither male nor female, is between or beyond genders, or is some combination of genders. This identity is usually related to or in reaction to the social construction of gender, gender stereotypes, and the gender binary system.

Intergender*: person whose gender identity is between genders or a combination of genders.

Pangender*: person whose gender identity comprises all or many gender expressions.

Sex: medical term designating a certain combination of gonads, chromosomes, external gender organs, secondary sex characteristics, and hormonal balances. Because usually subdivided into male and female, this category does not recognize the existence of intersex bodies.

Transandrogyny*: gender diverse gender expression that does not have a prominent masculine or feminine component.

Transgender: person who lives as a member of a gender other than that expected based on anatomical sex. Sexual orientation varies and is not dependent on gender identity. A transgender person may or may not be preor post-operative; if s/he is, the individual is likely to refer to him/herself as transsexual. This has become an umbrella term for nonconforming gender identity and expression. Often associated with this term is FTM/F2M (female to male) and MTF/M2F (male to female).

Transsexual*: person who identifies psychologically as a gender/sex other than the one to which they were assigned at birth. Transsexuals often wish to transform their bodies hormonally and surgically to match their inner sense of gender/sex.

Two-Spirited*: Native persons who have attributes of both genders, have distinct gender and social roles in their tribes, and are often involved with mystical rituals (shamans). Their dress is usually a mixture of male and female articles and they are seen as a separate or third gender. The term *two-spirit* is usually considered specific to the Zuni tribe. Similar identity labels vary by tribe and include *one-spirit* and *wintke*.

*terms from *Trans and sexuality terminologies* (Green and Peterson (2004)).

Appendix B: Young Adult Literature

(texts and films taken from pp. 43–44 of Miller, 2007a, *Unpacking the Loaded Teacher Matrix*)

Middle School Texts

Including gay/lesbian/bisexual/transgender themes:
Alice Alone, Phyllis Reynolds Naylor
Alice on the Outside, Phyllis Reynolds Naylor
The Eagle Kite, Paula Fox
I Feel a Little Jumpy around You: A Book of Her Poems & His Poems Collected in Pairs, Naomi Shihab Nye
   and Paul B. Janeczko
From the Notebooks of Melanin Sun, Jacqueline Woodson
The House You Pass on the Way, Jacqueline Woodson
Risky Friends, Julie A. Peters
The Misfits, James Howe
The Skull of Truth, Bruce Coville and Gary A. Lippincott

High School Texts

Heterosexual (*made into a film)
Boys Lie, John Neufeld
Lucky, Alice Sebold
Out of Control, Shannon McKenna
Shattering Glass, Gail Giles
*Speak,** Laurie Halse Anderson
*To Kill a Mockingbird,** Harper Lee
Unexpected Development, Marlene Perez

GAY/BISEXUAL THEMES

Alt Ed, Catherine Atkins
Am I Blue?, Marion Dane Bauer and Beck Underwood
The Drowning of Stephan Jones, Bette Greene
Geography Club, Brent Hartinger
The Perks of Being a Wallflower, Stephen Chbosky
Rainbow High, Alex Sanchez
Rainbow Boys, Alex Sanchez
Shattering Glass, Gail Giles
Simon Says, Elaine Marie Alphin
What Happened to Lani Garver?, Carol Plum-Ucci

LESBIAN/BISEXUAL THEMES

Am I Blue? Marion Dane Bauer and Beck Underwood
Annie on My Mind, Nancy Garden
The Color Purple, Alice Walker
Empress of the World, Sara Ryan
Keeping You a Secret, Julie Anne Peters
Kissing Kate, Lauren Myracle
Name Me Nobody, Lois-Ann Yamanaka
Out of the Shadows, Sue Hines

TRANSGENDER THEMES

Define "Normal," Julie Anne Peters
The Flip Side, Andrew Matthews

Luna, Julie Anne Peters
My Heartbeat, Garret Freymann-Weyr
Standing Naked on the Roof, Francess Lantz
Written on the Body, Jeanette Winterson

Films

We encourage you to have discussions with your cooperating teacher, clinical supervisor, university instructor, and administrator if you intend to use any of these films. Some of these films are better suited for the methods classroom.

A Girl Like Me, Billy Elliot, Boys Don't Cry, Beautiful Thing, But I'm a Cheerleader, Camp, Confronting Date Rape: The Girl's Room, Date Violence: A Young Woman's Guide, It's So Elementary, This Boy's Life, Ma Vie En Rose, Normal, School Ties, Speak, You Ought to Know: Teens Talk about Dating and Abuse

Appendix C: Bands with Gender-Fluid People

The Cliks
Rolling Stones
REM
New York Dolls
All the Pretty Horses
Scissor Sisters
Girl Friday
David Bowie
Grace Jones
Lipstick Conspiracy
Lisa Jackson & Girl Friday
Katastrophe
Peecocks
Storm Florez
Pepperspray
Veronica Klaus
Angel Wayward
Georgie Jessup
Harisu
Bambi Lake
Bitesize
Gurlfriendz
Transisters
Angela Motter
Peter Outerbridge
Imperial Drag

Appendix D: More Resources about Gender and Sex Issues

Binnie, J. (2004). *The globalization of sexuality.* Thousand Oaks, CA: Sage.
Bohjalian, C. (2000). *Trans-sister radio.* New York: Random House. Bornstein, K. (1995). *Gender outlaw.* New York: Vintage.
Browning, F. (1994). *The culture of desire.* New York: Random House.
Eugenides, J. (2002). *Middlesex.* New York: Picador.
Feinberg, L. (1993). *Stone butch blues.* Ithaca: Firebrand.

Foucault, M. (1991). *History of sexuality, Vol. 1.* New York: Vintage.

Halberstam, J. (1998). *Female masculinity.* Durham: Duke University Press.

Hennessey, Rosemary. (2000). *Profit and pleasure: Sexual identities in late capitalism.* New York: Routledge.

Lorde, A. (1983). *Zami: A new spelling of my name.* Trumansburg: Cross Press.

Moraga, C., & Anzaldua, G. (1981). *This bridge called my back: Writings by radical women of color.* New York: Kitchen Table/Women of Color Press.

Rubin, G. (1998). Thinking sex: Notes for a radical theory of the politics of sexuality. In P. M. Nardi & B. Schneider (Eds.), *Social perspectives in gay and lesbian studies.* New York: Routledge.

Russo, V. (1987). *The celluloid closet: Homosexuality in the movies.* New York: Harper & Row. Sedgwick, E. K. (1991). *Epistemology of the closet.* Berkeley: University of California Press. Seidman, S. (1997). *Difference troubles: Queering social theory and sexual politics.* Cambridge: Cambridge University Press.

Signorile, M. (1997). *Life outside.* New York: HarperCollins.

Signorile, M. (1993). *Queer in America.* New York: Doubleday.

Sullivan, A. (1996). *Virtually normal.* New York: Random House.

Sullivan, N. (2003). *Critical introduction to queer theory.* New York: New York University Press. Warner, M. (2000). *The trouble with normal: Sex, politics, and the ethics of queer life.* Cambridge, MA: Harvard University Press.

Wittig, M. (1992). *The straight mind and other essays.* Boston: Beacon Press. Woolf, V. (1928). *Orlando.* New York: Penguin

Note

1. For more information on transgender rights and current laws see the ACLU, http://www.aclu.org/getequal/trans.html; the Human Rights Campaign, http://www.hrc.org/index.html; the Transgender Law and Policy Institute, http://www.transgenderlaw.org/; the National Gay and Lesbian Task Force (NGLTF), http://www. thetaskforce.org/ourprojects/tcrp/; and http://www.mappingourrights.org for current rulings on discrimination by state.

References

Apple, M. (2002). *Official knowledge.* New York: Routledge.

Barton, D., & Hamilton, M. (2000). Literacy practices. In D. Barton, M. Hamilton, & R. Ivanic (Eds.), *Situated literacies: Reading and writing in context* (pp. 7–15). New York: Routledge.

Bhabha, H. A. (1994). *The location of culture.* New York: Routledge. Bourdieu, P. (1980). *The logic of practice.* Stanford: Stanford University Press.

Butler, J. (1990). *Gender trouble: Feminism and the subversion of identity.* New York: Routledge.

Danielewicz, J. (2001). *Teaching selves: Identity, pedagogy and teacher education.* Albany: State University of New York Press.

de Beauvoir, S. (1973). *The second sex.* (Trans. E. M. Parshley). New York: Vintage Books. deLauretis, T. (1987). *Technologies of gender: Essays on theory, film and fiction.* London: Macmillan.

Foucault, M. (1980). *Power-knowledge: Selected interviews and other writings, 1972–1977.* New York: Pantheon. Foucault, M. (1986). Of other spaces (J. Miskowiec, Trans.). *Diacritics, 16*(1), 22–27.

Freire, P. (1970). *Pedagogy of the oppressed.* New York: Continuum.

Gee, J. P. (1996). *Social linguistics and literacies: Ideology in discourses* (2nd ed.). New York: Falmer Press. Gilman, C. P. (1979). *Herland.* New York: Pantheon.

Green, E., & Peterson, E. (2004). *Trans and sexuality terminologies.* Retrieved January 8, 2008 from http://www.transacademics.org.

Hagood, M. (2002). Critical literacy for whom? *Reading Research and Instruction, 41,* 247–266.

Irigaray, L. (1985). *The sex which is not one.* (Trans C. Porter & C. Brooke). Ithaca: Cornell University Press. Leander, K. (2002). Locating Latanya: The situated production of identity artifacts in classroom interaction. *Re-search in the Teaching of English, 37,* 198–250.

Lefebvre, H. (1991). *The production of space.* Oxford: Blackwell.

Lewinson, M., Flint, A. S., & Van Sluys, K. (2002). Taking on critical literacy: The journey of newcomers and novices. *Language Arts, 79*(5), 382–392.

McCarthey, S., & Moje, E. (2002). Identity matters. *Reading Research Quarterly, 37*(2), 228–238.

Miller, s. (2007a). The loaded matrix in classroom and school environments. In sj. Miller & L. Norris, *Unpacking the loaded teacher matrix: Negotiating space and time between university and secondary English classrooms* (pp. 33–83). New York: Peter Lang.

Miller, s. (2007b). The loaded matrix: Theoretical and practical framework. In sj. Miller & L. Norris, *Unpacking the loaded teacher matrix: Negotiating space and time between university and secondary English classrooms* (pp. 11–31). New York: Peter Lang.

Miller, s. (2007c). Social justice and sociocultural issues as part of the loaded matrix. In sj. Miller & L. Norris, *Unpacking the loaded teacher matrix: Negotiating space and time between university and secondary English classrooms* (pp. 157–203). New York: Peter Lang.

Rose, G. (1993). *Feminism and geography: The limits of geographical knowledge.* Cambridge: Polity Press.

Soja, E. W. (1996). *Thirdspace: Journeys to Los Angeles and other real-and-imagined places.* Malden: Blackwell.

Street, B. V. (1995). *Social literacies: Critical approaches to literacy in development, ethnography, and education.* London: Longman.

Tolan, S. (1991). *Plague year.* New York: Random House.

Witting, M. (1983). The point of view: Universal of particular? *Feminist Issues, 3*(2), pp. 63–69.

PART IV

More than Methods: Authentic Teaching

CHAPTER 14

Breakbeat Pedagogy

Brian Mooney

My break beat is to break away from yo thang.

—Arrested Development

Breakbeat Pedagogy: A Framework

The term "Hip-Hop based education" (HHBE) has been used to describe the curricular and pedagogical uses of Hip-Hop's four elements—DJing, Breakdancing, Rapping, and Graffiti Art. However, the theoretical and practical applications of HHBE remain unclear and there is sufficient need to question, clarify, and reimagine what HHBE might look like in schools. There is no shortage of critics who deem this kind of teaching and learning as "gimmicky," superficial, and ambiguous.

I propose a new framework, based on HHBE, which aims to clarify what this pedagogy looks like when a school more fully integrates the elements of Hip-Hop via the performance art space. It is built on theory, but ultimately is based in reality. This framework is called Breakbeat Pedagogy (BBP).

Breakbeat Pedagogy is the art of the Hip-Hop event. It involves the process of creating a poetry slam or Hip-Hop event, alongside students, to initiate a democratic space for the elements to live and thrive within a school community. Hip-Hop has a long tradition of "the event"—from South Bronx block parties to community centers to back-to-school jams at 1520 Sedgwick Ave. (Chang, 2005). "The event" is where the breakbeat first moved the crowd, united b-boys, and exemplified the performative, yet unpredictable and exciting nature of Hip-Hop culture. Nowhere have the elements been more clearly on display than the Hip-Hop event.

In order to clarify this pedagogy, I turn now to an important publication, *The BreakBeat Poets: New American Poets in the Age of Hip-Hop* (Coval, Lansana, & Marshall, 2015), from which my book draws its name and its inspiration. It is the most comprehensive anthology of Hip-Hop generation poets ever published and an indispensable resource for educators. The following excerpt is from the section "Ars Poeticas & Essays":

The *break* is the moment when everything in a song stops—except for the drums and bass or the drums alone. When Kool Herc, as we know, took two copies of the same record and spun the break back and forth, he extended the drum beat for as long as people on the floor wanted it to last. Thanks to Herc, the break wasn't just a fissure, a brief account, a short reprieve; it was the ongoing pulse, the call to what Afrika Bambaataa calls the Godself. Instead of thinking of it as a moment that comes and goes, the whole music was a sustained breaking. Herc changed the notion/the practice/the role of the break in history. He changed history, music as intervention, the ticks on the clock become the proverbial *break* o'dawn. (Rosal, 2015, p. 323)

Sustained Breaking

The break, manipulated by Kool Herc for the sake of dance, represents the most elemental nature of Hip-Hop. When everything is stripped away, we are left with a drum pattern, reduced to its most simplistic form, yet infinitely complex in its implications for teaching and learning. The break, like storytelling itself, is fundamental to Hip-Hop culture. If teachers and schools want to practice HHBE, I suggest looking back in time to what brought us all together to begin with—the breakbeat.

If the break is the moment when everything stops, we need to create pedagogical sites that suspend the space-time of traditional teaching and learning, looking to the Hip-Hop event as the primary opportunity for us to honor the complex literacies, talents, interests, and stories of our students. The breakbeat is about unity, but also fracture. It is about harmony, but also discord. As Kevin Coval (2015) writes, it is to "break from the norm ... a break in time ... a rupture in narrative ... a signifying of something new."

Events like *Word Up!*—the Hip-Hop and spoken word event that I created with my students—represent the application of Breakbeat Pedagogy (BBP). The event, which features student-poets, MCs, graffiti writers, breakdancers, and DJs, is a communion of the elements both within and without. It exists inside the school, in the Black Box Theater, an institutional space, but it also exists somewhere between classrooms, between the officially sanctioned spaces, somewhere inside the breakbeat—a place uninterrupted by school bells and disruptive announcements.

The event is fundamental to BBP theory because it creates an "ongoing pulse." It isn't a momentary departure from traditional schooling, but a continuum of democratic unity, a metaphysical cypher that transcends the school calendar, giving students and teachers and parents a reason to come together. Like Kool Herc extending the break, the schoolwide Hip-Hop event literally and figuratively extends the school day. It breaks or departs from previously charted waters, which scares many administrators and teachers. *What will students say with all that freedom?*

Word Up!—our Hip-Hop event—symbolizes what Patrick Rosal (2015, p. 323) calls a "sustained breaking." It is a break not only from the institutional structures of the school day, but also from the scattered applications of critical pedagogues trying to implement HHBE in isolated spaces. It is a pedagogical coming together of the elements, generated by students, to celebrate, showcase, and champion youth voice. The Hip-Hop event breaks from what Freire (1970) calls "the banking model of education" in a radical way. It positions the student as curator / presenter / teacher / storyteller / director / lecturer / organizer / and planner.

When students build a communal storytelling space—through poetry, rap, graffiti art, breakdancing, and even sonically, through DJing / turntablism—new kinds of incentives arise from the ashes of the archaic, rote methodology of Eurocentric pedagogies. Students begin to anticipate people showing up to listen. They know there will be a show, an event, a showcase, a reason to unite, a reason to stay after school and catch the late bus on a Friday because the slam team is performing and there's a guest poet coming from New York City that we've all seen on YouTube. They know someone will be working lights and sound, and selling tickets, and music will be playing—and there will be performances, entertainment, storytelling, a communal cypher that has been circulating since the last show, and which we are eager to continue.

Lights/Camera/Break!

The excitement surrounding a Hip-Hop event is unparalleled. It is the essence of youth culture in a school. When student-poets and MCs know there is going to be a room or theater full of peers listening intently, there is a heightened level of motivation to perform well. The event is a catalyst for students to invest in the creation process. The real value is in the weeks and months leading up to the event, when students are engaged in critical conversations about race, class, gender, and identity. The real value can be found in the art-making process of workshopping poems, giving feedback, practicing performance techniques, refining stories, designing artwork, assembling playlists, and choreographing dance routines. This process is completely interest driven and student centered, with the teacher functioning as co-facilitator/planner.

Breakbeat Pedagogy depends on our willingness to embrace the idea that "flaws and fractures are the substance of imagination" and that "breaking is making" (Rosal, 2015, p. 325). When students and teachers create an art space that integrates elements of Hip-Hop culture, there is a simultaneous breaking and building. Students, in their ontological vocation to become fully humanized (Freire, 1970), break from the structures and pedagogies that have been confining them to the margins of the classroom. Equipped with voice and microphone, their stories are a kind of shattering. They shatter preconceived notions about "articulateness" and literacy. They shatter stereotypes. They shatter dominant narratives and ideologies that have excluded them. They shatter identities, rebuilding them in the same breath. Ultimately, they shatter despair and what Maxine Greene (1995) calls "the mundane." All these forms of breaking are also forms of building. But this kind of building can take place only in a democratic space that is open to the whole school.

Many schools and districts likely won't allow a "Hip-Hop event." Sometimes we must frame the events as "poetry readings" or "poetry slams," which are essentially the same kinds of gatherings, but without the stigma of "Hip-Hop." Until the powers that be will accept Hip-Hop as a legitimate culture, we must find ways to transgress so that the work continues, regardless of those who try to silence us.

If there aren't facilities that can accommodate an event of this kind, a classroom, cafeteria, or gymnasium will do, as long as it can be opened to the community. Too often we relegate student performances to "presentation days" in our classrooms, limiting the performances to an audience of twenty-five or thirty peers. Our students are worthy of large audiences. This we know.

Bearing Witness

Breakbeat Pedagogy is a form of therapeutic intervention. It is a disruption of both form and content, interjecting itself into spaces previously closed off to Hip-Hop, such as schoolwide assemblies in the gymnasium and shows in the performing arts theater. BBP sanctions a space for itself in a physical way. It reclaims the school building and says, "We're here in the spirit of peace, unity, love, and having fun." It says, "We're here on behalf of democracy." It says, "We're here to take over this theater and make it dope." It says, "We don't just study Hip-Hop lyrics; we create and perform and showcase and invite the school to participate in our cypher, to build with us, and to come bear witness."

For participants in a Hip-Hop community to bear witness there must be a physical coming together. We must exist in the same space with one another's bodies. BBP invites us to reclaim our bodies in a communal space. It channels the energy of a theater or gymnasium and translates that energy into snaps, moans of sympathy, verbal affirmations, head nods, and hands waving in the air. BBP reminds us that call-and-response works best when there's a crowd! BBP asks us to reflect on the moments that have moved us beyond our self-centered fear. BBP insists there is a power greater than ourselves at work when people come together in the spirit of unity. How we define that power is truly up to us.

I'll turn for a moment to the idea of the academic conference, a space in which professionals gather to share, present, build, and network. We know the feeling of the conference. It affirms that we are part of something. It's exciting to be in the presence of brilliant educators, people who share our vocation and our passion for teaching and learning. We sense there is an unspoken connectivity that materializes only when we come together in the physical. Many of us communicate via social media and participate in Twitter chats to share ideas and resources, but the ancient gathering of bodies in the same room prevails. Dialogue. Conversation. Listening. Performance. These things sustain us.

So what kinds of spaces do we create for our students to acquire this same kind of sustenance? It's true that some of our students attend out-of-school conferences such as Comic-Con, gatherings that bring together people who share similar interests, but why can't this happen in schools? Why must we make students leave their identities at the classroom door, forcing them to seek affirmation outside of the school building? Perhaps we should vacate our classrooms and head for the gym or theater. Perhaps our classrooms have served only to isolate teachers and students from one another, barring us from communal spaces that celebrate youth culture. This old design needs breaking. It needs reimagining. It needs poetry slams and Hip-Hop events. It needs Breakbeat Pedagogy.

Critical Hip-Hop Language Pedagogies

In my research, I have been particularly interested in the empowerment of school communities through Hip-Hop pedagogy, spoken word performance, and the resistance to what Samy Alim (2007) calls "the language ideological combat that is being waged inside and outside of our classroom walls." We must recognize that waging a grammar war against speakers of different English dialects is an injustice, and that while most teachers devote exorbitant amounts of energy to cultivating an academic language, many students are busy "celebrating, highlighting, and consciously manipulating diverse language varieties" (Alim, 2007, p. 164). I have sought ways to celebrate this variety not only by integrating Hip-Hop music and lyrics in the classroom, but also by employing the surrounding culture of graffiti art, DJing, breakdancing, and spoken word poetry in the larger school community. The synthesis of these elements is what I mean by Breakbeat Pedagogy.

Alim (2007) argues that "Critical Hip Hop Language Pedagogies, or CHHLPs, engage in the process of consciousness-raising, that is, the process of actively becoming aware of one's own position in the world and what to do about it" (p. 166). Breakbeat Pedagogy aims to develop this awareness, extending this consciousness-raising to the larger school community through the Hip-Hop and spoken word event. Literacy is a participatory practice, a performative event in the truest sense, learned through critical and democratic social engagement in spaces that affirm identity, voice, and empowerment.

The use of Hip-Hop in the classroom is not a simple gimmick disguised to get students interested in the literary canon (Morrell & Duncan-Andrade, 2002), although it can be used for that. The real value of Breakbeat Pedagogy is the dialogue it generates. Conversations about race, class, privilege, power, masculinity, and misogyny were common in my classroom when preparing for *Word Up!* This kind of dialogue speaks to the Freirean (1987) nature of Breakbeat Pedagogy because it asks students to "read the world" through a critical lens, developing a capacity for what Maxine Greene calls "wide-awakeness" (1995). The kinds of conflict that Hip-Hop presents (Low, 2011) actually provide us with opportunities to confront oppression in a critical way, ultimately developing the capacities needed to become critical consumers and producers of texts in the twenty-first century (Low, 2011; Morrell, Dueñas, Garcia, & López, 2013). It isn't enough to have students engage in dialogue about sexism in Hip-Hop. They need to produce a response, a reinterpretation, a talking back—and share these new understandings in a community space that extends beyond the classroom walls. We must invite the community, including administration, *into* our new understandings if our hope is for Hip-Hop pedagogy to transform education.

Breaking the Common Core

One misconception is that Hip-Hop and spoken word are not academically rigorous, when in fact the study of Hip-Hop can be highly academic and aligned to the Common Core Standards. Morrell and Duncan-Andrade (2002) suggest that if we want to empower urban students to analyze complex literary texts, "Hip Hop can be used as a bridge linking the seemingly vast span between the streets and the world of academics" (p. 89). In my Hip-Hop Lit class, we regularly engage in close-reading practices such as making inferences and predictions, identifying figurative language, analyzing theme, making connections, and synthesizing knowledge. One Common Core Standard that we address frequently is ELA Standard #6 under the Reading Literature cluster:

> CCSS.ELA-Literacy.RL.9–10.6 Analyze a particular point of view or cultural experience reflected in a work of literature from outside the United States, drawing on a wide reading of world literature.

Some would argue that Hip-Hop texts, such as lyrics from American rappers, do not constitute "a work of literature from outside the United States." However, if we think about Hip-Hop as a cultural artifact that has been shaped by colonialism and the African diaspora, we can understand Hip-Hop as a cultural production that has always been "outside" the dominant narrative of the United States. The term "outside the United States" is open to interpretation. It asks us to consider the voices, identities, and stories of groups that have traditionally been silenced and marginalized within our borders, and within our curriculums.

It's also worth noting that Breakbeat Pedagogy meets many of the Speaking and Listening standards of the Common Core because poetry slam–style events carry on the oral tradition of Hip-Hop culture. During a show, participants and audience members are engaged in an exchange that is dialogic in nature. There is a profound transaction happening between performers and audience members.

Dialogue as Pedagogy

Creating spaces to engage in critical dialogue with students has led me to believe that dialogue actually shapes the production of creative writing in a classroom and thus the event itself. Dr. Maisha Fisher (2005) observed a classroom in New York City that celebrated spoken word culture, calling the space a "Participatory Literacy Community" that allowed "students to be co-constructors of their learning community" (p. 116). My students and I constructed a similar environment through *Word Up!* I argue that this kind of shared literacy atmosphere is essential to our development as readers, writers, and performers.

The creative writing and performances that my students have demonstrated are coupled with empathy and awareness on the part of the audience. Each week before the slam, my classroom is typically filled with snaps and cheers as students listen closely to their peers share original raps, freestyles, and poems. Most afternoons, the room is filled to capacity. We have created "a forum to expose and access multiple truths and experiences while fostering a particular kind of listening" (Fisher, 2005, p. 118). The listening itself is a literacy practice and the transactions taking place happen within that "culture of listening" (Fisher, 2005, p. 117).

Hip-Hop fosters this kind of attentive listening and participation because young people are always waiting for the punch line. They want to be moved. They want to affirm themselves and one another. In my experience, the nature of student poems and raps is almost always positive, healing, and transformative when the space includes adults who are modeling this kind of writing and thinking. On the occasion when a student presented a poem that was sexist, homophobic, or violent, we were able to generate a dialogue around those issues to interrogate different perspectives, redirecting when needed, and using the experience as a learning moment.

Snapping represents affirmation, engagement, and participation in one another's literacy development. The result at our school was a growth of empathy that extended to the larger school community. At *Word Up!*, an observer would hear a cacophony of snaps and cheers in a theater filled to capacity with teachers, students, parents, and administrators.

My students spoke in what Patrick Camangian (2008) calls "a critical voice," which means "finding the power to be heard, felt and understood while communicating transformative ideas in ways that effectively impact and challenge listening audiences" (p. 39). Some students wrote poems about struggling with sexual identity, while others wrote about bullying and anxiety. It was common to hear sighs of identification, groans of sympathy, and cheers of celebration. As co-constructors of the event, students became the center of their own learning process.

If breaking is a form of "making," of "risk and mistake" (Rosal, 2015, p. 325), then the Hip-Hop poetry slam is the ideal site for the practice of Breakbeat Pedagogy. When students approach the microphone with a story, they are both breaking and mending a part of themselves. Patrick Rosal (2015) reminds us that "an artist breaks only by being vulnerable to his own breaking" (p. 325). Breakbeat Pedagogy gives students an opportunity to "break into" experiences that have been previously closed off to them under lock and key. All we really need is one mic.

Mic Check
(a persona poem in the voice of a microphone)
When the spotlights are blaring
and their sweaty hands twist the stand,
lowering or raising me to their height,
I never get over how brave they are.
how infinite, how vulnerable,
to be made of blood and flesh,
how warm it must be to have organs
instead of metal in your chest.
I love the lights.
When they go dim that means
no one moving between whisper and scream,
no particles of spit being embedded
into my porous silicone membrane,
nothing to be amplified,
given volume,
translated into waves
and vibrations for ears.
I miss the way the freshman girl
always spoke her Ps too hard,
making me stab the audience
in the eardrum for a split second,
how I long to putter, pat, P, Puh, Puh,
grab me, hold me, lower me to your neck
and raise me again like a sunrise.
We are not so different—
both giving kids a way to tell stories,
adding volume to voice,
vividly inventing the very identity of everything.
I want sold-out crowds, listeners,
snaps, rhythm, volume, snaps, volume,
soft Ps, hard Ps, Ls, lots and lots of Ls,
whispers, shouts, screams, bass, thud, voice.
And when I die, I just want to go in front of someone's lips.

References

Alim, H. S. (2007). Critical hip hop language pedagogies: Combat, consciousness, and the cultural politics of communication. *Journal of Language, Identity, and Education, 6*(2), 161–176.

Camangian, P. (2008). Untempered tongues: Teaching performance poetry for social justice. *English Teaching: Practice and Critique, 7*(2), 35–55.

Chang, J. (2005). *Can't stop, won't stop: A history of the hip hop generation.* New York, NY: St. Martin's Press.

Coval, K., Lansana, Q., & Marshall, N. (Eds.). (2015). *The breakbeat poets: New American poets in the age of hip-hop.* Chicago, IL: Haymarket Books.

Fisher, M. T. (2005). From the coffee house to the school house: The promise and potential of spoken word poetry in school contexts. *English Education, 37*(2), 115–131.

Freire, P. (1970). *Pedagogy of the oppressed.* New York, NY: Continuum.

Freire, P., & Macedo, D. P. (1987). *Literacy: Reading the word & the world.* South Hadley, MA: Bergin & Garvey.

Greene, M. (1995). *Releasing the imagination: Essays on education, the arts, and social change.* San Francisco, CA: Jossey-Bass.

Low, B. E. (2011). *Slam school: Learning through conflict in the hip hop and spoken word classroom.* Stanford, CA: Stanford University Press.

Morrell, E., Dueñas, R., Garcia, V., & López, J. (2013). Critical media pedagogy: Teaching for achievement in city schools. New York, NY: Teachers College Press.

Morrell, E., & Duncan-Andrade, J. (2002). Promoting academic literacy with urban youth through engaging hip hop culture. *The English Journal, 91*(6), 88–92.

Rosal, P. (2015). The art of the mistake: Some notes on breaking as making. In *The breakbeat poets: New American poets in the age of hip-hop.* Chicago, IL: Haymarket Books. pp. 322–326.

CHAPTER 15

Contextualizing the Possible for Transformative Youth Leadership

Shirley R. Steinberg

Introduction: What's Wrong with You?

An often-told story to my students relates to when I was hired as a high school drama teacher in 1987. At that time, it was expected that I "bring" back a dying theatre program by producing and directing an enormous musical production. Creating a theatrical community while mounting *Grease* was part of my own personal mandate. The students, musicians, stagehands, all of us, became parts of a dynamic whole. The group was a social and artistic organism, enjoying one another. Jeremy was cast as Kenickie, the hell-raising greaser who becomes the potential father attached to Rizzo's possible pregnancy. Lanky, funny, and flexible, Jeremy had a dynamite voice, he was perfect for the part. Early one morning, following the previous evening's run-through of "Greased Lightning," my office phone rang:

Hello.

I'm looking for Ms. Steinberg.

You found me, can I help you?

This is Reverend Farnsworth.

I'm so glad you phoned, Jeremy is doing so well, he is amazing.

That is why I am calling. I have a problem with you.

In what way?

I don't like the play you are directing, I don't like the part Jeremy is playing, I think it sends the wrong messages to our children, and I don't like what I hear about you.

Is there anything else?

I don't like that these young adults are doing, what I think you call, improvisation. Drama games. They are not following scripts. The whole play and the drama program are not what we want them to be learning. This is a school, and your values are not appropriate.

What is it you want me to do?

My son refuses to quit the play. I think you should tell him he can't have the part.

I can't do that. Jeremy deserves the part, it is his decision.

That's precisely the problem, you are teaching a program that allows students to make the decisions.

I'm sorry you feel that way, you are welcome to discuss it with the administration; however, they approved this production.

Obviously, I can't get anywhere discussing this with you.

Thank you for calling.

Wait, just one more thing … this is what I really want to ask you. …

(pause)

What is wrong with you, Ms. Steinberg?

Wrong with me?

There has to be something wrong with you. The students stay late after school; you take them to plays; you all go out for dinner.

Yes.

No one likes teenagers. Only someone with something wrong inside wants to be around them that much.

Reverend Farnsworth was right. Most people (grown-ups) don't like teenagers, they don't trust them, and certainly wanting to be around them is suspect. It was then that I decided to devote my career to facilitating young adults to become leaders, to be viewed as worthwhile, trustworthy, and brilliant. The old boy was speaking the language of the dominant North American parent: *kids are bad, kids are sneaky, kids raise hell, kids are not capable of making good decisions.*

Our son, Ian, and his best friend, Nathan, were hanging out a few years later, I was working on a book about schooling and asked the boys a few questions. Nathan was up to answering:

You are 16. You are in school. What do you think the purpose of school is for you?

To keep us in.

In?

Yeah, to keep us out of trouble, off the streets until we learn how not to get into trouble. They just want to keep us in.

Fear of Youth

Historically, adolescents and youth were not a distinct societal subculture. Indeed, until the twentieth century, North American "teens" were often working at a young age, and certainly few were educated. In the 1950s, the notion of the rebel youth appeared, poster child James Dean became a grown-up's nightmare, along with rock n' roll, the hell-raising 1950s led into the tune in, turn on, drop out 1960s.

Popular images of youth created a suspect society driven by desire and the ability to terrify adults. Psychologists and sociologists struggled to deal with youth; psychologizing, pathologizing, and institutionally marginalizing youth became the practice. What was wrong with youth? Everything.

Schools attempted to balance out youth subcultural movements by counter images of *the good girl* and *the manly, responsible boy*. Certainly, the Cleavers (*Leave it to Beaver*) never had problems with Wally or the Beaver; Patty Duke (*The Patty Duke Show*) complied; Father always knew best (*Father Knows Best*), and popular television created images of teens who did not question, did not rebel, and certainly did not emulate Kenickie on the stage. Notions of drag racing, hoods, loose girls, and back talking to parents were lower class behaviors, by the kids from across-the-tracks. Leadership by teens was reduced to two categories: *Preppies* (my word), the scrubbed kids with starched shirts and ties: and *Hoods* (ganstas), those from lower or blacker/browner social classes who ran in gangs. Popular culture throughout the first thirty years of television did not portray empowered, functional youth as leaders.

Empowerment was not discussed. Schools did not address the possibility of creating a curriculum of leadership for youth … sort of like they don't do this now. Historically, and presently, the idea of youth leadership is not engaged. Youth are to be feared, controlled, contained, and, as Nathan noted, "kept in."

A fear of youth is part of our fabric. Woven between the threads, young men and women are unloved, often not understood, and often feared. Academic, school, and parent discourse address issues *about* youth in constant discussions about:

- eating disorders

- bullying

- teen mothers

- gangs

- youth suicide

- homelessness

- disrespect for parents

- boredom in school

- failure to succeed

- lack of initiative

- sexualities

- identities

- language (as in slang, crude, or nonstandard)

Conversations about youth reveal that *they are a problem*. Yet, we do not have the conversations about why *we* perceive a problem. Curricula are designed to make sure youth know that they need to change, they need to take responsibility, and yes, Nathan was right, they need to be kept in.

All this to say, that in this chapter, I will not look at the "youth problem" nor articulate any confirmation that youth are "at risk." I will engage in a conversation about youth leadership, its possibilities and challenges. Bottom line, youth are not a deficit in our culture or educational system. The deficit vision of youth is psychologized, pathologized, institutionalized, and marginalized … in a phrase, adults fear youth.

How Do We Discuss Youth Leadership if We Don't Want Youth to Lead?

Leadership is a clumsy term to deal with, the nontransformative kind. I'm not sure how to replace it, but want to state upfront, I don't like it much. It implies a hierarchy with the leader at the top, and then the leadees following below. Some may be given tasks or delegated responsibility, but leadership tends to expect that the leader will ultimately have the power. As a critical theorist, leadership for me becomes problematic. In a critical pedagogical world, noting how power works and replicates itself, how does one become a leader without assuming power? And, how do we work with youth to become leaders who do not intend to wield power? This is a tough one, and I want to keep it in mind in this discussion.

The notion of transformative youth leadership must be grounded in the articulation that youth are distinct beings and citizens, with specific needs, cultures, and views of the world. Instead of seeing youth as mini us, we need to redefine youth by seeing how youth define themselves—they are not a subculture; they are young men and women with cultures. Within these youth cultures, subcultures are created (usually by the youth themselves). I have observed in my work with youth that many adults are reluctant to name youth cultures, instead discuss them with distain, pathology, or marginalization: *She's in her Goth phase. Snapchat has taken them over. Instagram is consuming him. World of Warfare is just his way of avoiding being with the family. I was the same way, I hated all adults. She just needs to understand that her appearance is not acceptable in our home. This music is out of control. He thinks he is gay; we are ignoring it; he will grow out of it. This hip-hop thing, it is violent; we don't allow it in our home.* Rarely are young women and men given credit and respect for the decisions they make on a daily basis. Issues of identity become points of ridicule, and many teachers and caregivers view choices as phases, stages, or unimportant fads.

Certainly, teacher education does not prepare secondary and middle school teachers to facilitate youth leadership and empowerment; most parents and caregivers are not wired to assist empowerment, rather to squelch it. Often citing yellowed memories from their own lives, adults forget that they somehow made it through adolescence and teen years and actually did lots of good things during that time. Memories from adults are often categorized in two ways:

> 1. I did it, regret it, and don't ever want my kids to know I did it or to do "it" themselves: or 2. When I was that age, I did what I was told, what was expected, did not ask for my own "space," I was part of a family.

Incanting the term, *youth leadership,* most educators and parents speak out of both sides of their mouths, giving the term, and taking the power … no one seems to want kids to lead, to make responsible decisions, and to eventually replace a stagnant status quo. Ironically, it will happen. Thirty years ago, no one would have ever guessed that a presidential nominee's theme song would be one by Fleetwood Mac. There is almost a "get over it" pedagogy that we must enact in order to overcome the youth phobia shared by many adults … especially those who design curriculum and create pseudo-leadership roles for youth.

What We Need to Know

Creating a socially just youth leadership curriculum has obstacles, and the more urban the area, the more disenfranchised, the harder the challenge becomes. However, we must use the dialectic of challenges and opportunities. We must view our youth as novel entities, who may be similar or dissimilar from other young men and women. We rid ourselves of assumptions and create a space and pedagogy of leadership for schools and students, researching and observing each group on its own. We must focus attention on:

- The sociocultural context of a school or community organization

- The backgrounds of each young man and woman

- The positions of empowerment and disempowerment from which each youth operates

- The knowledges youth bring to the classroom or organization

- The languages spoken by the youth, both cultural and subcultural

- The ways these dynamics mold teaching and learning

Keeping in mind the complexity and contradictions of the category of youth leadership, we must look at the unique features in creating a transformative youth leadership program. These are features which be kept in the forefront, especially in working with urban and marginalized youth.

- What are the considerations of population density as it applies to where youth live?

- Sizes of schools, availability of community centers. Are large suburban and rural counterparts more prepared to serve higher numbers of lower socioeconomic class students? Are many students likely to be ignored and overlooked in the crowds of an urban area? In this context, it is difficult for urban and marginalized students to create and feel a sense of community. This creates an alienation which often leads to low academic performance, high dropout rates, and unanticipated leadership, gang affiliation, and negative subculture associations.

- What does the examination of geographic areas marked by profound economic disparity reveal? Disproportionate percentages of minority students and their families are plagued by centralized urban poverty, which hampers their quest for academic success on a plethora of levels. In urban schools and drop-in community centers (if they exist), there are an appalling lack of resources, financial inequalities, horrendous infrastructural violations, dilapidated buildings, and no space ... no space for youth to just be ... to be trusted, to make decisions.

- Urban areas have a higher rate of ethnic, racial, and religious diversity. In densely populated urban locales, people come from different ethnic, racial, and religious backgrounds, not to mention economic, social, and linguistic arenas, and they live close to one another. Nearly two-thirds of these urban youth do not fit the categories of White or middle class, and within these populations high percentages of students receive a free or reduced price lunch. Achievement rates for poor minority youth consistently fall below those of Whites and higher socioeconomic classes, and often their failures are the final proof that quitting school, engaging in illegal activity, is success.

- How does our work reach gay, lesbian, bisexual, transgendered, and questioning youth?

- Where do Indigenous youth fit into a closed definition of youth? Immigrant and migrant youth?

- Adults who sit on school boards, city councils, and youth task forces experience and factionalize infighting over issues on resources and influence, and often fighting is reduced to the youthphobia notion that they are not to be leaders ... as the reverend told me, *there has to be something wrong with me.* How could I tolerate and trust youth? There are no attempts to incorporate the voices of youth within these boards, councils, and task forces. Youth are discussed as the societal deficit ... the youth problem.

- Often administrators and leaders who work with teachers are undermined by ineffective business operations. Where are kids supposed to go? The facilities rely on basic resources, especially in urban settings, and no one has the ability to change the reality. I work with youth in East New

York (Brooklyn) now and have made it a point to count the amount of play yards with function-ing hoops for basketball, basketballs, and a minimum of jump ropes and hand balls. Youth drop centers are often in the cast-off basements or temporary buildings of a past era, and groups are reluctant to add financially to the structure of a soon-to-be condemned building and space.

- Work with youth does not tend to include initiatives for health and well-being. Naturally, the more socially deprived the youth, the worse the health and safety issues. School administrators will be more concerned with providing a warm building on a cold day than fixing unsanitary and disease-producing bathrooms—poor spaces for youth, if any are provided for them to meet. The community fears youth meeting in groups; malls are closed during certain hours, or kids must be accompanied by adults. Street corners, steps of stores, these become the places for youth to meet.

- A mobility issue also haunts disenfranchised and urban schools. Students, teachers, and com-munity leaders, especially administrators, leave frequently. Good work may be done but halts when an adult is replaced. Analysts have noted that the poorer the student, the more moves he or she is likely to make. High teacher turnover, one out of every two teachers in urban and poor schools leaves in five years … community organizers are volunteers or so poorly paid that they are unable to advocate for even a minimal raise.

- Urban and poor schools serve higher immigrant populations. Each group experience has needs particular to their own ethnic group, yet they have little governmental or educational help to get them started.

- Urban schools have characteristic linguistic challenges. In New York City, for example, over 350 languages and dialects are spoken. Because the leaders and teachers are White or middle class, it is hard to have the general sense of heritage and educational backgrounds to make use of linguistic diversity. Indeed, linguistic diversity is seen as a problem, rather than a unique opportunity.

- Context is important. We know the responsibilities many young men and women carry. Once again, in lower socioeconomic strata, or in specific cultures, youth take on adult roles as small children. Minding baby brothers and sisters/nieces and nephews, tending to aged grandparents, translating personal and medical knowledge between adults and doctors or social workers … these conditions throw youth into powerless leadership positions of trans-lation and decision making.

- Mentors, teachers, and social workers are less likely to live in a community, which is profiled economically or culturally. Consequently, youth do not have consistent leadership models upon which to build or seek advice.

Eschewing the Modernist Constructions of Youth

Along with contextualizing the above thoughts is a short deconstruction of previous notions and defini-tions of youth. Keep in mind that "teenager," as a separate designation of *an older kid*, started to appear in literature in the late 1930s, early 1940s. No historical reference launches fireworks for *the* day that the word first was used. Originally, it described literally kids who were in the teens, 13–19. Most who work in adolescent and youth studies have different definitions. I loosely look at the ages between 11 and 21 but also can see that teenager or youth are tentative words, and along with them come expecta-tions both cognitively and performatively. Jean Piaget addressed the notion of adolescence, observing that sometime around the age of 12, adolescents began to enter the formal operational stage, a more enlightened and sophisticated cognitive developmental stage. He saw that scientific, logical, and abstract thought was enacted by this age group and understood that many young people could stretch concrete thought to abstractions. He saw them as able to understand words and ideas in meaning-making terms, consider relationships, and have an operating knowledge of concepts like justice, morals, fairness, etc. My criticisms of Piaget have been discussed in the work done with Joe Kincheloe in postformal thinking (Kincheloe & Steinberg, 1993). Our main issue was that Piaget as the final word in youth construction was exactly that … and there are no final words. Piaget's developmentalist approaches are limited, essentialistic, and not capable of considering the nuances of youth … especially in a postmodern era. We cannot work with youth, teach youth, or facilitate youth empowerment for leadership using the tired methods of developmentalism … with a redefined notion of youth, adulthood, and the cultural capital of technology and cyberspace, the development of youth has changed (of course, I would argue that the Piagetian model never created the appropriate read on youth).

Youth development is not in stages: it is culturally and socially defined by the surroundings and experience of each young adult. Facilitating youth to become socially aware and ethical leaders requires a deep read of the lived world of each young man or woman. There are no ways to methodologize youth, no applicable clipboard charts that can take place to acknowledge the importance of working with youth to create individualized and contextualized leadership empowerment. The discussions with youth on empowerment and leadership must be tentative and ongoing, and they must be done with those who *like* youth, who are not afraid of youth, and who are committed to a vision of engaged youth leadership.

A Transformative Critical Pedagogical Youth Leadership

We must ask, in the critical pedagogical fashion of dialogue: *what can be done in youth leadership?* What is it we are trying to facilitate and enact? Freire (1970) reminds us that empowerment cannot be taught; rather, we can act as conduits to creating safe spaces and opportunities for empowerment/enlightenment to take place. As critical educators, we learn first to view the world from the eyes of those who are not part of the dominant culture. In this case, we view from the perspectives and ways in which youth see the world. How do youth see power? Do they identify with their place in the world, in the web of reality? Do they recognize opportunities? Are they comfortable with becoming leaders and mentors? What is it like to be a young man or woman today? How can one organize? Can character be built? What are the ethics of leadership? How does trust fit in with leadership? What communication skills are needed in leadership? Is there an attitude of leadership? Leaders are not born, they develop, and it is our mandate to secure dialogue and place in which to mentor and usher development. Youth leadership in a critical sense includes character, responsibility, respect, and knowledge. Those who work with youth to create viable leadership opportunities acknowledge each of these traits … and in this context, I would assert that respect is paramount in youth engagement. Our work with youth should be committed to facilitating the development of a democratic citizen, one who is conscious of being part of a whole, of society.

We encourage and mentor the notions that a young leader learns to articulate vision and understands his or her place within power structures and society in general. We encourage leadership by listening, collaborating, doing, and modeling; and by seeking/researching those who lead but may not be known as leaders. I use the example of the Canadian athlete Terry Fox, a young amputee with cancer, who was determined to run the width of Canada in order to bring awareness to cancer research. Fox began in Newfoundland with little fanfare, just a kid with a metal leg and a vision. Momentum gathered, and he became a symbol of persistence, faith, and leadership. Fox was a leader who did not seek to lead but to do good work. Leadership can be created by good works. This is not to confuse the notion of leader with role models or heroes. Often media-driven, those who are defined as role models are part of the Hollywoodization of leadership. Many are called heroes but incorrectly. A hero is one who does not seek to do heroic deeds but is thrust into being a hero through altruistic motivation and selflessness. It is an important pedagogical act to differentiate between a leader and a role model or hero. A leader does not aspire to be "followed," but she or he aspires merely to do *good work*. Paulo Freire also serves as an example of a leader, a quiet intellectual with political indignation, who was imprisoned and exiled. Freire didn't seek fame; he sought to create socially just dialogue that would serve to open paths to empowerment. Engaging in a conversation about youth leadership demands that youth identify those who serve to define leadership and good work. Part of a critical pedagogy of youth leadership asks that young men and upon deliberate upon what characteristics a youth leader needs and who exemplifies those characteristics.

Youth can be engaged in defining youth leadership; discussions about listening, respect, desire to learn, sharing, delegation, life-long learning are part of coming to terms with leadership qualities. We ask when one should lead and when a leader supports another to lead. Leadership also means giving up the lead. Youth should be leaders, they are leaders; however, with the decades of seeing youth as hood-lums, gangstas, thugs, and reprobates, it will take time to change, not only society's view of youth, but the self-identity of youth themselves.

Leaders rise from need. In the 1960s and 1970s, youth in the United States became leaders embed-ded in the rallying cry against the Vietnam War; organized and angry, driven by fear and fury, they cre-ated a citizen force refusing to be quieted. Global youth movements followed, and they didn't slow down. Those antiwar protest led the groundswell that eventually culminated in the end of the war. Youth have participated in democratic demonstrations and leadership in spite of adults. Recent gun violence and school shootings created youth voices that refused to be silenced. After almost two decades of mass mur-ders in American schools, following the death of 17 students and teachers at Stoneman Douglas High School in Broward County, Florida, youth refused to wait for adult action. After years of false promises by government officials to curb gun violence, surviving youth from the high school organized the #Nev-erAgain movement to legislate for safe schools, enforced gun registration, and to abolish the availability of semi-automatic and automatic weapons. Refusing to allow politicians to silence them, the students created a network of hundreds of thousands, assuring their voices would be heard (Steinberg, 2018).

Youth today are not going to wait to be found and respected; they understand that through social media, their voices become as strong and evident. Elections, governments, and curriculum will be chal-lenged more and more by our youth, and it is essential that as educators, we are available to facilitate with respect and awareness.

Only a Beginning

Avoiding the platitude-laden liberal tripe about youth, we name the needs, issues, and social conditions surrounding our youth. We act as mentors, and treat youth as young leaders … young colleagues, engaging in respect and collegiality as we create a safe and healthy leadership vision. We ask that youth contribute to the vision, lead the vision, that it is not imposed upon them, and that we assist in discovering their abilities and potentials as leaders. We do not create a definition of a leader but a flexible, changeable view of one who leads. Some will be tacit leaders, some will be overt, some will share leadership, and some will support it … youth leaders are not the new curricular *thing*, the new *chic* of pedagogical lexicons; youth leaders are necessary to nurture in order to create a healthy and optimistic environment. And, my final word on working with and teaching youth … it is a profession that requires we understand and like the students we work with. We have an obligation as teachers to ensure that we are working within a school and grade (age group) which we respect and comprehend, teaching can never be "a job," it is a commitment and our way of life, it is essential that we know where we can do the most with those students we understand and protect. A critical pedagogy of transformative youth leadership can impact youth in a global context, creating a space for youth leadership studies, research, mentorship, internships, and empowerment.

References

Freire, P. (1970). *Pedagogy of the oppressed.* London: Continuum Books.

Kincheloe, J. L., & Steinberg, S. R. (1993). A tentative description of post-formal thinking: The critical confrontation with cognitive theory. *Harvard Educational Review, 63*(3), 296–321.

Steinberg, S. R. (2018). *Activists under 30: Global youth, social justice and good work.* Leiden, NL: Brill/Sense Publishing.

CHAPTER 16

Lost in the Shuffle

Re-calling a Critical Pedagogy for Urban Girls

Venus Evans-Winters and Christie Ivie

I n this chapter, we draw from the multicultural, social justice, and feminist literature to explore the possibilities of a critical feminist pedagogy for urban girls. We use the term "urban girls" to refer to young women being educated in central cities or high-poverty communities, who are economically disadvantaged and/or members of racial/ethnic minority groups. These are young women who have been marginalized or excluded from society and from discussions of equal educational opportunity in the United States. In 1992, the American Association of University Women (AAUW) released to the nation a report on the state of education for American girls. The widely received report suggested that schools were shortchanging girls.

In particular, the AAUW (1991) authors cited findings that girls were falling behind their male peers in the areas of math and science, had lower self-esteem and less confidence about themselves and their abilities, and were called on less by teachers in class (Orenstein, 1994; AAUW, 1991). For both the general public and the education community, the report suggested that girls were not allowed the same economic and social opportunities in our society as boys due to being left behind and excluded in the early school years, and more so, in the middle-school grades. Unfortunately, the AAUW report was not as inclusive in detailing the educational experiences of young women of color and girls from economically disadvantaged groups.

Other feminists and female scholars of color have noted the unique educational experiences of young women of color, urban female students, and those students from economically disadvantaged groups (Evans-Winters, 2005; Fine, 1991; Fordham, 1996; O'Conner, 1997; Smith, 1982). Students from racial/ethnic minority groups, economically disadvantaged backgrounds, and minority-language students are more likely to live in central cities. These groups of students are more likely to be from single-parent households; to attend high-poverty or under-funded schools or schools with high dropout rates; to live in hyper-segregated communities; and to encounter teachers who are from racial and social classes different from their own. Unlike their White female and male middle-class counterparts, many girls attending schools in urban communities are more likely to experience racism, sexism, classism, and other forms of discrimination at school. In the 1980s and early 1990s, at the height of multicultural paradigms in education, scholars (Smith, 1982; Ladner, 1987; Leadbeater & Way, 1996) attempted to call attention to the social and educational needs of urban girls.

More recently, however, the educational and pedagogical needs of urban girls have been ignored or overlooked because of the attention from the scholarly community and public being given to the educational experiences of boys in American schools. The new argument in academia and by the masses is that boys are being left behind and shortchanged by our schools. People inside and outside of academia point to the high reading and writing competencies of girls compared to boys; the closing gap between boys and girls in standardized scores in math and science; and the fact that girls are less likely than boys to repeat a grade, be placed in a special education classroom, and be reported for problem behavior in the classroom (see Pollack, 1998; Kunjufu, 2005; Sommers, 2000; Wilgoren, 2001). Scholars and educational advocates of color also point out the disparity between Black males and females, with Black girls making up the majority of classrooms, graduating from high school, and outnumbering Black men in the attainment of higher-education degrees (Wilgoren, 2001). The reports and research findings over the last fifteen years have raised much debate about the schooling of both boys and girls in the United States and inspired much discussion about the best practices for educating boys, girls, and students from marginalized groups.

Unfortunately, in this boys-versus-girls debate, the educational needs of urban girls have been left out of the discussion. By focusing exclusively on gender, researchers, theorists, and practitioners fail to acknowledge the unique needs and potential of urban girls. Much of the debate centered on the educational accomplishments or failures of boys and girls overlooks the role that race and class play in the educational experiences and outcomes of many girls. In the past, feminists have looked to feminist classrooms and pedagogies as a possible solution to close the gap between boys and girls. Other scholars, interested in positive educational development for boys, have called for separate classrooms for males and females, male role models in the classrooms, and mentors outside of the school environment. In this discussion, we look to pedagogies grounded in the multicultural, social justice, and feminist' literature to call for pedagogical practices that work to improve the educational experiences of urban girls and prepare them to be change agents in the social world.

Feminist Pedagogy

The concept of feminist pedagogy has its roots in the second wave of feminism in the United States in the 1960s and 1970s. During this time of extreme social change, leaders of the feminist revolution like Betty Friedan advocated education as the key to women's liberation. The idea of consciousness-raising or talking about women's oppression and liberation, became popular as women across the nation created safe spaces for themselves and one another to discuss sexism and resistance strategies (Fisher, 2001). As women began to gain access to the academy, they began to apply the principle of consciousness-raising in higher education classrooms, especially in women's studies classrooms and programs. By exploring political and social issues through discourse, both teachers and students were able to reach new levels of understanding about the teaching and learning process and society. Thus, the concept of feminist pedagogy began to grow and take shape at institutions of higher education.

The goals of feminist pedagogy in higher education, like the definitions, are fluid and highly context specific. First, the concept of mutual learning is a goal for both students and professors in feminist classrooms. In this paper, we use the term "feminist classroom" as a classroom in which the instructor has a concept of feminist pedagogy which s/he deliberately applies to teaching. While these instructors may lecture or employ other traditional teaching techniques, the students' input is also valued, and learning becomes a dynamic process. Typically this means that the students benefit from the wider knowledge of the professor, and the professor benefits from the fresh perspectives provided from the students. Once a space for mutual learning has been established, the students can explore gender, identity, power structures, and social justice issues in relation to the subject matter. A second objective is to cultivate personal engagement in the material among the students in an attempt to analyze their own positions in society and to achieve a better understanding of one another. A third goal of a feminist classroom in higher education is to teach students how to thrive in the larger society, while simultaneously challenging that social order in which they were taught to succeed (Fisher, 2001, p. 27). This social change includes, but is not limited to, working toward gender equality.

Certainly no universal model of feminist pedagogy exists because the concept has as many diverse meanings and applications as feminism itself. It is highly contingent on a teacher's "political and educational values, the models of teaching and learning she [or he] has encountered and adopted, and the institutional and social conditions under which she [or he] teaches" (Fisher, 2001, p. 25). Despite the many difficulties involved in defining feminist pedagogy, feminist scholars have attempted to understand and share their own meanings. Fisher (2001) describes it as "teaching that engages students in political discussion of gender injustice" (p. 44). A more inclusive conceptualization is articulated by Maher and Tetreault (2001), who seek "an education that is relevant to their [the students'] concerns, to create their own voices in relation to the material" (p. 4). A common theme found throughout the literature on feminist pedagogy is "collective and cooperative learning" (Fisher, 2001, p. 38). Consistent with its foundation in consciousness raising, feminist teaching emphasizes learning through open discussion, self-disclosure, and active listening without judgment. Students and teachers are encouraged to understand and analyze oppression and power imbalances and explore the meanings of social justice. Ideally, this understanding will inspire activism and social change; thus, it can be described as action oriented (Fisher, 2001). Although the meanings given to feminist pedagogy seem to have certain values that serve as guidelines, it is important to remember that actual techniques vary within different contexts.

Also, because many administrators, teachers and parents feel that educators should not impose their values on students, many teachers are hesitant to enact their feminist values in the classroom. Another challenge in reaching a universal concept of feminist pedagogy is the contestable nature of traditional White Western liberal feminism, which is sometimes viewed as a "private white cult" (Maher & Tetreault, 2001, p. 7). A common criticism of traditional mainstream feminism is that it overlooks race, sexuality, age, and class-based inequalities, with the presumed intention of not distracting from the central issue of gender inequality (Davis, 1983; hooks, 1990; Collins, 1990). Unfortunately, the needs of urban girls have been lost in the shuffle, between efforts to save middle-class White girls and boys and latest efforts to save young Black boys from dropping out and being pushed out of school.

Multicultural and Social Justice Education

Obviously, as pointed out by Evans-Winters (2005) in her book *Teaching Black Girls: Resiliency in Urban Classrooms*, any feminism or pedagogy that avoids issues of racism, sexism, and classism renders itself inapplicable to urban school communities and classrooms. This outdated notion of gender as being separate and above other forms of oppression and social justice struggles has prevented a unified concept of feminism in today's world, let alone feminism's application to diverse urban educational systems. As pointed out above, research has looked at the contribution of feminist pedagogy and teaching practices in colleges and university settings, and over the last few years, more research has looked at the application of feminist pedagogy in K–12 classrooms.

However, very little research exists about its relevance to urban K–12 classrooms. What are the possibilities/possible benefits of a feminist curriculum in elementary and secondary education? What would it "look like"? What are some practical suggestions for integrating race, class, gender and social justice issues into K–12 education? To begin to answer these questions, we must look to the multicultural and social justice literature. In the *Handbook of Research on Multicultural Education* (Gay, 2004) defines multicultural education "as a set of beliefs and explanations that recognize and value the importance of ethnic and cultural diversity in shaping lifestyles; social experiences; personal identities;

and educational opportunities of individuals, groups, and nations" (p. 33). Furthermore, multicultural education furthers principles of social justice because it uses critical pedagogy as its underlying philosophy and focuses on knowledge, reflection, and action (Gay, 2004, p. 34). Traditionally, scholars and advocates of multicultural and social justice education have centered on the needs of students from marginalized groups.

According to Banks (2004), a major goal of multicultural education is to reform educational institutions so students from diverse racial, ethnic, and social class groups will experience quality education and to give male and female students opportunities for academic success. In the following excerpt, Banks (2004) provides an even more comprehensive view of the underpinnings of multicultural education:

> There is a general agreement among most scholars and researchers that, for multicultural education to be implemented successfully, institutional changes must be made in the curriculum; the teaching materials; teaching and learning styles; the attitudes, perceptions, and behaviors of teachers and administrators; and the goals, norms, and culture of the school. (p. 4)

Scholars have pointed out the tensions between multiculturalism and feminism, with claims that multiculturalism ignores struggles for gender equality and women's everyday realities (Ladson-Billings, 2004). We add to this recognized and acknowledged tension that both multiculturalism and feminism, with their commitments to social justice in mind, fail to contribute to discourse and practice on improving the state of education for urban female children and adolescents. However, it is the authors' belief that, together, feminism and multiculturalism have the potential to shape curriculum, practice, and policy that serve to enhance the educational, social, economic, and cultural opportunities for urban girls. From a social justice perspective, we also argue by increasing the educational and social opportunities for urban girls, educational communities are also contributing to the overall empowerment of all those living and being schooled in urban school communities.

Toward a Critical Multicultural Feminism

Fisher (2001, pp. 46–52) identifies six values around which she centers her knowledge of feminist pedagogy: access, caring, community, transmission, performance, and critical thinking.

- Access: including, accommodating, and benefiting all students equally

- Caring: showing genuine interest in a student's emotional, social, and intellectual wellbeing

- Transmission: passing on knowledge and skills to students

- Performance: awareness of one's own interpretation of education and her/his role of educator

- Critical thinking: reasoning and problem solving

The first value expressed by Fisher (2001) is access, which is ideally achieved by ensuring that the material, method of teaching, environment, educator, classroom, and the overall climate are not causing any students to feel excluded. An example might be teaching abstinence-only education to sexually active teens, thus depriving them of knowledge about their own sexuality and sexual health and denying them chances to make informed, healthy decisions. Another example would be ensuring that all students, regardless of gender, language abilities, mental and physical abilities, etc., are fully included in the social, cultural, educational experiences of the classroom and school environment. Such a focus on full access is especially important at a time when more research is detailing the number of students of color, especially African American males and females, being segregated within schools into special education classrooms or lower ability tracks, being more likely to be suspended and expelled, and less likely to have access to higher quality teaching (Harry & Anderson, 1994; Serwatka, Deering, & Grant, 1995; Cooper, 2002). A critical multicultural classroom and curriculum theorized here will assure that all students will have full access to culturally relevant (Ladson-Billings, 1994) teaching practices and methods, with a central focus on the intersection of race, class, and gender.

Fisher's (2001) second value is caring. Effective teachers embrace a meaningful pedagogy that places caring and the student's well-being at the center of pedagogy. Angela Valenzuela (1999) explores this topic in her research on U.S.-Mexican youth and their experiences with education. She found that many Latino/a students prefer a process of schooling based on respectful and caring relations. Yet, the students in the study felt that the teachers did not care for them, while the teachers felt that the students did not care about school. This cultural incongruence caused many of the Mexican and Mexican American students in her study to resist schooling. Her study suggests that urban high school classrooms would benefit from increased caring based on mutual understanding.

Valenzuela (1999) argues that "the most important step is to introduce a culture of authentic caring that incorporates all members of the school community as valued and respected partners in education" (p. 99). The value of community is defined as creating an environment of mutual responsibility and care, group cohesion (Fisher, 2001, p. 48). This value aims to fulfill the students' need of belonging (p. 49) and combat the anonymity that so many students feel today especially in large culturally and ethnically diverse urban schools. The third value of feminist pedagogy, according to Fisher (2001), is transmission or "the process of passing knowledge and disciplinary skills that lie at the center of our own academic identities" (p. 49). For many feminist teachers, the preferred method of transmission is mutual or cooperative learning. Nancy Barnes (2000), in her essay "Teaching Locations," explores alternate techniques of transmission as she teaches her college students how to position themselves as teachers in urban schools. In the process, she challenges the students' belief in the importance of personal experience and encourages them instead to investigate the perspectives of the high school students themselves. This type of exercise in pre-service teacher education could prove particularly valuable in multicultural urban classrooms where the teacher's personal experience may differ significantly from that of his/her students.

Performance, the fourth value defined above, can be described as awareness of the "dramaturgical performance" of education. Meaning, by examining the "complex selves" (p. 51) urban teachers bring to the classroom, teachers can better analyze our own biases and how they affect teachers' approaches to teaching and pedagogy (and students' multiple identities). Douglas E. Foley (1990) explored the role of dramaturgical performances in the school setting and how they contribute to cultural reproduction. In his study of a Texas high school, he found that those students who mastered performing their different roles were ultimately the ones who succeeded in sports, academics, and the real world. For educators, analyzing their own performance can help determine which aspects of each of them to bring to the classroom (and, possibly, which to suppress), for the benefit of the development of the student. Even more, a multicultural feminism would assist and encourage students to reflect on, critique, and embrace their own multiple identities. Such self-reflection is critical for urban children and adolescents because too often, others (e.g., researchers, school administrators, policymakers, and the media) are defining, constructing, and exploiting their identities for them.

Critical thinking is the next value that shapes Fisher's (2001) theory and practice of feminist pedagogy. Critical thinking is the mental process of acquiring information, then evaluating it to reach a logical conclusion or answer. The Bush administration enacted No Child Left Behind (NCLB) in 2001, which aims to standardize and narrow the curriculums of elementary and secondary public schools. Schools are pressured to perform well on standardized tests and face budget deductions if they do not. Many scholars have argued that standardized tests and curriculum have only contributed to devaluing critical thinking in classrooms, especially urban classrooms with economically disadvantaged students and students from racial/ethnic minority groups (Apple, 1993; Kozol, 2006; Ladson-Billings, 2004). Unfortunately, this means that children in K–12 classrooms are being deprived of opportunities for creativity and self-expression, especially poor and minority students, who are more likely to be affected by the mandates of NCLB. A multicultural feminist curriculum and pedagogy, although quite possibly incompatible with the principles of NCLB, would encourage young students to use critical thinking and problem-solving techniques.

Implications for Practice

Using these applications of Fisher's (2001) six values of feminist pedagogy to elementary and secondary education, we have hypothesized several possibilities/possible benefits of their integration into K–12 curricula, focusing specifically on urban classroom settings. An important benefit would be the creation of spaces for identity work and self-expression (Fine & Weis, 2000). While college students in many liberal institutions of higher education are asked to analyze the intersection of race, class, and gender, and how these variables shape their experiences, younger students are not given the same opportunity. Thus, they are often robbed of chances to (re)create and explore their own identities. In addition, a curriculum based on social justice underpinnings would better meet the social, emotional, and cultural needs of younger students.

Another possibility of multicultural feminist pedagogy in K–12 classrooms is to increase the level of student engagement, by allowing female and male students to teach *and* be taught. This concept of mutual learning, when applied to children and youth, could empower students by encouraging them to value, question, and expand their own innate knowledge. Furthermore, a multicultural feminist curriculum would work toward the development of a social consciousness and sense of community in all students. The possibility to prepare students to be socially responsible citizens and work together toward gender and racial equality and social justice would prove invaluable in today's society. A significant thematic thread runs throughout all these possible benefits, and that is the idea of reaching students earlier.

Given these possibilities/possible benefits of a critical multicultural feminist curriculum in elementary and secondary education, what might a sample curriculum "look like" in the urban K–12 classroom? First of all, there would be plenty of opportunities for self-expression through media such as art, writing, and discussion. The students would further develop their own voice and social imagination through open, relevant discussions of social roles, stereotypes, and inequalities. These conversations can be used to address racism, classism, sexism, heterosexism, ageism, and help the students make sense of conflicts and power imbalances in their own lives.

With increased opportunities for the students to expound on their own knowledge, there would be less "banking" and more interactive learning. Banking refers to Freire's theory that the teaching and learning process in classrooms becomes an act of depositing, in which the students are the depositories and the teacher is the depositor (Freire, 2007). Ideally, in a feminist classroom, the environment, subject matter, language, and material would be accessible and context specific to meet needs of urban children and adolescents, keeping in mind the realities in which they live, work, and play. In addition, there would be less "busy work," and more critical-thinking exercises. Most importantly, themes of gender equality, social justice, and social activism would be woven throughout any and all materials.

With these possibilities, goals, and expectations in mind, we have merged the tenets of multicultural education and feminist-based discourse to locate and create some practical suggestions for curriculum activities that would integrate the values and goals of multicultural feminist pedagogy into K–12 curricula. For practicality purposes, we have separated secondary and elementary education into three levels: K–5th grade (primary school), 6th–8th grade (secondary/middle school), and finally, 9th–12th grade (high school). Some suggestions for K–5 are:

- Field trips to local arts/cultural events

- Learn about different cultures

- Conflict narratives

- Gender narratives

- Learn about and volunteer time/money as a class/grade/school project to a worthy cause (e.g., Habitat for Humanity, Heifer International)

- Class discussion of gender issues. Sample questions: Why is it important for boys and girls to be friends? Do you ever feel like you are expected to act a certain way (play with certain toys, etc.) because you are a girl/boy? Have you ever been called a hurtful name like faggot or tomboy? How did it make you feel?

Conflict narratives, as defined in the essay "Narrative Sites for Youths' Construction of Social Consciousness" by Colette Daiute (2000), are narratives that serve "to develop social consciousness rather than being a passive reflection of social capacity or risk" (p. 211). In these exercises, students write about a conflict they have faced and how it was solved. After several months, the young students in Daiute's study (2000) began to show more depth and develop a social consciousness or what Freire (2007) calls *conciencizacion*. They begin to analyze their own role as well as other participants' and move past an aggressor/victim model. This creative approach to conflict resolution could be especially useful in schools with high incidences of neighborhood or community conflict. Gender narratives, as suggested by McClure (1999), help children identify and confront gender inequalities. One example she gives for this activity is as follows:

Recall an event in your childhood, one which is clearly etched in your memory. Write a brief but detailed narrative of the experience. Rewrite the narrative, changing your gender. Review both texts, highlighting or underlining the passages that were altered because of the gender change. (p. 80)

These exercises, like conflict narratives, aim to promote the child's social imagination. As students move on to higher grade levels and stages of development, the activities also can become more complex by building on previous knowledge and activities. Some suggestions for 6th–8th grades are:

- Relevant class discussions of social roles, expectations, stereotypes

- Sexuality education as part of sex education

- Have students choose and research a social justice group

- Writing assignments. Sample topics: What does racism mean to you? Pick a classmate that you admire and write about why. Identify a "clique" that you feel exists at school (Do not use specific names of classmates). How would it feel to be a member of that group for a day?

- Study contributions of both genders in core subjects, like famous women in math, physics, biology, etc.

- Have students conduct research reports on well-known African Americans, Latino/as, Native Americans, etc.

- Have students conduct oral histories with a female relative

- Institute a rites of passage program at your school for young men and women

Sexuality education as part of sex education could be very controversial. However, consistent with the goals of analyzing and discussing oppression through feminist pedagogy, it would be an important step forward in reaching out to gay, lesbian, bisexual and transgendered youth, and combating heterosexism beginning at an earlier age. It should be noted that writing and oral communication are both valuable in the multicultural feminist classroom, and gender is an intricate part of class discourse. Gender-based discussions and observations are not simply add-ons in the curriculum, and neither are topics of race and class. Some suggestions for 9th–12th grade questions and activities are:

- Field trip to local women's shelter, home for battered women, etc.

- Watch a movie as a class and identify race/class/gender stereotypes and inequalities portrayed.

- Work with a partner of the opposite sex and write ten adjectives describing him/her. How many are gender specific? How many are positive?

- Research a social issue (affirmative action, reproductive rights, etc.) and lead a class discussion on your topic.

- Bring in nontraditional guest speakers to talk about their experiences after graduation (teen mother, army veteran, stay-at-home father, female factory worker, policeman/woman, etc.).

- Write a paper examining your childhood and how different events shaped your personality/biases.

- Write about a time you felt like a valued member of a group and a time you felt you were on the "outside."

- Emphasize critical thinking and creative expression in all disciplines.

- Have students organize girls-only groups at their school

- Require students to participate in community service projects.

- Attend a school board meeting and have students analyze issues of power

In order to make educational experiences more relevant to the lives of the students, it would be helpful to bring in classroom visitors whose life chances resembled those of the student participants. For example, in school neighborhoods with high teenage pregnancy rates, it may be beneficial to bring in a single parent to talk about her goals, dreams, and challenges. Similarly, it is important to invite other community members in the classrooms, who have (or are) overcoming societal challenges and barriers. The goal of multicultural classrooms is to place at the center of pedagogy the experiences of those social actors who we want to most benefit from a more just society.

The possibilities/possible benefits for feminist pedagogy for urban multicultural classrooms at the K–12 level are endless; however, they need to be explored. The authors are the first to admit the limitations of the suggested classroom practices and curricula; however, we know what it is like to yearn for a classroom that embraces all of our identities (hooks, 1990). We yearn for a pedagogy that considers place and urbanicity, race and racism, sexuality and sexism, social class and classism, voice and language, history and tradition, family and individualism, age and agency in educational spaces. We argue that although the students would benefit from applying the principles of access, caring, community, transmission, performance, and critical thinking, teachers too would benefit. By creating a caring community within a class, teachers could feel more connected to their students. A multicultural feminist curriculum would also alleviate the pressure currently placed on teachers to "teach to the test" and allow them more flexibility and creativity. By making the material relevant to the experiences of the students, we can assume that the students would become more excited about education; therefore, teaching might become a more rewarding process for all the participants in the teaching and learning process. Multicultural feminist pedagogy at the K–12 level has the possibility of creating a more caring, community-based, engaging, and socially just concept of education, especially for those who otherwise may be lost in the shuffle.

References

American Association of University Women. (1991). *How schools shortchange girls: A study of major findings on girls and education*. Washington, DC: AAUW Educational Foundation, The Wellesley College Center for Research on Women.

Apple, M. W. (1993). *Official knowledge: Democratic education in a conservative age*. New York: Routledge.

Banks, J. A. (2004). Multicultural education: Historical development, dimensions, and practice. In J. A. Banks & C. A. Banks (Eds.), *Handbook of research on multicultural education* (3rd ed., pp. 3–29). New York: Wiley.

Barnes, N. (2000). Teaching locations. In Fine, M. & Weis, L. (Eds.), *Construction sites: Excavating race, class and gender among urban youth* (pp. 196–210). New York: Teachers College Press.

Collins, P. H. (1990). *Black feminist thought: Knowledge, consciousness, and politics of empowerment*. London: Unwin Hyman.

Cooper, P. (2002). Does race matter? A comparison of effective black and white teachers of African American students. In J. J. Irvine (ed.), *In search of wholeness: African American teachers and their culturally specific classroom practices* (pp. 47–63). New York: Palgrave.

Daiute, C. (2000). Narrative sites for youths' construction of social consciousness. In Fine, M. & Weis, L. (Eds.), *Construction sites: Excavating race, class and gender among urban youth* (pp. 211–234). New York: Teachers College Press.

Davis, A. (1983). *Women, race and class*. New York: Vintage Books.

Evans-Winters, V. (2005). *Teaching black girls: Resiliency in urban classrooms*. New York: Peter Lang. Fine, M. (1991). *Framing dropouts: Notes on the politics of an urban high school*. New York: SUNY Press.

Fine, M. & Weis, L. (2000). *Construction sites: Excavating race, class and gender among urban youth*. New York: Teachers College Press.

Fisher, B. M. (2001). *No angel in the classroom: teaching through feminist discourse*. New York: Rowman & Littlefield.

Foley, D. E. (1990). *Learning capitalist culture: Deep in the heart of Tejas*. Philadelphia, PA: University of Pennsylvania Press.

Fordham, S. (1996). *Blacked out dilemmas of race, identity, and success at Capital High*. Chicago, University of Chicago Press.

Freire, P. (2007). *Pedagogy of the oppressed*. New York: Continuum.

Gay, G. (2004). Curriculum theory and multicultural education. In J. A. Banks & C. A. Banks (Eds.), *Handbook of research on multicultural education* (3rd ed., 30–49). New York: Wiley.

Harry, B. & Anderson, M. G. (1994). The disproportionate placement of African American males in special education programs: A critique of the process. *Journal of Negro Education*, 63(4), 602–618.

hooks, b. (1990). *Yearning: Race, gender and cultural politics*. Boston: South End Press.

Kozol, J. (2006). *The shame of the nation: The restoration of apartheid schooling in America*. New York: Three Rivers Press.

Kunjufu, J. (2005). *Keeping black boys out of special education*. Sauk Village, Illinois: African American Images.

Ladner, J. A. (1987). Introduction to tomorrow's tomorrow: The Black woman. In S. Harding (Ed.), *Feminism and methodology* (pp. 74–83). Bloomington, Indiana: Indiana University Press.

Ladson-Billings. (1994). *The dreamkeepers: Successful teachers of African American children*. San Francisco, CA: JosseyBass.

———. (2004). New directions in multicultural education: Complexities, boundaries, and critical race theory. In J. A. Banks & C. A. Banks (Eds.), *Handbook of research on multicultural education* (3rd ed., pp. 50–65). New York: Wiley.

Leadbeater, B. J. R., & Way, N. (Eds.). (1996). *Urban girls: Resisting stereotyping, creating identities*. New York: New York University Press.

Maher, F., & Tetreault, M. (2001). *The feminist classroom: Dynamics of gender, race, and privilege*. New York: Rowman & Littlefield.

McClure, L. J. (1999). Wimpy boys and macho girls: Gender equity at the crossroads. *English Journal*. V 88(3), pp. 78–82.

NCES (2007). *Statistics and trends in the education of racial and ethnic minorities*. Washington, D.C.: U.S. Department of Education Institute of Educational Sciences.

O'Connor, C. (1997). Dispositions toward (collective) struggle and educational resilience in the inner city: A case analysis of six African-American high school students. *American Educational Research Journal*, 34(4), pp. 593692.

Orenstein, P. (1994). *Schoolgirls: Young women, self-esteem and the confidence gap*. New York: Doubleday. Pollack, W. (1998). *Real boys: Rescuing Our Sons from the Myths of Boyhood*. New York: Henry Holt.

Serwatka, T. S., Deering, S., & Grant, P. (1995). Disproportionate representation of African Americans in emotionally handicapped classes. *Journal of Black Studies*, 25 (4), 492.

Smith, E. J. (1982). The Black female adolescent: A review of the educational, career, and psychological literature. *Psychology of Women Quarterly*, 6 (3): 261–288.

Sommers, C. H. (2000). *The war against boys: How misguided feminism is harming our young men*. New York: Simon & Schuster.

Valenzuela, A. (1999). *Subtractive schooling: U.S. Mexican youth and the politics of caring*. New York: SUNY Press.

Wilgoren, J. (2001). *Girls rule*. New York Times Upfront, 133 (13), pp. 8–13.

CHAPTER 17

Punk Rock, Hip-Hop, and the Politics of Human Resistance

Reconstituting the Social Studies Through Critical Media Literacy

Curry Malott and Brad Porfilio

Nearly one hundred years ago, the social studies discipline was formally introduced in North America as a possible school subject. Business leaders and corporate leaders saw social studies as an avenue for indoctrinating the millions of immigrants, who were entering North America from predominantly European countries, with values conducive to becoming a *productive* worker as well as beliefs that promoted American and Canadian patriotism and colonialism (Russell, 2002). Progressive educators, on the other hand, had a quite different vision of the discipline. They viewed it as a way of fostering within students the ability to critically reflect on their world and take action for social justice. Unfortunately, business and governmental leaders used their privileged position to ensure their vision for this discipline came out victorious; consequently, it became the official model for the social studies curriculum across the educational landscape. We have been left with the legacy that has, while serving the interests of capital, which include fostering the development of an uninformed spectator-oriented citizenry, failed to meet the intellectual needs of the majority of its populace.

Despite the ongoing struggle and subsequent attempts over the past several decades made by progressive educators/activists to revamp the social studies curriculum for creating a more socially just education and wider social structure, the discipline, officially, has not strayed from its state-building, pro-capitalist function. For instance, in classrooms across North America, youths rarely learn about "the contributions, perspectives, or talents of women or those outside the mainstream culture" (Nieto, 2002, p. 9). Consequently, the social studies curricula, textbooks, and standardized examinations still reflect the values and beliefs of North America's economic and political leaders. In-service teachers in contemporary classrooms frequently alienate and thus fail to engage youths by centering their curriculum on historical narratives that valorize the lives of dead White men as well as the conquests and expeditions of Western society.

Likewise, the test-driven environment within public schools and teacher education programs has limited teachers' sense of empowerment and thus willingness to engage in critical multicultural social studies (Malott & Pruyn, 2006). Unable or willing to take the risks needed to spark student interests, teacher educators, and classroom teachers often turn to the "banking model" of education. The pedagogy is inextricably linked to promoting a passive type of citizenship, where the great majority of students become apathetic toward social, political, and economic issues, but become complicit in internalizing dominant beliefs, values, worldviews, and social practices (Case & Clark, 1997, p. 20).

It would not be a stretch to say the social studies curriculum "seems meaningless to almost every student, regardless of race, class or gender" (Kornfeld & Goodman, 1998, p. 306). Contemporary youths have been positioned to lack what Paulo Freire (2005) refers to as "a passion to know"; therefore, they are without the drive to develop the self-discipline needed to learn to not only read the word, but the world as well, a process designed to lead to critical consciousness and ultimately a sense of empowerment needed to transform our dull reality, that is, the material world. For Freire (2005) and others (see Freire & Macedo, 1987; McLaren, 1995) this is what it means to be fully literate and thus equipped with the intellectual tools to participate in the production and reproduction of our world. In short, this is critical literacy. This chapter is a foray into critical media literacy. For us, critical media literacy (Kellner & Share, 2005) is a pedagogical tool that provides us with the theoretical ballast needed to uncover the liberatory potential of countercultural formations and puts forth possible ideas of intervention for teachers, preservice teachers, professors (including ourselves), and other community and cultural workers interested in reinforcing the more transgressive moments in our cultural manifestations—punk rock and hip-hop serving as primary examples in this essay.

To revitalize the social studies for the purpose of ensuring it has the potency to be a viable part of the move toward creating a more democratic social order—a society predicated on the principles of equity, social justice, freedom, and diversity—we believe critical theory must be central in this mission. Within critical theory, we can still find examples of unwavering resistance that are withstanding the corporate takeover of higher education. It is within these examples of vibrant militancy that we theoretically depart. These traditions continue to help educators "link learning to social change and education to the imperatives of a critical and global democracy" by focusing our critical lens on cultural artifacts such as music (Giroux, 2005). Current transformative educators also provide us with the theoretical tools necessary for both knowledge construction and action, assisting our awareness of how educational policies and practices are linked to the social production of labor, the lifeblood of capital, and how we can teach against these draconian formations through a revitalized critical/revolutionary pedagogy (McLaren & Jaramillo, 2005; Allman, McLaren, & Rikowski, 2005). In other words, critical theory provides us with the theoretical tools to not only analyze countercultural formations for their transformative potential against the process of value production, but also challenges us to unearth the unjust practices and social formations that foster economic and social injustices across the globe. In the following analysis, we take a critical approach guiding our analysis and pedagogical project. It is our intent in the pages that follow to provide a theoretically rich project for a critical multicultural social studies (Malott & Pruyn, 2006).

Specifically, we will document how two alternative subcultures—punk rock and hip-hop—at their most radical moments, have the potency to provide in-service and pre-service teachers with a critical reading of the word and the world and opportunity to be a part of changing the relationships that define our lives through conscious intervention, to paraphrase Paulo Freire (1998, 2005). By examining these youth subcultures within the context of teacher education programs, we argue schoolteachers will begin to take inventory of the economic, social, and historical forces creating social inequalities within schools and the wider social world, recognize the urgency to develop critical forms of pedagogies for the purpose of ensuring that today's youths are equipped to make sense of the constitutive forces causing injustice and oppression in their own social worlds, take action as empowered agents of change, and understand the importance of linking their pedagogical projects with their students and other global citizens to excavate various forms of injustice in our increasingly morally bankrupt society. What follows is, therefore, first an overview of punk rock and hip-hop lyrics that provide a critical analysis of the contemporary social historical world. What is more, we pay particular attention to how the politics of these artists transcends the forum of music. Next, we discuss pedagogical implications for how this body of work and movement can be used by teacher educators, in-service teachers, administrators, and other cultural workers for the purpose of revitalizing the social studies, empowering youths, and transforming the world.

Subcultures in Context

Both punk rock and hip-hop emerged during the 1970s and 1980s in the United States as a response to the increasing success of the economic elites' ability to wage warfare on working people through economic policies and a highly skilled propaganda machine (Chomsky, 2005; Giroux, 1994; McLaren & McLaren, 2004; Malott & Peña, 2004; Porfilio & Malott, 2007) (see Malott & Peña, 2004, for a discussion on the British punk rock movement). That is, policies that have ultimately led to deindustrialization, the increasing globalization of capital through policies such as the North American Free Trade Agreement (NAFTA), the militarization and privatization of everyday life, and a mean-spirited discourse blaming young people for their own dispossessed conditions, which resulted in a material reality that left many youths alienated from the dominant society, and therefore searching for meaning in a seemingly meaningless world. Armed with a largely intuitive response to the downsizing of their futures, many youths took to their creative impulses. They forged what is now known as punk rock and hip-hop.

Both hip-hop and punk rock first drew breath in New York City's European American and Afro-American, Latin, and Afro-Caribbean working-class communities, while punk rock was simultaneously born out of the rubble of Los Angeles' "White" and Latina/o barrios (Dancis, 1978; Cohen, 1980; Dimitriadis, 1996; Malott & Peña, 2004). Existing on the fringes of cultural life, both subcultures, at their more critical moments, gained strength and credibility through a creative process of building something out of nothing.

For punk rockers, this pedagogical approach has come to be known as DIY, or Do It Yourself, that is, creating something new within the remains of the old, such as small fanzines, record labels, bands, styles, modes of analysis, and ultimately a movement and way of life. DIY has, therefore, served as a rallying cry for those punk rockers who take pride in surviving against an economic social structure that does not serve their own interests, a system that grows more powerful the more surplus value or unpaid labor hours it is able to extract from the majority of the world's working people.

Similarly, the more progressive elements of hip-hop draw on an identity of independence often manifesting itself as a "fight the power" sentiment, which is imbued with Afrocentric pedagogy, as expressed by New York City's Public Enemy (PE). For example, in "Fight the Power" on the *Fear of a Black Planet* (1990) record Chuck D of PE exclaims:

... I'm Black and I'm proud ...
Most of my heroes don't appear on stamps
Nothing but rednecks for 400 years if you check ...
Power to the people no delay ...

Contemporary radical hip-hop groups such as Dead Prez and Immortal Technique have built on pro-Black counterhegemonic messages from PE and other groups such as the Poor Righteous Teachers and X Clan. Their music has added a more sophisticated class analysis to the hip-hop scene. Brooklyn's Dead Prez (DP), emerging as one of the leading voices in hip-hop's cultural and material revolution, identifying themselves as "revolutionary but gangsta, RBG," has upped the radical ante. For instance, the group's song "it's bigger than hip-hop" refers to the social revolution they argue is needed at this particular social juncture, an epoch marred by growing global poverty, hunger, a resurgence in White supremacy, among many other indicators of an out-of-control transnational capitalist elite. In the following lyric, like Public Enemy, DP assumes an Afro-centric stance while advocating for a humane social and economic system:

Organize the wealth into a socialist economy
Cause the world is controlled by the white male
Dead Prez (2000). "Police State." *Let's Get Free.*

DP often refers to the Black Panther Party as a source of pedagogical inspiration. Their music is informed by community activism, Black pride and power, and a desire to create a society predicated on symmetrical power relationships (discussed below). They postulate their music is a cross between PE and NWA, and if they had come of age during the 1970s, they would have been Panthers. Coming from Oakland, California, where the Huey P. Newton and Bobby Seale started the Black Panther Party for Self-Defense, The Coup stands as an exemplary example of today's African American revolutionary West Coast U.S. hip-hop. Although offering anti-racist sentiments through their songs, The Coup offers a more class-based perspective on what causes systemic oppression. They have also successfully melded their social commentary with political satire in songs such as *Wear Clean Draws* and *5 Million Ways to Kill a CEO* that, respectively, address the issue of African American female body image and how to create the conditions whereby oppressors, motivated by greed, are lured into self-destructing. In the introduction to their album *Party Music* (2001), The Coup chants "every broke motherfucker gonna form a gang, and when we come we're takin everything." In this song The Coup presents a non-racially specific message to working and poor people in general. In another track, "Ghetto Manifesto," The Coup offers a serious yet slightly humorous rallying call against the state and capital. Consider their words:

This is my resume slash resignation
A ransom not with proposed legislation
A fevered ultimatum you should take it verbatim …

The class analysis and anti-racism offered by The Coup and other hip-hop artists highlighted above have also been prevalent in the lyrics of many punk rock bands from early groups such as the Dead Kennedys and Bad Religion to more contemporary artists like AntiFlag, Leftover Crack, and the Fartz. Rising out of San Francisco's underground punk and hardcore scene in the late 1970s and early 1980s the Dead Kennedys (DK) emerged as a leading satire-infused unity punk band with overtly leftist political messages. For example, in their first release, "Nazi Punks Fuck Off" (1979/1980) Jello Biafra, DK lead vocalist, takes a stance against White supremacist infiltrations into the punk scene, exclaiming:

You still think swastikas look cool
The real nazis run your schools
They're coaches, businessmen and cops …

Rather than taking aim at hegemonic/counter-revolutionary elements within the scene, Anti-Flag, more recently, offers a devastating blow to the corporate-dominated military complex, which, they allude, usurps both the labor power and physical bodies of working people as cannon fodder. These are key forces in promulgating U.S. imperialism across the globe. Consider their words:

Isn't everybody tired of the killing?
Isn't everybody tired of the dying?
Isn't everybody tired of the hatred?
Anti-Flag, 2002, "911 for Peace," *Mobilize.*

In another song Anti-Flag extends their plea for peace with a solid analysis of the deleterious effects of the alienating nature of selling one's ability to labor for a wage, thereby contributing to the creation of a world that benefits the few at the expense of the many.

To join the corporate army
For god and country give up your life,
Don't try to figure out what's wrong of right
Anti-Flag, 2002, "Their System Doesn't Work for You," *Mobilize.*

Coming from a similar theoretical/political perspective as Anti-Flag and the Dead Kennedys, although employing a more reggae-dub/punk/hardcore sound, New York City's Leftover Crack in "Super Tuesday" connects the North American legacy of colonization and slavery with current economic policies of the World Bank and the International Monetary Fund:

It ain't a mystery, that US History
Was built upon the graves
Of Native ways and beaten slaves ...

Beyond the Lyrics

Beyond the messages transmitted through their songs, teacher educators, teachers and students can look to the community activism of hip-hop and punk artists as guideposts for possible *paths of dissent.* Here we will detail the activism of several key figures highlighted above. They are actions that can lead us beyond our unjust social and economic systems and their hegemonic manifestations, such as patriarchy, White supremacy, and homophobia. Lead singer of Leftover Crack, Stza Sturgeon, has been vociferous in his condemnation of North America's mass media and Bush's presidency. Over the past several years, Sturgeon has conducted several interviews for the purpose of unveiling the mass media's role in concealing how U.S. global policy spreads violence and injustice across the globe, while concomitantly, throwing light on how the Bush regime and the mass media espouse "ultranationalist propaganda to squelch dissent" aimed at their unjust policies and practices (McLaren, 2005, p. 198). He has urged his fans to reflect critically upon the dominant narratives generated by the media and state, and to support political movements designed to bring about a democratic state. On September 11, 2005, he brought his messages to the stage by performing a protest concert with Choking Victim. He made it clear to over 2000 fans that Western imperialism, neoliberal economics, and xenophobia are to blame for the 9/11 attacks. Here he implicates Bush and the media for creating false narratives about the causes of terrorism:

> George Bush's brother Marvin Bush was head of security at the World Trade Center up until 9–11, and they were doing nefarious things, ... They wanted another Pearl Harbor to install the Patriot Act and take us to war. Don't listen to the media; the media is there for maximum security—to tell you lies! (Ferguson)

Likewise, the *raison d'être* of Anti-Flag's work and social projects is to "play the role of educator to fans" about U.S. government and business leaders' 'current war on terrorism' (Usinger, 2004). In contrast to many artists who have taken part on the Warped Tour, AntiFlag has openly renounced the United State involvement in Iraq. Not only were the band's shows geared to raise young people's consciousness about 9/11, terrorism, and U.S. imperialism, but they were designed to encourage action against unjust policies perpetuated by greed. Offstage, band members have worked to empower youths alongside U.S. Representative Jim McDermott, who, in 2004, "gave a speech in the House of Representatives, praising Anti-Flag for working to encourage young people to register and vote" (http://en.wikipedia.org/wiki/Anti-Flag). The group has been actively involved in several endeavors that they feel will bring about a more just and humane society. They have taken part in anti-war demonstrations in Washington, DC, and Pittsburgh, backed PETA's stance for humane treatment of animals by bringing members from the organization to its shows, as well as taking part in interviews surrounding animal rights, and started a campaign http://militaryfreezone.org/ to end military recruitment in public schools.

Anti-Flag's central theme of social protest and change is representative of a long tradition of punk rock pedagogy, at its most critical moments. Perhaps one of the most influential punk rock activists since the 1979/1980 release of the aforementioned song, "Nazi Punks Fuck Off," is Jello Biafra and the establishment of Alternative Tentacles Records. Beyond the turbulent and controversial legacy of the Dead Kennedys, wrought with internal conflict that persists to this day (see Malott & Peña, 2004), is the existence and focus of Alternative Tentacles itself, which sarcastically boasts of "25 years of cultural terrorism" (www.alternativetentaclesrecords.com). In 1983 the Dead Kennedys were taken to court and charged with the "distribution of harmful matter to minors," for an insert on their "Frankenchrist" record of a reproduction of a painting by Swiss artist H. R. Giger, "Penis Landscape." However, the prosecution's case did not focus on the insert of "Penis Landscape," but rather on the legacy of the Dead Kennedys, considering it was presented to the court through such tactics as blowing up DK lyrics on large poster boards. The case was eventually overturned, but the trial tore the Dead Kennedys apart and nearly bankrupted Alternative Tentacles as a result of costly court fees and the banning of Dead Kennedys records in most retail outlets with the exception of small independent record stores.

As a result, Jello Biafra, a self-proclaimed "information junky," engaged in a series of spoken word tours, resulting in over 10 spoken words records on Alternative Tentacles. Biafra continues to tour and lecture at colleges and universities throughout the United States and elsewhere on issues from censorship to unjust imperialist wars. In addition to publishing Biafra's lectures, AT also continues to put out original independent music through its many signed artists who, brags Biafra, have 100% artistic freedom, which is antithetical to how mainstream corporate labels tend to be run. Making AT especially significant is its publishing of the lectures of noteworthy radical academics, writers, and activists such as Jim Hightower, Angela Davis, Noam Chomsky, Howard Zinn, Mumia Abu-Jamal, and Ward Churchill, to name a few. The coexistence of such radical thinkers with independent musicians under one label provides the opportunity of many AT music fans to be exposed to political ideas of critique and the possibility for large-scale social change otherwise not happening (Malott & Peña, 2004). Embracing the notion that punk rock is more of an ideology than a style, AT has signed critical artists from Earth First! folk singers, hillbilly country acts, schizophrenic eccentrics, and radical rappers.

However, beyond the efforts of AT, rappers one of the most influential Rap music icons, Public Enemy, continue in their quest to "fight the power" for the sake of forging a democratic society. PE founder, Chuck D, has utilized the radio and television airwaves to condemn the United States' involvement in Iraq. On his (co-hosted with Gia'na) Air America show, *On the Real,* he provides a space for youths and other progressive speakers to be heard on "how life, politics and the history of the American culture work (and who gets sacrificed for it)" (http://shows.airamericaradio.com/onthereal/about). For instance, the show helped to educate youths about the racist and classist response by Washington in the aftermath of Hurricane Katrina, one of the biggest crises, faced primarily by working people, in this country. Along with providing a space for discussion on this crisis, he composed a poem for his listeners, which was eventually turned into the band's song "Hell No We Ain't Right," to express his outrage at today's "new world order:"

> *New Orleans in the morning, afternoon, and night*
> *Hell No We Ain't Alright*
> *Now all these press conferences breaking news alerts*

Chuck D has also shared his insight in relation to social issues at college campuses across North America. In his discussion, "Race, Rap, and Reality," he has "lambasted America's anti-intellectualism and its obsession with celebrity. He criticized the lack of substance in today's rap music and suggested that technology distances us from our fellow man" (Rivers, 2006). His social commentary has spilled over to film. In the short documentary, *Bling: Consequences and Reproductions,* Chuck D's narration illustrates how the Revolutionary United Front has killed between 50,000–75,000 people and amputated many other individuals' limbs to secure Sierra Leone—the most diamond-rich country in the world (Cornish, 2005). The question remains: how can the music, messages, and movements highlighted above be used to enhance and make relevant a social studies curriculum that is if not dead, terminally ill?

Making Connections and Creating Passion Through Music: CMSS

Pedagogically, what role can punk rock and hip-hop play in the formation of revolutionary praxis? Drawing on critical media literacy, in the following paragraphs, we put forth the beginnings of a revitalized K–12 social studies education, a possible pedagogical and curricular place of departure.

More so now than ever, students who enter our classrooms, be it classrooms in universities, elementary schools, or high schools, are bringing with them the cultural commodities of punk rock and hip-hop. Within these cultural artifacts are embedded ways of understanding and viewing the self and the larger world (as demonstrated within the examples of punk and rap outlined above). It is imperative for educators to understand how our students know. Honing in on this pedagogical necessity Freire (2005) argues:

> ... our relationship with learners demands that we respect them and demands equally that we be aware of the concrete conditions of their world, the conditions that shape them ... Without this, we have no access to the way they think, so only with great difficulty can we perceive what and how they know. (Freire, 2005, p. 58)

Understanding the ways in which students perceive the world enables teachers to begin to create a culturally relevant and engaging education, which are key components in fostering *a passion to know*. For example, in our work teaching high school social studies and teacher education social studies methods courses, we have had students bring in songs that relate to particular social issues such as racism, sexism, among countless other foci. Discussing the messages presented within these songs has offered our classes a focus of critique and an opportunity for us to share more revolutionary/critical examples from the genres, as outlined above.

Such an approach has also provided a powerful and engaging method to teach students about the internal workings of capitalism. Focusing on the commodification and cooptation of punk rock and hip-hop has provided our students with a critical lens to better understand the predatory nature of capital, as well as other social forces creating injustices in society. Using critical media literacy in this way has consistently led many of our students to more informed visions of their own subjectivities and the ways in which they are shaped by market forces and capital's divisive hegemonies such as White supremacy. However, because "... we are programmed but not predetermined, because we are conditioned but, at the same time, conscious of the conditioning, that we become fit to fight for freedom as a process and not as an endpoint ..." (Freire, 2005, p. 70). In other words, our approach does not focus on awareness alone, but calls for action.

The activism of the artists described above has allowed many of our students to, first, envision themselves as agents of change, and then, once empowered, be able to overcome their own fear of freedom and to take action for social justice. For example, some of our students have begun with actions such as writing letters to record companies and politicians. While such actions, it can be argued, are ultimately ineffective in their attempts to convince the powers that be to change their policies, they are effective at providing students with that first step at seeing themselves as participants rather than observers. This step is fundamental in their development as critically literate global citizens. Actions our students have taken are by no means limited to letter writing. Other examples include, but are not limited to, joining activist organizations and groups, attending demonstrations, publishing critical work/becoming radical scholars, and developing progressive curricula.

Given the current trends in privatization and standardization, which, together, threaten the democratic potential of the social studies curriculum in particular, and education in general, critical theory, along with critical media literacy, must assist us to meet the democratic challenge put forth by humanity's unrelentless demand for dignity and respect.

References

http://shows.airamericaradio.com/onthereal/about). Retrieved, January 22, 2006

Allman, P., McLaren, P., & Rikowski, G. (2005). After the box people: The labor-capital relation as class constitution and its consequences for Marxist educational theory and human resistance. In P. McLaren (Ed.), *Capitalists & conquerors: A critical pedagogy against empire* (pp. 135–165). New York: Rowman and Littlefield.

www.alternativetentaclesrecords.com Retrieved, January 28, 2006 *Anti-Flag: Biography.* Retrieved, January 28, 2006, from http://en.wikipedia.org/wiki/Anti-Flag.

Case, R., & Clark, P. (1997). Four purposes of citizenship education. In R. Case & P. Clark (Eds.), *The Canadian anthology of social studies: Issues and strategies for teachers* (pp. 17–28). Vancouver, BC: University of British Columbia Press.

Chomsky, N. (2005). *Imperial ambitions: Conversations on the post-9/11 world.* New York: Metropolitan Books.

Cohen, P. (1980). Subculture conflict and working-class community. In S. Hall, D. Hobson, A. Lowe, & P. Willis (Eds.), *Culture, media, language: Working papers cultural studies 1972–1979* (pp. 78–87). Birmingham: The Center for Contemporary Cultural Studies, University of Birmingham.

Cornish, M. J. (2005, December 9). *Chuck D narrates 'bling: Consequences and repercussions.'* Retrieved, February 7, 2006, from www.nobodysmiling.com.

The Coup. (2001/2004). *Party music* [CD]. Los Angeles, CA: Epitaph Records.

Dancis, B. (1978). Safety pins and class struggle: Punk rock and the left. *Socialist Review, 8* (39), 58–83. Dead Kennedys. (1979/1980). Nazi punks fuck off. *In God We Trust, Inc.* San Francisco, CA: Alternative Tentacles Records.

Dead Prez. (2000). "Police State." *Let's Get Free.* New York: Loud Records.

Dimitriadis, G. (1996). Hip-hop: From live performance to mediated narrative. *Popular Music,* 15(2), 179–194.

Ferguson, S. (12 September 12, 2005). 9–11 Conspiracists invade Ground Zero. *The Village Voice.* Retrieved, February 6, 2006, from http://www.villagevoice.com/news/0537,fergusonweb2,67726,2.html

Freire, P. (1998). *Pedagogy of the oppressed.* Boulder, CO: Continuum.

Freire, P. (2005). *Teachers as cultural workers: Letters to those who dare teach.* New York: Westview Press. Freire, P., & Macedo, D. (1987). *Literacy: Reading the word and the world.* South Hadley, MA: Bergin and Garvey.

Giroux, H. A. (1994). Doing cultural studies: Youth and challenges of pedagogy. *Harvard Educational Review, 64(3),* 278–308.

Giroux, H. A. (2005). Cultural studies in dark times: Public pedagogy and the challenge of neoliberalism. *Fast Capitalism, 1*(2). Retrieved, January 22, 2006, from http://www.henryagiroux.com/.

Kellner D., & Share J. (2005). Politics of education towards a critical media literacy: Core concepts, debates, organizations and policy. *Discourse: Studies in the Cultural Politics of Education,* 26(3), 369–386.

Kornfeld, J., & Goodman, J. (1998). Melting the glaze: Exploring student responses to liberatory social studies. *Theory into Practice, 37(4),* 306–314.

Malott, C., & Peña, M. (2004). *Punk rockers' revolution: A pedagogy of race, class, and gender.* New York: Peter Lang.

Malott, C., & Pruyn, M. (2006). Marxism and critical multicultural social studies. In W. Ross (Eds.) *The social studies curriculum: Purposes, problems, and possibilities (3rd Edition)* (pp. 157–170). Albany: State University of New York Press.

McLaren, P. (1995). *Rethinking media literacy: A critical pedagogy of representation.* New York: Peter Lang.

McLaren, P. (2005). *Capitalists & conquerors: A critical pedagogy against empire.* New York: Rowman and Littlefield.

McLaren P., & Jaramillo, N. (2005). God's cowboy warrior: Christianity, globalization, and the false prophets of imperialism. In P. McLaren (Ed.), *Capitalists & conquerors: A critical pedagogy against empire* (pp. 261–334). New York: Rowman and Littlefield.

McLaren, P., & McLaren, J. (2004). Afterword: Remaking the revolution. In C. Malott & M. Peña (Eds.), *Punk rockers' revolution: A pedagogy of race, class, and gender* (pp. 123–127). New York: Peter Lang. www.militaryfreezone.org/Retrieved, January 22, 2006

Nieto, S. (2002). Affirmation, solidarity and critique: Moving beyond tolerance in education. In E. Lee, D. Menkart, & M. Okazawa-Rey (Eds.), *Beyond heroes and holidays: A practical guide to K-12 anti-racist, multicultural education and staff development* (pp. 7–18). Washington, DC: Teaching Change.

On the real: About the show. Retrieved, January 25, 2006, from http://shows.airamericaradio.com/onthereal/about.

Porfilio, B., & Malott, C. (2007). Neoliberalism. In G. L. Anderson & K. G. Herr (Eds.), *Encyclopedia of activism and social justice.* New York: Sage.

Rivers, K. (2006, February 4). *Chuck D finds a new public enemy.* Retrieved, February 6, 2006, from www.SouthBendTribune. com.

Russell, R. (2002). Bridging the boundaries for a more inclusive citizenship education. In Y. Hebert (Ed.), *Citizenship in transformation in Canada* (pp. 134–149) Toronto: University of Toronto Press.

Usinger, M. (2004, July 8). *Anti-Flag backs up its bashing.* Retrieved, January 24, 2006, from www.straight.com.

CHAPTER 18

Alternative Media
The Art of Rebellion

Zack Furness

Scholars and activists frequently debate the role of mass media in society, but it is commonly understood that media contribute to the formation of cultural practices and political opinions, the evolution of journalism and art, the construction of ideologies (collective ideas about the way the world "should" work) and the development of national, regional, and self-identities. Mass media are an integral part of everyday life, but ironically most people are never taught to understand, evaluate or critically analyze the ways that media work. Media education is virtually absent from most public schools in the United States and until recently the phrase "media literacy" was rarely used in connection with primary or secondary education. Slowly but surely, school districts are beginning to incorporate media education into their standard curricula, but most teachers—aside from those trained in communication, film, or cultural studies—have not been taught how to develop effective media literacy programs.

Effective forms of media literacy require people to develop their critical thinking skills, and students are often very surprised (or shocked) when they begin to learn about the intersecting problems between media conglomeration, production, advertising, representation and reception. Sorting through history, misinformation and misconceptions is a difficult process and doing so can seem overwhelming to even the most educated person. However, critical media studies can be both rewarding and empowering if approached in the right way. The problem is that many educators feel as if the only way to empower students is to overwhelm them with information and statistics about the insurmountable problems related to mass media without adequately discussing the ways in which people either challenge media power or create alternatives to it. Moreover, teachers often fail to understand why students do not *do* anything with this knowledge once they have been "empowered." The reason why is because teaching media literacy in this manner is not a form of empowerment—it is paralysis.

For any program in critical media literacy/education to be successful, several factors must be present. First of all, students must be willing to develop their critical thinking skills, to engage both their peers and their teachers, and to challenge their own assumptions. Teachers must also be willing to engage in critical dialogue, but they have the additional responsibility of creating an environment that encourages students to learn from one another. Students generally have a vast knowledge of media technologies and media content, and it is important for teachers to help their students utilize such knowledge in the classroom. Most importantly, though, teachers must choose reading materials and topics that address both the problems of mass media as well as some of the viable alternatives to a corporate media model.

In an ideal world, teachers would have the time, resources, and/or freedom necessary to adequately explore media practices that challenge the status quo. However, we all know that the realities of public education in the U.S. are much more grim—students can consider themselves lucky if they attend a district that has adequate funding for books, much less a media literacy curriculum. Nevertheless, teachers who facilitate media literacy programs have a responsibility to expose their students to diverse media content and media practices that are not profit-governed. One of the best ways to achieve such goals is to utilize *alternative media* in the classroom. The study of alternative media can, and should be, incorporated into any media curriculum that aspires to motivate and empower students. In what follows, I will discuss what alternative media are, why people create alternative media, and how alternative media production promotes the ethics of participation and dissent over consumption and passivity.

What Are Alternative Media?

Mass media in the United States have a long history of corporate ownership, from the empire established by newspaper mogul William Randolph Hearst in the 1920s through the contemporary dominance of multinational corporations like Murdoch's News Corporation and Time Warner (Bagdikian 2004, McChesney 2004). The production of alternative media emerged as a response to the problems posed by a profit-driven media system in which only a few corporations (an *oligopoly*) largely determine what types of media will be produced, which topics will be discussed, which forms of expression will be seen/heard, and whose voices will ultimately be silenced. Alternative media is part of a vibrant spectrum of dissent against consolidated media power (Couldry & Curran 2003) that includes the efforts of media reform groups (who advocate structural change through policy), media watchdog groups (who critique mass media content) and media education organizations (who advocate media literacy). Alternative media could best be defined as non-corporate media that are driven by content, as opposed to profit, and based upon a "Do It Yourself" (DIY) ethic. Political literature, pirate radio, independent record labels, zines, Web zines, "comix" (underground comic books), and blogs are some of the most notable forms of alternative media that differ from mass media in their production, content, and purpose. By appealing to smaller, specialized audiences through a more personal approach to content that is not dependent on corporate advertising, the producers of alternative media can utilize different formats for their own needs, whether one's goal is to make a hip-hop record or circulate pamphlets on radical feminism. In other words, people have greater control over what types of media they can produce and what their media "say." This situation is radically different when compared to the corporate model because corporations have almost exclusive control over the content of their media and they largely base their decisions to feature certain types of media on whether they can sell that product to advertisers. Before I go into more depth about specific types of alternative media, it is useful to explain a little more about the context for alternative media and the relationships between production, content, and purpose.

Production, Power, and Content

Media corporations and advertisers are specifically interested in a group that Eileen Meehan (1990) calls the commodity audience—those people in a given media audience who have disposable income or spending money. A perfect example of the role of the commodity audience can be found in television production. With regard to the content of television programming, the executives of a corporation like NBC do not care whether they show an investigative news program, a made-for-TV movie, or a still photo of the *Friends* cast for an hour, as long as they can convince advertisers that the commodity audience will be watching their station at that particular time. Both corporations and advertisers use rating systems to (roughly) determine who is watching, and they then proceed to haggle about the price of advertising time. To put this more simply, the product being bought and sold is the audience's attention—not the program. Ultimately, the media corporations decide on the content, and the advertisers can influence those decisions based on the prospects of either buying more advertising time or pulling their financial support altogether. While the specific dynamics of the relationship between producers, advertisers, and audience vary between different media industries, the prevailing norm in corporate media is based upon the strategy of making money … lots and lots of money.

Although there are some exceptions to the rule, people who make alternative media do so in a much different way, meaning that they do not have to work within a rigid hierarchical (top-down) system, and they have the ability to largely determine what is made, how much it will cost, and where it will be available. More importantly, their purpose for making media is not profit-motivated. People sometimes confuse the idea of profit vs. profitmotivated, and it is an important distinction to keep in mind when considering how alternative media are different from corporate media. Profit is not necessarily bad because it is an important way to generate money for new media projects and to reimburse people for their energy, time, and/or services. For example, some alternative media companies, such as independent record labels, may seem like smaller or scaled-down versions of corporate record labels because they have small staffs of paid employees and they advertise their products. However, there are important differences with regard to content, creative control, profit distribution, decision-making and ownership that distinguish these companies from their corporate counterparts. Generally speaking, independent recording artists are not expected to sacrifice creative control, or to compromise their artistic expression, in the name of profit. Media corporations not only exercise power by controlling the content of their media, they also exert power by restricting access to anyone who is not part of their system. We are led to believe that the media industry is a free market, where anyone can take part, but unless a person has millions of dollars and/or access to satellites, studios, airwaves, or distribution networks, he or she cannot broadcast or circulate his or her chosen medium through corporate channels, never mind having the chance to directly compete with them. In other words, there are extremely high financial and technological barriers to entering the corporate media system. In light of this situation, it is easy to see how production, power and content are interrelated, and why these circumstances are loathed by people who view media as a means of creative expression, a form of education, and/or a vital component of a democratic society.

DIY Media

While it is true that most people lack the financial and technological means to take part in the corporate media system, it is a mistake to think that people who make alternative media want to be part of that system in the first place. Most alternative media producers are strongly opposed to the corporate model, and many hate everything it represents. However, this may not be the primary focus of one's work, or the reason why one makes media in the first place. People create media for a number of different, equally important reasons that should be acknowledged and respected.

One of the most basic reasons why a person creates alternative media is because there are no forms of media available that address one's interests, or represent them in any way. For example, science fiction fans in the 1930s created their own publications called "fanzines," or "zines," in order to write about their favorite sci-fi authors, to review books and films, and to debate issues in science fiction. Science fiction zines also included contributors' contact information so that zine readers could exchange letters, books and writing with one other. At the time there were no publications available that interested hardcore sci-fi fans, so they started their own! By including their contact information, they used fanzines such as *The Comet* (the original fanzine) to create a grassroots community of science fiction fans. The basic model of the zine was widely popularized in the 1970s through the circulation of punk zines like

Sniffin' Glue and *Punk*. Like their sci-fi predecessors, punk zines featured interviews, editorial columns, reviews and news about a subculture that was generally ignored by mainstream print media. Since the 1970s, people have made zines about thousands of other topics or issues including thrift store shopping, bicycling, feminism, "temp" work, soccer, celebrity murders, ferrets, afros, queer culture, and just about anything else you could think of (in addition to lots of things you would have never thought of).

The "lo-fi" approach to media production embodied in the cheap, photocopied format of the zine is certainly one way in which individuals have learned how to develop their own voices in an environment of mass produced media, but zines are merely one part of a wider DIY movement against corporate media that is manifested through the independent production of nearly every type of medium including books, film, photography, music, posters, radio programs, and Web sites. Through the use of techniques that range from wheat pasting to html coding, alternative media enthusiasts have not only learned how to use a variety of tools to get out their messages, they have also pushed the creative and artistic boundaries of their respective mediums. For example, some of the most innovative and passionate music to emerge throughout the last 30 years was created by artists who either started their own record labels or worked with independent labels that were founded and operated by other musicians. Despite the fact that media corporations have been actively purchasing entire independent music labels or parts of labels that once played a key role in the production of anti-corporate music (such as Rawkus, Sup Pop, Matador) there are thriving independent music scenes throughout the world that are buttressed by the fiercely anti-corporate ethics of labels like Rough Trade, SST, Warp, Dischord, Anticon, K Records, Definitive Jux, No Idea, Ninja Tune, Constellation, Plan-it-X, and the list goes on and on and on.

> My point here is not to privilege music above other forms of alternative media, but merely to provide a basic example of how artistic expression is often fostered in noncorporate environments. The DIY response to mass media production has been, and continues to be, shared by millions of people who create media to represent and address their own specific interests. Participation is the key ingredient to alternative media, which makes it fundamentally different from media models in which producers are seen as separate from audiences. Stephen Duncombe, a professor and political activist, suggests that people who make alternative media erode the lines between producer and consumer and they "challenge the dichotomy between active creator and passive spectator that characterizes our culture and society." (1999, p. 127)

With the development of the Internet and digital publishing technologies, the DIY ethic of participation has not only been more visible to wider audiences, it has also resulted in the creation of interactive forums by groups of eager media producers who work outside of, or directly against, corporate media channels. A perfect example of a participatory, Webbased alternative medium is the online news Web site, Indymedia.org, which was started by activists who wanted to document the events of the 1999 World Trade Organization protest in Seattle. In the years since the WTO protest, there have been Indymedia Web sites developed in almost 200 cities throughout the world, and people have used the interactive resource as a way to cover news stories, debate political issues, publish investigative journalism, and organize activists for protests on a wide range of political issues.

The DIY approach to media production does not solve socioeconomic problems, but it promotes the idea that anyone can learn how to make their own media. In this way, DIY ethics cross race, class, and gender lines and connect different alternative media practices throughout history. However, there are crucial differences to consider when looking at why or how people end up "doing it themselves." For example, White people have an incredible degree of privilege compared to people of color, so it is wrong to suggest that White suburban teenagers who put out political punk records in the twenty-first century are the same as African American abolitionists who printed their own newspapers in the nineteenth century. There are *worlds* of difference between these two groups including their respective historical/cultural contexts, their motivations, and their access to money, materials and volunteer labor.

In addition, there are obvious differences in the actual content of their messages, i.e. what is being said and how it is being said. However, the bond that connects these different groups is a mutual recognition that people must create their own media outlets when none exist—because corporations are certainly not going to do it for us. Media scholar Chris Atton sums this up when he says that alternative media offer "the means for democratic communication to people who are normally excluded from media production" (2002, p. 4).

Radical Media

One of the most important reasons why people make alternative media is because they want to express opinions and views that are too critical, confrontational, and/or political for mass media. Media scholar John Downing (2000) refers to this lineage of media production as *radical media* or media that express an oppositional stance against both mainstream society and popular culture. Radical media have a long history in Western countries where people had early access to printing press technologies and opposition to radical media is just as old. For example, the English government passed a large tax on newspapers in 1797 in order to put limits on the radical press. Despite the historical power wielded by governments, churches, and multinational corporations, radical media have continued to thrive through the production of newspapers, pamphlets, posters, music, zines, documentaries, films, Web sites, and blogs that challenge the politics, ethics, and logic of the status quo. Radical media have played an especially important role in labor struggles and social movement activism throughout the last 150 years because they have been a way for disenfranchised and oppressed peoples to articulate their experiences, grievances, and perspectives that are consistently ignored, or grossly misrepresented, by the mass media.

Mass media, particularly news, have a powerful agenda setting function, which means that the media do not necessarily tell us what to think, but they give us an extremely limited option for "what to think about and how to think about it" (McChesney 2004, p. 70). Through this process of coercion (toward a particular set of beliefs) and consent (people's willingness to embrace mass media) a dominant, or hegemonic, paradigm evolves in a given society and ideas that challenge the dominant ideology are viewed with skepticism, anger, or outright hostility. Radical media, in the form of propaganda (intentionally persuasive information) and journalism (reporting about facts and events with a more "objective" approach) directly challenge this model by introducing new ideas into public discourse, by critiquing institutions of power, by documenting cultures that exist under the radar of popular/consumer culture, by promoting participation, and by encouraging solidarity with others who have similar beliefs about how the world should work.

For the millions who do not benefit from capitalism, consumerism, globalization, and concentrated governmental authority, radical media create spaces where people can both discuss and demand alternatives to prevailing socioeconomic and cultural norms. Some notable examples of radical media in this vein are newspapers and pamphlets produced by groups like the Industrial Workers of the World (IWW) and the Black Panther Party for Self-Defense (The Black Panthers). The IWW began as an anarchist/socialist union that argued for the political organization of all working people into "one big union" that could overthrow the wage system through direct action, i.e., strikes, boycotts, and various forms of civil disobedience. At its height in the early 1900s, the IWW had over 100,000 members who were dedicated to the idea that "an injury to one is an injury to all." Publications like *The Industrial Worker*, the IWW newspaper, were used to keep members informed and educated about relevant news, events, and opinions of fellow workers throughout the country.

A similar example of radical media used in support of a political party can be found in the organization of the Black Panthers, a civil rights and self-defense organization started in 1966 by African American activists who spoke out openly against police violence, capitalism, and centuries of racism against Black people. The group's principles were laid out in a document called the "Ten Point Program," which was widely circulated in Black communities throughout the United States. Along with the oratory skills of their leadership and the development of successful community programs, the Panthers' literature played an important role in the development of Black consciousness in the United States, and it aided in the recruitment of new party members during the late 1960s. In addition to the "Ten Point Program," the Panthers published books, newspapers (*The Black Panther),* and various educational pamphlets about community resources, constitutional rights, and the dangers of drug abuse (to name a few topics).

Activists in recent decades have become more media-savvy by studying both the victories and defeats of media campaigns waged by social movements of previous eras. Their efforts have not only resulted in the production and distribution of radical media throughout the world, they have helped to organize activists involved in the environmental movement, the animal rights movement, the anti-globalization movement, the queer rights movement and the anti-war movement. Radical media has been globally utilized by a diverse wave of activists that range from peasant revolutionaries in Mexico to urban anarchists in the U.K., to peace activists in the Israeli-occupied Palestinian territories.

Creating Networks

The production of alternative media is not just about the creation of media texts, it is also about creating a shared sense of community with people who have similar views, interests and beliefs. This is one of the reasons why alternative media has played such a central role in political organizations and subcultures throughout the world. As new forms of media emerge, new channels of communication open up, new communities develop, and the cycle continues. With the added advantage of Web-based communication, the once-small network of alternative media producers, distributors and retailers has grown enormously in recent decades. As a result, it is easier than ever for media producers to gain access to basic materials and distribution networks, assuming that one has the financial means to do so.

Distribution and sales networks are crucial to alternative media production because it is very difficult for people to find places where they can sell media that might be considered "weird," foreign or overtly political. The emergence of giant media retailers (chain stores) and the subsequent closure of "mom and pop" establishments across North America has resulted in fewer stores that are willing to acquire and sell media that are not shipped from a corporate distributor. This also means that fewer stores are willing to support local musicians, writers, artists, and other media producers. Fortunately, there have been diligent media enthusiasts and activists who have devoted incredible amounts of energy to the circulation and distribution of alternative media—oftentimes without being paid. For example, it is not uncommon to see tables set up at DIY punk and/or hip-hop shows where people have boxes of records and CDs for sale from bands whose music will never see the light of day in a Best Buy, Wal-Mart, or Virgin Megastore. At some of the same shows, you will often see touring bands selling music, books, or art from their friends and fellow artists in their hometowns. These types of alternative media distribution networks are often intentionally small and therefore very personal. However, there are certain cases in which these same networks can expand into larger organizations that subsequently help out other independent publishers and distributors.

A case in point is AK Press, a worker-owned collective that publishes political literature and distributes what might be the biggest selection of radical media in the world. AK Press was founded by Ramses Kanaan, an anarchist zine editor who started his distribution network in Scotland. During the late 1980s and early 1990s, Ramses sold political zines while he was on tour with punk bands in Europe, and in 1991 AK Press was turned into a worker-owned cooperative (Vale 1996, p. 106). In recent years, AK has published new books, reprinted older and/or "out of print" books and widened their distribution list to include clothing, buttons, CDs, films, magazines, hundreds of zines and thousands of books—including the entire catalogues of over a dozen independent book publishers/distributors. Through this network, AK Press is not only able to make political literature more widely available, they are also able to help develop and strengthen other alternative media networks that include activists, writers, artists, radical bookstores and "infoshops" (small, volunteer-run collectives that sell and distribute political media). By creating successful, self-sufficient distribution networks, organizations like AK provide vital outlets for people who would otherwise have no substantial means to sell and/or distribute their work. This not only allows alternative media producers to reach new audiences, it also supports people who want to take artistic/political chances with their media.

Conclusion

While I have only been able to provide a (very) brief glimpse into the world of alternative media, it is easy to see how there are viable options that exist for people who want to create alternative media and others who want access to such resources. Given the vast scope of media produced under the alternative rubric, it is crucial for media scholars, teachers, and students to recognize the ways in which alternative media can enhance, redefine, and challenge our engagement with media in the twenty-first century. Similarly, it is also important to contextualize alternative media as part of a wider resistance movement against corporate power structures that will not save the media on their own account. It is ignorant to dismiss alternative media as a "fringe" activity, but it is also foolish to credit alternative media as being implicitly revolutionary. Alternative media certainly have a distinct role to play in revolutionary politics, and they also have the potential to revolutionize the way in which media are made throughout the world. However, we must not be content with the idea of simply creating alternatives to a commercial, corporate media system that excludes dissent, discourages participation, and negatively represents both the interests and beliefs of billions throughout the world. What we need is more organization among media critics, more pressure applied to corporate media producers, more support for media reform groups, more dialogue, and more media education.

Alternative media teaches us that anyone who wants to make media can do it on their own terms. It teaches us that media production does not require a vast knowledge of media institutions or a great deal of money. It can inform us about a vast array of perspectives on politics, culture, economics and the media industry. Finally, alternative media emphasizes the idea that culture is a "whole way of life" (Williams 1953, p. viii) defined by creation and participation—culture is not simply a product to be consumed.

Learn. Create. Participate. Resist.

References

Atton, C. (2002). *Alternative media.* London: Sage.
Bagdikian, B. (2004). *The new media monopoly.* (2004). Boston: Beacon Press.
Downing, J. (2000). *Radical media: Rebellious communication and social movements.* London: Sage.
Couldry, N., & Curran, J. (Eds.). (2003). *Contesting media power.* Lanham, MD: Rowman & Littlefield.
Duncombe, S. (1997). *Notes from underground: Zines and the politics of alternative culture.* London and New York: Verso.
McChesney, R. (2004). *The problem of media.* New York: Monthly Review Press.
Meehan, E. (1990). Why we don't count. In Mellencamp (Ed.), *Logics of television: Essays in cultural criticism* (pp. 117–137). Bloomington: Indiana University Press.
Vale, V. (1996). *Zines!* San Francisco: V/Search.
Williams, R. (1953). *Culture and society: 1780–1950.* New York: Columbia University Press.

Further Reading

Armstrong, D. (1984). *A trumpet to arms: Alternative media in America.* Cambridge, MA: South End Press.
Atton, C. (1999). The infoshop: The alternative information centre of the 1990s. *New World Library, 100*(1).
Atton, C. (2005). *An alternative Internet.* Edinburgh: Edinburgh University Press.
Buhle, P., & Schulman, N. (Eds.). (2005). *Wobblies: A graphic history of the industrial workers of the world.* London and New York: Verso.
Jones, C. E. (Ed.). (1998). *The Black Panther Party reconsidered.* Baltimore: Black Classic Press. Marcos, S. (2004). *Ya Basta! Ten years of the Zapatista uprising.* Oakland: AK Press.
McCombs, M., & Shaw, D. (1972). The agenda-setting function of mass media. *Public Opinion Quarterly, 36*, 176–187.
McKay, G. (1996). *Senseless acts of beauty.* London: Verso.

McKay, G. (1998). *DIY culture: Party and protest in Britain*. London: Verso.

Morris, D. (2004). Globalization and media democracy: The case of the independent media centers." In D. Schuler & P. Day, *Shaping the network society: The new role of civil society in cyberspace*. Cambridge, MA: MIT Press.

Newton, H. P., & Morrison, T. (1995). *To die for the people: The writings of Huey P. Newton*. New York: Writers and Readers Publications.

Nogueira, A. (2002). The birth and promise of the Indymedia revolution. In B. Shepard & R. Hayduk (Eds.), *From ACT UP to the WTO: Urban protest and community building in the era of globalization*. London: Verso.

Renshaw, R. (1967). *The Wobblies: The story of the IWW and syndicalism in the United States*. New York: Doubleday.

Roger, S., & Triggs, T. (2002). *Below critical radar: Fanzines and alternative comics from 1976 to Now*. New York: Codex.

Spencer, A. (2005). *DIY: The rise of lo-fi media*. London: Marion Boyers.

Stein, R. L., & Swedenberg, T. (Eds.). (2005). *Palestine, Israel and the politics of popular culture*. Durham: Duke University Press.

Internet Resources

*AK Press (www.akpress.com)
*Democracy Now! (www.democracynow.org)
*International Progressive Publications Network (www.ippn.ws/)
*Microcosm Publishing (www.microcosmpublishing.com)
*The Zine and E-zine Resource Guide (www.zinebook.com)

Contributors

Philip M. Anderson is Professor Emeritus of Education at Queens College and the Graduate Center of the City University of New York. He earned a Ph.D. in curriculum and instruction from the University of Wisconsin-Madison and worked as a faculty member in Wisconsin public schools and at Brown and Ohio Universities. He has taught students and teachers in eighth grade through graduate school and published extensively on curriculum and cultural theory, language and reading, and teaching the arts and humanities in schools.

Roymieco A. Carter, M.F.A., is Associate Professor and Director of the Visual Arts Program and University Galleries at North Carolina A&T State University. He teaches courses on graphic design, digital media, visual literacy and theory, and social criticism. He is a graphic designer of print, web, and motion-based media. His work has received local, national, and international recognition. He has written articles on graphic design education, art education, gaming, human computer interaction, and graphics computer animation. He can be reached at roymieco.carter@gmail.com.

Venus E. Evans-Winters is Associate Professor of Education in the Department of Educational Administration and Foundations at Illinois State University. She holds a doctorate in educational policy studies and a master's degree in school social work from the University of Illinois at Urbana-Champaign. Her research interests are school resilience, urban education, critical race theory, critical pedagogy, and feminism(s).

Zack Furness is Associate Professor of Communications at Penn State Greater Allegheny and an interdisciplinary cultural studies scholar. He is the author of *One Less Car: Bicycling and the Politics of Automobility*, the editor of *Punkademics*, and co-editor of *The NFL: Critical and Cultural Perspectives*.

Elizabeth E. Heilman is Associate Professor of teacher education at Michigan State University. Her recent articles appear in *Teachers College Record*, *Educational Theory* and *Teaching Education*. She is the editor of *Harry Potter's World: Multidisciplinary Critical Perspectives* and co-editor of *Democratic Response in an Era of Standardization*.

Christie Ivie is a sociology student at Illinois Wesleyan University with an interest in early childhood education in developing countries.

Tricia M. Kress is Associate Professor and Director of the Urban Education, Leadership and Policy Studies Doctoral Program at the University of Massachusetts Boston. She is co-editor of the book series *Imagination and Praxis: Criticality and Creativity in Education and Educational Research* with Sense Publishers. In April 2014, she and her co-editor Robert Lake (Georgia Southern University) received The Society of Professors of Education Book Award for *Paulo Freire's Intellectual Roots: Toward Historicity in Praxis*.

Virginia Lea is Professor at the University of Wisconsin-Stout. Her work includes Lea, V., Lund, D., & Carr, P. (Eds). (2018). *Critical Multicultural Perspectives on Whiteness: Views from the Past and Present*. New York: Peter Lang; and Lea, V. (2014). *Constructing Critical Consciousness: Narratives That Unmask Hegemony, and Ideas for Creating Greater Equity in Education*. New York: Peter Lang. Virginia sees her scholarship, research, teaching, and The Hegemony Project, which she founded and co-directs (www.thehegemonyproject.org), as a means of developing greater understanding about how cultural hegemony works to create and reproduce socioeconomic, cultural and educational inequities in our time; and to take social action for equitable social change. Virginia also co-directs the nonprofit The Educultural Foundation with her partner, Babatunde Lea.

Curry Malott is Associate Professor in the Department of Educational Foundations and Policy Studies at West Chester University of Pennsylvania. Malott is a leader in his union and an organizer with the ANSWER (Act Now to Stop War and End Racism) Coalition, the Party for Socialism and Liberation, and the People's Congress of Resistance. His most recent book is *History and Education: Engaging the Global Class War* (Peter Lang).

Elizabeth J. Meyer is Associate Professor in the School of Education at the University of Colorado Boulder and Associate Dean of Students. She is the author of *Gender, Bullying, and Harassment: Strategies to End Sexism and Homophobia in Schools* (Teachers College Press, 2009) and *Gender and Sexual Diversity in Schools* (Springer, 2010). She is a former high school teacher and Fulbright Teacher Exchange Program Grantee. She completed her M.A. at the University of Colorado–Boulder and Ph.D. at McGill University in Montreal, Quebec. Her research has been published in academic journals such as *Gender and Education*; *Teachers College Record*; and *The Journal of LGBT Youth*. She blogs for *Psychology Today* and is also on Twitter: @lizjmeyer.

sj Miller is a transdisciplinary award-winning teacher/writer/activist/scholar and is an expert on gender identity and its intersections with schooling practices. sj presents globally, sits on a number of LGBT Advisor Boards, co-edits two book series, is a U.S. representative on gender identity with UNESCO, and recently won the 2017 AERA Exemplary Research Award for *Teaching, Affirming, and Recognizing Trans and Gender Creative Youth: A Queer Literacy Framework*, which is being used in Chile, Australia, New Zealand, South Africa, and across Latin America.

Brian Mooney is an educator, scholar, and poet who explores the intersections of hip-hop, spoken word poetry, literacy, and urban education. He is the author of *Breakbeat Pedagogy: Hip Hop and Spoke Word Beyond the Classroom Walls*. His work has been featured by national news outlets including *The New York Times, NBC, Rolling Stone, NPR, SiriusXM, MTV* and others.

Brad J. Porfilio is Associate Dean of Research and Programs and Full Professor at Seattle University. His research interests and expertise include: urban education, gender and technology, cultural studies, neoliberalism and schooling, and transformative education.

Nelson M. Rodriguez is Associate Professor of Women's, Gender, and Sexuality Studies in the School of Humanities and Social Sciences at The College of New Jersey. His current research areas span queer studies and education, critical masculinity studies, and Foucault studies. His recent publications include *Critical Concepts in Queer Studies and Education: An International Guide for the Twenty-First Century*; *Educators Queering Academia: Critical Memoirs*; *Queer Masculinities: A Critical Reader in Education*; and *Queering Straight Teachers: Discourse and Identity in Education*.

George J. Sefa Dei is Professor of Social Justice Education and Director of the Centre for Integrative Anti-Racism Studies at the Ontario Institute for Studies in Education of the University of Toronto (OISE/UT). In 2000 he co-edited *Indigenous Knowledges in Global Contexts: Multiple Readings of Our World* with Budd Hall and Dorothy Goldin Rosenberg. His most recent books include *Teaching Africa: Towards Transgressive Pedagogy*; *Fanon and Education: Pedagogical Challenges*, co-edited with Marlon Simmons (Peter Lang Publishing, 2010); *Fanon and the Counterinsurgency of Education*; *Learning to Succeed: Improving Educational Achievement for All*; and *Reframing Blackness and Black Solidarities through Anti-Colonial and Decolonial Prisms* (Springer, New York 2017). In July 2007, he was installed as a traditional chief in Ghana, namely the Gyaasehene of the town of Asokore-Koforidua in the New Juaben Traditional Area of Ghana. His stool name is Nana Adusei Sefa Tweneboah.

Marlon Simmons is Assistant Professor at the Werklund School of Education, University of Calgary. His research interests include culture and leadership, and governance of the self in educational settings. Marlon's scholarly work is grounded within the Diaspora and communicative network practices of youth. Related to Marlon's educational inquiry are the scholarship of teaching and learning and the role of sociomaterial relations with enhancing student learning.

Nina Zaragoza has taught at Florida International University, in the public schools of Miami-Dade County, Florida, and in Vladimir, Russia. She taught in the New York City public school system and also served as NY Education Director for World Vision. She currently travels the globe to empower those most marginalized to reach their fullest potential.

Index